2001	CENTURY CITY: ART AND CULTURE IN THE MODERN METROPOLIS
2002	DOCUMENTA 11
2005	VENICE BIENNALE 2005: ALWAYS A LITTLE FURTHER / THE EXPERIENCE OF ART
2007	GLOBAL FEMINISMS: NEW DIRECTIONS IN CONTEMPORARY ART
2007–09	WACK! ART AND THE FEMINIST REVOLUTION
2009	EVERYWHERE: SEXUAL DIVERSITY POLICIES IN ART (EN TODAS PARTES: POLÍTICAS DE LA DIVERSIDAD SEXUEL EN EL ARTE)
2009–11	ELLES@CENTREPOMPIDOU
2010	ARS HOMO EROTICA
2010–12	HIDE/SEEK: DIFFERENCE AND DESIRE IN AMERICAN PORTRAITURE
2011–12	THE GLOBAL CONTEMPORARY: ART WORLDS AFTER 1989
2011–13	RE.ACT.FEMINISM #2 – A PERFORMING ARCHIVE
2015	VENICE BIENNALE 2015: ALL THE WORLD'S FUTURES
2015–17	ART AIDS AMERICA

CURATORIAL ACTIVISM

MAURA REILLY

FOREWORD BY LUCY R. LIPPARD

CURATORIAL ACTIVISM

TOWARDS AN ETHICS OF CURATING

WITH 107 ILLUSTRATIONS

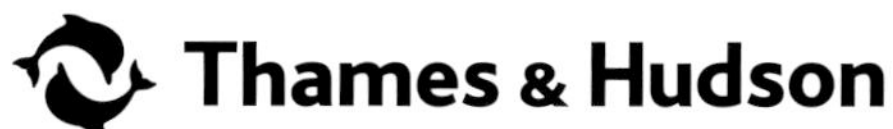

ACKNOWLEDGMENTS

There are many people who helped make this book happen. I'd like
to thank my colleagues worldwide for the multiple speaking invitations
that allowed me to tease out a lot of the ideas discussed herein:
Jo Holder, Jonathan Katz, Fiona MacDonald, Anne Marsh, Jacqueline
Millner, Catriona Moore, Lara Perry, Caroline Phillips, Avril Quaill,
and Susan Fisher Sterling, as well as the institutions and art fairs
that hosted me: Armory Show, New York; Art Basel Miami; Art Gallery
of New South Wales, Sydney; Migros Museum, Zurich; Monash
University, Melbourne; Museum Folkwang, Essen, Germany; National
Museum of Women in the Arts, Washington, DC; Stony Brook
University, New York; Tate Modern, London; and Victoria College
of the Arts/University of Melbourne. I'd also like to thank Sarah
Douglas from *ArtNews* for publishing an earlier version of Chapter
Two, and Alex Greenberger for his fine editing, as well as Amelia Jones
and Lucy Lippard, my feminist heroes. As always, I must express
my sincere gratitude to Linda Nochlin, my mentor and dear friend,
who is a daily source of intellectual inspiration. To Sophy Thompson,
Publishing Director at Thames & Hudson, thank you for believing
in this project from the start, and to all your amazing colleagues
who shepherded it through to completion, including Poppy David,
Flora Spiegel, Diana Loxley, Helen Farr, Nicola Chemotti, and
Ginny Liggitt. And to all of the curatorial activists highlighted in this
book, your intelligent, inclusive and diverse projects are changing
the course of art history, now and into the future; for that, I am forever
grateful. Above all, I'd like to thank my partner extraordinaire, without
whose love and patience this book would not have been possible.

Portions of the text of this book were previously published
in different form as Maura Reilly's 'Introduction: Toward
Transnational Feminisms' in the exhibition catalogue *Global
Feminisms*, edited by Maura Reilly and Linda Nochlin and
published by the Brooklyn Museum and Merrell Publishers
in 2007.

First published in 2018 in the United States of America
by Thames & Hudson Inc., 500 Fifth Avenue, New York,
New York, 10110

www.thamesandhudsonusa.com

Reprinted 2019

Library of Congress Control Number 2017945427

ISBN 978-0-500-23970-4

Printed and bound in China by C&C Offset Printing Co. Ltd

FOREWORD
BY LUCY R. LIPPARD

THE MORE THINGS CHANGE...

Curatorial activism comes from within, and Maura Reilly has been on the internal front lines, especially as the inaugural curator of the Elizabeth A. Sackler Center for Feminist Art at the Brooklyn Museum, New York City. Her own exhibitions, like this book, can be considered forms of institutional critique. Her core question: "How can we get people in the art world *to think about* gender, race, and sexuality, to understand that these are persistent concerns that require action?" Maura Reilly's book *Curatorial Activism* focuses on significant, large-scale exhibitions at major museums that broke the rules by introducing identity-driven social issues. In the process, of course, all such shows are attacked for disregarding "quality"—that elusive bailiwick for the conservative wing of the art-for-art's-sake crowd. Smart, brave curators are often denigrated for daring to be sensitive, or, god forbid, "politically correct." Then there are the others, who remain oblivious to those issues. Reilly's meticulous documentation of statistics, artworks, and critical responses to exhibitions including and not including artists who are female, of color, and LGBTQ are illuminating, if often depressing for those of us who thought we were changing the world in the 1960s and 1970s.

Since I began my occasional forays into curating in 1966, the selection and installation of art exhibitions has become a highly specialized profession, increasingly academic, subject of many serious books. Fifty years ago it was the province of art historians who gravitated to museums. (The renowned MoMA curator Dorothy Miller had no Ph.D.) Commercial galleries, and then "alternative spaces," were beginning to offer freer zones where artists or freelance writers like myself could try out new ideas: spreading temporary public works out across a city, incorporating "non-art" materials or popular culture on equal status with "high art," or creating street corner "museums" and all the forerunners of the "pop up" show. Increasingly, these ventures were invited into mainstream museums.

Although I have occasionally been invited in, much of my own activism has involved protesting museums for their exclusion of audiences as well as artists. MoMA (my alma mater in a sense, as the site of my first and only real job) has often been the target. Reilly notes that it continues to receive "the worst grade for gender and race discrimination." I was startled to read that the only "non-white artists" in its 2004 expansion show were Diego Rivera and other Mexican muralists. (Frida Kahlo often fills the token "artist of color" slot: her father was European and her mother was a *mestiza*, of mixed European and Amerindian ancestry; as a bisexual, she's a triple whammy for today's statistic collectors.) Reilly notes that the new Whitney opened in 2015 with a show of 600 works, of which just 31% were by women and 23% by artists of color—but this was progress, at least since Ad Hoc Women Artists protested the old Whitney in 1970, demanding 50% women and 50% "non-white" artists. We succeeded in raising the number of women from 4.5% in the previous Painting Annual to 22%. It took years to improve on that figure. The more things change...

Reilly also cites ArtSlant's 2015 April Fools' joke that MoMA would devote the year entirely to women, echoes of Ad Hoc's fake press release from the Whitney supporting our 1970 goals, which brought the FBI to our doors. Micol Hebron's 2013 Gallery Tally updates the research of feminist groups in the early 1970s and the Guerrilla Girls since the mid-1980s. She found that less than a third of artists represented in US commercial galleries were women. And yet between 65% and 80% of US art students and around 70% of MFA students are women. What becomes of them? And of course we also have to ask are these "women artists" feminists as well? (My 1976 book *From the Center* was subtitled *Feminist Essays on Women's Art*, and this also became a contentious issue when naming the Sackler Center.)[1]

While the feminist battle for equal representation has gone on longer and is therefore more frustrating for some of us, we don't have as many stats for the other two constituencies Reilly discusses. For instance, there is no data on students of color or LGBTQ, but Pussy Galore's 2016 tally of commercial galleries found that only 21% of the artists were non-white. (In addition, "non-white," which maintains white as the measure, is obviously a debatable term, especially within the Latino/a population.) And so it goes, on and on. Reilly remarks on the stereotyping that is inevitable in most identity-specific shows, quoting Cuban critic Gerardo Mosquera on the way Third World artists are routinely required to "display their identity," and Kobena Mercer on "the burden of representation." She dissects blockbusters like the multicultural and multi-located *Decade Show*, the flawed but significant *Magiciens de la terre* (an improvement on MoMA's 1984 *"Primitivism" in Twentieth-Century Art*), and the Whitney's vital but much-maligned 1993 "political biennial," in which white male artists were for the first time in the minority.

For all the importance of statistics that make us angry, and make us act, for the artists themselves—artists "of color" or those from "other" (e.g. non-Eurocentric) cultures, and for women and queers too—the real issue is not to be invited to more "special" or thematic exhibitions (though they have been historically effective). More appealing is to be simply included in the pool of respected artists when shows are being selected. When we protested the Whitney in 1970 we were most concerned that curators visit the studios of those hitherto ignored. We were confident that once the work of women and artists of color was seen, and considered, they would be included. Turns out that it wasn't that easy.

Curatorial identity and ethics clearly make a difference. The "appalling statistics" of the Venice Biennales were amended once, in 2005, when both curators were women and so were 38% of the artists. In October 2016, Victoria & Albert curator Sonnet Stanfill wrote in a hardhitting op ed in the *New York Times* that while women claim about 70% of the curatorships in US art museums, the step up to director is a different story.[2] She pointed out that in 2015 the world's top twelve art museums (based on attendance)—"the directors' dozen"—were all led by men: "This gender gap extends from Europe to North America, where only five of the thirty-three directors of the most prominent museums (those with operating budgets of more than $20 million) are women." Stanfill also noted that when Frances Morris became the director of the Tate Modern in April, "she became the first woman to join the club." Change was immediate. Reilly cites the Tate Modern's "recalibration of their permanent collection to more accurately reflect the world we live in."

LGBTQ issues are more complicated, as demonstrated by Harmony Hammond's groundbreaking *A Lesbian Show* in New York in 1978, and by Great American Lesbian Art Show (GALAS) in Los Angeles in 1980. Not only was "self outing" a personal risk, but few of the works referenced the sexuality that contextualized them in the first place. (This should have pleased those who dislike specificity in art.) Even more than race or gender, sexual "sensibility" is an elusive and often subversive subject. Out of the closet and into the museum was quite a leap, simultaneously helped and hindered by the AIDS crisis. The unique trajectory of David Wojnarowicz's art and activism is a case in point. Challenging the heteronormative canon was a milestone, whether or not the exhibitions were well received. Reilly describes *In a Different Light* (1995) as "not a show of gay and lesbian images, but instead a mapping of queer practice in the visual arts over the past thirty years."

One might assume that the more "exotic" and unfamiliar arts would be welcomed by a market-driven art world that thrives on novelty, "breakthroughs," and planned obsolescence. ("Art's What Sells" was a SoHo graffiti decades ago.) However, Reilly's work suggests that it is "easier" to introduce women and even lesbians into the mainstream than it is to embrace artists of color from the USA. Okwui Enwezor's "postcolonial curatorial strategy" at *Documenta 11* in 2002, which emphasized theory and dialogue over objects and highlighted contradictions in the broader context, was something of a tipping point, its unabashedly political vision providing a powerful alternative. However, for all the 21st-century's art-world globalism, and the surge of artists of color in aid of decolonization, reliance on the familiar canons remains strong.

Not all the curatorial alternatives are improvements. In 2016, Jean-Hubert Martin, curator of *Magiciens de la terre*, presented *Carambolages* ("double whammy, ricochet shot in billiards, car crash or 'pile up'") at the Grand Palais in Paris. An "ahistorical, non-chronological, anti-categorical selection" of objects from across a millennium, many of which are "anonymous," were presented "context-free." In its return to formalism and disregard for cultural roots, this doesn't sound like the solution. On the other hand, in 1992, one of the most effective (and accepted) instances of true curatorial activism shared some of these characteristics precisely by emphasizing context. Artist Fred Wilson's brilliant *Mining the Museum* has served as a model for a number of artist-curated shows drawn from museum collections, including 2016's *Ground* at the Pomona College Museum of Art in 2016, in which Native American artist Rose B. Simpson chose mundane objects relating to women's work, like grinding stones, to accompany her striking post-apocalyptic figures and masks.

Reilly also addresses the touchy subject of curatorial laziness, an unwillingness to think beyond the precedents, out of the box, around the block, out of the comfort zone that can result in involuntary misogyny, racism, homo/lesbophobia. As Jude Kelly, artistic director of London's Southbank Centre for Performing Arts, has said, being inclusive is not about "standing in the middle and saying, 'I'd like to include you'—you have to stand in a different place."[3] I remember being asked by a museum curator in the 1980s, when I was writing *Mixed Blessings: New Art in a Multicultural America*, where on earth I found all these people?[4] At the time the Studio Museum in Harlem, the Museum of Contemporary Hispanic Art, the Asian American Cultural Center, and the American Indian Community House were all going strong and producing provocative shows, not to mention the innovative art that is always buried in studios. Having worked for some thirty years with Native American artists, I am constantly appalled at the mainstream ignorance about their work. It seems they are still "hard to find."

Reilly's examination of various counter-hegemonic strategies
is a valuable part of this book, which should be a mandated text for
up-and-coming curators as well as for those considering external
activism. She advocates a "leveling of hierarchies" and "a fundamental
redefining of art practice, transnationally." She demotes revisionism,
which is always popular at the beginning of such long journeys and
can correct some past deficiencies, providing a base for contemporary
work. But, as Reilly points out, revisionism ultimately accepts the
centrality of the white male Western canon, and can even strengthen it
by maintaining criteria that are prejudicial or inapplicable to disparate
cultures. She also raises the highly controversial question of whether
quotas should be enforced, by whom, and how. Ethical aesthetics
cannot be regulated like pay equity, which is also hard to come by.
At best the data presented here will spark conscious and even
unconscious examinations of curatorial inclusion, an awareness
that if the percentages are lousy, you need to do more work.
Don't say, as some Whitney staff did during the run up to the 1970
Sculpture Annual, "there are no good women sculptors" (or
conceptual artists, or anything else). Diversify museum boards,
advises Reilly. (In 1969 the Art Workers' Coalition demanded that
artists—who would have been all white males at the time—be
represented on all New York museum boards in order to protect artists'
rights.) Don't let commercial galleries off the hook. They form the
reservoirs from which most museum shows are selected. And private
collectors? Well, they are private, but they are usually ambitious
and vulnerable to art-world peer pressure. Artists themselves should
not be let off the hook. Reilly calls on them to speak up too, and
"make trouble," as they have in the past.

Curatorial interventions can open the eyes of viewers.
It remains to be seen how much courageous curators can get away
with in the current context. Thanks to the pioneering efforts detailed
here, ethical curation is more broadly accepted, if not necessarily more
popular. And of course there are other kinds of curatorial activism
aside from those based in identity. There is unabashed "political art"
that takes on systemic racism, economic inequality, police brutality,
immigration, and war. There is ecological art that confronts climate
change, gentrification, agriculture, the fossil-fuel industry. All of
these are as necessary and demanding of hard work and courage
as identity-based curating. But that's another book.

Lucy R. Lippard

PREFACE

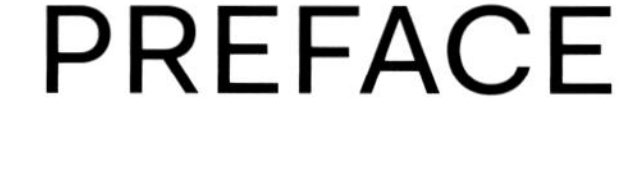

During the 1990s, while pursuing my graduate degree at New York
University, I worked in the Education Department of the Museum
of Modern Art (MoMA). I presented gallery tours of the museum's
permanent collection to the general public and conducted special
exhibition walk-throughs on topics as varied as Alexander Rodchenko
and the Russian Avant-Garde, Julia Margaret Cameron, Sigmar Polke,
and Jackson Pollock. The experience was invaluable. I gained
tremendous knowledge during my years at MoMA and could present
its permanent collection with my eyes closed, following the art-
historical trajectory as it had been laid out by Alfred H. Barr, the
institution's founding director, whose tenure spanned 1929 to 1943.

The permanent exhibition galleries at MoMA, representing art
produced from 1880 to the mid-1960s, are arranged to tell Barr's "story"
of modern art, beginning with Monet's water lilies and Cézanne's
Post-Impressionist paintings, leading into Picasso's Analytic Cubism
(exemplified stunningly by *Les Desmoiselles d'Avignon*, 1907), then
Futurism à la Boccioni, followed by the Surrealism of Marcel Duchamp
and André Masson, and culminating after World War II with the
triumphal drip paintings of Jackson Pollock. Barr's narrative emphasizes
a shift of avant-gardism at the turn of the 20th century, from Western
Europe—Paris/Berlin—to New York, epitomized most spectacularly
by Abstract Expressionism.

Barr's (MoMA's) "story" of modern art has achieved iconic status, one that other museum collections have sought to mimic. It is a story that forms the basis of most art-history textbooks and curricula in the West—and it has become so deeply entrenched and naturalized that it exists, largely unquestioned, as *the* history of modern art. Yet it is a narrative that is structured by the exclusion and/or subordination of those outside the established norm, a narrative that perpetuates, as Griselda Pollock argues, "a selective tradition which normalizes, as the *only* modernism, a particular and gendered set of practices."[1] For example, according to Barr's/MoMA's definition, "modern art" is a synchronic, linear progression of "isms" in which one (heterosexual, white) male "genius" from Europe or the USA influences another, younger version who inevitably must trump or subvert the previous master, thereby producing an avant-garde progression. Women, artists of color, and those who are not from Europe or North America—in other words, all Other artists—are rarely encountered. Indeed, the *New York Times* art critic Holland Cotter recently re-named MoMA's long-running permanent-collection galleries the "Modern White Guys: The Greatest Art Story Ever Invented."[2]

Thus it was in February 2017 that the curators at MoMA made an extraordinary decision: to replace some works in the museum's fifth-floor permanent collection galleries with eight works by artists from some of the majority-Muslim nations whose citizens had been blocked from entering the USA by a controversial immigration order enacted by President Trump. Although eight works might seem insignificant amidst a display of more than two hundred, the intervention—instigated and executed by staff who felt compelled to react to unsettling political circumstances—was unprecedented in the museum's history.

The additions ruptured MoMA's traditional narrative of Western Modernism, broadening the geographical and cultural scope, as well as the political implications, of its collection galleries. Alongside each work was a wall text that plainly stated the museum's intentions: "This work is by an artist from a nation whose citizens are being denied entry into the United States, according to a presidential executive order issued on Jan. 27, 2017. This is one of several such artworks from the Museum's collection installed throughout the fifth-floor galleries to affirm the ideals of welcome and freedom as vital to this Museum as they are to the United States."

This stealth activism on the part of MoMA's concerned curators garnered press, worldwide. To disrupt the museum's tightly woven narrative was a daring act. And yet, while the curators must be

credited for their chutzpah, why did it take a Muslim ban to spark
an intervention? How long will this tokenistic infiltration into the
permanent galleries last? And why has this never been done for
women artists or artists of color, who are woefully under-represented
in these same spaces? Instead of a monologue of sameness, why
not a presentation of Modernism as multi-vocal, global, diachronic?
As artist Cheryl Donegan has urged, "Modernism should not be seen
as biblical; it should be seen as Talmudic."[3] Instead of a synchronic,
static, linear narrative, why not follow a more Talmudic, Wikipedia-
like approach that would enable innumerable voices to comment,
debate, and shape tradition? Group exhibitions can play a big part
in this endeavor and grant the opportunity for many curators, non-
mainstream and mainstream alike, to showcase a wide assortment
of works, representing a multiplicity of voices, under the aegis of
a single curatorial thematic.

In the chapters that follow, I examine group exhibitions that
embody the various strategies associated with curatorial activism,
as outlined in Chapter 1, beginning with the 1976–1977 exhibition
Women Artists: 1550–1950 (Chapter 2), and ending with *Art AIDS
America* in 2015–2017 (Chapter 4). I discuss some landmark
exhibitions, as well as ones that are less familiar—but all of them
greatly expand the discourse of modern and contemporary art by
showcasing a more inclusive (vs. exclusive) selection of artists.
The coverage of each exhibition includes a selection of key images,
an overview of the show's theme and curatorial aim, and a summary
of its critical reception. These elements are not intended as critical
analyses but rather as overviews that, hopefully, will prompt further
scholarly and critical research.

It is important to point out that the selection of exhibitions
in this book has been informed by my identity as a white woman from
the USA, a seasoned curator and art historian, one who has visited
exhibitions internationally, but most often in Europe and North
America. Additional research needs to be undertaken in areas outside
this limited geographic region so that new definitions and agendas
for curatorial activism can be established.

1. WHAT IS CURATORIAL ACTIVISM?

"In the West, greatness has been defined since antiquity as white, Western, privileged, and, above all, male."[1]

Linda Nochlin

Statistics demonstrate that the fight for gender and race equality in the art world is far from over. Despite decades of postcolonial, feminist, anti-racist, and queer activism and theorizing, the art world continues to exclude "Other" artists—those who are women, of color, and LGBTQ. Discrimination against these artists invades every aspect of the art world, from gallery representation, auction-price differentials, and press coverage to inclusion in permanent collections and solo exhibition programs. In most mainstream museums, visitors are still required to actively search out work by them. There was, for example, dismal representation of women and non-white artists in the re-opening of the Tate Modern, London, in 2016—of the three hundred artists represented in the re-hang of the permanent collection, less than a third were women and fewer still were non-white.[3] Similar statistics were recorded the previous year, when the Whitney Museum of American Art opened its new location in New York with an inaugural exhibition entitled *America Is Hard to See*, showcasing works in its permanent collection and spanning a period from the 20th century to the present.[4]

While these facts are dismaying, it is the Museum of Modern Art (MoMA), New York, that gets the worst grade for gender and race discrimination. In 2004, it re-opened its greatly expanded exhibition spaces and unveiled the reinstallation of its prestigious permanent collection, featuring art from 1880 to 1970. Of the 410 works in the fourth- and fifth-floor galleries, only a paltry 16 were by women. There were even fewer works by non-white artists, and those who were given exhibition space were segregated in a single room dedicated to Diego Rivera and Mexican muralism. A dash through the same exhibition galleries in 2015 and 2016 revealed improvements, but continuing problems.[5] In 2014, as testament to the museum's lack of inclusiveness, the editors at ArtSlant started a rumor—an April Fools' joke, in fact—that MoMA would devote the year 2015 entirely to women.[6]

Blockbuster exhibitions are also subject to appalling levels of discrimination. The gender and race breakdowns of the Venice Biennale are a case in point. In the 2017 edition, entitled "Viva Arte Viva," curated by Christine Macel, women artists comprised only 35% of the participants. (By comparison, the tally was 37% in 2015, 26% in 2013, and 43% in 2009.) European and North American artists dominated the 2017 edition, with 61% of participants coming from the two continents. The racial demographics of the show were particularly disheartening, especially given the widespread vocal activism of groups such as Black Lives Matter: a mere 5 of the 120 artists were black—just one of whom (Senga Nengudi) was a woman. To my knowledge, not one critic has yet noted these gross disparities.[7]

In 2014, however, critics slammed the Whitney Biennial for its blatant racism and sexism, with protests in the galleries—by a group of artists calling themselves the "cliterati"—about the lack of women artists on display: of the 103 artists, just 37 were women. The Yams art collective withdrew their work from the Biennial in disgust at the show's lack of black and female artists. And within a month of the Biennial's opening, a protest show was organized, with the humorous title *Whitney Houston Biennial: I'm Every Woman*: it featured 22 artists, 10 of whom were women. Despite this public criticism of their 2014 Biennial, the Whitney's *America Is Hard to See* show the very next year was an astonishing 69% male and 77% white. The 2017 Biennial no doubt sought to redress the gross disparities: 25 of the 63 artists in the exhibition were women, several participants were gender fluid, and there was an almost equal percentage of white and non-white artists.[8]

GUERRILLA GIRLS' 1986 REPORT CARD

GALLERY	NO. OF WOMEN 1985-6	NO. OF WOMEN 1986-7	REMARKS
Blum Helman	1	1	No improvement
Mary Boone	0	0	Boy crazy
Grace Borgenicht	0	0	Lacks initiative
Diane Brown	0	2	Could do even better
Leo Castelli	4	3	Not paying attention
Charles Cowles	2	2	Needs work
Marisa del Rey	0	0	No progress
Allan Frumkin	1	1	Doesn't follow directions
Marian Goodman	0	1	Keep trying
Pat Hearn	0	0	Delinquent
Marlborough	2	1	Failing
Oil & Steel	0	1	Underachiever
Pace	2	2	Working below capacity
Tony Shafrazi	0	1	Still unsatisfactory
Sperone Westwater	0	0	Unforgivable
Edward Thorp	1	4	Making excellent progress
Washburn	1	1	Unacceptable

Source: Art in America Annual 1985-6 and 1986-7

A PUBLIC SERVICE MESSAGE FROM **GUERRILLA GIRLS** CONSCIENCE OF THE ART WORLD
532 LaGUARDIA PLACE, #237 · NY, NY 10012
email guerrillagirls@voyagerco.com
© Guerrilla Girls 1986

PUSSY GALORE'S 2015 REPORT CARD

GALLERY	% OF WOMEN	GALLERY	% OF WOMEN
303 Gallery	33%	Luhring Augustine	22%
Alexander & Bonin	27%	Matthew Marks	16%
Mary Boone	17%	Marlborough	7%
Leo Castelli	14%	Metro Pictures	25%
Cheim & Read	37%	Pace	16%
Paula Cooper	32%	Postmasters	30%
Derek Eller	18%	PPOW	53%
Ronald Feldman	29%	Andrea Rosen	27%
Zach Feuer	59%	Salon 94	48%
Gagosian	21%	Tony Shafrazi	5%
Marian Goodman	23%	Jack Shainman	47%
Casey Kaplan	14%	Sikkema Jenkins	52%
Paul Kasmin	13%	Sonnabend	28%
Yvon Lambert	21%	Sperone Westwater	9%
Lehmann Maupin	45%	Edward Thorp	38%
Galerie Lelong	64%	Tracey Williams	59%
Lombard Fried	20%	David Zwirner	24%

A PUBLIC SERVICE MESSAGE FROM **PUSSY GALORE** KICKING IDIOCY IN THE ARSE
© Pussy Galore 2015

The Guerrilla Girls' 1986 Report Card alongside Pussy Galore's 2015 Report Card

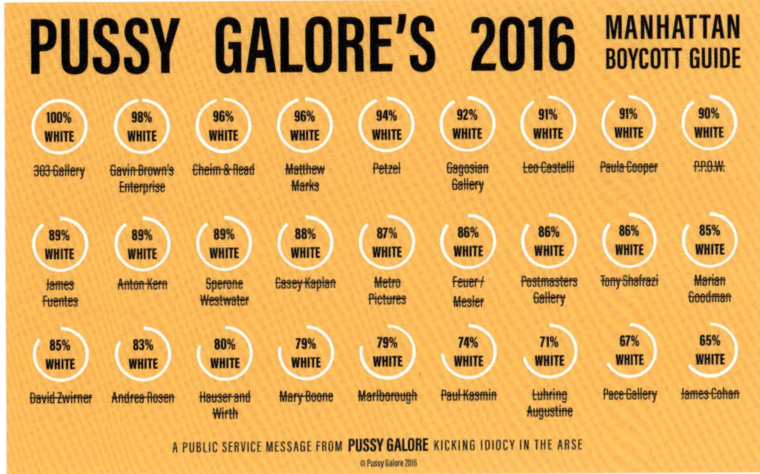

Feminist art activists such as the Guerrilla Girls have been protesting gender and race disparities for decades, calling out specific galleries and holding them accountable—most spectacularly in their Guerrilla Girls' 1986 Report Card, which displayed the number of women artists in New York gallery rosters, offering comments when and if there was improvement or deterioration.[9] More recently, art activists Pussy Galore updated the Guerilla Girls' statistics for those New York galleries that were still open, and added others to the mix. Of the galleries that were open in 2015, and comparing the statistics from 1986, the worst offenders were Sperone Westwater and Tony Shafrazi galleries. On a more positive note, some New York galleries were representing women half the time or more, including PPOW, Sikkema Jenkins, Zach Feuer, Tracey Williams, and Galerie Lelong.[10]

In 2013, the artist Micol Hebron, propelled by the predominance of male artists in gallery advertisements in *Artforum* magazine and in galleries themselves, launched the project Gallery Tally, which collects data on the ratios of male and female artists in contemporary galleries. Hebron estimated that less than a third of the artists represented by commercial galleries in the USA are women. According to her, there remains a "real problem" with who is being assisted, exhibited, collected, promoted, and written about.[11] An audit of the galleries in London by East London Fawcett (ELF) produced similar figures.[12]

The statistics highlighted by Gallery Tally, the Guerrilla Girls, Pussy Galore, ELF, and others are all the more shocking in view of the fact that in 2016 women made up between 65% and 80% of the students enrolled in studio art and art history programs.[13] (Statistics on non-white students are not available.) There is, then, an immense discrepancy between the number of female art students and the number of men represented by the galleries.

In 2016, the ever-vigilant Pussy Galore collective compiled statistics on racial discrimination in New York galleries. Tallying 34 galleries, they discovered that only 21% of the artists represented were non-white; the worst offenders were 303 Gallery, which was 100% white, and Gavin Brown Enterprise, which was 98% white.[14]

The availability of works by non-white and female artists at galleries obviously has a powerful impact on the amount of press coverage they receive and the degree of interest they generate from collectors, museums, and so on; this, in turn, directly affects their market and monetary values. There are now several publications and online rankings that collectors can turn to for insights into the market viability of an artist who may be of interest to them. For example, *Kunstkompass*, an annual publication (which for many years was published by the German business magazine *Capital* and is now published by *Manager Magazin*), reported what it claimed to be "The World's 100 Greatest Artists," basing its statistics on the frequency and prestige of exhibitions, publications, and press coverage, and the median price of one work of art. In the 2014 edition of *Kunstkompass*, three of the twenty "great artists" were women; all the artists were white.

Artnet.com also compiles rankings, which are based on art-market sales: in 2016, it presented a list of the "Top 100 Lots by Living Artists, 2011–16"—one woman (Cady Noland) and six non-white artists were listed. A second list unveiled the "Top 100 Living Artists," based on the total value of secondary market sales from January 2011 through mid-May 2016, ranking artists by the total value of works sold, along with the number of artworks at auction. In addition to Yayoi Kusama and Cindy Sherman, female artists on this 2016 list included Vija Celmins, Marlene Dumas, Bridget Riley, Tauba Auerbach, Julie Mehretu, and Cady Noland—giving a grand total of eight out of a hundred artists. Forty-five out of a hundred were non-white artists, the majority of whom lived in China.[15] These "Best of" listings of course do not equate with the aesthetic worth of the artist. They are, however, symptomatic of widespread discrimination.

While some ratios have improved for women and non-white artists, the statistics remain quite grim. It is important not to be seduced by what appear to be signs of equality—women and non-whites have never been, nor are they yet, treated on a par with white men. The existence of a few superstars or token achievers does not mean that Other artists have attained equality. The art world has not yet fully incorporated diverse or Other voices into the larger discourse—except, of course, as "special" (read separatist) exhibitions such as Latin American Art, Women Artists, Islamic Art, African Art, and so on. The master narratives of art—those that exclude large constituencies of people and present constructed boundaries and hierarchies as *natural* ones—continue to be discriminatory discourses that are rarely challenged. Sexism and racism have become so insidiously woven into the institutional fabric, language, and logic of the mainstream art world that they go almost entirely undetected. Once ferreted out, however, their prevalence cannot be denied. The statistics speak for themselves.

My aim as a scholar and curator is precisely *to ferret out*—to tally, to count, and to throw inequities into high relief, laying bare the powerful ideological mechanisms that ensure some artists are celebrated while others are marginalized. I have dedicated the past twenty-five years of my career to attempting to ensure that the under- or un-represented, the silenced, and the "doubly colonized" —those subjected by both empire and patriarchy, for example—are no longer ignored. I take as my operative assumption the fact that the art "system"—its history, institutions, market, press, and so on—is hegemonic, that it privileges white male creativity to the exclusion of all Others. My driving force as a curator is therefore wholly activist; my aim is to be consistently counter-hegemonic.

These imperatives have led me to examine global art history, to query the canon's Euro-US-centrism, and explore ways of rethinking it. Scholars who are focusing on race and postcolonial studies have had a particular impact on my critical thinking, as have those who are working on issues surrounding the canon and curricula. I have attempted to put into curatorial practice some of the strategies outlined in their approaches, with the *Global Feminisms* exhibition (2007) being my most ambitious attempt at a combined feminist/comparative-studies model, as originally envisioned by scholars such as Ella Shohat, Chandra Talpade Mohanty, and Kimberlé Crenshaw, among others.

The pursuits outlined above have led to this book, which ultimately asks: how can we get people in the art world *to think about* gender, race, and sexuality, to understand that these are persistent concerns that require action?; how can we all contribute to ensuring that the art world becomes more inclusive?

Several curators throughout the world are addressing, or have addressed, this issue of discrimination head-on. For example, Lucy R. Lippard, Jean-Hubert Martin, Okwui Enwezor, Rosa Martínez, Jonathan Katz, Camille Morineau, Michiko Kasahara, Juan Vicente Aliaga, Cornelia Butler, Simon Njami, Linda Nochlin, Amelia Jones, and others, are working for equal representation. While their strategies vary enormously, each is a "curatorial activist"—a term I use to describe people who have dedicated their curatorial endeavors almost exclusively to visual culture in, of, and from the margins: that is, to artists who are non-white, non-Euro-US, as well as women-, feminist-, and queer-identified. These curators, and others in similar fields, have committed themselves to initiatives that are leveling hierarchies, challenging assumptions, countering erasure, promoting the margins over the center, the minority over the majority, inspiring intelligent debate, disseminating *new* knowledge, and encouraging strategies of resistance—all of which offers hope and affirmation.

These curators—and others like them interested in art world injustices—have curated everything from biennales and retrospectives to large-scale thematic exhibitions, focusing on both historical and contemporary material. Some have tackled the historical canon, inserting artists into a narrative that had hitherto omitted them because of their sex and/or sexuality. Others have organized large monographic exhibitions of artists who have been historically overlooked, while others still have curated thematic exhibitions of modern and contemporary art that account for a wider range of voices. All these projects are widening the scope of artists on display and thereby expanding the historical canon and/or the contemporary art discourse in general.

THE CANON

The realization that Western art historical canons are problematic is not new. As early as 1971, in her pioneering essay, "Why Have There Been No Great Women Artists?," Nochlin cautioned against women attempting to name female Michelangelos or Picassos. "There are no women equivalents for Rembrandt, Delacroix or Cézanne, Picasso or Matisse," she argued, "any more than there are black American equivalents for the same."[16] The problem, she insisted, is systemic: it lies not in our hormones, if we are women, or in the color of our skin, if we are people of color—but in our institutions and our education. The question of equality centers on the very nature of institutional structures themselves, on patriarchy, and on the white, masculine prerogative that is assumed as "natural." It is precisely this ideological stronghold over women and non-white people that has prevented them from succeeding historically.

If the canon of art history is a hegemony—which I think we can all agree that it is—then, in the words of Griselda Pollock, how can we "difference it"?[17] Which counter-hegemonic strategies can we employ to ensure that more voices are included, rather than the chosen, elite few? What can we do as arts professionals to offer a more just and fair representation of global artistic production? Should we be working towards a global art history, an art without borders? Should we aim to abolish canons altogether, arguing that all cultural artifacts have significance—in other words, should our goal be a totalizing critique of canonicity itself? Should we be creating new, alternative canons?

In the pages that follow—and drawing on research from the last five decades of postcolonial, race, feminist, and queer theory—I discuss what I believe to be the most successful tactics for addressing inequality. Rather than pursuing unproductive critiques of the existing canon, I have attempted to pry it apart, and in the process uncover strategies for eroding, destabilizing, and dismantling it.

STRATEGIES OF RESISTANCE

REVISIONISM

The most frequently cited counter-hegemonic strategy addressing exclusion in the canon is a "revisionist" one, whereby individuals are reclaimed from history and the canon itself is re-written, the principal aim being to include those who had hitherto been refused, forgotten, or hidden. A revisionist approach to the canon typically asks questions such as: who were the women artists from the Renaissance-Baroque period?; who were the main African American painters in Abstract Expressionism?

In the 1970s, when many revisionist projects began—around the same time as the women's and civil-rights movements—it was argued that the resurrection of Others from history should be undertaken before analysis and deconstruction of the canon could begin. As Adrienne Rich argued in 1972, "Re-vision—the act of looking back, of seeing with fresh eyes, of entering an old text from a new critical direction—is for women far more than a chapter in cultural history: it is an act of survival."[18] A revisionist approach, then, rediscovers what the canon conceals and suppresses; it questions the adequacy of accepted conceptual structures, and looks for the "sins and errors of the past."[19]

Revisionist strategies enable curators to present a more inclusive and integrated selection of works and artists in relation to a particular subject—as was the case, for example, with Norman Kleeblatt's exhibition, *Action/Abstraction: Pollock, De Kooning, and American Art, 1940–1976* at the Jewish Museum in New York in 2008, which revised the timeworn narrative of Abstract Expressionism to include Helen Frankenthaler, Lee Bontecou, Joan Mitchell, Ann Truitt, Lee Krasner, and Norman Lewis—five women and an artist of color who had previously been excluded.

Similarly, feminism can be used as a methodological strategy for exhibitions related to historical periods. For example, at the Brooklyn Museum in 2007, I co-curated with Edward Bleiberg *Pharaohs, Queens, and Goddesses: Feminism's Impact on Egyptology*, which was dedicated to powerful female figures from Egyptian history. In this exhibition of thirty-five objects, the central object was an important granite head from the Brooklyn Museum's collection of Hatshepsut, the fifth pharaoh of the Eighteenth dynasty (1539–1292 BCE). She was shown alongside the queens Cleopatra, Nefertiti, and Tiye and the goddesses Sakhmet, Mut, Neith, Wadjet, Bastet, Satis, and Nephthys, among others. The exhibition demonstrated how the discipline of Egyptology has been transformed by feminism and the women's movement: conditions in the academic world have improved greatly, with many more women Egyptologists than there were at the beginning of the 20th century; as they observe changes in modern society, both male and female Egyptologists are now more willing to accept that women wielded political power in the ancient world. For example, the older interpretations of Hatshepsut's reign as a violation of Egyptian protocol have fallen out of favor. Today, Egyptologists recognize that Hatshepsut preserved her family's claims to the throne while the male heir was still a child—in recent years, she has metamorphosed from the villain to the heroine of her own story. In much the same way, Egyptologists now recognize Tiye and Nefertiti as their husbands' equal partners in ruling Egypt, rather than as women who attempted to claim more power than was appropriate for a queen. Even Cleopatra— whose reputation among the ancient Romans, and countless historians, was essentially negative—is today recognized primarily as the legitimate guardian of her country's political interests. These fundamental reassessments of historical figures stem from a viewpoint that has been hugely influenced by modern feminism.

While revisionism is an important curatorial strategy, it nevertheless assumes the white, masculinist, Western canon as its center and accepts its hierarchy as a natural given. So, within a revisionist strategy, a fundamental binary opposition is retained, which means that the Other will always necessarily remain subordinated. And as feminist literary theorist Elaine Showalter cautions, "the feminist obsession with correcting, modifying, supplementing, revising, humanizing, or even attacking male critical theory keeps us dependent upon it and retards our progress in solving our own theoretical problems."[20] We must also be wary of a revisionism that becomes a kind of homage.[21] As Susan Hardy Aiken warns, "One might, by attacking, reify the power one opposes."[22]

Revising the canon to address the neglect of women and/or so-called minority artists, then, is fundamentally an impossible project because, as Pollock argues, "such revision does not grapple with the terms that created that neglect."[23] So, after decades of feminist and postcolonial work that attempts to rectify gaps in the archive, we still face the question posed by her: "How can we make the cultural work of women [and minorities] an effective presence in cultural discourse which changes both the order of discourse and the hierarchy of gender [and race] in one and the same deconstructive move?"[24] (The canon is "politically 'in the masculine' as well as culturally 'of the masculine'"[25]—just as it is politically and culturally "in/of the white".)

Despite these shortfalls, the benefits of the revisionist strategy are many. For example, not only do they address critical exclusions, but they can also provide a deeper, more contextual understanding of key issues by creating space within white male institutions and mainstream discourses that help audiences understand visual culture from a wholly different perspective.[26] In revising the art historical canon to include Other artists such as Elisabeth Louise Vigée Le Brun, Berthe Morisot, and Norman Lewis on an equal footing with their white and/or male counterparts, curators have succeeded in integrating them into the Western canon, thereby offering a broader, more comprehensive view of art history.

AREA STUDIES

While revisionism involves an integrative approach, "area studies" produces new canons and supplements the traditional discourse by focusing on work that is based on either racial, geographical, gendered, or sexual orientation. This type of approach may encourage exhibitions that spotlight Women Artists, African American Art, LGBTQ Art, Middle-Eastern Art, and so on. Again, anything outside the (white, male, Western) center requires "special" attention, and is designated a separate "area."

Since the 1970s, numerous exhibitions in Europe and the USA have adopted this strategy, including *Old Mistresses* (1972), *Women Artists: 1550–1950* (1976), *Sense and Sensibility: Women Artists and Minimalism in the Nineties* (1994), *Mirror Images: Women, Surrealism, and Self-Representation* (1998), *Africa Remix* (2005), *Hide & Seek* (2010–12), *Women of Abstract Expressionism* (2016), *Queer British Art,*

1861–1967 (2017). Each of these shows added Others to the dominant narrative, but as separate categories of either gender, race, or sexuality. Again, while such projects are inherently revisionist, an area-studies focus is often seen as the most effective way to diversify the historical canon and/or contemporary discourse. These exhibitions are sophisticated and complex studies, but they are viewed as entirely separate from the canon. This is why many postcolonial and feminist theorists have argued against them, claiming that they are ghettoizing, segregating, and culturally and/or biologically essentialist insofar as they isolate artists on the basis of their gender, nationality, and sexuality—or indeed, any other difference—and create specialized, separatist museums and exhibition spaces (for example, the Jewish Museum, the National Museum of Women in the Arts, the Center for Feminist Art at the Brooklyn Museum, the Leslie Lohman Gay and Lesbian Museum).

Specialist exhibitions are not always looked upon favorably in the art world itself. In 2004, for example, Christian Rattemeyer, then a curator at Artists Space (an avant-garde institution in New York that has traditionally supported work from the margins), rejected shows on African and LGBTQ art (the latter entitled *Living Legacy: Queer Art Now*) because, according to him, "it is no longer the time to make such limiting judgments for selection," and "we should shy away from exhibitions of works by Women artists, Black artists, or, as in the most recent example, African artists, selected solely on the basis of gender, ethnicity, or nationality."[27] He also argued that there is no longer a need for exhibitions on so-called marginalized groups because they have now been included in contemporary art shows.

On hearing of Rattemeyer's response, the Guerrilla Girls sent him the following letter:

> Dear Sir
>
> We were privileged recently to see a letter that you sent to Harmony Hammond and Ernesto Pujol declining an exhibition proposal they had submitted to your institution.
>
> We are writing to say that we couldn't agree more with the views you expressed in your letter!!!!! You are right that in this post-ethnic era there should no longer be exhibitions of works by "Women artists," "Black artists," "African artists," or, as in the co-curator's proposal, "Queer Artists," or any shows selected solely on the basis of gender, ethnicity, or nationality.

But we feel you didn't go far enough. Let's get real, here!
In this post-studio era, how can you justify shows of
"video artists," "painters," "sculptors" or "photographers?"

In fact, since, any curatorial intervention limits the reading
of artists' work, by pushing it into some thesis or other,
we propose there should be no more exhibitions at all!

Sincerely,
Käthe Kollwitz for the Guerrilla Girls

This letter poses important questions, such as: is there no longer
a need for exhibitions of work by queer artists, African artists, women
artists, or any other groups?; and are we really living in a post-black,
post-feminist, post-queer world? In thinking about these issues,
it should be noted that some curatorial positions universalize artistic
production—for example, we should not assume that the few freedoms
LGBTQ individuals have achieved in the USA are replicated in other
countries. We cannot claim to live in a post-queer world when in some
countries being queer, gay, bisexual, or transgender is punishable
by death and in many more it is a criminal offence. It is a grave mistake
to assume that the social climate of apparently liberal cities such
as Manhattan, Los Angeles, and London is also the social climate
of the world, just as we cannot assume that the issues "queers" face
in New York are the equivalent to the issues they face in Nebraska.
There is, then, a real need for shows that examine what it means
to be "queer" on a global scale.

We should perhaps be thinking less about the potentially
ghettoizing effects of these types of specialist exhibitions, and more
about their positive aspects—for example, as curatorial frameworks
that allow us to present outstanding works of art to the public, often
for the first time. As Lippard pointed out when she was asked why she
had curated the women-only exhibition *26 Contemporary Women
Artists* in 1971: "The show itself, of course, is about art. The restriction
to women's art has its obvious polemic source, but as a framework
within which to exhibit good art it is no more restrictive than, say,
exhibitions on German, Cubist, Black and white, soft, young, or new art."[28]

Another key aspect of specialist exhibitions is that they
function as curatorial correctives. While many of us long for a time
when there will no longer be a need for shows focused exclusively
on race, gender, or sexuality, we have not yet reached that point.
Without "area studies" exhibitions, Other artists will continue to

be marginalized and made invisible. The key concept here is *visibility*, which is crucial in terms of prominence in the marketplace and in art history. In the 1976 exhibition *Women Artists: 1550–1950*, for example, the curators Linda Nochlin and Sutherland Harris literally resurrected works by women artists, such as Italian painters Lavinia Fontana (1552–1614) and Sofonisba Anguissola (1532–1625), from museum storage in the USA and Western Europe. Previously obliterated from history, these artists are now highly visible—they are taught in schools, colleges, and universities, and feature in academic dissertations as well in the major textbooks of art history. In short, women-only exhibitions have had a transformative impact on the art world.

This is also true of exhibitions that have focused exclusively on sexuality—as in *Queer British Art, 1861–1967*, curated by Clare Barlow at Tate Britain in 2017. The blockbuster show sought to present art and (some) ephemera from Britain that reflects, celebrates, and reveals the nuances of non-binary, non-heterosexual, and gender-fluid identities, with a timeframe spanning the abolition of the death penalty for sodomy in 1861 to the de-criminalization of male homosexuality in 1967. From Duncan Grant's homoerotic sketches, Simeon Solomon's veiled lesbo-erotic work, and Man Ray's portrait of Virginia Woolf to Gluck's mannish self-portrait, Joe Orton's library-book collages, and Noël Coward's dressing gown—and ending with explicit works by Francis Bacon and David Hockney—the exhibition was brimming with extraordinary stories and vibrant perspectives. Presenting more than one hundred objects (the majority of which were produced by white males), the show was designed not only to adjust the fact that art history has ignored and glossed over queer artists and artworks but also to showcase works that give voice to oppressed identities. In other words, as Adrian Searle explained in his review in *The Guardian*, the exhibition—which he considered "strange, sexy, heart-wrenching"—was "about stories and lives, and conflicting social mores, as much as of images and objects." [29] Importantly, it included never-before- or rarely-seen objects that the curator had unearthed from the art world's less-travelled paths, including, among many others surprises, tiny lockets designed by Charles Ricketts for Edith Cooper and her life partner Katherine Bradley, and a full-length portrait of Oscar Wilde by Robert Harper Pennington, which was hung beside the actual door to Wilde's cell in Reading jail, where Wilde was imprisoned in the late 19th century for "gross indecency" with other men.

Writing in *The Independent* in 2016, Janet Street-Porter accused Tate Britain of "lumping together" LGBTQ artists, criticizing the view of "queer art" as a movement, and the exhibition's premise as "highly questionable."[30] However, Barlow was by no means presenting "queer art" as a movement, but rather presenting, in one exhibition, works and objects produced by non-heteronormative artists. Her choice of the word "queer" was intended to designate a fluid term for people of different sexualities and gender identities, and using it in this way allowed her to recount a complicated story of sexuality and desire through works that are often as coded and veiled as they are explicit. As Barlow explained, "We [were] absolutely not presenting it as a closed canon. It [was] the start of a conversation."[31] And it is a conversation that must continue.

Until Other artists have a far stronger foothold in the system and have achieved equality in representation, it is important that we preserve these exhibitions, spaces, curatorial positions, and labels such as "black," "woman," or "queer," even though we may recognize that they are inherently essentialist, ghettoizing, exclusionary, and universalizing, and fail to account for important differences between and among artists' lived experiences. Gayatri Spivak's concept of "strategic essentialism," as outlined in her book *In Other Worlds: Essays in Cultural Politics* (1987), is particularly useful in this context. For Spivak, groups may act temporarily "as if" their identities are stable in an effort to create solidarity, a sense of belonging and identity to a group, race, or ethnicity, for the purposes of social or political action. For instance, strategic essentialism might involve the bringing together of diverse agendas of various women's groups to work for a common cause, such as abortion rights or domestic violence. The Women's March on Washington in 2017, initiated by the uproar concerning Donald Trump's election as president of the USA, was a particularly powerful example of strategic essentialism: a million people—of every gender, ethnicity, and religion—came together as "women" protesting. Their causes and concerns were not identical by any means, but they united under an "essentialist" identity, that of women. So, in strategic essentialism, the "essential attributes" are acknowledged to be a construct—that is, the (political) group, somewhat paradoxically, acknowledges that the attributes (black, queer, woman, for example) are not intrinsically essential, but are invoked if they are considered to be strategically and politically useful. Moreover, members of the group maintain the power to decide when the attributes are "essential" and when they are not. In this way, strategic essentialism can be a potent political tool.[32]

RELATIONAL STUDIES: EXHIBITION-AS-POLYLOGUE
In her postcolonial analysis of college curricula, cultural studies scholar Ella Shohat proposes a "relational approach" as the most efficient way

to address Euro-US-centrism and sexism in the classroom.[33] This approach begins with questions such as: what if history was re-conceived as dialogic instead of synchronic? So, instead of thinking, for example, of Modernism and postmodernism as a series of interlocking, related, "-isms," arranged along a linear historical line, they could perhaps be re-conceived as multivocal. Similarly, what if time itself was understood to be wide or kaleidoscopic as opposed to linear?[34] What if works of art and literature were presented ahistorically, ignoring national borders or periodic categories, or were arranged thematically or without a coherent thesis? Or if we were to abolish historic canons, arguing that all art has significance (including cultural artifacts), non-Western and Western alike? Or again, if oppositions and hierarchies (high/low, West/East, white/black) were dismantled? How would such radical redefinitions of the field and transformations in perception affect the contemporary global art world?

Aiken argues that by employing a relational approach we can present multiplicity in terms of an ongoing dialogue—or, more accurately, a polylogue (a term she borrows from philosopher, psychoanalyst, and literary critic Julia Kristeva): "an interplay of many voices, a kind of creative 'barbarism' that would disrupt the monological, colonizing, centristic drives of 'civilization.'"[35] Such an approach becomes not merely what Rich terms "an act of survival," but also a way to "perpetual regeneration."[36] A relational approach to curating, then, is interested not in a monologue of sameness, but in a multitude or cacophony of voices speaking simultaneously. The result, as Pollock explains, is that "the cultural field may be reimagined as a space for multiple occupancy where differencing creates a productive covenant opposing the phallic logic that offers us only the prospect of safety in sameness or danger in difference, of assimilation to or exclusion from the canonized norm."[37] In this type of exhibition, for example, contemporary "Aboriginal art" would not be considered as Aboriginal art but as contemporary art, and would be exhibited alongside art from Japan, the USA, Argentina, Africa, and so on—with no hierarchical implications. It should be emphasized that this strategy is concerned not with assimilation, but with a leveling of hierarchy. It is a fundamental redefining of art practice, transnationally.

A relational approach to curating presents art as if it were a polysemic site of contradictory positions and contested practices. This focus goes beyond a mere description of discrete regions and cultures; it transcends the "additive" approach, collapses the destructive center-periphery binary, and is essentially postmodern in nature: it is textual, dialogic, and "writerly." According to French literary critic and theorist Roland Barthes—whose work also addresses and has had an immense impact on how we perceive the visual world—a writerly text is characterized by heterogeneity and incoherence. It is "a multi-dimensional space in which a variety of writings, none of them original, blend and clash."[38] In a "writerly" exhibition, then, the reader, or viewer, can be seen as an active participant in the construction, or "writing" of meaning with respect to the works on view.

Examples of exhibitions that have used a relational approach to curating include *Magiciens de la terre* (1989), *Documenta 11* (2002), *Global Feminisms* (2007), and *Carambolages* (2016), among others. Curatorially, the relational approach pertains to group (versus monographic) exhibitions as it aims to ensure multiple voices. But a group exhibition alone does not always embody the approach, as it is a *deliberate* tactic, a conscious decision on the part of the curator(s) to look beyond Europe and the USA, beyond sex, gender, and race, to arrive at a more equitable representation of contemporary art. It is also an approach that is specific to contemporary art (only rarely is it adopted for exhibitions that focus on artists from the past). Such an exhibition may, for example, focus on 20th-century art that was global in scope, perhaps arranged thematically, and did not assume the "-isms" derived from Western discourse (Cubism, Abstract Expressionism, and so on) as defining moments globally, but rather as context-specific to one region of the world or another. One such example would be the exhibition *Century City* (see pp. 130–37).

Curators who adopt a relational approach highlight cultural differences by presenting a collection of voices that, as Mohanty suggests, "tell alternate stories of difference, culture, power, and agency."[39] Using a model of relational analysis, the curators can place diverse works in dialogic relation to one another in order to underscore what Mohanty refers to as "common differences"—that is, the significant similarities as well as the localized differences between artists across cultures.[40] With careful juxtaposition of works, then, curators are able to draw attention to important differences in the artists' treatment of similar themes. In so doing, they offer a fresh and expanded definition of artistic production for a transnational age, one that acknowledges important differences among artists globally. However, the issue with exhibitions that are thematic, ahistorical, and transnational is that they are rarely understood and often criticized, as with the permanent-collection installations at Tate Modern (organized by Iwona Blazwick) in 2000 and at Reina Sofía, Madrid, in 2009. Ultimately, people are wary of shows with *unfamiliar* artists and without a strict chronology.

At other times, these exhibitions embody a visual culture paradigm. *Carambolages*—organized by Jean-Hubert Martin in 2016 for the Grand Palais in Paris—is one such example. In this show, Martin (who also curated the iconic *Magiciens de la terre* in 1989), presented an ahistorical, non-chronological, anti-categorical selection of 184 objects, ranging over thousands of years. They consisted of both artworks and artifacts and were chosen for their formal similarities or poetic affinities. For example, a sculpture of a cat by Giacometti was shown alongside a two-thousand-year-old sculpture of a mouse from Oceania; and an 18th-century self-portrait by Flemish artist Nicola van Houbraken—in which the artist peeps through a hole in the canvas— was juxtaposed with a "slash painting" by Lucio Fontana. Importantly, many of the works and artists included in the exhibition were relatively unknown—a feature that was derided by several critics, who longed for masterpieces by more famous artists.[41] Each group of works was arranged in a continuous sequence, with every work not only somehow dependent, either visually or conceptually, on the one that preceded it, but also "announcing" the one that followed it, rather like a game of billiards, where—as Martin points out—a single ball

Installation view, *Carambolages*
Réunion des Musées Nationaux –
Grand Palais
March 2, 2016–July 4, 2016
curated by Jean-Hubert Martin

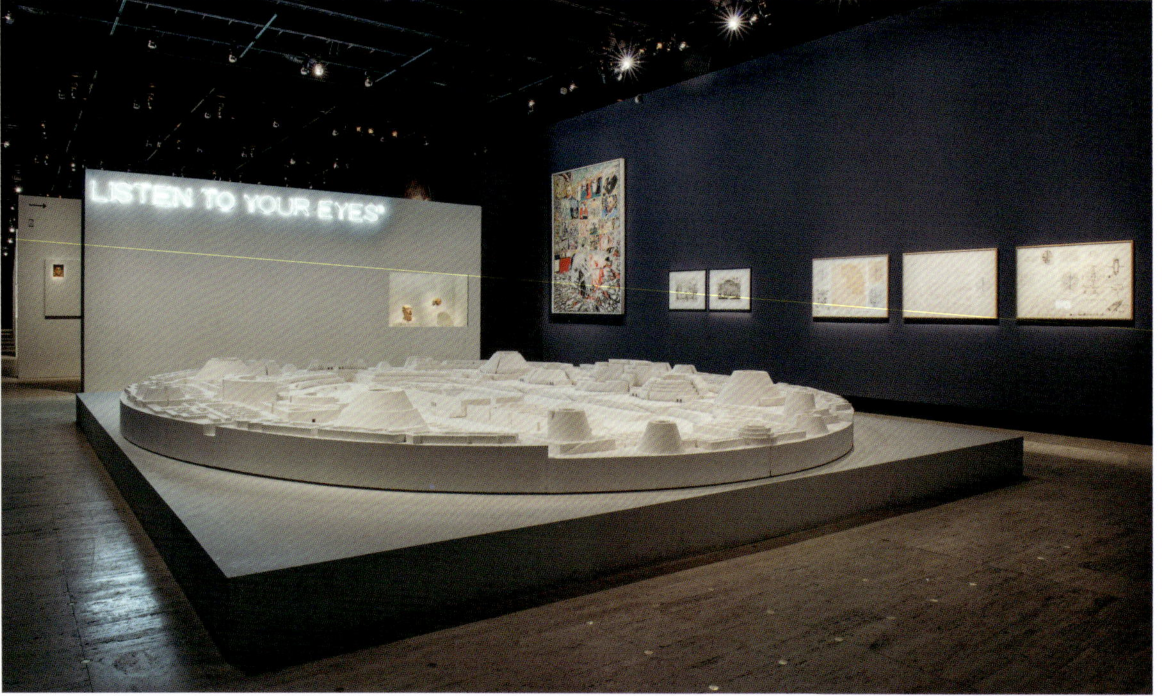

can impact two other balls.[42] Hence the title *Carambolages*, which translates from French as: "double whammy"; "ricochet shot in billiards"; "car crash" or "pile-up."

In the exhibition catalogue, Martin acknowledges Aby Warburg's influence on cross-cultural exhibitions, emphasizing that he (Martin) is not the first curator to organize works of art and artifacts in a personalized manner. Much like Warburg in his picture atlas, *Mnemosyne Atlas* (1927–29), or Sir John Soane in his eccentric London museum, or Duc d'Aumale, in Château de Chantilly, or André Malraux's *The Museum without Walls* (1947), Martin's exhibition underlined the importance of individual interpretation on the part of the viewers, who were perceived as active participants in the construction of meaning. As in Barthes's concept of the writerly text, these "readers" are encouraged to perceive the exhibition as "multiple, irreducible, coming from a disconnected, heterogeneous variety of substances and perspectives."[43] *Carambolages* demonstrated no overarching or coherent thesis: objects were presented context-free—that is, without wall labels (although visitors with smartphones could download captions at the entrance). In the exhibition, Martin invented what he called "an artistic game," with no captions, but with the eye as the medium for enjoying the exhibition. "Listen to your Eyes" by Maurizio Nannucci was used as a motto in neon letters in the first room. According to the curator, "You don't need cultural references to enjoy a work of art."[44] Instead, the viewers' senses were guided so that they could understand what they saw with reference to other works from different periods and styles. Martin's expressed aim was to break down the traditional approach to art so as to transcend the borders of genres, eras, and distinct cultures.

Carambolages was a postmodern cabinet of curiosities that swerved far from the strict periodic categories once typical of the museum and art history. As Martin explained, "The history of art is only one factor among others when it comes to understanding a work…It is imperfect because instead of there being a succession of big historical shifts, there is on the contrary an enormous continuity between those who painted the Chalet cave and today's artists. Artists have asked themselves the same questions across time."[45] In this heterogeneous, ahistorical show, unknown artists and artisans were presented as equals to the "celebrity" artists—and deliberately so. In arguing that all cultural artifacts have significance, Martin's show was a totalizing critique of canonicity itself.

2. RESISTING MASCULINISM AND SEXISM

"Do you see art as a man's world? Yes, it is a world where men and women are continually trying to satisfy the power of men."[1]

Louise Bourgeois

Women have come a long way since Linda Nochlin wrote her landmark essay, "Why Have There Been No Great Women Artists?" in 1971 (see p. 22).[2]

Today, women artists are featured in important museum and private collections; they are the subjects of monographs, represented in art-history textbooks, and visible in galleries, in the media, and in the art scene in general. In recent years, numerous women have received grants from the Guggenheim Foundation, New York, and the MacArthur Foundation, Chicago; Yayoi Kusama, Georgia O'Keeffe, Cady Noland, and Frida Kahlo, among others, made headlines in 2016 with their off-the-chart auction prices; and the luminaries of the 1980s and 1990s—artists such as Cindy Sherman, Kiki Smith, Mona Hatoum, and Tracey Emin—have demonstrated the immense possibilities for women artists in the modern world.

Over the past two decades, curators have shown greater interest in integrating women more fully into major group exhibitions. For example, in the Venice Biennale of 2009, organized by Daniel Birnbaum, almost half the featured works were by women.[3] One-woman museum shows and retrospectives are also on the rise; and feminist art exhibitions have been far more frequent in recent history, especially post-2000. Access to art education—to which women had historically been denied—is now possible for many with financial means, and there are far more female than male students in art programs in the USA. Moreover, the institutional power structures—which, as Nochlin pointed out, made it impossible for women, whatever their talent, to succeed on the same footing as men—have been shifting, albeit slightly.[4] And women themselves, whom she cautioned against "puffing mediocity," have since taken the risks and "leap[s] into the unknown" that she felt were necessary for them to achieve "greatness."[5]

Given such advances, one might think that women's improved status and visibility in the art world were indicators of significant and irreversible progress. However, while these are all optimistic signs that certainly represent a shift in a positive direction, *they are by no means seismic*. Full equality has not been achieved and there are still major systemic problems that need to be addressed. Progress for women has always come in fits and starts: one step forward, one back, and so on. The year 2013, for example, saw some major setbacks for women artists, to the extent that the overall situation seemed to be deteriorating rather than improving over the years. Whereas Birnbaum's 2009 Venice Biennale, for instance, had been a step forward for women, the 2013 Biennale, under Massimiliano Gioni, was a disaster, with the number of female artists represented plummeting to a dismal 16%. And by September of the same year, the New York art world was abuzz with speculation about a male take-over in the art world. There was tremendous media attention on the fact that the majority of museums in New York City were holding major solo exhibitions highlighting male artists—from René Magritte at the Museum of Modern Art (MoMA) and Robert Indiana at the Whitney Museum of American Art, to Robert Motherwell at the Guggenheim and Balthus at The Metropolitan Museum of Art, New York—and that a powerful, highly visible gallery such as the Gagosian was presenting a group exhibition in London showcasing thirty-five artists, only one of whom was female. On WNYC radio, art critic Deborah Solomon took the temperature of the moment in one of her "Art Talks": "This," she said, "is an art season that could make you think that the feminist movement had never happened."[6]

During her broadcast, Solomon also posed the provocative question: should New York's museums give equal time and space to female artists? In other words, should quotas be enforced? This triggered a firestorm of responses. Some argued, why not? It has worked in other fields. One critic, John Powers, suggested establishing a kind of "Title IX" program at art museums (modeled on Title IX in the 1972 US federal law, designed to abolish gender discrimination in higher education). Title IX had been particularly effective in college athletics, boosting participation in women's sports substantially. In the art world, such a measure would require gender proportionality in funding for art exhibitions, acquisitions, and so on. Powers even suggested that MoMA should be sued under Title IX, especially as museums share the same organizational definitions and nonprofit, tax-exemption status that makes universities Title IX-eligible. Many media critics agreed wholeheartedly. At worst, suing the organization on the grounds of gender discrimination would force some revisions to a predetermined rubric; at best, it would broaden definitions of greatness, redefine some tired rules, and better reflect the world outside. Those opposed to affirmative action suggested that we are beyond that now, and that suing MoMA for discrimination was absurd. They argued that women are treated equally in the art world now and that the prevalence of shows dedicated to male artists is simply a coincidence, not outright prejudice. They cited artists such as Emin, Sherman, and Marina Abramović as examples of female art stars, represented by blue-chip galleries, and garnering record prices at art auction. This kind of cognitive dissonance needs addressing. Political action is obviously still necessary.

GENDER REFORM IN THE ART WORLD

Since the 1970s, there have been a series of women's and feminist art exhibitions that have acted as correctives to the omission of women artists from art-historical records. In the 1970s and 1980s, shows in the UK, Europe, Canada, and the USA drew attention to women artists as important cultural producers worthy of consideration.[7] Some of the projects reclaimed and excavated these artists from history and inserted them into the historical canon from which they had been excluded; others celebrated contemporary artists whose work embodied the 1970s feminist dictum "the personal is political," and whose politics were most often played out on the body itself, with women artists using their bodies as a canvas upon which to act out their ideas. In *Up to and Including Her Limits* (1973–76), for example, Carolee Schneemann used her nude body as a tool or instrument to create a canvas, while Hannah Wilke, in *S.O.S. Starification Object Series: An Adult Game of Mastication* (1974–75), stuck tiny vulval-shaped sculptures made from chewing gum onto herself.

In the 1990s, feminism continued its forward momentum, with a number of benchmark exhibitions.[8] By calling attention to non-male cultural producers, this series of shows challenged the broader framework of contemporary art and its exhibition practices for being unconditionally masculinist. As counter-hegemonic projects, they expanded the canons of art history and contemporary art discourses to include what the canon hitherto refused—women, in particular.

From the beginning of the 21st century there has been a wealth of high-profile feminist art exhibitions that has generated important debate about feminist artistic production.[9] Each show specifically addressed the art world's inherent biases by offering up a counter-discourse and/or parallel narrative that focused on stellar work being produced by artists from women's and feminist communities, on an international scale.[10] Indeed, 2007 was referred to as the "Year of the Woman" and "the year of institutional consciousness-raising" in the mainstream press, in recognition of the fact that women and feminist artists were drawing tremendous public attention around that time.[11]

This widespread interest in feminist art post-2000—displayed not only in shows, but in books, magazines, symposia, and panels—reflected the rise of powerful female curators, art historians, and, most notably, patrons, who were working to change art institutions from the inside. In 2001, for example, art philanthropist Elizabeth A. Sackler purchased the iconic installation *The Dinner Party* (1979) by Judy Chicago, conserved it at The Getty Center, Los Angeles, and then gifted it to the Brooklyn Museum in 2002, when it was presented as a special exhibition to around eight thousand people over a four-month period. It was during this special exhibition of *The Dinner Party* that discussions began between Sackler and Brooklyn Museum director Arnold Lehman about establishing not only a permanent installation for Chicago's work, but also an 8,300 sq. ft (770 sq. m) exhibition and public programming space devoted exclusively to feminist art, which would represent the first space of its kind in the USA, if not the world. Later in 2002, the Brooklyn Museum made a formal announcement that it was in conversation with Sackler about the initiative. There was considerable debate thereafter about whether the space should be called a center for "women's art" or "feminist art." The museum finally settled on the latter, recognizing the profound impact feminism has had on post-1960s cultural production. In emphasizing "feminist," the museum also acknowledged how feminism's challenging ideas, theories, and methodologies—and the myriad ways in which those are manifest in the visual realm—have influenced every aspect of contemporary art.

The Elizabeth A. Sackler Center for Feminist Art, for which I was founding curator, opened in March 2007 with three inaugural exhibitions: *Pharoahs, Queens and Goddesses: Feminism's Impact on Egytology*, which I co-curated with Edward Bleiberg; the permanent installation of Chicago's *The Dinner Party*; and *Global Feminisms: New Directions in Contemporary Art*, which I co-curated with Nochlin (see pp. 74–79). There was massive international press coverage at the opening, and the Center was recognized as an unprecedented museological intervention, and as a significant milestone—not only in the history of museums, but in the history of art itself.

In 2005, MoMA experienced its own moment of institutional consciousness-raising, when arts patron Sarah Peter approached the museum with a request to find ways for it to support women artists more effectively. Her offer provoked internal discussion, which led to the decision that curators would research the women artists in the museum's collection—the ratio of male to female artists was about 5:1 at the time. What started as a book about female artists at MoMA eventually led to the establishment of the Modern Women's Fund (MWF), which is now the umbrella organization for a series of ongoing initiatives. The aim of the MWF is to reassess the traditionally masculinist canon and to make room for women artists incrementally, on a long-term basis. The MWF also manages an acquisitions fund devoted to purchasing work by women artists for the collection. These acquisitions are supported by dues paid by a funding group of trustees and collectors. The MWF initiative has resulted in many important changes since 2005, including extensive educational and public programs, support for major solo exhibitions dedicated to women artists, and the staging of international symposia focusing on women's issues in the art world. Sarah Suzuki, the current curatorial chair of the MWF, and curator of drawings and prints, says that the effects of the Fund only continue to reverberate and amplify within the institution. A newly reconstituted internal group, the Modern Women's Leadership Council, has recently brought together female staff from across MoMA's departments to find further meaningful ways to make the contributions of women artists more visible, with an eye towards sharply recalibrating the 5:1 ratio previously seen in the permanent galleries. While the MWF has chosen "women" and not "feminist" in the Fund's name, their project is wholly feminist. It is rooted in a desire to right the wrongs of past histories within the institution and to make "correct" decisions in the present and moving forward. They have the full backing of the institution from the top down, strong funding, and an inspired staff to ensure success.

The Moderna Museet in Stockholm was also making a concerted effort around this time to address gender disparity in its permanent collection. From 2006 to 2008, under the direction of Lars Nittve, the museum created the "Second Museum of Our Wishes," which was a call for the government to allocate funds for the acquisition of works by women artists. Such initiatives should obviously be celebrated as they function to grant women artists increased visibility. In this case, however, it was disappointing that the museum enhanced its collection by only twenty-six works by fourteen artists. Also, the initiative lasted for just three years and did not raise funds to guarantee the acquisition of works by women in perpetuity. Some critics therefore considered the museum's actions to be largely tokenistic.

Another initiative that contributed to the recognition of women and feminist artists during the early 21st century was the establishment of The Feminist Art Project (TFAP) in 2006, which I co-founded with Arlene Raven, Judy Chicago, Dena Muller, Judy Brodsky, Ferris Olin, and Susan Fisher Sterling. Its initial aim was to spark initiatives throughout the USA that would build on the momentum created by the announcement that the Sackler Center would be opening in 2007. We conceptualized TFAP as a conscious effort to jumpstart a new movement through the grassroots promotion of feminist art exhibitions, events, education, and publications.[12] The project is a strategic intervention against the ongoing erasure of women from the cultural record, and is one that continues today. Each year at the annual conference for the College Art Association, there is an entire day programmed by TFAP that is dedicated exclusively to women's and feminist art. With regional groups rapidly developing and international networking in place, perhaps some of those necessary systemic changes will and can take place in the future—first and foremost (since it is primarily an academic-based project) via the dismantling and re-structuring of fine art and art historical curriculums.

Other more recent initiatives have included the donation, between 2014 and 2015, of sixty-eight works by women artists to the Institute of Contemporary Art, Boston, by philanthropist, political activist, and collector Barbara Lee, representing the most expensive gift the museum had ever received. The Barbara Lee Collection of Art by Women, as it is now called, is an ongoing project that aims to put women in the spotlight at the institute and, as Lee explains, allows it "to tell urgent and under-told histories of postwar and contemporary art."[13] Similarly, a UK-based project, launched in 2015, entitled "Valeria Napoleone XX," seeks to address gender imbalance in museum collections. Institutions are invited to apply for support from the project, which donates a work by a leading woman artist to a different UK museum each year. The chosen museum not only receives a work by the selected artist but also hosts an exhibition of her art.

Art patrons, collectors, and philanthropists are playing major roles in addressing systemic sexism—as are museum directors. In 2016, the Tate Modern, London, hired its first female director, Frances Morris, who has made a public commitment to showcasing women artists. "It isn't like we are celebrating women for six months and then all the chaps come back," she reported in *The Guardian*. "There is a commitment now to show the real history of art and the contribution made by many women who have been overlooked for many reasons."[14] However, substantive changes to programming and exhibition checklists have yet to be seen—for example, as discussed previously, of the three hundred artists displayed in the 2016 re-hang of the permanent collection, less than a third were women.

Women-only exhibitions are on the rise, according to the *New York Times*. At least a dozen galleries and museums featured women-themed surveys in 2016, including: *Revolution in the Making: Abstract Sculpture by Women, 1947–2016* at Hauser Wirth & Schimmel, Los Angeles, which showcased an intergenerational lineup of thirty-four sculptors; *Champagne Life* at the Saatchi Gallery in London, which exhibited the work of fourteen emerging artists; *No Man's Land* at the Rubell Family Collection in Miami, which celebrated work produced by more than a hundred women artists; *O'Keeffe, Stettheimer, Torr, Zorach: Women Modernists in New York*, at the Norton Museum in West Palm Beach, Florida; *Women of Abstract Expressionism* at the Denver Art Museum, which was conceptualized to counter the male-oriented view of Abstract Expressionism; as well as the spring season at The New Museum in New York, which was devoted to five solo exhibitions by women artists. Each of these exhibitions is shining light on neglected artists and raising the visibility and commercial viability of others. These shows, as Barbara Kruger points out, are "playing catch-up after centuries of women's marginality and invisibility."[15]

Curated by
Linda Nochlin and
Ann Sutherland Harris

WOMEN ARTISTS: 1550 – 1950

Los Angeles County Museum of Art, 1976
Brooklyn Museum, New York, 1977

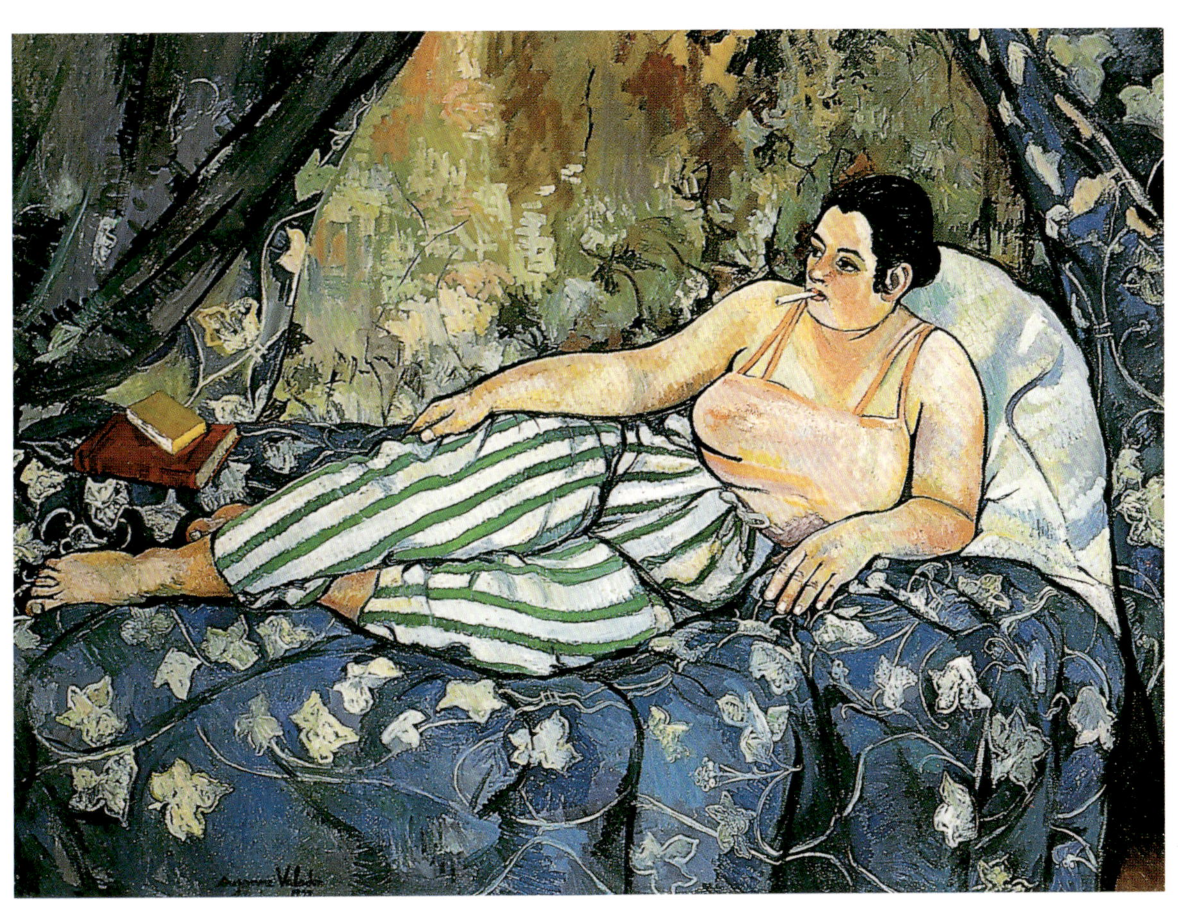

Suzanne Valadon
The Blue Room
1923

By far the most significant curatorial corrective in the USA in the 1970s to the occlusion of women as cultural contributors from the larger historical record was the pioneering exhibition *Women Artists: 1550–1950*, organized in 1976 by Nochlin and Ann Sutherland Harris.[16] The exhibition, which *Time* magazine hailed as "one of the most significant theme shows to come along in years," was the first large-scale museum exhibition in the USA dedicated exclusively to women artists from a historical perspective.[17] Its central aim was the reclamation of women artists and their insertion back into the traditional canon of art history from which they had been lost, or forgotten, or simply dismissed as insignificant. The show presented more than one hundred and fifty works by eighty-four painters, from 16th-century miniatures to modern abstractions, including examples by Lavinia Fontana (Italy), Artemisia Gentileschi (Italy), Judith Leyster (The Netherlands), Elisabeth Louise Vigée Le Brun (France), Berthe Morisot (France), and Georgia O'Keeffe (USA). It by no means claimed to be a comprehensive survey of painting by women artists over the four-hundred-year period—as if that were possible—but should be seen as a compilation of significant and, in some cases, "great" women artists.

From the moment they conceptualized the project in 1970, the two scholars were off and running on a five-year course through museums, libraries, and private collections in the USA and abroad. "It was like doing the whole history of art with a feminist cast," Nochlin explained at the time.[18] And it was an overwhelming task. Art-historical literature about women artists was scant, monographs devoted to women were an absolute rarity, and museums and galleries were negligent about, if not averse to, exhibiting work by women at that time. Indeed, many of the paintings in the exhibition were excavated from the dusty basements of museums to which they had been relegated like castoffs.[19] The already daunting task of mounting the largest exhibition of women artists to date was made more difficult by misunderstandings and a general lack of interest among many of the curators' peers: for example, the curators often had to make strenuous efforts to persuade museum administrators to loan works, because many of them had difficulty understanding that an exhibition of women artists could be a serious or scholarly enterprise.

It did not help that most of the artists the curators were interested in were unknown at the time, even to seasoned scholars working in areas from the Renaissance to the modern era. In 1976, when *Women Artists* was on view at the Los Angeles County Museum of Art, the museum's director, Kenneth Donahue, reported that when a group of art historians from the College Art Association came to see the exhibition, "We heard them say over and over again that they didn't know women artists were doing anything before Rosa Bonheur or Mary Cassatt." [20] Yet what the exhibition and its catalogue made clear was that, although present-day scholars were largely unaware of these artists' work, the neglect did not derive from a lack of accomplishment or success during the artists' lifetimes. Many of these so-called unknown artists in the exhibition had in fact been hugely celebrated in their own day, including such figures as Swiss painter Angelica Kauffman (1741–1807), one of the founding members of the Royal Academy of Arts in London, where she was admitted in 1768; Dutch artist Rachel Ruysch (1664–1750), whose specialty of fruit and flower paintings brought her international fame in her lifetime; and French painter Anne Vallayer-Coster (1744–1818), whom French philosopher and art critic Denis Diderot considered a near-rival of the 18th-century French painter Jean-Baptiste-Siméon Chardin. [21] The fact that scholars of the 1970s were unaware of the work of these artists reflects widespread discrimination against women, historically, and the persistent erasure of their cultural production. As Sutherland Harris argued in her catalogue essay, since the Renaissance women had been systematically denied access to a proper art education and had been institutionally prohibited from achieving success on a par with men, regardless of their talent or genius. [22]

Women Artists was an inherently feminist project that challenged not only the masculinist canon of art history, but also the history of museum exhibition practices, which had helped to sustain the canon institutionally for centuries. But the canon against and within which Nochlin and Sutherland

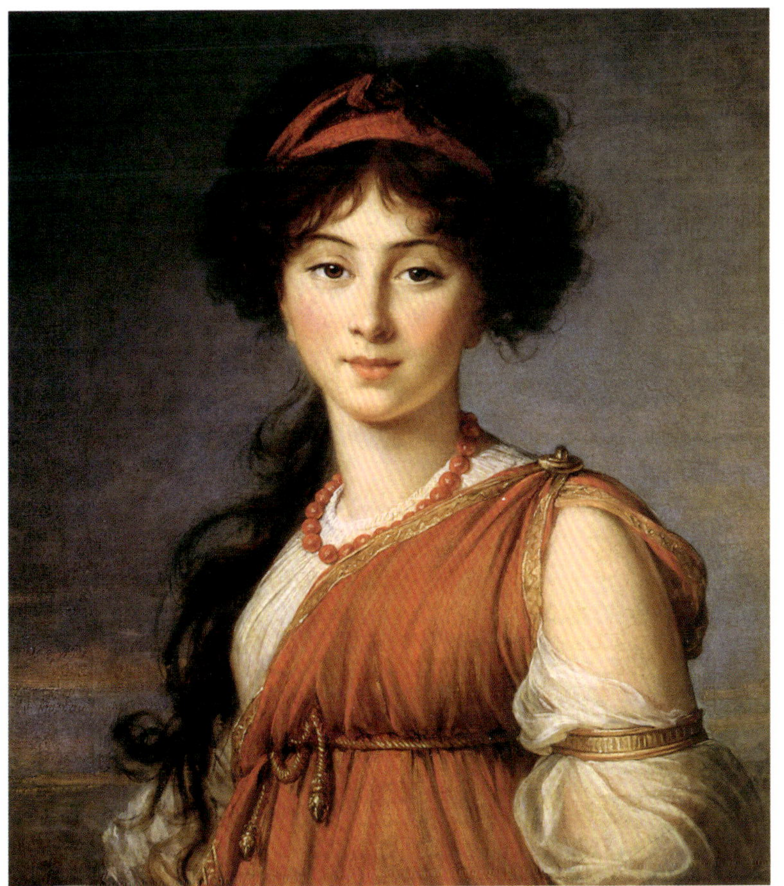

Elisabeth Louise Vigée Le Brun
Varvara Ivanovna Ladomirskaïa
1800

Harris chose to work, and within which they were trained as art historians, was the dominant, Western one: in 1976, no one even thought to question the fact that the exhibition focused solely on artists from the USA and Western Europe, or that it included only one woman of color (Frida Kahlo). It was understood and accepted that this was the chosen object of analysis. The academic canons of art history, literature, and philosophy were being challenged by feminists at that time mainly for their masculinist tendencies, not for their Eurocentric and imperialist bias. It was not until the 1980s that the hegemony of the Western canons began to be questioned (see pp. 24–25).

In his review of *Women Artists*, US art critic John Perrault announced that, "the history of Western art will never be the same again"; "research has proved," he said, "that there have been women artists of great accomplishment all along." [23] The exhibition had a considerable and immediate impact on the art historical paradigm against which it was working. Museums lending to the exhibition began exhibiting their works by women artists more regularly once they had returned from the tour. The exhibition spawned countless articles and monographs, as well as extensive dialogue about the importance of women's artistic production. It also had an impact on all subsequent women's and feminist art exhibitions.

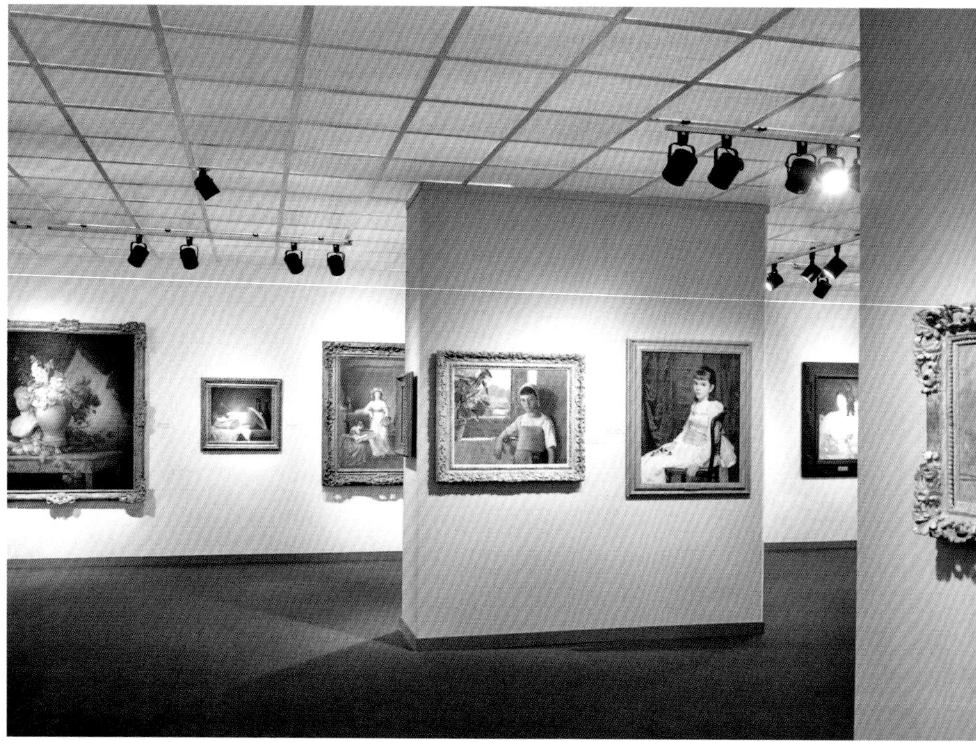

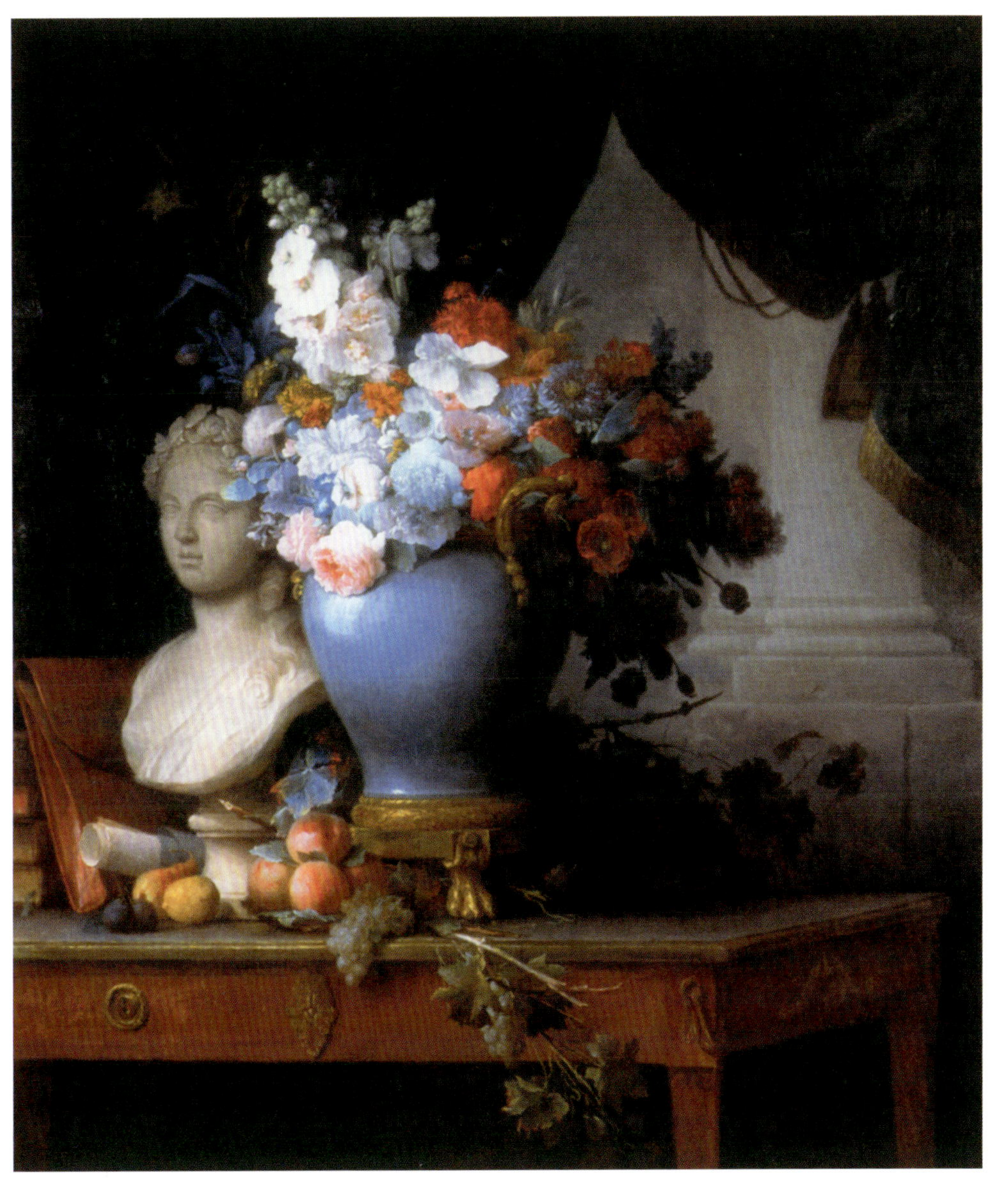

Anne Vallayer-Coster
Vase of Flowers with a Bust of Flora
1774

Installation view at the Brooklyn Museum
Women Artists: 1550–1950
October 1, 1977–November 27, 1977
Curated by Linda Nochlin and
Ann Sutherland Harris

1993 and 1994

Curated by
Kate Bush,
Emma Dexter,
and Nicola White;
Marcia Tucker;
Marcia Tanner

BAD GIRLS

Institute of Contemporary Arts, London, 1993
The Centre for Contemporary Arts, Glasgow, 1994 (a presentation)
(curated by Kate Bush, Emma Dexter, and Nicola White)

New Museum of Contemporary Art, New York, 1994 (two-part show)
(curated by Marcia Tucker)

Bad Girls West
Wight Art Gallery, University of California, Los Angeles, 1994
(curated by Marcia Tanner)

 Note: the US versions of *Bad Girls* were organized independently from the UK version.

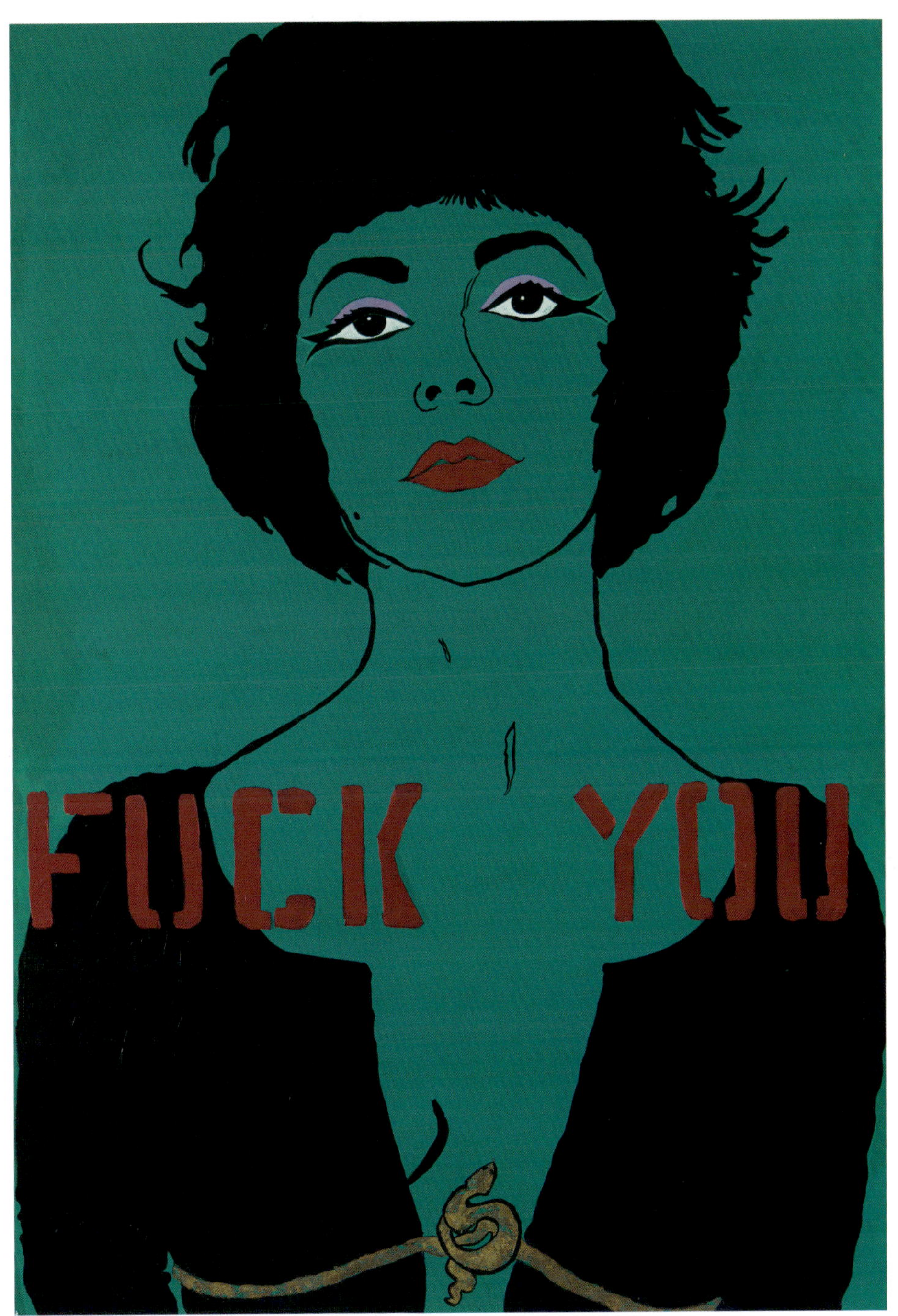

Kathe Burkhart
Fuck You: From the Liz Taylor Series (Cleopatra)
1984

Throughout the 1980s and 1990s, in the wake of *Women Artists*, numerous group exhibitions in North America and Western Europe dedicated themselves to the history of women's artistic production, past and present—but in these instances, with a specific focus, for the most part, on post-1970 feminist artistic production. The most controversial of these exhibitions were the multiple *Bad Girls* shows—in London, Glasgow, New York, and Los Angeles. The first to be presented—an exhibition organized separately from the US-based ones but with the same title—was *Bad Girls* at the Institute of Contemporary Arts (ICA), London, in 1993 (followed by a presentation at the Centre for Contemporary Arts in Glasgow, in 1994). Curated by Kate Bush, Emma Dexter, and Nicola White, the exhibition celebrated a new spirit of playfulness, tactility, and perverse humor in the work of six British and American women artists: Helen Chadwick, Dorothy Cross, Nicole Eisenman, Rachel Evans, Nan Goldin, and Sue Williams—each of whom was represented by several works.

The term "bad girls" was defined in the London catalogue as "sly, in-your-face, disturbing, provocative, haunting, subtle, sensual, shocking, sexy." [24] The exhibition sought to celebrate the multiplicity of feminisms in the 1990s, undermining tendencies toward the essentialist and didactic voices of early feminist work. "Irreverent, personal, shocking, funny, and fey," the curators explained, "*Bad Girls* dares to attack on two fronts at once: offending proscriptive feminism as well as the reactionary forces of patriarchy." [25] The curators' aim was not to present work in the lineage of 1980s artists such as Cindy Sherman, Barbara Kruger, and Jenny Holzer—whose works, they argued, "put a feminist gloss upon the power and manipulations of the media, movies and advertising"—but rather to harken back to "the surrealist traditions of Louise Bourgeois and Meret Oppenheim as well as the aggressive camp of Judy Chicago's *Dinner Party*." [26] It did not purport to be a definitive survey of current trends within feminist art, but rather a "sympathetic grouping" that allowed for "intriguing and provocative correspondences" between the works. [27]

Highlights of the London exhibition included Eisenman's drawing *Betty Gets It* (1992), which parodies the happy heterosexuality of the characters Betty and Wilma—from the 1960s animated television series *The Flintstones*—as a lesbian couple; Williams's *A Funny Thing Happened* (1992), which depicts a series of rape scenes in stark black acrylic on white canvas, with scrawled texts reading, "We don't know if she enjoyed it or not"; Chadwick's sculpture *Glossolalia* (1993)—a circular table on which several golden pelts are arranged like a trophy below a cone centerpiece with lapping lambs' tongues cast in glistening bronze; as well as photographic portraits by Goldin of drag queens and those living with AIDs. Also on view were images of Amazons castrating pirates (Eisenman), platonic romance (Evans), and surrealist juxtapositions (Cross). In all, it was a selection of powerful works exemplifying what one critic called "the very highest fuck-you-fem Mae West tradition."[28]

The London exhibition received mixed reviews. Brian Sewell, writing in the *London Evening Standard*, complained that the works on view demonstrated "anti-male prejudice at its silliest and most obsessive—hysterical and violent propaganda utterly contemptible as art,"[29] and Katy Deepwell called it "an incomprehensible babble."[30] Laura Cottingham, writing in *Frieze* magazine—but who, ironically, also wrote for the ICA catalogue—was fiercely critical of the exhibition, taking particular issue with the title itself, as did Iwona Blazwick, who noted that it stressed an "infantile, naughty, rebellious posture whereas there was actually a very serious and powerful thrust to a lot of the work in the show."[31] Cottingham argued that the exhibition presented some of "the artistic products of feminism's partial success in the form of an apology, a laugh." The curators, she said, attempted to appeal to "the tritest cliché of male chauvinist charges—that feminists have no sense of humor." The "girlie giggle," she continued, "an unconscious social signifier women deliver as a sign that you (men) need not take us seriously, is put forward as the controlling rhetoric. This 'It's So Funny!' curatorial posture betrays both feminism and art: none of the artists included in this exhibition is either a failed or an aspiring comedian and all are undeservedly trivialized by this mockery."[32] Others were more forgiving. Ekow Eshun wrote in *Elle* magazine, for example, that while the images were disturbing and confrontational, they also challenged a history of art in which women are merely passive subjects: "And bleak as their subject matter is, the cumulative effect of the new generation's work is liberating rather than depressing."[33]

A year later, in 1994, curator Marcia Tucker organized a two-part *Bad Girls* exhibition at the New Museum of Contemporary Art in New York, and Marcia Tanner curated *Bad Girls West* at the Wight Art Gallery, University of California, Los Angeles (UCLA), which was a "sister exhibition" to Tucker's.[34] Although the two curators inspired and assisted each other, and shared the same catalogue, the two exhibitions were organized independently. Both of them were interested in examining a phenomenon they had observed in the early 1990s: "a new wave of female artists who were using humor (often bawdy, raucous 'unladylike' humor) in their work as a strategy to

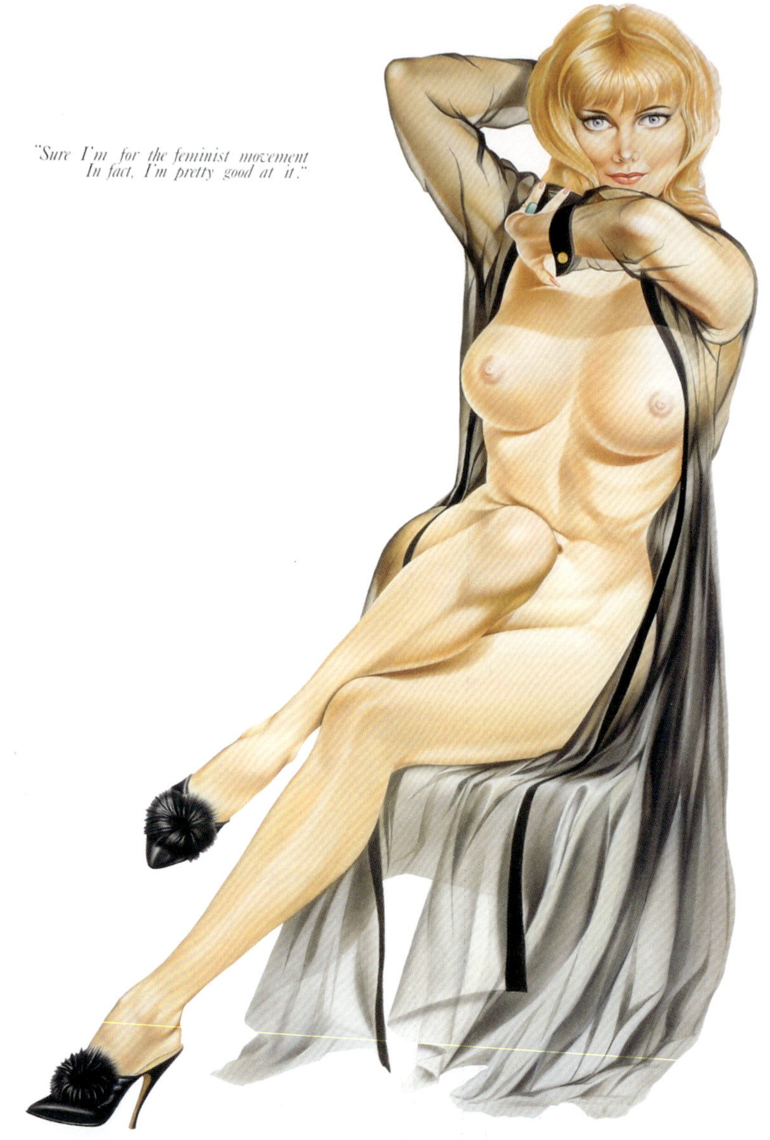

Lutz Bacher
Playboys (Feminist Movement)
1993

engage viewers with feminist issues."[35] Tanner explained that what
distinguished this new wave from earlier feminist work was its use
of humor as a subversive strategy operating outside the bounds
of feminine propriety.[36] In both curators' catalogue essays, laughter is
presented as "an antidote to being silenced, defined, and objectified,"[37]
and as these artists' "most transgressive strategy."[38] Tucker's concept
for the exhibition called for art that is "funny, really funny," and that
goes "too far";[39] Tanner's was to showcase work that is "irreverent,
anti-ideological, non-doctrinaire, non-didactic, un-polemical and
thoroughly un-ladylike."[40]

Subversive humor was the connecting force between the more
than one hundred artists, performers, filmmakers—women and
men—featured in *Bad Girls* and *Bad Girls West*. The works ranged
from sculptures to wall texts to photographs, videos and comics,
and addressed such issues as marriage, child-rearing, food, genitalia,
lesbianism, motherhood, gender identity, role reversal, aging, sex,
race, class, and violence. Stand-outs from the New York presentation
included Xenobia Bailey's *Sistah Paradise's Revival Tent* (1993), a tent
of brightly colored, beautifully patterned knitted wool that is part
shelter, part headdress, part woman's head; Renée Cox's larger-than-
life photograph *Mother and Child* (1993), a nude self-portrait of the
artist holding her son; Jacqueline Hayden's images of heavyset elderly
women in the nude, which point up the obsession with beauty and
youth; Portia Munson's *Pink Project: Table* (1994), a large table laden
with an orderly, densely packed array of things pink—from combs,
brushes and hair slides to children's toys, dildos, and a garbage can—
in all, two thousand instances of femininity reinforced; stripper/
photographer Cammie Toloui's *Lusty Lady Series* (1992), a slideshow
of patrons masturbating, snapped in her place of business, "The
Pleasure Palace," which you could ogle through a set of peepholes;
and Yasumasa Morimura's *Portrait (Futago)* (1988), a photographic
self-portrait of the artist playing the role of both maid and model in a
scrupulously reconstructed image of Edouard Manet's *Olympia* (1863).

West Coast highlights included an example from Lutz Bacher's
Playboys series, entitled *Feminist Movement ("Sure I'm for the feminist
movement. In fact, I'm pretty good at it.")* (1993), which was based on
the sensual, large-breasted and blithely smiling pin-ups by the
illustrator Antonio Vargas, which appeared in *Playboy* in the 1960s and
1970s; Deborah Kass's *Four Debras* (1992), a Warhol spoof with a Jewish
twist; Kathe Burkhart's painting *Fuck You: From the Liz Taylor Series
(Cleopatra)* (1987); a series of needlepoint works by Charles Gute's
Ludwig von Beethoven Quotations series (1988); a wacky sculpture by

Rona Pondick, entitled *Double Bed* (1989), comprised of a mattress, pillows, and dozens of baby bottles; and a sculpture by Sue Williams, *Manly Footwear* (1992), which featured a series of squashed-in women's faces made of silicon rubber, in reference to violence against women.

The *Bad Girls* exhibitions in the USA drew mixed reactions from art critics. Most took aim at the title, arguing that it was "trendy," "angry," "a cheap hook," and that it "eclipsed any real debate around the work." [41] Some claimed that the exhibits were based on a weak idea and actually trivialized the work of women artists. [42] Others stated that the concept was backward, or like "a byline for a fashion magazine." [43] As Jan Avgikos explained in *Artforum*, "Once feminist-oriented art has been disparagingly categorized as the work of 'bad girls' it can be laughed off, crated up, and shipped out to sea." [44] She continued, "This curatorial misadventure…is particularly egregious, given that the show's organizers happen to be women." [45] And while some praised the quality of the work on view, [46] others claimed that it "…is not 'bad' enough, it's creepily safe or academically naughty, neutralized further by the didactic museum context." [47] Benjamin Weissman from *Artforum* agreed: "The badness is elegant, safe, conventional, and, most important, museum-ready." [48] Roberta Smith of the *New York Times* was disappointed by Part I of the New York City exhibition. She had hoped for a "reasonably accurate view of the new, angrily ironic feminist art…that has been percolating up through the galleries and alternative spaces in the last few years." She argued that this third generation of feminist artists to emerge since the 1970s has, "built on the attitudes of the photo-appropriation feminists of the 1980s (Barbara Kruger, for example), confidently branching out into painting and sculpture and installation art. It's a good time to assess their efforts and consider the issues they raise." [49] She believed the exhibition fell short of doing so. Yet, a critic from the *New York Observer* argued that "*Bad Girls*' satirical sendup of feminism is refreshing…excess and outrageousness is the rule." [50] And Elizabeth Hess of the *Village Voice* declared, "Tucker should be congratulated for staking her territory smack in the middle of current feminist debates." [51]

Portia Munson
Pink Project: Table
1994

Installation view, *Bad Girls (Part I)*
New Museum of Contemporary Art
1994
Curated by Marcia Tucker

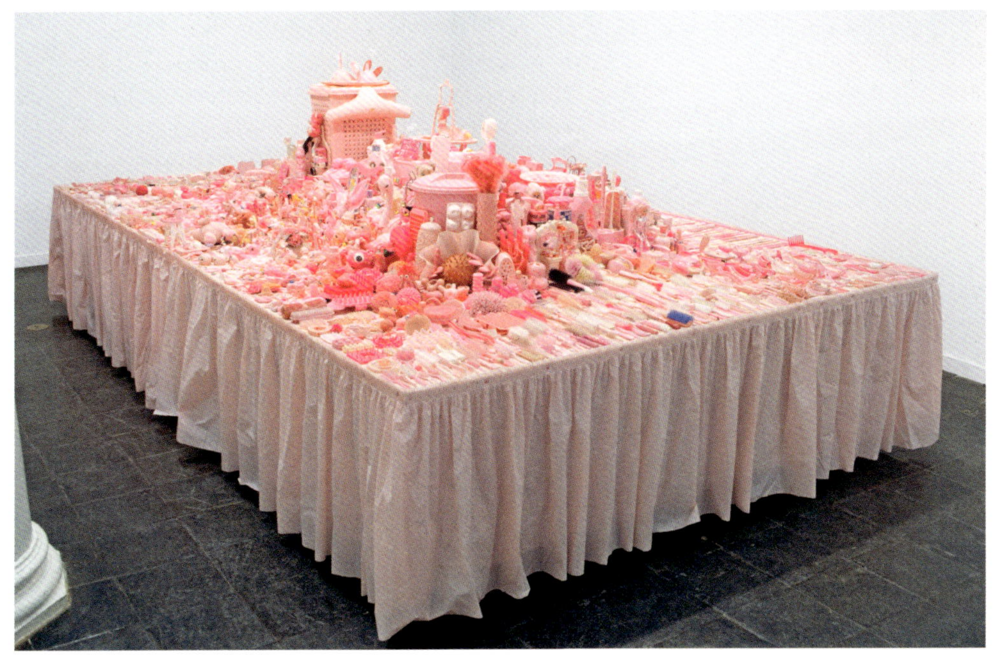

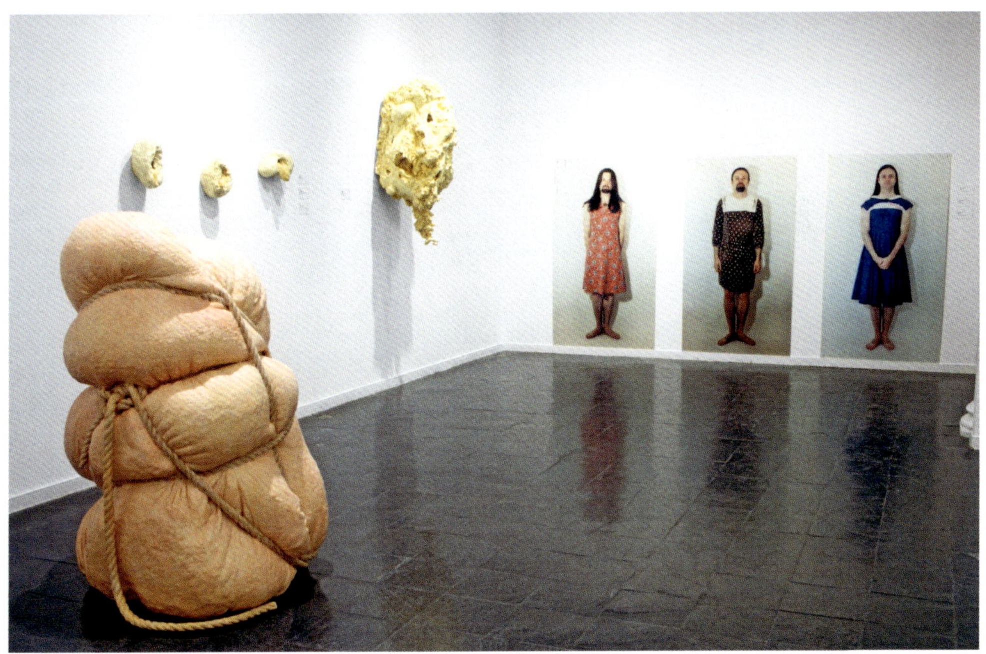

Curated by
Catherine de Zegher

INSIDE THE VISIBLE: AN ELLIPTICAL TRAVERSE OF 20TH CENTURY ART IN, OF, AND FROM THE FEMININE

Béguinage of Saint-Elizabeth, Kortrijk, Belgium, 1994–1995
Institute of Contemporary Art, Boston, USA, 1996
National Museum of Women in the Arts, Washington, DC, 1996
Whitechapel Art Gallery, London, 1996
Art Gallery of Western Australia, Perth, 1997

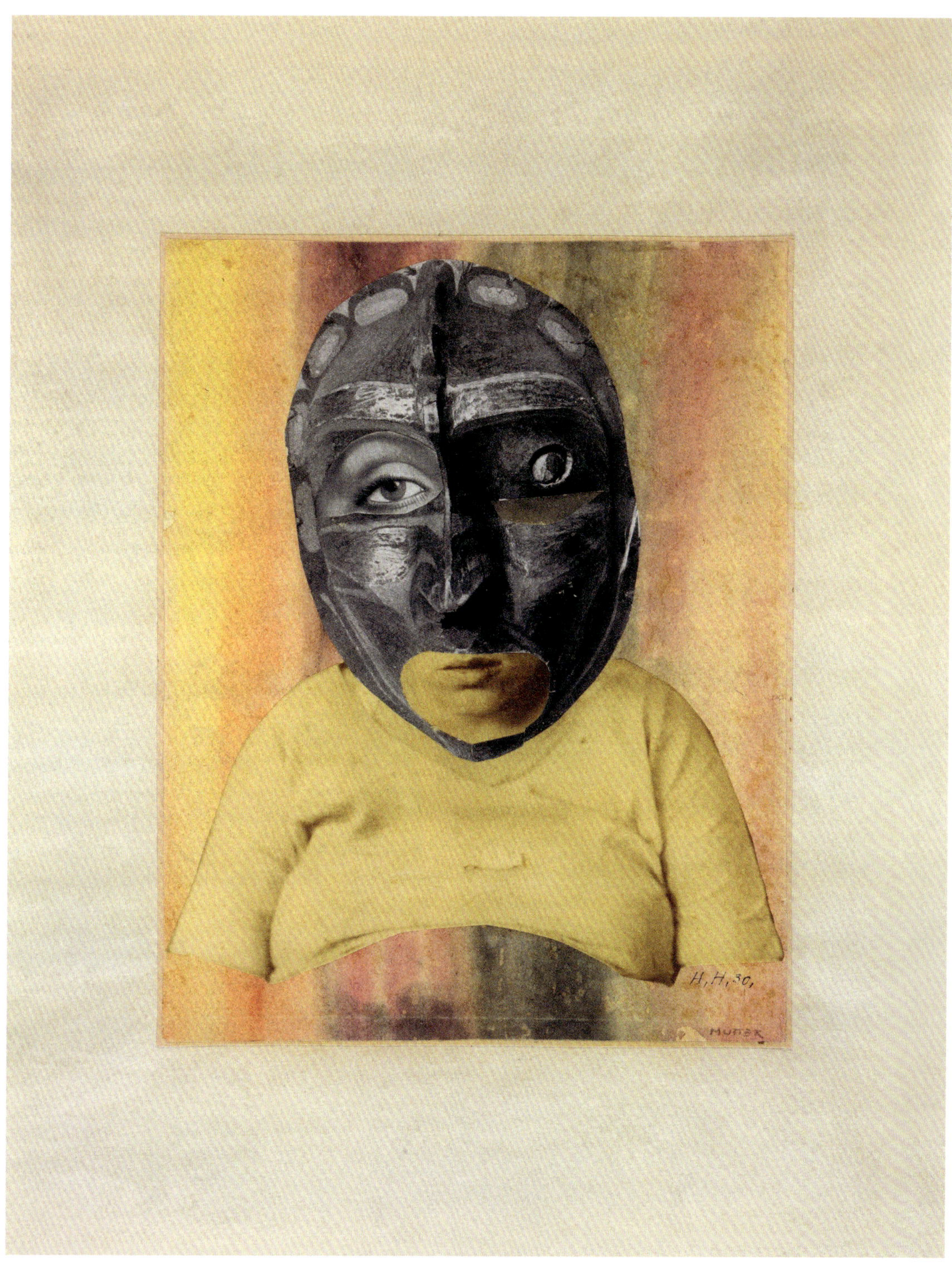

Hannah Höch
Mutter
c. 1930

Inside the Visible: An Elliptical Traverse of 20th-Century Art in, of, and from the Feminine, curated by Catherine de Zegher, premiered in 1994 at the Béguinage of Saint-Elizabeth in Kortrijk, Belgium, and then traveled to the Institute of Contemporary Art in Boston, USA, in 1996, where it was expanded; thereafter, it moved to the National Museum of Women in the Arts in Washington, DC, the Whitechapel Art Gallery in London, and the Art Gallery of Western Australia in Perth (1997). The exhibition comprised more than 250 objects by 37 women artists, dating from the late 1920s to the mid-1990s, from South as well as North America, Eastern as well as Western Europe, the Middle East and Asia. In part, it was an international survey of 20th-century women's art, with numerous well-known names,[52] as well lesser-known artists—Katarzyna Kobro and Gego, for example—and provocative younger artists who were just making their critical mark in the 1990s, such as Nadine Tasseel and Ellen Gallagher.

The exhibition was divided into four sections, "Parts of/for," "The Blank in the Page," "The Weaving of Water and Words," and "Enjambment: La donna è mobile" ("Rhythm: woman is fickle"). Much of the art within each grouping bore stylistic similarities, even though it may have been produced decades apart. All the works in "Parts of/for," for example, dealt with fragmentation and the dismembered female body as fetish—either through actually cutting and pasting, as in Hannah Höch's Dadaist collages and Martha Rosler's anti-war collages from the 1970s, or through surrealist juxtapositions, as in Carol Rama's watercolors. The works in the section "The Blank in the Page" included either actual bits of text or obvious mark-making—for example, Spero's diary-like paintings, such as *Codex Artaud* (1971–72), and Hanne Darboven's obsessive writings from the 1960s and 1970s were paired with Charlotte Salomon's diaries of life as a Jew in fascist Germany. Similarly, the works in "The Weaving of Water and Words"

Nancy Spero
Panel X of *Torture for Women* (detail)
1976

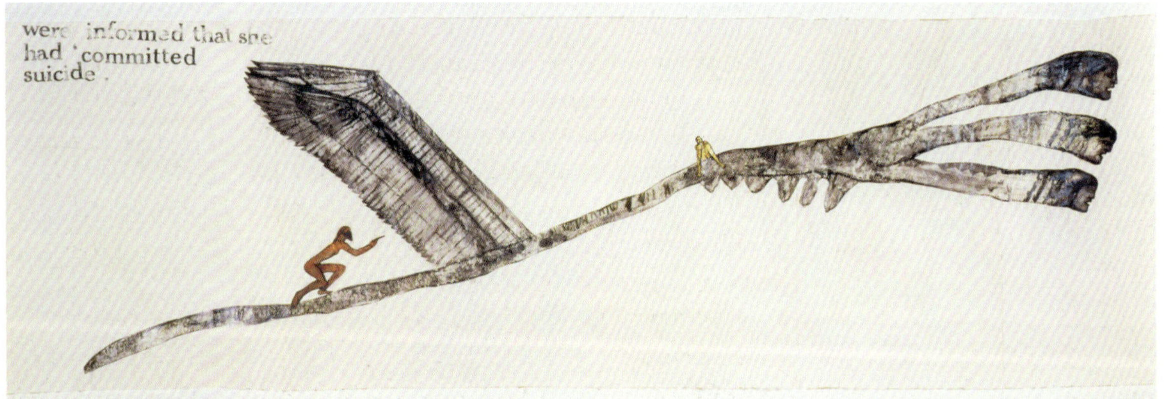

dealt with linear elements such as string (Gego), the grid (Agnes Martin), and strands of woven hair (Mona Hatoum), or raw wool (Cecilia Vicuña). The works in the final section, "Enjambment (Rhythm)", all required viewer interaction—from Lygia Clark's "sensorial helmets," set out on a table for visitors to try on, to more ethereal works, including those by Joëlle Tuerlinckx, whose fragile sculpture made of flour was affected by whatever activity took place around it.

The exhibition, and the formal juxtaposition of objects therein, constructed (as suggested by the show's title) "an elliptical traverse" of crossings and repetitions that weaved through 20th-century art —a criss-cross that resisted the conformity of linear narratives of art historical progression and development—and that made the viewer aware of art's fluidity, of how issues continue to occupy artists in different ways in different time periods, and how similar visual elements are used by many artists to different effect. De Zegher explained in the catalogue how there is often an urge in moments of crisis "to deconstruct existing representational codes to search for 'new beginnings' in order to imagine the world anew." [53] However, rather than divine origins, such "new beginnings" generally take the form of historical returns and repetitions, which recur to produce different meanings differently experienced by different audiences in different locations. [54] Therefore, as she explained at the time, "The interesting question isn't who was first, but why these ideas keep coming back." [55] Indeed, one of the exhibition's revelations was that what the 1970s and 1980s saw as a new concern with gender and identity (as in the work of Cindy Sherman) had been evident in women's art since at least the 1920s (with Claude Cahun's self-portraits, for example). Seventies feminism, then, could no longer be seen as a point of origin cut out from the past because, as British scholar Sue Malvern argued, "to do this is to risk murdering the mothers of this one moment of new beginning." [56]

Today, *Inside the Visible* is considered a defining exhibition, but the critical reception at the time was mixed. As de Zegher explained, "Depending on the country of the touring exhibition and the author (mostly male), the reviews went from critical to very positive." Some critics were "perplexed," she continued, "because the exhibition wasn't mainstream and it appeared not to be about feminist issues, although it addressed many." [57] As for the women artists represented in *Inside the Visible*, de Zegher regards them "as having developed positions of general resistance in relationship to other dominant themes in the 20th century: dictatorship in Latin America, fascism in Europe, racism in America." [58] The "feminine" in the exhibition's full title, then, was posited by the curator as a force of resistance, not as an essence, nor as a term in opposition to a masculine norm.

London-based scholar and art critic Katy Deepwell has argued that de Zegher's use of the term "feminine" as a "mark of difference"—not as a means to define women—in the exhibition demonstrated the ways in which "women artists had generated distinct practices which explored, critiqued, and questioned concepts of the feminine and 'otherness' in aesthetic terms." [59] In "[d]eveloping a framework fluid enough to avoid creating artificial constructs which would be read as 'fixed,'" de Zegher acknowledged (according to Deepwell), "each woman's individuality in her practice without firmly establishing a category known as 'women's art.'" [60] Not all critics have agreed. While the exhibition purported to refute essentialism's debilitating effects, some criticized its women-only focus itself as essentialist—as Amelia Jones asks, "what brings together such disparate artists across time and space other than an assumption that they are joined by their 'women's experience'?" [61] Adrian Searle of *The Guardian* agreed, and went further, describing the exhibition as "a mess of the bad, the brilliant and the plain naff." [62] He continued, "Too often the exhibition looks tackily bunched-up, though it is undoubtedly intended to be meaningfully heterogeneous and disruptive," and as "a show not so much traversing as strangulating itself." [63] Others criticized the exhibition's catalogue as simultaneously "intriguing, stimulating, and annoying," [64] and its essays as too dense: "The language is often verbose and laden with the jargon of current critical analysis. Everybody from Duchamp and Freud to Lacan and Kristeva down through Hal Foster and Umberto Eco are cited and a casual reading is difficult." [65]

Some critics celebrated the exhibition as a model for feminist curation, arguing, for example, that "de Zegher's purpose was not… to 'correct' an existing canon, nor to accumulate 'great women' but to identify and articulate a body of practice that doesn't 'fit' past histories and current debates, which has existed in its byways, and whose 'non-fit' speaks to aporias within modernism, and indeed within contemporary feminist theory." [66] So, while the content of the works was not always "feminist," the curatorial methodology was, insofar as it showcased 20th-century women artists in a new spotlight, granting many of these formerly invisible artists visibility.

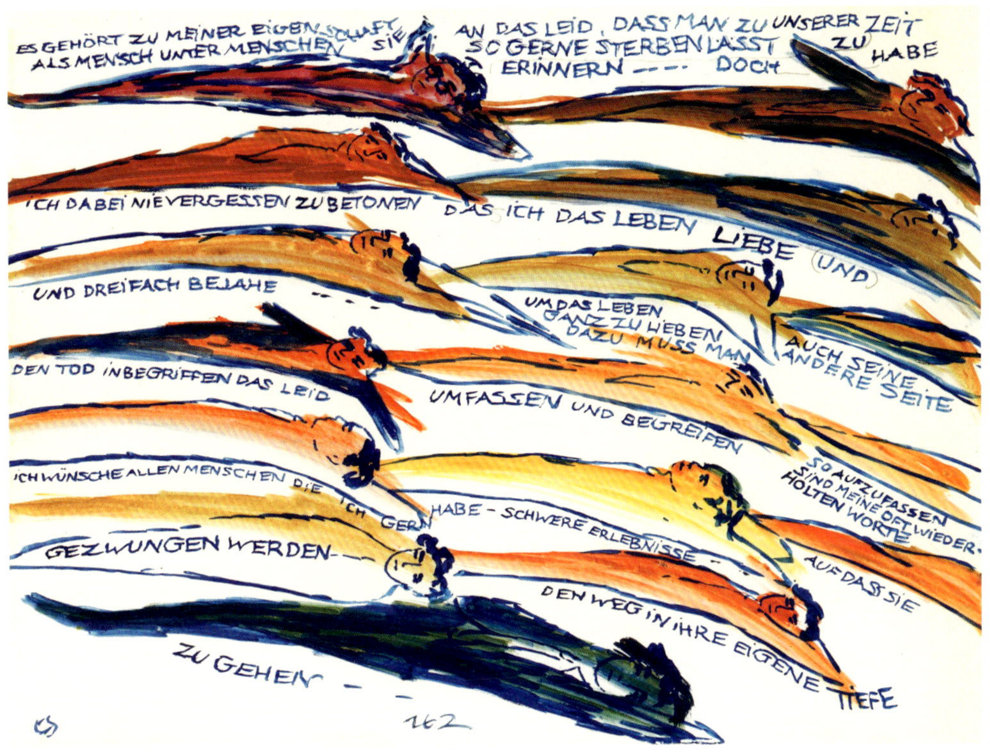

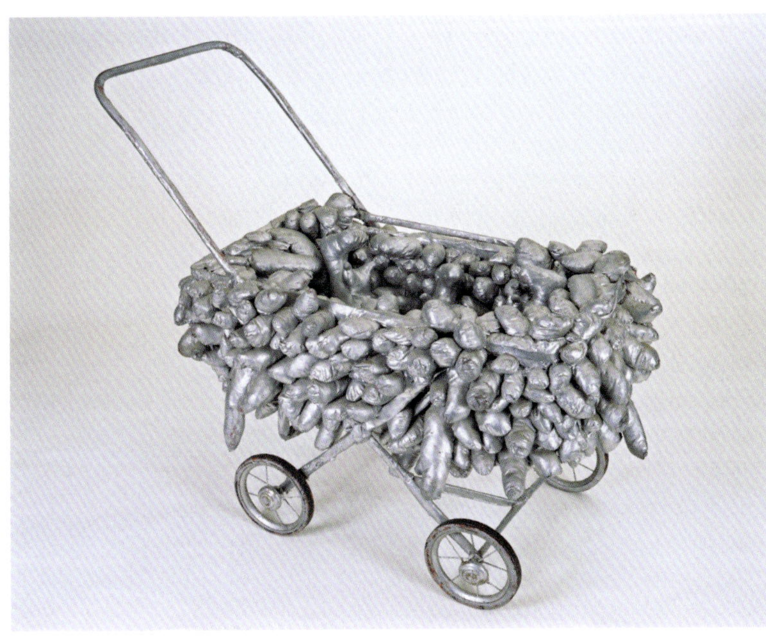

Charlotte Salomon
From the series *Life? or Theater?*
1940–42

Yayoi Kusama
Baby Carriage
1964

Curated by
Amelia Jones

SEXUAL POLITICS: JUDY CHICAGO'S "DINNER PARTY" IN FEMINIST ART HISTORY

The Hammer Museum, University of California, Los Angeles

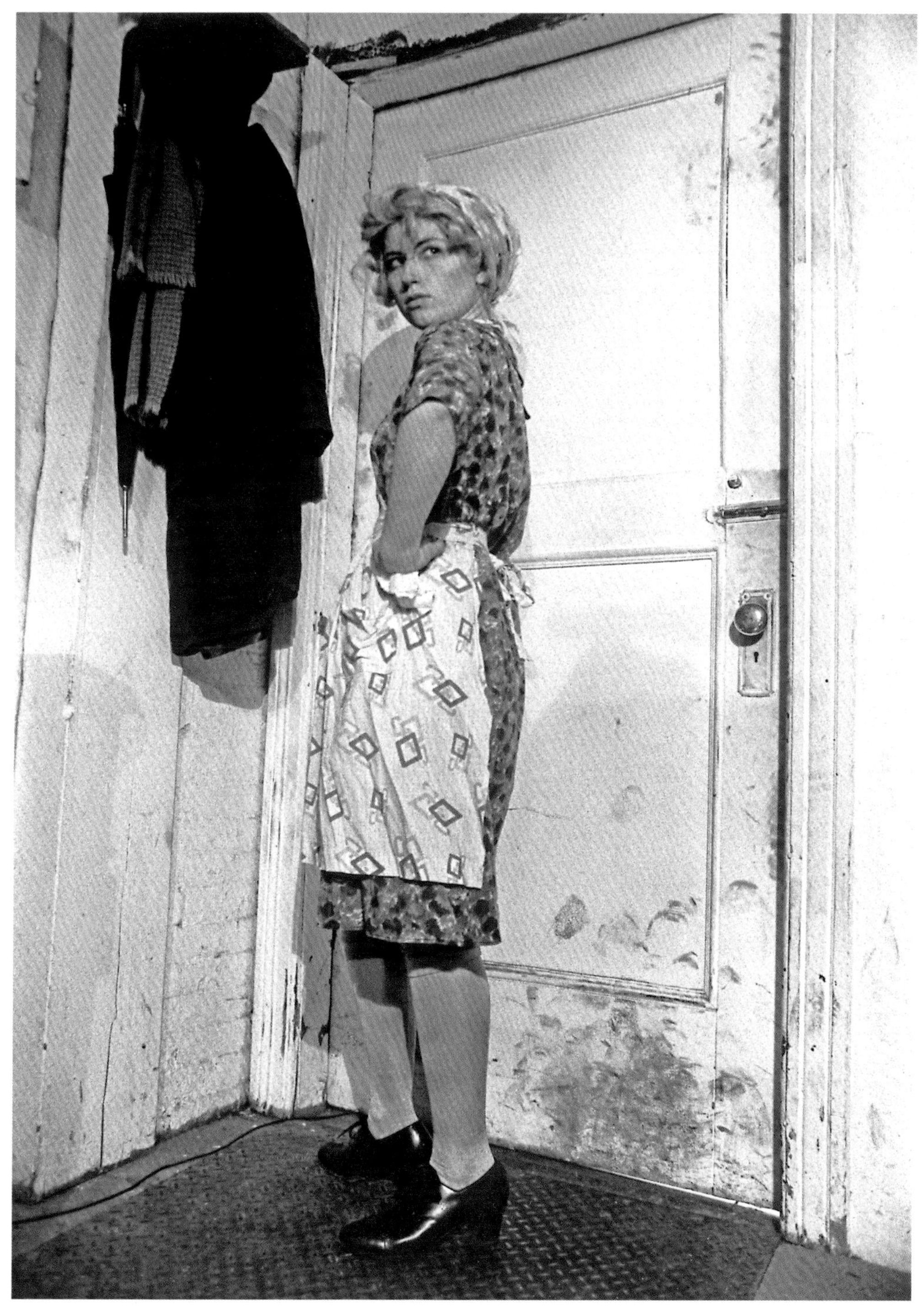

Cindy Sherman
Untitled Film Still #35
1979

The year 1996 was an important one in the history of feminist curating in the USA because two blockbuster exhibitions—*Inside the Visible* and *Sexual Politics*—garnered tremendous press attention and attracted large audiences. *Sexual Politics: Judy Chicago's "Dinner Party" in Feminist Art History* (1996), was curated by Amelia Jones and presented at the UCLA Hammer Museum. It was a large-scale exhibition that sought to reappraise Chicago's highly controversial installation *The Dinner Party* (1979) within a broader context of works ranging from the 1960s to the present. While Chicago's massive work was installed on the museum's ground floor, the remainder of the exhibition, presented upstairs, featured the other fifty-six artists, and was divided into several themes that covered the gamut: cunt imagery, maternity, menstruation, the domestic sphere, violence, autobiography, eroticism, goddesses, and diversity, among others. Within these themes, second-generation US-based feminist artists (including Faith Wilding, Joan Semmel, Hannah Wilke, and Carolee Schneemann) were juxtaposed with a younger generation (such as Rene Cox, Millie Wilson, Lauren Lesko, Marlene McCarty) in order to highlight a feminist continuum of ideas from the 1970s to the present.

In the section entitled "Female Imagery: The Politics of 'Cunt Art'," for example, Jones juxtaposed 1970s core works by Wilding and Tee Corinne with more recent vaginal imagery, such as Wilson's *Wig/Cunt* (1990), which appropriates 19th-century scientific representations of lesbian genitalia in order to expose the heterosexism and misogyny that informs empirical representations of the female body. While the subject-matter—cunt imagery—is similar, the later artist interrogated the negative connotations of this imagery, unlike the earlier artists whose imagery could be characterized as celebratory. Similarly, in the section "Menstruation, Birth, Maternity," the subject of motherhood was represented by Mary Kelly's iconic *Post-Partum Document* (1973–79), as well as by recent works by artists like Cox, *Yo Mama* (1993), and Rona Pondick, *No* (1990), which demonstrated not only a continued interest in the theme by feminist artists, but also the multifariousness of responses to the subject of motherhood itself.

While many critics praised the survey portion of the exhibition as successful in exploring a number of the contentious issues that grew out of 1970s feminism, some agreed with the argument that, "the arrangement of the work of all participating artists under these inclusive, reductive, labels argues for the persuasiveness of Chicago's influence in all areas of feminist art."[67] Others felt that despite Jones's stated goal of reassessing the *The Dinner Party*, the exhibition largely re-presented it in much the same way as it had been shown at its premier in 1979—which is to say, installed in a darkened space, carefully lit, creating an ecclesiastical aura, and "inspiring viewers to discuss the work in hushed, reverential tones as they made their pilgrimage around its perimeter." [68] So it seems that many visitors had been hoping for a fresher take on the iconic work. What critics did not understand, however, is that installation is a self-curated work of art with, in this case, a strict installation guide written by Chicago herself.

Jones acknowledged in the catalogue that the exhibition was "inevitably flawed as a curatorial project by the dominance of the piece itself (a dominance that underlines its contentious but undeniably important position in feminist and contemporary art histories)." Despite this, she encouraged viewers "to question the reasons for the almost automatic dismissal of *The Dinner Party* by Modernists, postmodernists, and many feminists alike." [69] More recently, Jones

Judy Chicago
The Dinner Party
1979

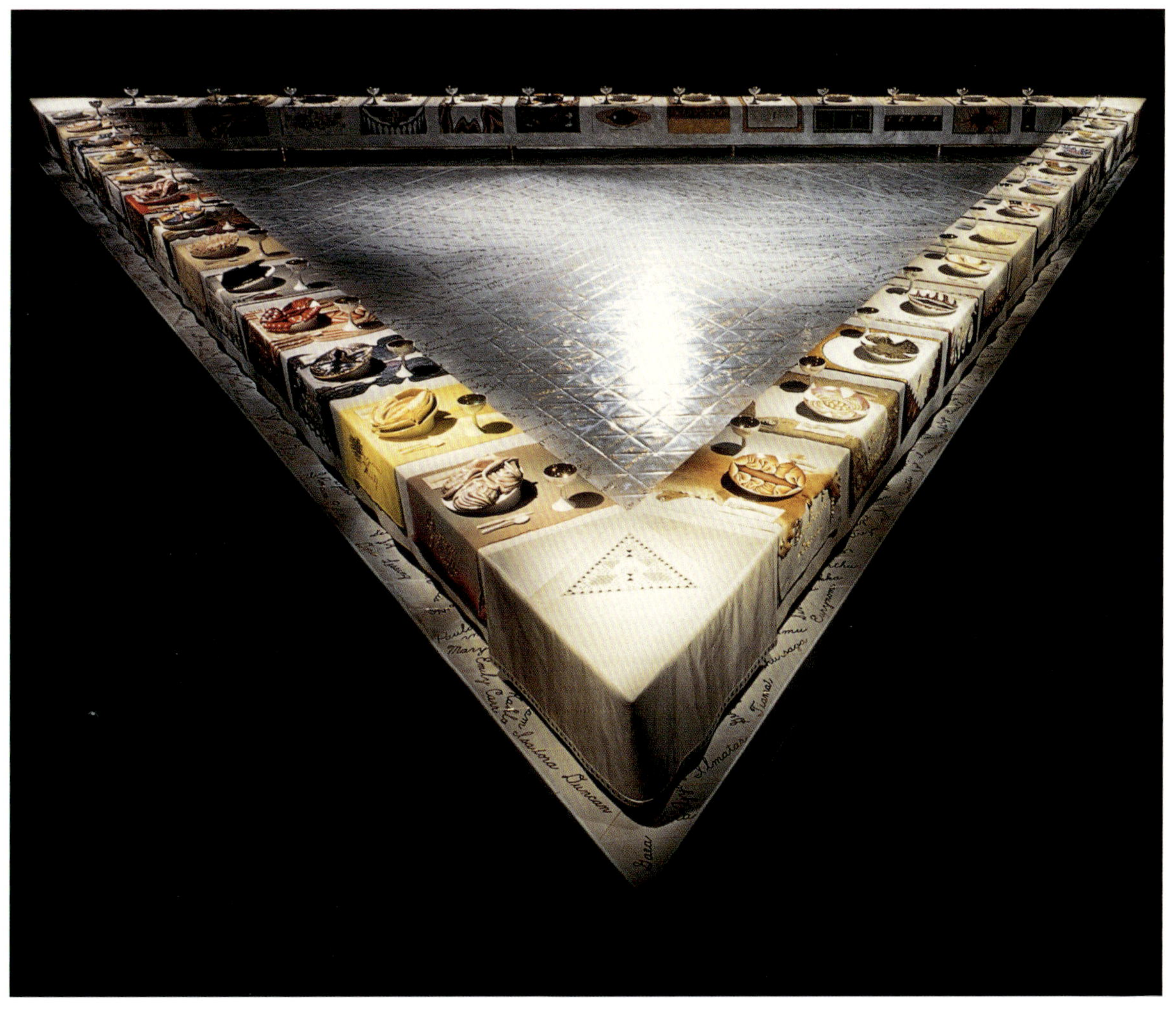

explained that her curatorial aim had been to: "…use a major work that had been effectively excluded by the most empowered forces even in feminist art discourse (*The Dinner Party*) as a pivot around which other works could be arranged, so that the vast range of strategies being deployed by feminist artists could be more clearly understood. I made a point of including work by artists considered 'essentialist' and those self-proclaimed as 'anti-essentialist' in order to show the continuum and to challenge the polarity."[70] She has also admitted that she had been naive: "I had no idea about the kind of animosity—that's probably the best word—that *The Dinner Party* engenders among certain parts of the feminist art and art history worlds."[71]

The Dinner Party's centrality in the show posed significant challenges, especially in trying to persuade prominent artists to take part in an exhibition that showcased Chicago as the epicenter of feminist art. Indeed, Mary Beth Edelson, Joyce Kozloff, Miriam Schapiro, Joan Snyder, and Nancy Spero all objected to the show's "heroization" of Chicago and requested that none of their works be represented. As Jones noted at the time, "I had no idea that this exhibition…would prove as controversial as the piece itself."[72] And controversial it was. Writing for the *Los Angeles Times*, Christopher Knight called it "the worst exhibition I've seen in a Los Angeles museum in many a moon," a "fiasco," a "blunder," and a "curatorial failure."[73] *Sexual Politics* "isn't really about art at all," he argued. "Instead, it's a history of contemporary feminist theory. Works of art have been deployed as mere illustrations, picturing the twists and turns of feminist argument since 1970." Feminist theory was privileged over art practice, he argued, and the art's efficacy was "undermined by curatorial trivialization." Gary Kornblau agreed, calling it the "worst exhibition of 1996."[74]

Sexual Politics did have its defenders, however. Art historian Donald Preziosi called the show "landmark," and "a breath of fresh air": "Jones and the Hammer are to be congratulated for mounting a critically and historically important exhibition," he argued.[75] Similarly, scholar and critic David Joselit wrote in *Art in America* that the hostility of the mainstream critics toward the exhibition had more to do with the fact that it was "an openly feminist project," and that the "often mean-spirited buzz of disapproval" was "only exacerbated by widespread complaints about Chicago's perceived careerism."[76]

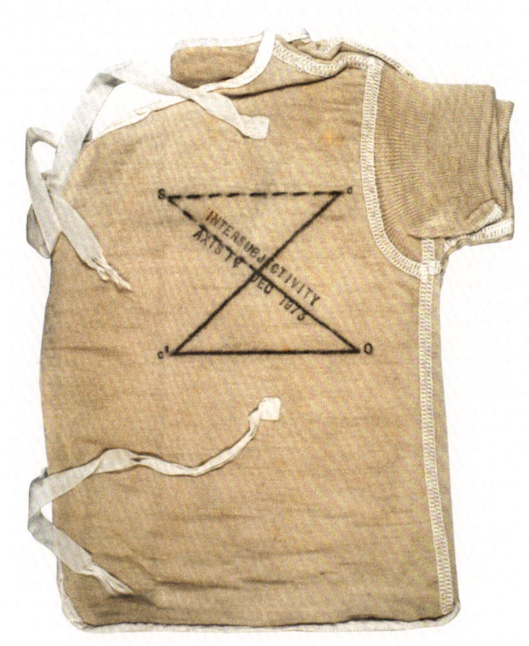

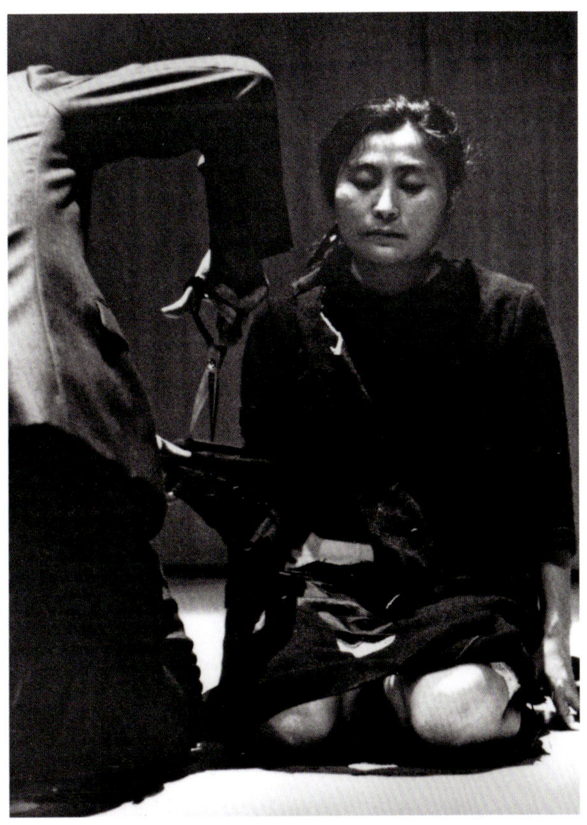

Mary Kelly
Post-Partum Document: Introduction
1973

Yoko Ono
Cut Piece
Performed at Sogetsu Art Center, Tokyo
1964

Curated by
María de Corral and
Rosa Martínez

VENICE BIENNALE 2005: ALWAYS A LITTLE FURTHER / THE EXPERIENCE OF ART

The Italian Pavilion and the Arsenale, Venice, Italy

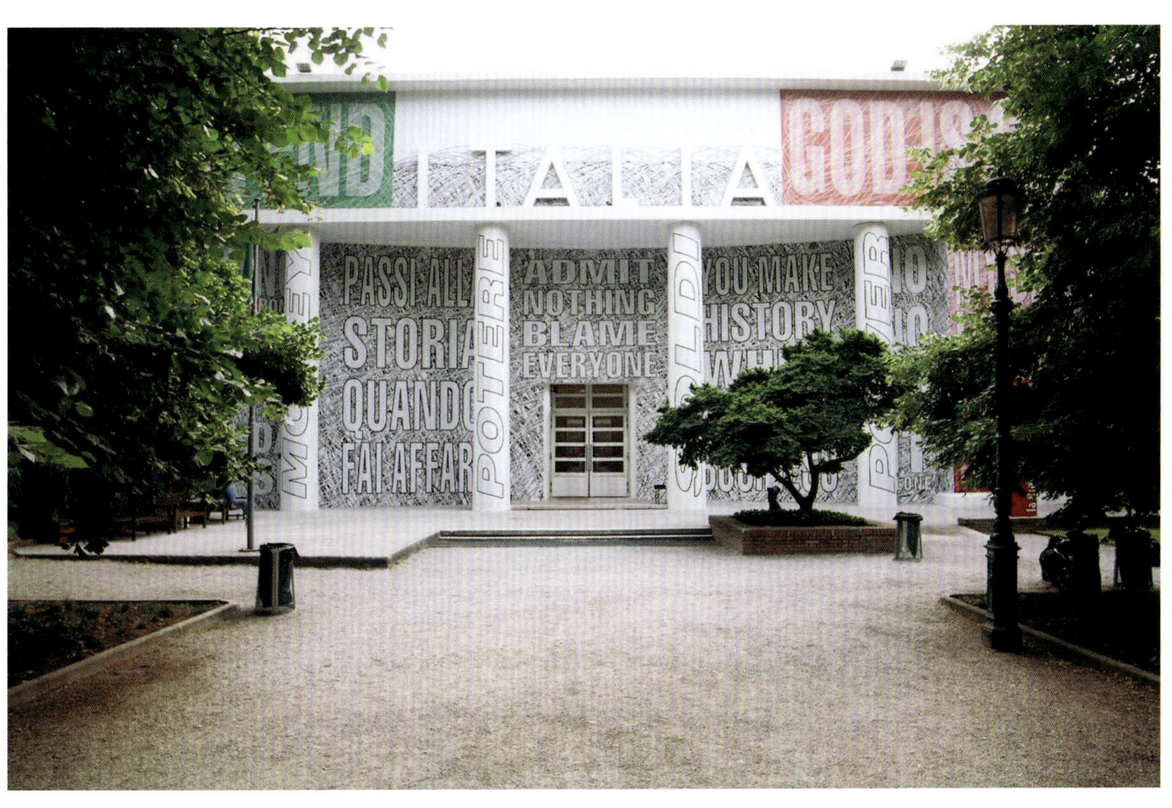

Barbara Kruger
Entrance to the Italian Pavilion at the 51st Venice Biennale
2005

During the first decade of the 21st century, feminism continued its momentum in the Western European and US art worlds with a myriad of high-profile exhibitions. The 2005 Venice Biennale was a standout among these shows—principally because the exhibition, organized by Rosa Martínez and María de Corral, was the first in the Biennale's then-110-year history to be directed by women. Both Martínez and de Corral, who curated the group shows *Always a Little Further* and

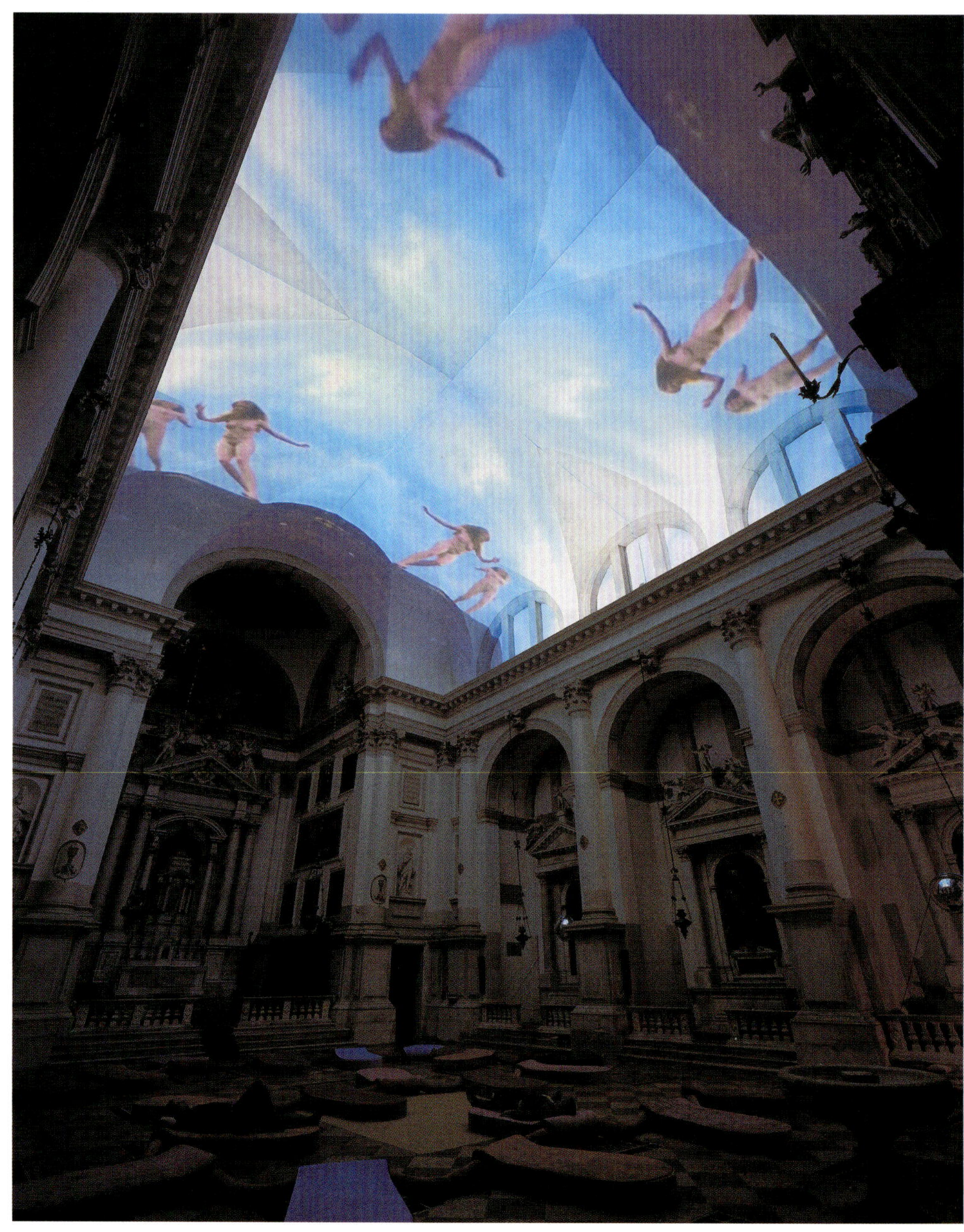

The Experience of Art at the Arsenale and Italian Pavilion, respectively, selected numerous female artists for their exhibitions.[77]

It was clear from both their exhibitions that Martínez and de Corral wanted to identify their curatorial practices as feminist. De Corral, for example, awarded Kruger the most prominent position in the show—the white facade of the Italian pavilion itself, upon which she placed an enormous vinyl mural with her signature direct-address phrases such as "Admit Nothing. Blame Everyone"; "Pretend Things Are Going As Planned"; and "God Is on Our Side." Similarly, Martínez turned over the first few rooms of the Arsenale to the feminist collective the Guerrilla Girls, whose statistics, irony, and humor about gender biases at the Biennale and in Italian museums roused audiences from the start, and left no doubt that the show that lay ahead would inflect other feminist sentiments, such as those put forward by Emily Jacir, Shahzia Sikander, Kimsooja, Pipilotti Rist, Pilar Albarracín, Eija-Liisa Ahtila, Donna Conlon, Berni Searle, and many others.

The critical reception to the Biennale was mixed. While Adrian Searle of *The Guardian* and Christopher Knight of the *Los Angeles Times* found much to praise, *Artforum*'s Alison Gingeras was downright dismissive. She condemned the exhibition's thematic frameworks as "nothing more than a string of vanilla platitudes," and while she admitted that Martínez's feminist pronouncements certainly "raised eyebrows," she argued stridently that, "it takes more than an increase in women artists (with a statistical breakdown courtesy of the Guerrilla Girls) and a return to *Womanhouse* aesthetics (such as Joana Vasconcelos's tampon chandelier) to instigate a mordant debate about gender politics and sexual difference."[78]

Marcia Vetrocq's review in *Art in America* was equally scathing. She argued that the exhibition came "wrapped in a self-satisfied mantle of better-late-than-never feminism."[79] The feminist declaration, she continued, felt "more wishful and nostalgic than pungent and present." Searle, on the other hand, while critical of Martínez's show as "a bit of a zoo," found de Corral's "a more satisfying, and at times troubling and moving, show than most of the efforts by the national representations in the Giardini."[80] Knight praised it as "the most thoughtful and, in several instances, bracing Biennale in ages," and was thankful the curators had chosen the open-ended but crucial theme of liberty, as it is "one that resonates because it is so broadly contested in daily life today."[81] And Jennifer Allen and Linda Nochlin, writing for *Artforum* and *Art in America*, respectively, agreed that the Biennale itself was an example of feminist theory translating effectively into curatorial practice, which both critics viewed as a much-needed shift for the Biennale, considering its sexist history.[82]

The Venice Biennale of 2005 was also far more global in scope than those before it. More countries were represented with national pavilions than ever before (not to mention more women), and the selection of artists in the group shows demonstrated the curators' concerted effort toward full transnational inclusion. Indeed, of the thirty-four feminist artists in the exhibition, seventeen were non-Euro-US. The global feminist scope of the exhibitions ensured that viewers were consuming feminisms, in the plural—that is, they were being offered not a consensus, but a multiplicity of points of view, and ones that emphasized differences among artists cross-culturally. By extension, theirs were curatorial projects that challenged the Euro-US-centrism of feminist, contemporary art trajectories as well. Given the fact that no biennale before this had been curated by women, let alone by self-identified feminist curators, in addition to the geographic breadth of works on display, the exhibition can perhaps be deemed the first transnational feminist Venice Biennale.

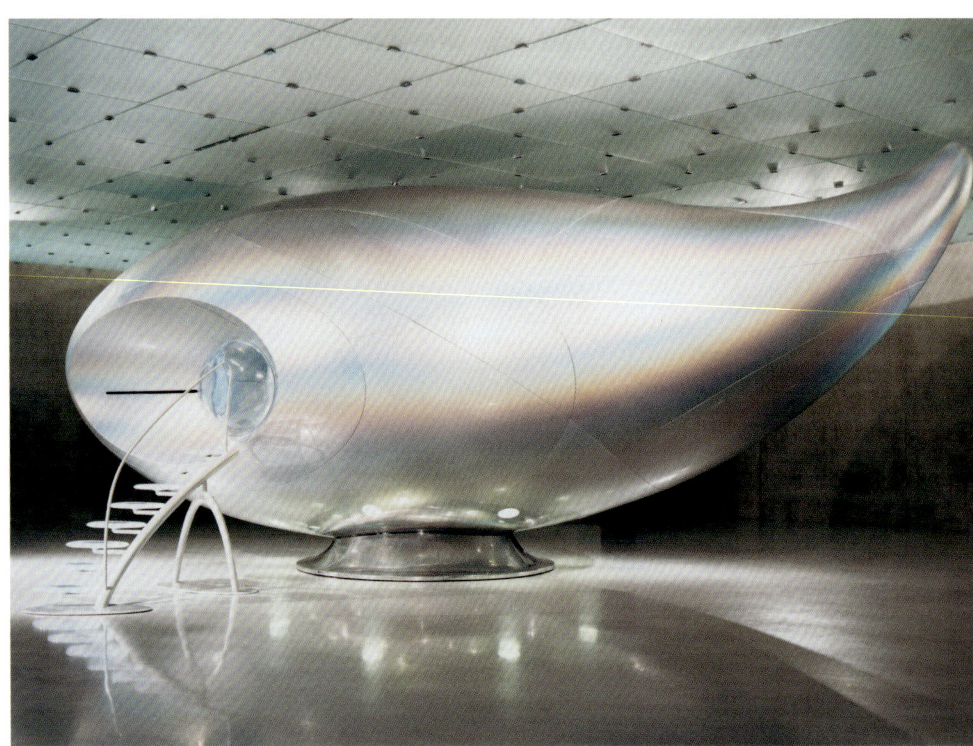

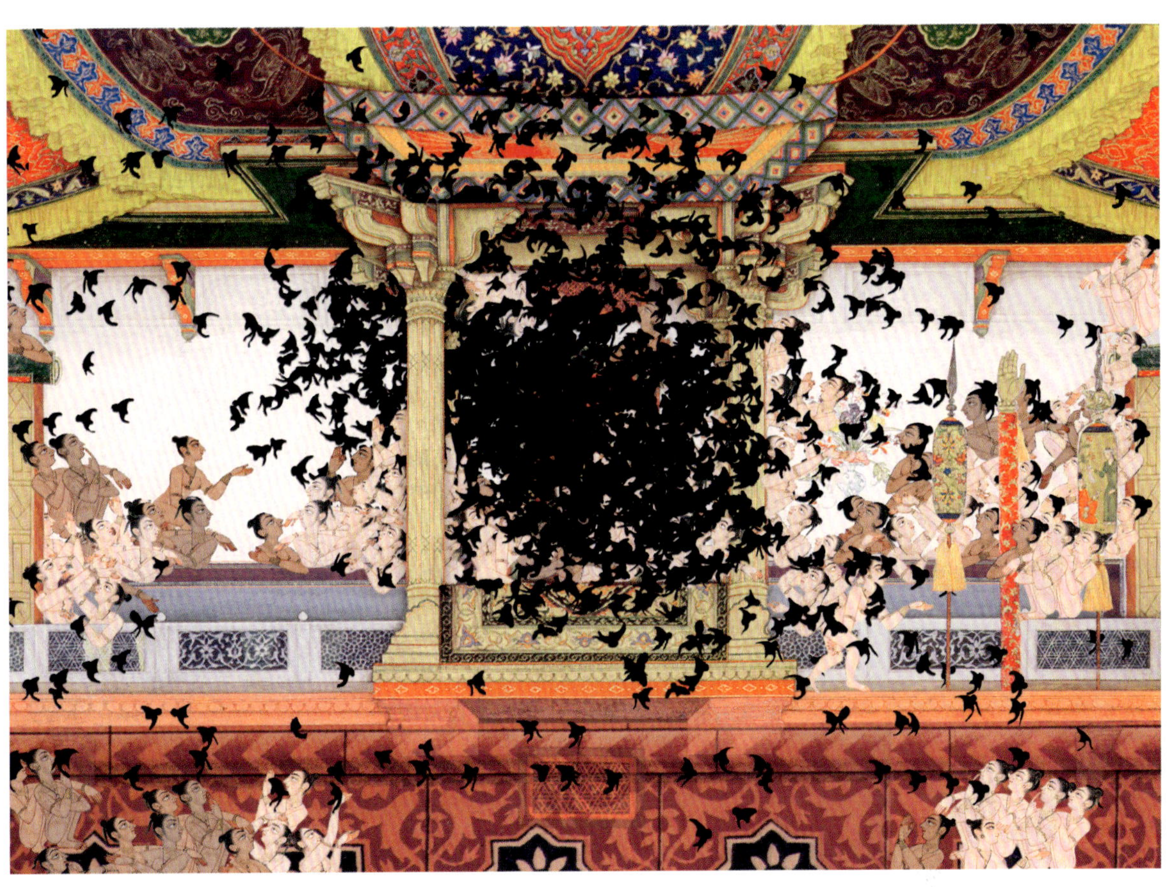

Mariko Mori
Wave UFO
1999–2003

Shahzia Sikander
Still from *SpiNN*
2003

Curated by
Linda Nochlin and
Maura Reilly

GLOBAL FEMINISMS: NEW DIRECTIONS IN CONTEMPORARY ART

Elizabeth A. Sackler Center for Feminist Art,
Brooklyn Museum, New York, 2007

The Davis Museum and Cultural Center,
Wellesley College, Wellesley, Massachusetts, USA, 2007

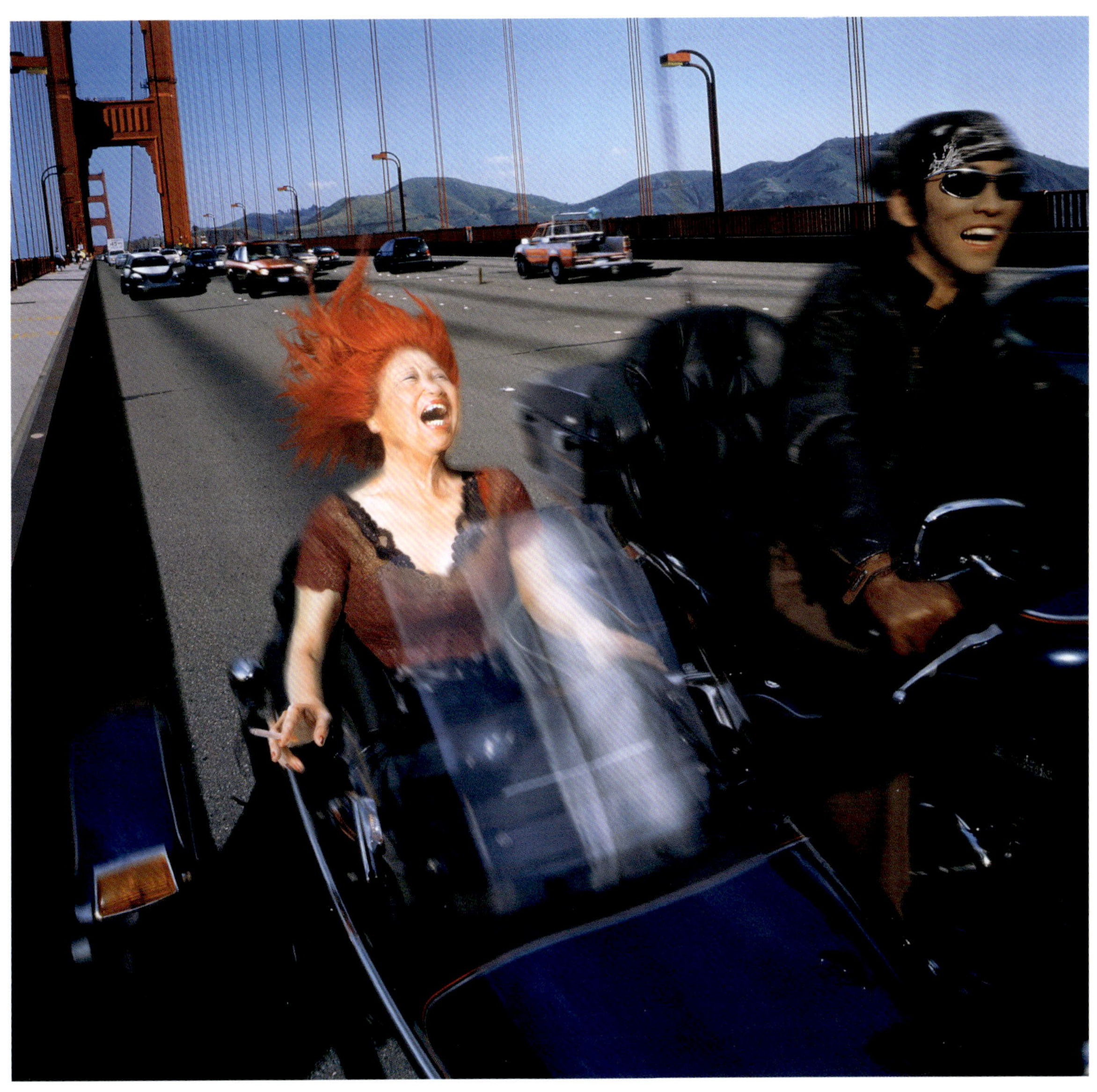

Miwa Yanagi
Yuka, from the *My Grandmother* series
2000

Global Feminisms: New Directions in Contemporary Art—which Nochlin and I organized at the Elizabeth A. Sackler Center for Feminist Art at the Brooklyn Museum in 2007[83]—called special attention to work by women as cultural producers across cultures, not just in the West, with the goal of challenging the broader framework of contemporary art as implicitly masculinist as well as Euro-US-centric. Presenting the work of eighty-eight female artists (only four of whom were born in the USA) from sixty-two countries, the exhibition featured a multitude of voices, calling attention to the fact that feminism is a truly global issue. In using a plural noun—"feminisms"—the curators implied that there is not one single, unitary "feminism," any more than there is a universal "woman." Similarly, *Global Feminisms* sought to challenge the concept of a "global sisterhood," a term that assumes a universal sameness among women without taking into account social, racial, ethnic, economic, sexual, and cultural differences.

Importantly, the year 2007 also marked the thirtieth anniversary of the *Women Artists: 1550–1950* exhibition's presentation at the Brooklyn Museum, also curated by Nochlin (with Sutherland Harris; see pp. 42–47). *Global Feminisms* integrated into its curatorial strategy developments in postcolonial feminist practice and theory that helped move contemporary art toward a new internationalism. In some senses, it functioned as a respectful update of *Women Artists*—a curatorial project that was specific to the 1970s. The two exhibitions thus served as conceptual bookends separated by thirty years of feminist artistic and curatorial practice.

The exhibition's installation was neither chronological nor geographical; instead, it was organized loosely into four sections that demonstrated both the interconnectedness and the diversity of women's histories, experiences, and struggles worldwide. The first section, "Life Cycles," charted the stages of life—from birth to death— in a non-traditional and subversive fashion, featuring artists who preferred to explore lesbian motherhood (Catherine Opie), primate wet-nurses (Patricia Piccinini), male pregnancy (Hiroko Okada), the dark underbelly of childhood (Loretta Lux), cyber-feminist marriages (Tanja Ostojić), hipster grandmas (Miwa Yanagi), and seductive tombstones (Pipilotti Rist). Section two, "Identities," took as its starting point feminist theorist Donna Haraway's declaration that identities are "contradictory, partial, and strategic," [84] and included works by Oreet Ashery, Cass Bird, Dayanita Singh, and others that sought to reveal that a person's identity cannot be restricted to a single definition, and that recognized identities—of race, class, gender, sex—are fluid, and never stable.[85]

The third section of the exhibition, "Politics," examined world politics through the eyes of women artists whose overt declarations demonstrated that the political has become deeply personal. It included works that explore the problematic relationship between the individual and those institutional or political forces that give rise to war (Lida Abdul and Michèle Magema), racism (Fiona Foley), sex trafficking (Skowmon Hastanan), suppression of female sexuality (Ghada Amer), colonialism (Tania Bruguera), geographical displacement (Emily Jacir), and industrial pollution (Yin Xiuzhen).

"Emotions," the final section, explored the representation of various emotional and psychological states—ranging from ecstasy to self-loathing, psychosis to contentment, sexual pleasure to hysteria—in an attempt to dismantle the confining structure of what is "natural" for women, and men, to feel and express. Many of the works in the section evoked strong emotional responses in the spectator, as one was confronted with passionate kisses (Tracey Moffatt), domestic violence (Julia Loktev), self-mutilation (Ryoko Suzuki), fits of laughter (Boryana Rossa), bouts of tears (Sam Taylor-Wood), or the display of sexually arousing poses (Aude du Pasquier Grall).

Global Feminisms received mixed reviews. Writing for *Artforum*, Carol Armstrong railed against the curators for not including male artists, and said she "came away depressed"; Peter Schjeldahl of *The New Yorker* described it as "a big, high-minded, intermittently enjoyable show"; and Roberta Smith of the *New York Times* as "a false idea wrapped in confusion." [86] The exhibition did have its fans, however. Helena Reckitt, writing for the international feminist art journal *n.paradoxa*, praised the exhibition's focus on non-Western artists, and the organizers' consultation with critics and curators in regions that were not traditionally part of the Western art-world's orbit—in so doing, they avoided mainstream curatorial tendencies to select artists who had already been rubber stamped by the international arts community.[87] Dena Muller agreed, writing that the exhibition was "impactful," "progressive and challenging," and argued that if critics found it "falling short of their bated anticipation," then they were ignoring curatorial intention altogether—intentions, she reminded readers, that are clearly outlined in the exhibition's wall texts and catalogue essays.[88]

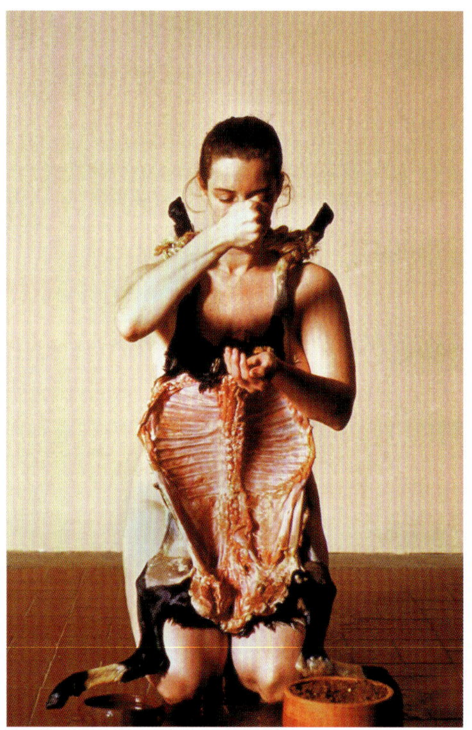 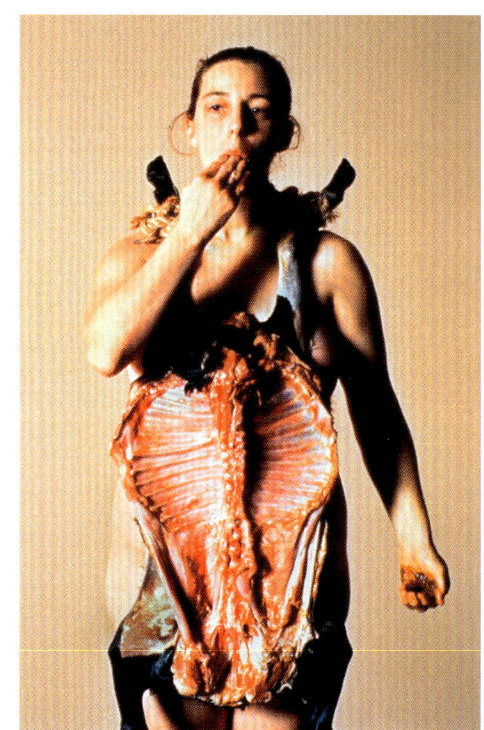

Tania Bruguera
The Burden of Guilt
1997–99

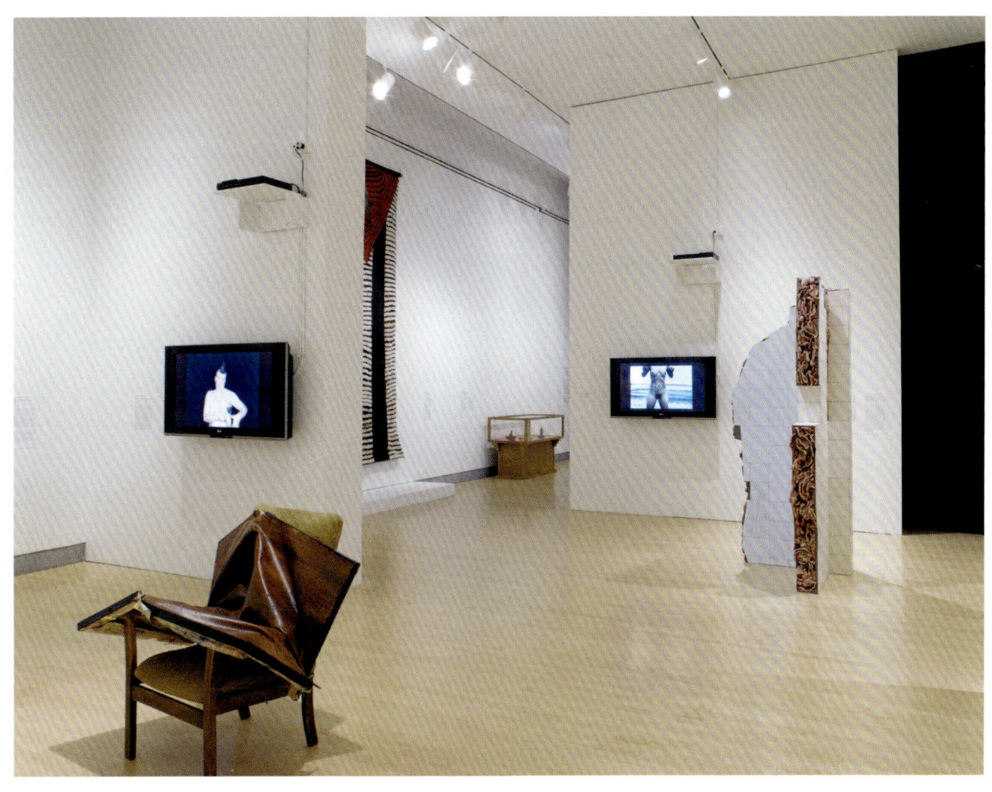

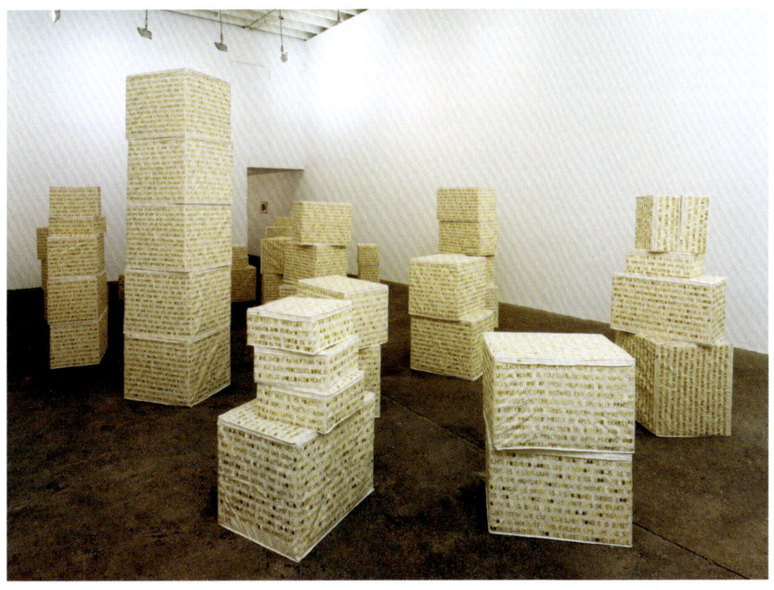

Installation view, *Global Feminisms*
Brooklyn Museum
Curated by Linda Nochlin and Maura Reilly
2007

Ghada Amer
Encyclopedia of Pleasure
2001

Curated by
Cornelia Butler

WACK!
ART AND THE FEMINIST
REVOLUTION

Museum of Contemporary Art, Los Angeles, 2007
National Museum of Women in the Arts, Washington, DC, 2007
MoMA PS.1 Contemporary Art Center, Long Island City, New York, USA 2008
Vancouver Art Gallery, Vancouver, Canada, 2008–2009

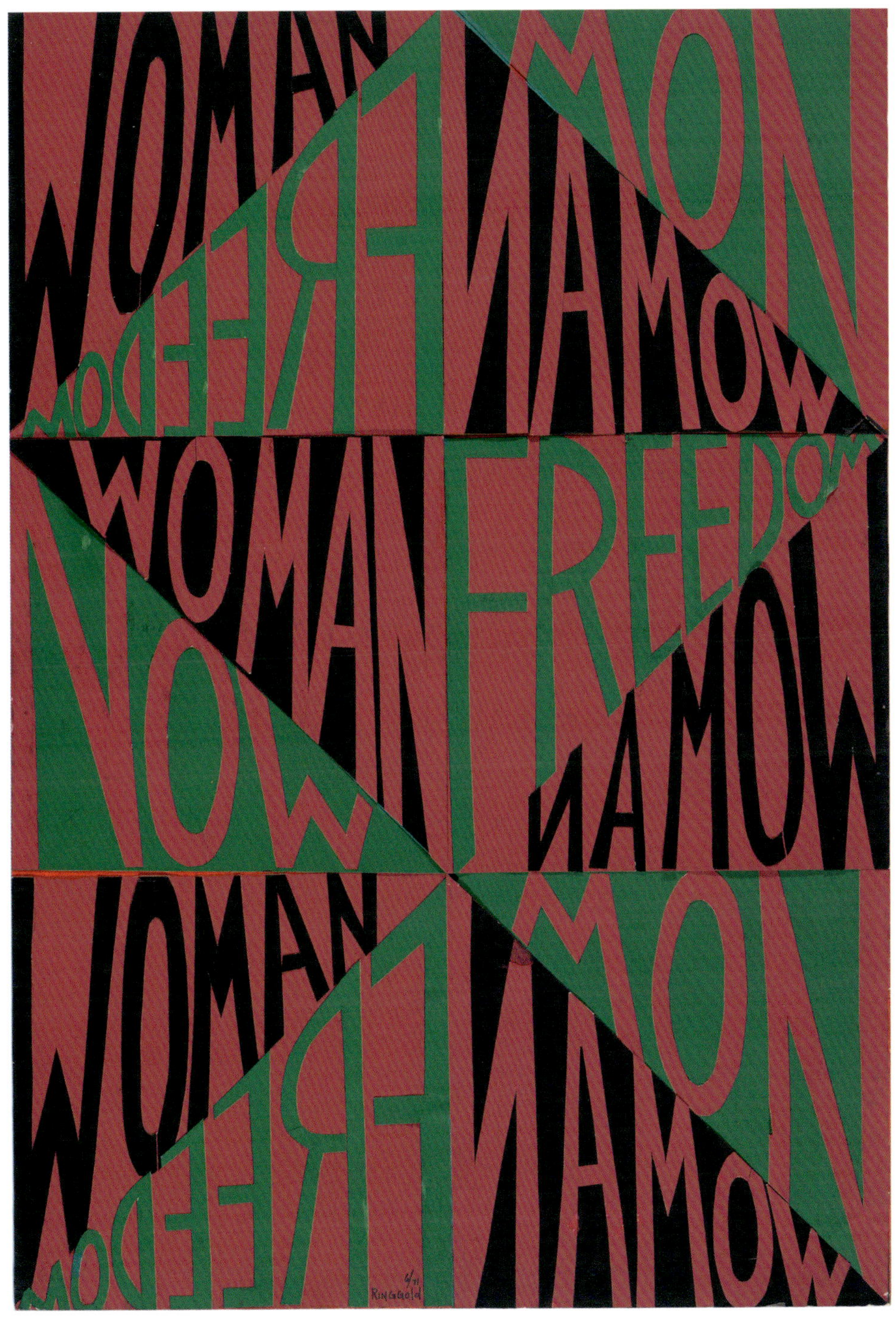

Faith Ringgold
Freedom Woman Now
1971

WACK! Art and the Feminist Revolution, curated by Cornelia Butler, first presented at the Museum of Contemporary Art in Los Angeles in 2007, was a historical exhibition that examined the international foundations and legacy of feminist art, and focused on the crucial period from 1965 to 1980, during which a vast amount of feminist activism and art-making occurred internationally. The exhibition included 430 works by 120 artists from 21 countries, including the USA, Central and Eastern Europe, Latin America, Canada, and the Asia-Pacific region. The exhibition explored intercontinental connections and themes based on media, geography, formal concerns, and collective aesthetic and political impulses.

Rather than imposing definitive categories or a chronological or geographical order, the exhibition was organized into a series of loose themes: "Goddess," "Gender Performance," "Pattern and Assemblage," "Body Trauma," "Taped and Measured," "Autobiography," "Making Art History," "Speaking in Public," "Silence and Noise," "Female Sensibility," "Abstraction," "Gendered Space," "Collective Impulse," "Social Sculpture," "Knowledge as Power," "Body as Medium," "Family Stories," and "Labor." The flexibility of these themes demonstrated that the show's logic was suggestive rather than authoritative, and allowed for a mixing and matching of artworks by well-known with lesser-known artists, with no implied hierarchy.[89] So, for example, in the gallery dedicated to "Abstraction," the 1970s works of (Italian-Brazilian) artist Anna Maria Maiolino and (French-American) Louise Bourgeois were presented side-by-side. As Armstrong argued in *Artforum*, "That there was no chronological order or clear thematic breakdown to this international barrage of wildly multimedia work…only enhances the sense of the thrilling (and exasperating) chaos of the moment, the all-over-the-place free-for-all that was those two decades."[90] Because there was no strict narrative, the experience of the exhibition felt free and open, "unfolding as commonalities and differences among works and artists were discovered."[91]

Highlights of the exhibition included Magdalena Abakanowicz's *Abakan Red* (1969), an enormous suspended fiber sculpture dyed a rich vermilion, suggesting a monumental vagina; Spero's *Torture of Women* (1976), a set of five horizontal scrolls filled with graffitti-like drawings, which read like a hallucinated record of human pain; Louise Fishman's six *Angry Paintings* (1973); Harmony Hammond's *Hunker Time* (1979), which resembled a ladder-shaped grid wrapped in strips of cloth; Lygia Clark's *Collective Head* (1975), a plywood headdress decorated with bits of plastic tarp, ropes, and paper to be worn while walking through urban streets; and Howardena Pindell's video *Free, White, and 21* (1980), in which the artist played the roles of a black woman talking about art-world racism and a white woman accusing her of paranoia. Only six African American artists were included in the exhibition.[92]

"My ambition for *WACK!*," Butler stated in the exhibition catalogue, "is to make the case that feminism's impact on art of the 1970s constitutes the most influential international 'movement' of any during the postwar period."[93] Reconciling a host of positions within feminism, Butler relied on US scholar Peggy Phelan's definition that feminism is "the conviction that gender has been, and continues to be, a fundamental category for the organization of culture. Moreover, the pattern of that organization favors men over women."[94] Butler said that the point was to show "feminist art's lofty and romantic striving for nothing less than a complete reorganization of cultural hierarchies," and to this end, "the presentation had to be above all attractive, to constitute a powerful visual experience of the kind that sticks in your mind."[95]

The exhibition was a huge success, with massive audiences, and major international press coverage. While some critics took issue with the show's title for, as one writer expressed it, "playing too readily into an antic, bad-girl take on feminist art that diminishes it and makes it a joke,"[96] and others railed against its token inclusion of non-Western artists, which was seen as maintaining a Western-centric narrative of feminist art,[97] the exhibition received mostly praise from the press. Its tremendous inclusiveness was credited with positing an alternative history of art from 1965 to 1980, detailing the symbiotic overlap between feminist art and styles as diverse as, for example, process art, pattern and decoration, and social sculpture.[98] Others, however, including Holland Cotter, argued that because feminist art history is complex and under-documented, the show was a "rough draft," but one that provided material for future drafts.[99] And while Ingrid Rowland of the *New York Review of Books* argued that "the quality of the work produced in these years ranges from sublime... to dreadful," "the general spirit is infectiously exuberant in its eagerness to conquer the world, not just the art world, and set it to rights."[100] The show was, Mike Sperlinger declared in *Art Monthly*, "a serious testament to feminism's unfinished business."[101]

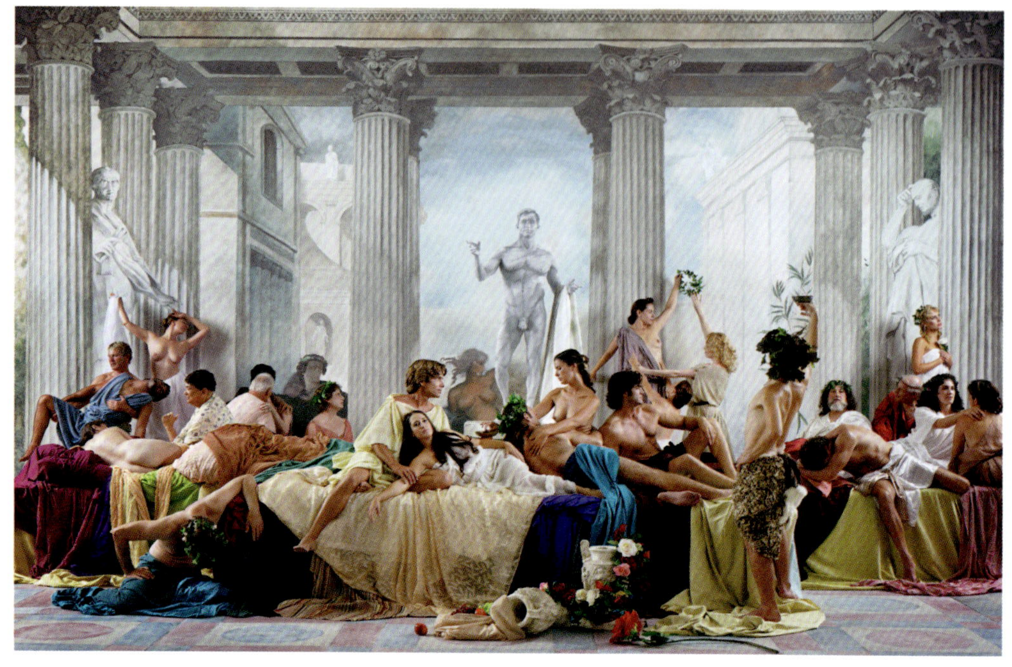

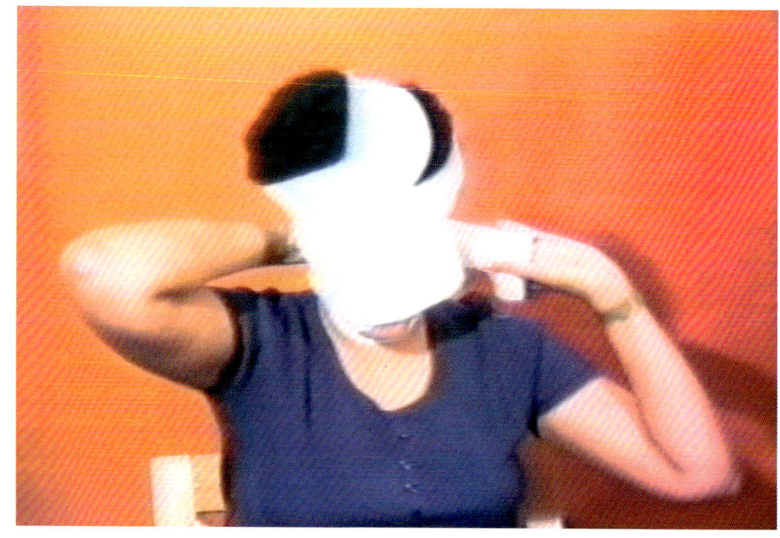

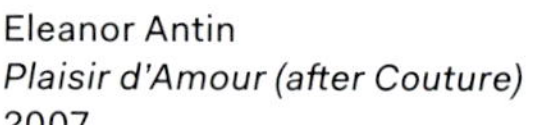

Eleanor Antin
Plaisir d'Amour (after Couture)
2007

Howardena Pindell
Free, White, and 21
1980

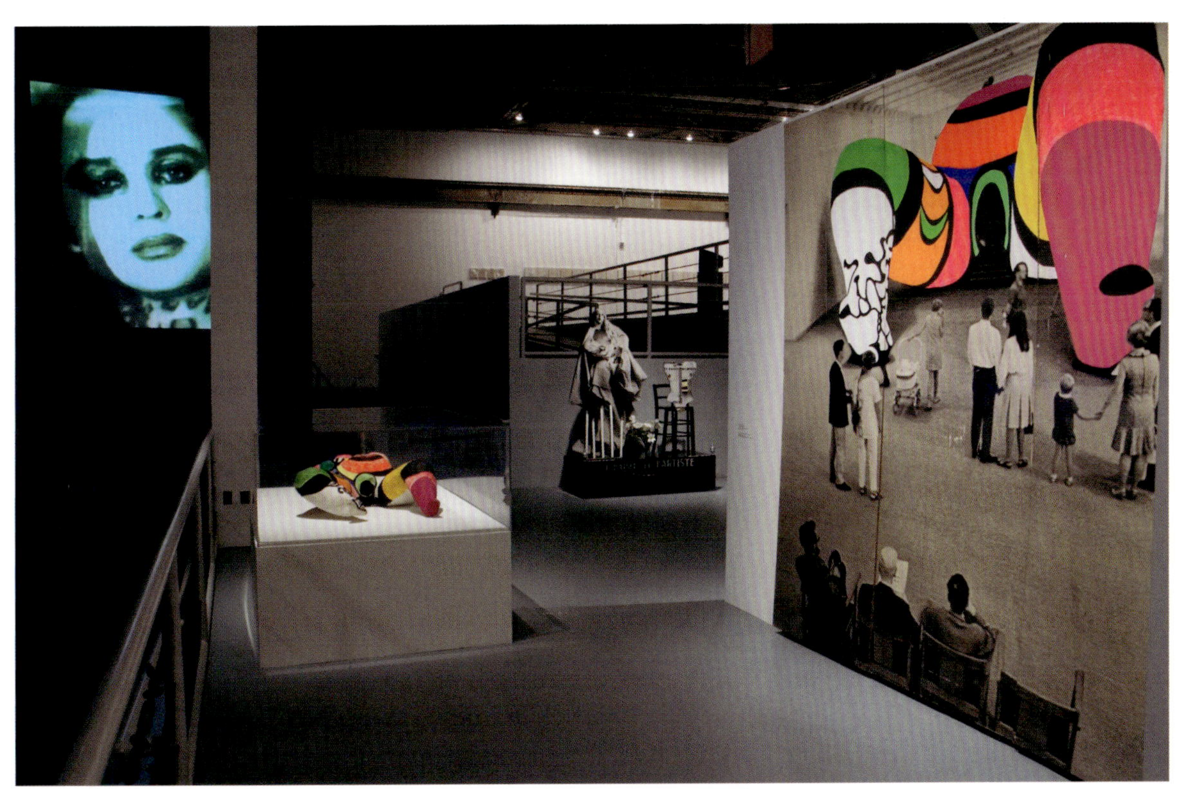

Installation view, *WACK! Art and the Feminist Revolution*
The Geffen Contemporary at the Museum of Contemporary Art, Los Angeles
March 4–July 6, 2007

2009 – 2011

Curated by
Camille Morineau [102]

ELLES@CENTREPOMPIDOU

Pompidou Center, Paris

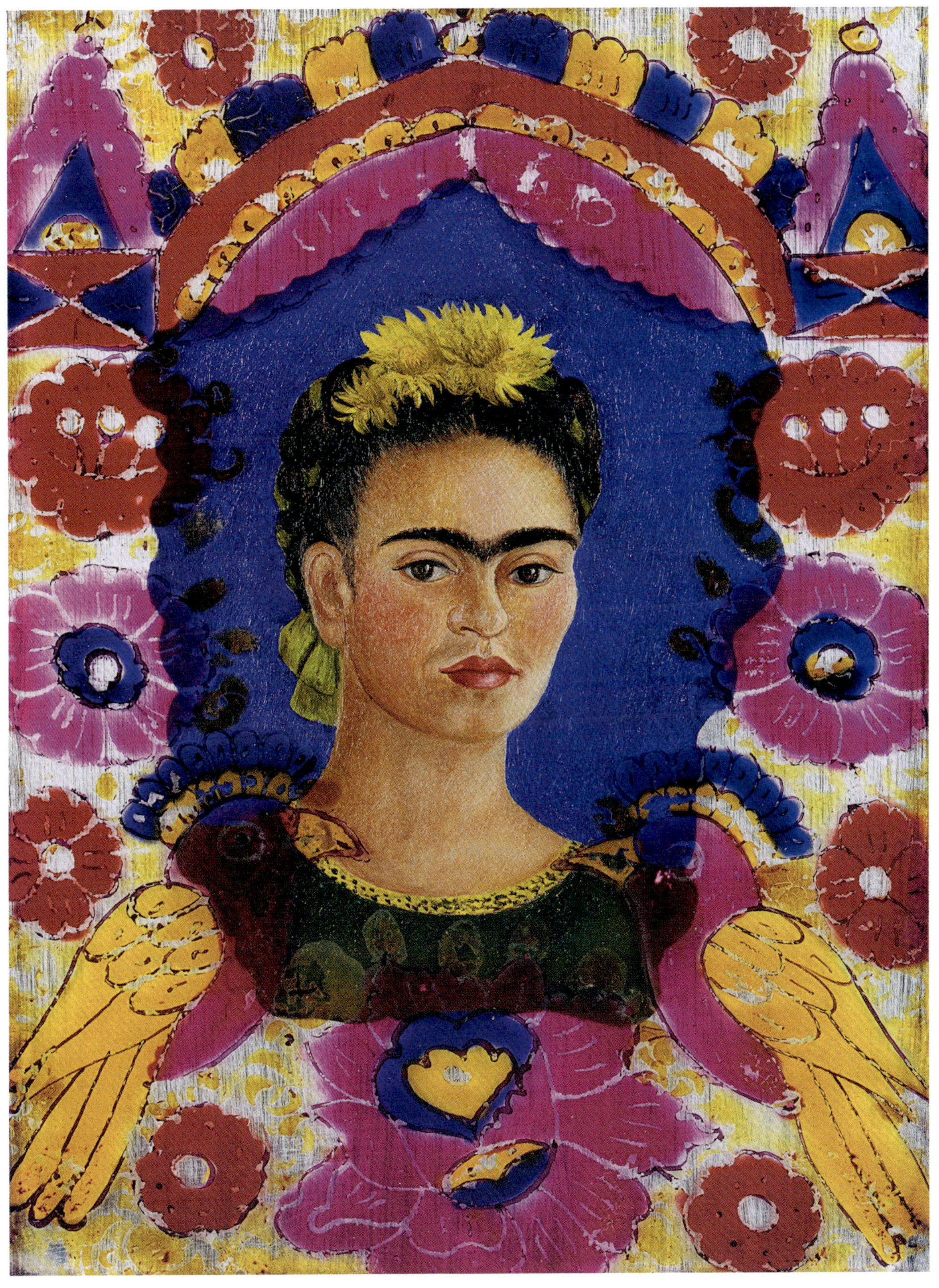

Frida Kahlo
The Frame
1938

In 2009, the Pompidou Center in Paris took the bold step of organizing a rotating exhibition that lasted for almost two years, entitled *Elles@centrepompidou*, in which the then-Head of the Contemporary Collections, Camille Morineau, along with a team of museum curators, reinstalled the museum's permanent collection with only women artists—presenting an alternative history of modern and contemporary art. In short, from May 27, 2009, to February 21, 2011, the museum put all the works by male artists in storage. The installation of about five hundred works by more than two hundred women was a hugely ambitious project, and began with early 20th-century paintings by French artist Suzanne Valadon and ended with works by more contemporary figures, such as Pipilotti Rist and Rachel Whiteread. The exhibition was hung in chronological order by themes—"Pioneer," "Free Fire," "Eccentric Abstraction," "Body Slogan," "The Activist Body," "A Room of One's Own," "Wordworks," and "Immaterials"—which were broad enough to accommodate both non- and proto-feminist as well as explicitly feminist work.

Elles was a particularly revolutionary gesture in the context of France. As Morineau later explained, "It was a very un-French thing to do. In France, nobody counts the number of men and women in exhibitions. Very few people notice that sometimes there are no women." [103] "That's why I decided to do the show," she said. "It's a little taboo. By putting women at the center, the question of marginalization disappears; you can rewrite history in the way you present the show." [104] It took her six years to convince the then-director Alfred Pacquement that an all-women exhibition was a sound proposal. Instead of offering to organize a blockbuster feminist show, which was her first choice, she suggested that it would be better to work with the collection because it would bring to light the history of taste. It would address fifty years of collecting, not just a particular curator's point of view. Pacquement eventually agreed. But it meant that the Pompidou's holding of women artists had to be expanded through purchases and donations—an effort that was supported by collectors, galleries, and artists who supplied works by missing artists. In fact, 40% of the works included in *Elles* were acquired in the five years preceding the exhibition.

In its way, *Elles* was a radical gesture of affirmative action—but one that was not long-lasting: as Morineau explained, in the post-*Elles* re-hang of the permanent collection in 2012, just 10% of the works on view were by women—exactly the same as it was pre-*Elles*. While all the works in *Elles* were produced by women, art by women comprised only 18% of the museum's entire collection at the time. Moreover, post-*Elles* the acquisition funds for women artists had almost immediately dried up; globalizing the collection became the new initiative, according to Morineau, who left the institution in 2012.[105]

Of all of the feminist curatorial activism around that time (*WACK!* And *Global Feminisms*, for example), the Pompidou Center was a standout among museums' efforts to pay more attention to women. If not the first such exhibition in the world, as advertised, it was certainly the first on such a grand scale. It was hugely successful, received tons of international press and, importantly, increased attendance figures to the permanent collection by a quarter.[106]

Elles received mostly positive reviews in the press. In *Artforum*, Okwui Enwezor called it an "informative, beautifully installed, and altogether engaging exhibition," [107] while Nicole Salez claimed that the presentation demonstrated definitively that art by women is as radical, strong, and complex as that by men in contemporary art.[108] Others argued that the simple act of making women's art visible on a grand scale acknowledged the diversity of their approaches.[109] Emmanuelle Lequeux suggested in *Le Monde*, however, that *Elles* ran the risk of relegating women artists to a ghetto.[110] Catherine Gonnard responded to that criticism: "Rather than isolating female artists in a ghetto, the exhibit took positive steps to address the paradoxical situation Joan Scott has identified. This is the dilemma where women have to 'fight against exclusion and for universalism while acknowledging sexual difference—the very same difference that led to their exclusion in the first place!'" [111] Germaine Greer's critique of *Elles* was particularly dismissive. In her article, "Why the world doesn't need an Annie Warhol or a Francine Bacon," she argued: "The effect of offering a sampler of the work of 200 women is to diminish the achievement of all of them. By lumping the major with the minor, and by showing only minor works of major figures, *Elles@centrepompidou* managed to convince too many visitors to the exhibition that there was such a thing as women's art and that women artists were going nowhere. Wrong, on both counts." [112] Jonathan Jones took issue with the women-only focus, as well, calling the endeavor "clumsy" and a "stunt." He asked whether this was the best way to rebalance history, and trivialized the show as "a slightly old-fashioned political art gesture." [113]

More recently, Amelia Jones has pointed to director Pacquement's implicit misogyny and fear of "the feminine," as indicated in the preface to the catalogue, where he noted that *Elles* signaled "'a possible development of a history of art in the feminine,' only to backtrack schizophrenically: 'it is [now] possible to unfold a full and entire history of art with *Elles*. A history about which there is nothing feminine at all.'" [114] Pacquement's statement reflects his apparent anxiety about "the feminine" and his reduction of radical feminist work to feminine qualities. Indeed, this anxiety was evident throughout the exhibition in that none of the wall texts mentioned the word "feminism," opting instead to refer to it as an exhibition "displaying the feminine side," and as "a feminine hanging of the collection." Regardless, Jones argued that despite the limitations of what was possible, "the show was a fantastic argument in favor of continuing to mount shows of 'women's art.'" [115]

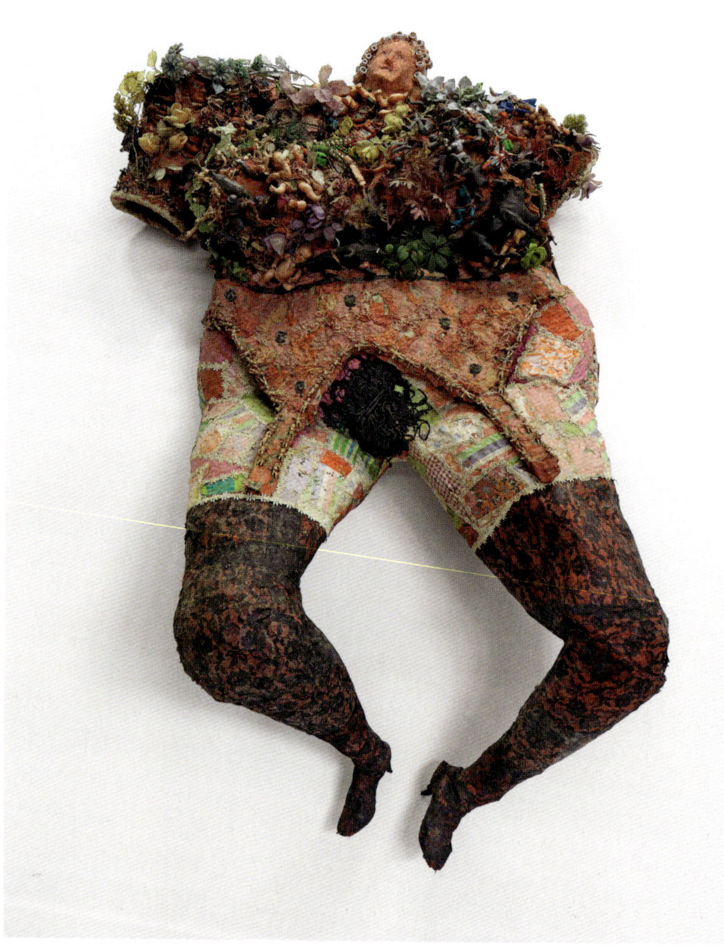

Niki de Saint Phalle
Crucifixion
c. 1965

Véronique Ellena
Les Calanques, from *Les Dimanches
(Sundays)* series
1997

Lee Bontecou
Untitled
1966

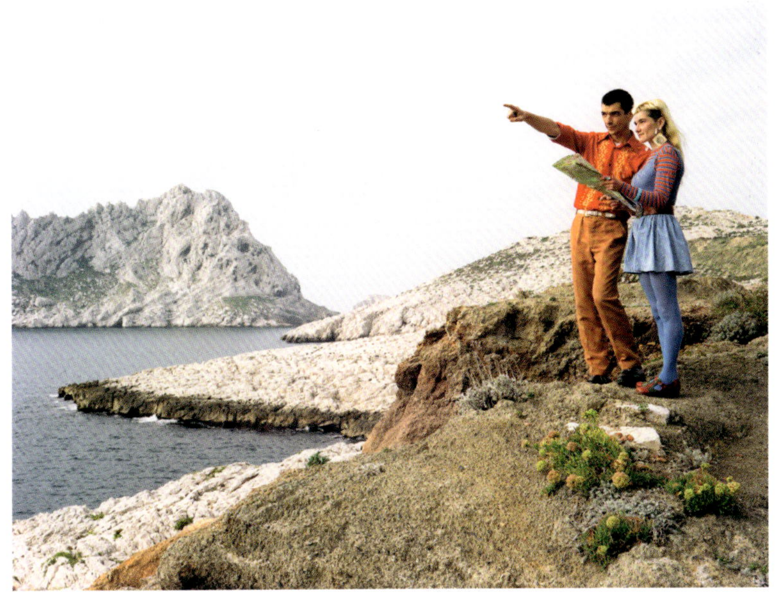

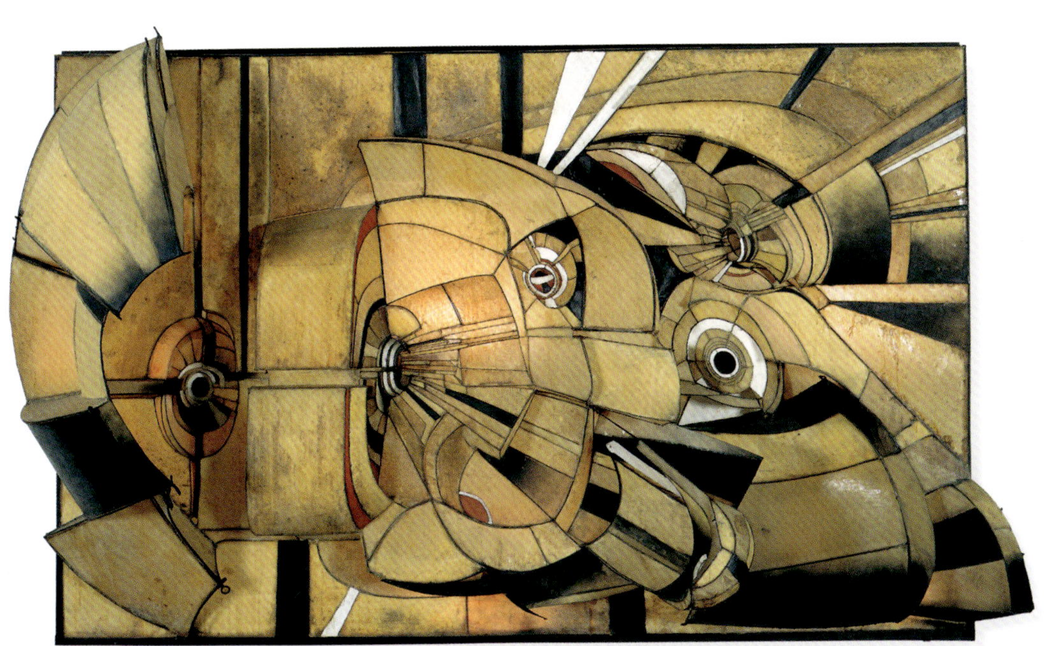

2011 – 2013

Curated by
Beatrice Stammer and
Bettina Knaup

RE.ACT.FEMINISM #2 — A PERFORMING ARCHIVE

Centro Cultural Montehermoso, Vitoria-Gasteiz, Spain, 2011
Wyspa Institute for Art, Gdansk, Poland, 2012
Galerija Miroslay Kralievič, Zagreb, Croatia, 2012
Museum of Contemporary Art, Roskilde, Denmark, 2012
Tallinn Art Hall, Tallin, Estonia, 2012
Fundació Antoni Tàpies, Barcelona, Spain, 2013
Academy of Arts, Berlin, Germany, 2013

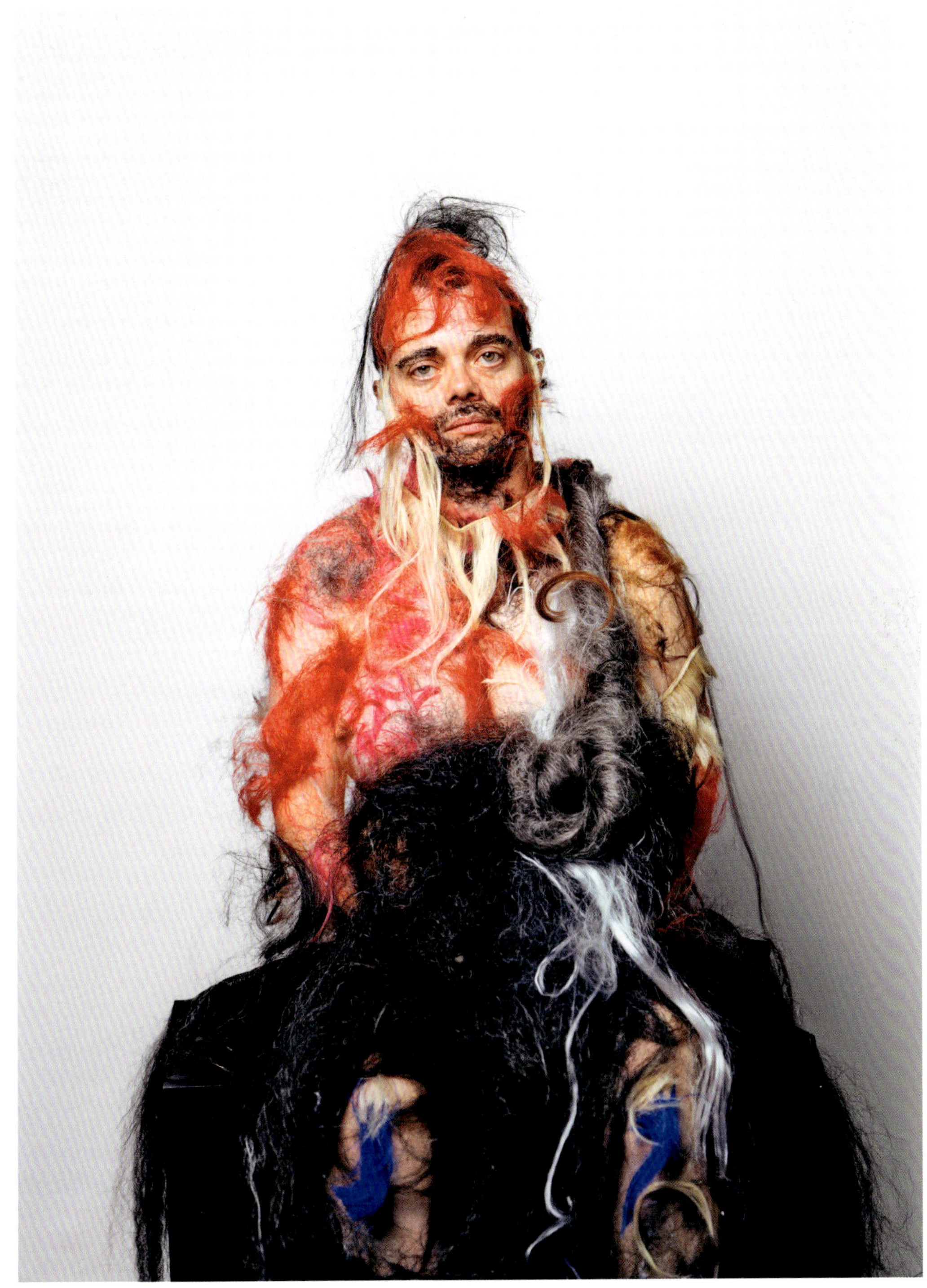

Oreet Ashery
Hairoism
2009–11

Curated by Beatrice Stammer and Bettina Knaup, *re.act.feminism—a performing archive*, began as an exhibition of women artists' videos, as well as photographic documentation and artifacts from performances, shown at the Academy of Arts, Berlin, from 2008 to 2009. It included a video archive, a series of live performances, and a conference. It then toured to Ljubljana, Slovenia, in reduced form as part of the City of Women International Festival of Contemporary Art, before finishing at the Kunsthaus Erfurt, Erfurt, Germany. Its second iteration, *re.act.feminism #2*, first presented in 2011 at the Centro Cultural Montehermoso in Vitoria-Gasteiz, Spain, comprised a larger archive of documented performances by more than 180 artists and artist collectives. It then toured to other venues in Europe (Poland, Croatia, Denmark, Estonia, and a second site in Spain) before finishing at the Academy of Arts, Berlin, in 2013. According to the project's program, *re.act.feminism #2* presented what the organizers called a "continually expanding, temporary and living performance archive," representing feminist, gender-critical, and queer performance art from the 1960s to the early 1980s, as well as contemporary works.[116] The research focus was on Eastern and Western Europe, the Mediterranean, and Middle East, the USA, and several countries in Latin America. As it traveled through Europe, the temporary archive continued to expand through local research and cooperation with art academies and universities. It was also "animated" through exhibitions, screenings, performances, and discussions along the way, which continuously supplemented the archive.

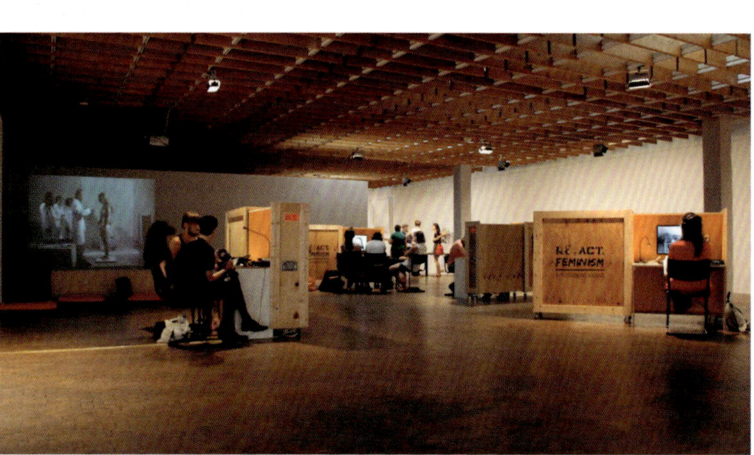

re.act.feminism #2—a performing archive
Workshop in re.act. open space with
Les Salonnières
Akademie der Künste, Berlin
2013

The heart of the project was a mobile, travel-ready archive comprised of a set of five foldable freight boxes with document cabinets, four of which housed mobile viewing and work stations, each including a DVD player, monitor, and headphones. The fifth crate housed an extensive archive of DVDs and photographs from and about performance art. An inventory book of the archive was available in the local language, which included short descriptions of works, artist biographies, and an overview of the entire selection. A museum guard functioned as an archivist, available for questions. Each installation was accompanied by an exhibition of related works, as well as live events—all with a regional/local focus. In Gdansk, for example, the host venue organized an exhibition of lesser-known films by Polish performance art from the 1970s and 80s. In Vitoria-Gasteiz, Spain, the curators worked with others to present a cross-section of the archive, following certain thematic threads.

Each venue was organized according to a series of thematic fields designed to emphasize connections, differences, and incompatibilities.[117] The section "Dis/appearing Subjects" presented performative works that wrapped, veiled, or fragmented the body, as either a means for scopophilic disruption, or for the exploration of multiple, malleable (or non-linear) identities, as in Ana Mendieta's *Bird Transformation* (1972), Boryana Rossa's *SZ–ZS* (2005), and Theresa Hak Kyung Cha's *Aveugle Voix* (Blind Voice, 1975), among others. "Resisting Objects" featured performance works such as Adrian Piper's *The Mythic Being* (1973), Oreet Ashery's *Hairoism* (2009–11), and Lorraine O'Grady's *Mlle Bourgeoise Noire*, 1980, in which, as the curators explained, "the objectified other or the freak is an important character," and where "the exaggeration of visibility, the enforcement of voyeurism and the disturbance of a seamless link between perception and legibility are common features of their performances, which use strategies of metamorphosis, masquerade and role-play to demonstrate the 'resistance of the object.'"[118]

The section "Labor of Love and Care" presented performance works that politicized or dramatized invisible housework (Mierle Laderman Ukeles's *Touch Sanitation*, 1978–80), reproductive work, and care giving; others criticized the capitalist exploitation of immaterial labor (Pauline Boudry and Renate Lorenz, *Charming for the Revolution*, 2009). "Relational Bodies/Extended Skins" presented body-art performances with a particular focus on gender-critical work: for example, Miriam Sharon's tent costumes produced for workers and nomads in Israel, and Marta Minujín's participatory sculptures, among others. The section "Body Controls and Measuring Acts" explored different practices of controlling the body. These practices ranged, Knaup explained, "from state oppression by authoritarian regimes and the surveillance of free movement and migration to sexualized and internalized violence—and the practice of resistance involved in re-claiming (public) space."[119]

The section "Working in Collectives" explored works associated with the history of—as well as current examples of—women-only collectives, including A Social Art Network (Suzanne Lacy and Leslie Labowitz), Disband, Corpus Deleicti, Icelandic Love Corporation, The Waitresses, Chicks on Speed, and Pussy Riot, among many others. Finally, in the "Feminine Drag and Pleasurable Acts" section, artists questioned, deconstructed, and/or reconstructed ideals of female beauty and heteronormative femininity. Many adopted female personae (Colette and Martha Wilson), stylized their bodies as feminine, androgynous, erotic, artificial beings (Manon and Narcissister), or embodied hybrid auto-erotic scenes (Orshi Drozdik)—all of which were strategies used to explore the concept of "feminine drag."

The exhibition *re.act.feminism #2* received numerous reviews in mainstream and art publications. Irmgard Berner, writing for the *Berliner Zeitung*, called it a "pioneering achievement," which, "like a mobile cinema" was helping to re-establish some long-lost female artists.[120] *Das Kunstmagazine* noted that it raised critical questions about the preservation and exhibition of performance, and referred to it as "a contemplative, immersive art experience" that offered the opportunity of entering into an "intensive dialogue" with the artworks.[121] Some critics were disappointed that there was too much material (180 works) to view in one sitting and that the selection was random. Nevertheless, others acknowledged that the sheer volume of work demonstrated not only the rich "field of feminist awakenings," but also, how fleeting its materiality was and, if left undocumented, how easily these works could be lost or forgotten.[122]

Lilibeth Rasmussen
Never Mind Pollock
2009

Ewa Partum
Selbstidentifikation (Selfidentification)
1980

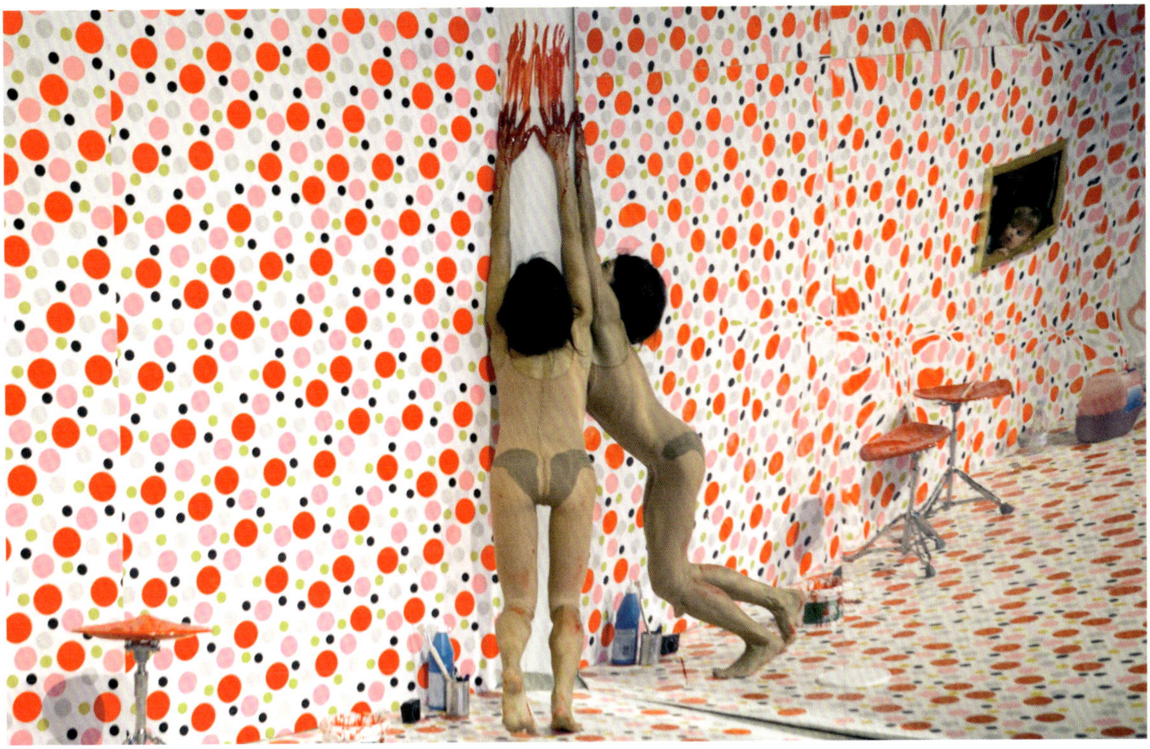

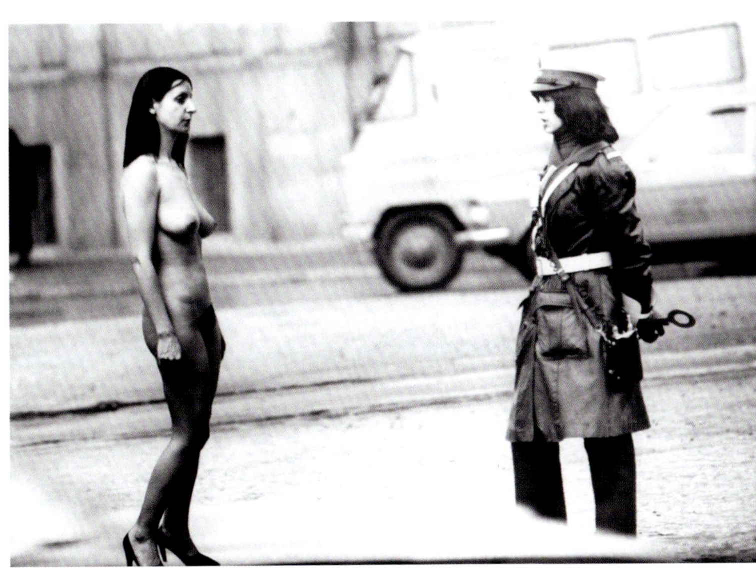

3. TACKLING WHITE PRIVILEGE AND WESTERN-CENTRISM

"[The art world] is one of the last bastions of white supremacy-by-exclusion." [1]

Judith Wilson

Between 1989 and 1995, several landmark art exhibitions were organized in Europe and the USA that departed from what had been the traditional curatorial practices of art institutions in those regions, including *Magiciens de la terre* (1989), *The Decade Show: Frameworks of Identity in the 1980s* (1990), *Mining the Museum* (1992–93), and the Whitney Biennial of 1993. While there had, of course, been exhibitions before these that were international and multicultural—namely, Documentas and Biennials—none had set out to be as consciously inclusive of the Other (defined in these exhibitions as non-Western and/or non-white). Each of the shows insisted that no evaluation of contemporary culture could ignore the marginalization of large groups of non-Western (and non-white) artists, and attempted to overturn the binary pairing of center/periphery and black/white upon which Modernism itself was founded. The framework of each exhibition posed an unprecedented challenge to the mainstream art world by calling into question its Western-centrism, while some—especially *The Decade Show* and the 1993 Whitney Biennial—resulted in the recognition and inclusion of more "hyphenated" artists into contemporary art discourse (Latin-Americans, Asian-Americans, and so on). Although the principal goal for many of these activist exhibitions was to give voice to "minority" artists, most were criticized for pandering to political correctness, to an ethos of identity politics, and were sometimes dismissed as having sacrificed quality in favor of multiculturalism.

A NEW, INCLUSIVE DISCOURSE?

These activist exhibitions of the late 1980s to the mid-1990s set the stage for subsequent endeavors in which curators sought to construct a new and inclusive discourse for art in an age of globalization, including, for example, *Century City: Art and Culture in the Modern Metropolis* (2001), *Authentic/Ex-Centric: Conceptualism in Contemporary African Art* (2001), *Documenta 11* (2002), *Africa Remix* (2005), *The Global Contemporary: Art Worlds After 1989* (2011–12), and the Venice Biennale of 2015—these shows, among others, self-consciously departed from Euro-US and monocultural perspectives. The curatorial aim of many of them was, as Nigerian-born curator, writer, and critic Okwui Enwezor explained, to articulate the "demands of the multitude"[2]—that is, to include rather than exclude the multitude of Other artists who deserved to take their place on the global art stage. But, again, many of the shows were criticized for their preoccupation with socio-political concerns, and for utilizing morality-based approaches; others were dismissed for exhibiting works characterized as political propaganda.[3]

Despite these widespread efforts since the late 1980s to address systemic racial discrimination in the art world, problems persist. The exclusion of artists of color and non-Euro-US artists from mainstream (non-activist) exhibitions is demonstrated by the 2014 Whitney Biennial—a group exhibition that was criticized at the time for epitomizing the concept of white privilege. Indeed, in 2014, *The New Inquiry* published an article by Eunsong Kim and Maya Isabella Mackrandilal, which railed against the show's lack of diversity:

Dear White Curators,
1. Diversity is not the inclusion of those not from New York. Diversity isn't more white women. Diversity isn't safe art. Diversity isn't black bodies put on display by white artists.

2. You don't get to appropriate diversity as a buzzword for your PR work. Besides, we know how to count. [...]

3. Your theory is tired, your reasoning bland and your politics telling. To use Sara Ahmed's term, your Biennial is a case study in "reproductive whiteness"—citation practices that privilege

whiteness, white thinkers and white history to perpetuate whiteness. We know how to read between the lines.

4. Your choice to reproduce a whitewashed art world has material effects on the lived experiences of people of color and denies the shifts taking place in our visual world.[4]

Their anger was more than justified, given that only 8 out of the 103 artists were non-white. That is a shocking statistic, and even more egregious when one considers that the museum billed it as "one of the broadest and most diverse takes on art in the United States that the Whitney has offered in many years."[5]

The same Whitney Biennial experienced more controversy when the collective HowDoYouSayYaminAfrican (known as Yams)—a group of thirty-eight artists of color—withdrew their video from the exhibition, expressing concern about the lack of black and female artists in the show. They stated that they had intended their initial participation to be an intervention into a white supremacist institution, and one they hoped would change the Whitney's systemic racism from within: "We are protesting institutional white supremacy and how it plays out," they explained.[6] "A main part of our message is that we want to move the idea of white supremacy away from caricatures: neo-Nazis, KKK members, crazy kids who live in the mountains of Arkansas. White supremacy is embodied in these institutions that tokenize us, that invite us into their spaces where they have absolutely no interest in ceding power." The museum's chief curator responded by saying that the institution maintains "a profound commitment to diversity" and welcomes debate on the subject.[7] Unfortunately, that debate never happened.

More recently, in 2016, there was a public protest led by US artist Chris Jordan over the lack of racial diversity in the exhibition *Art AIDS America*, on view at the Tacoma Art Museum, Washington: of more than one hundred featured artists only five were African American. The protestors publicized the event online with the hashtag #StopErasingBlackPeople and released a statement saying that the exhibition "paints HIV as an issue faced predominantly by white gay men, when in fact the most at-risk group are currently black trans women."[8] Given that African Americans bear the biggest burden of HIV/AIDS in the USA, the inclusion of only five African American artists was questionable and irresponsible.[9]

In both examples—the Whitney Biennial and *Art AIDS America*—non-white artists had been excluded, and/or reduced to token participants. This had effectively erased black experience from these exhibitions, rendering it virtually invisible. Protest against the practice of collective indifference has been at the heart of the campaign #OscarsSoWhite, initiated in 2015, which criticizes the lack of "minority" actors being nominated for Academy Awards. As Richard Brody indicated in *The New Yorker*, "The underlying issue of the Academy's failure to recognize black artists is the presumption that baseline experience is white experience and that black life is a niche phenomenon. The result is that only narrow and fragmentary views of the lives of African Americans ever make it to the screen."[10] For example, of the seven black actresses to ever win an Academy Award, two played slaves, and one played a maid. Writing in the *New York Times*, critic Parul Sehgal examined Brody's hypothesis (outlined in *The New Yorker* article) about how white audiences might "fully engage" with black lives. Sehgal noted that, according to Brody, "they would have to encounter their own complicity in black suffering, in the past and the present…" But, she observed, the situation is more daunting than that: "They would have to reckon with the fact that the work will not always speak to them, orient them, flatter them with tales of their munificence or infamy, or comfort them with stereotypes."[11] The omission, or "white-washing," of African American lives in Hollywood, as in the art world, is just one of the many mechanisms whereby those in power reinforce their own values and beliefs and suppress the experience of Others.

Kymberly Pinder, dean of the University of New Mexico's college of fine arts, has argued that when African American artists are featured in art-history textbooks, the works of theirs that are chosen tend to be case studies in racial stereotyping.[12] For instance, in a prime example of "artistic validation through subject matter," the 19th-/20th-century US artist Henry Ossawa Tanner is almost always represented in such books by a "black" genre scene, despite the fact that he made his international reputation as a painter of religious pictures.[13] Cultural theorist Stuart Hall has identified this type of black representation as that which "replaces invisibility with a kind of carefully relegated, segregated visibility."[14] (Regarding art-history textbooks, it was not until 1986 that African American, and women, artists were included in this genre for the first time when they appeared in the textbook *History of Art*—a classic work by the eminent Russian-born German-American scholar H. W. Janson. Native Americans were introduced in 1995.)

African American art historian Beryl Wright has explained that if black artists produce work that is not "visibly black," offering a point of resistance for white art historians, curators, and critics, it cannot be easily ghettoized, as "it's harder to control work that doesn't fit white people's perceptions of who black people are."[15] Erasure and other practices of exclusion can be detected by a preference for what Nigerian writer Chimamanda Ngozi Adichie calls the "single story"—easily legible narratives that reinforce the existing order. The danger of reproducing such uniform narratives, according to Adichie, is that complex human beings are reduced to a "single story," rather than being associated with a heterogeneous compilation of different stories.[16]

Exclusionary practices against non-white artists are everywhere visible in the art world—in the art galleries, museums, press, market, exhibitions, permanent collections, and so forth. For example, in their poster entitled "2016 Manhattan Boycott Guide," the Pussy Galore art collective revealed that only 21% of the artists represented in New York City galleries were non-white. Similarly, in their 2015 "Census Report," the BFAMFAPhD collective found that New York City's formally educated arts world (in this case, defined roughly as working artists and those with arts degrees) appeared to be 200% whiter than its general population.[17]

Tackling Eurocentrism in the contemporary art world is equally challenging. As the statistics throughout this book demonstrate, most exhibitions organized by Western institutions play lip service to non-Western artists. Rarely do they challenge the broader framework of contemporary art as implicitly Euro-US-centric. In other words, the so-called "global" art market is really not global at all: its signified is always the West, the privileged center of control.

While there have, of course, been several significant exhibitions since the late 1980s that have addressed the widespread Eurocentrism within cultural institutions, offering a more global perspective on visual culture—such as *Century City*, which represented four major continents, with no single origin of creativity (see pp. 130–37); and *Global Feminisms*, which presented work by eighty-eight female artists, only four of whom were born in the USA, from sixty-two countries (see pp. 74–79)—most mainstream (non-activist) exhibitions include only a few non-Western artists as exotic add-ons. (One need only examine a checklist for an exhibition that purports to be "international" to verify this.) These few add-ons, moreover, are usually artists who have already garnered attention in the West. As US artist and scholar Olu Oguibe argues convincingly in *The Culture Game* (2004), the global culture market sustains a firm grip on the entry and flow of non-Western contemporary art into the market to ensure that there is no "threat of an influx of aliens" on the scene and that "only a handful may gain visibility at any given time."[18] He explains further: "In effect, their 'discovery' is scrupulously managed and promotion firmly and methodically rationed to avoid an influx, while a fierce but silent competition rages between dealers as each battles to ensure that his or her non-Western artist, his or her 'global native,' as one Moroccan artist once put it, stays ahead of the game."[19] Non-Western artists are not considered successful until they have secured a gallery in Europe or the USA, preferably in New York, London, or Berlin. If they succeed elsewhere, outside of that geographic region, it is thought to be insignificant, as the work will not have real value until it enters the Euro-US market. In other words, artistic greatness (read market desirability) is still defined as white, male, and Western. The contemporary art scene, according to Cuban curator and art historian Gerardo Mosquera, is a "centralized system of apartheid."[20]

Moreover, instead of constructing a new and inclusive discourse for art in an age of globalization—one that confronts the limits of occidental power and thereby departs from hegemonic, Euro-US cultural perspectives and their exhibition projects—most mainstream (non-activist) exhibitions are only interested in including postcolonial Others as long as they speak of their Otherness.[21] For those artists who live outside the center, this global "culture game," as Oguibe calls it, has two important rules that must be understood and followed correctly in order to succeed. First, non-Western artists must recognize that it is a game, with rules written by the West; and second, that it is a game "of difference," in which artists must speak incessantly of their own Otherness, because the game's economy of signs is structured around the principle of irreducible difference.[22] Mosquera agrees: "Third World artists are constantly asked to display their identity...to look like no one else or to look like Frida [Kahlo]."[23] Mosquera argues that non-Western artists have no choice, in a way. Since it is the Euro-US art world that selects, legitimates, promotes, and purchases, non-Western artists are forced "to adapt in order to satisfy the preferences of the curating culture, not only looking for material benefits, but following the prestige of the paradigms legitimated by the centers."[24] A "burden of representation," as Kobena Mercer describes it, is established, whereby Other artists are expected to stand as representatives of a cultural group or its contributions.[25]

Many postcolonial critics are wary of the interest on the part of Western culture in all things non-Western, seeing it perhaps as an answer to global capitalism's persistent need for new commodities.

The question remains: by bringing artists and marginal centers of art to the purview of the West, are mainstream curators simply constructing the conditions for a new appropriation of the Other by the West, in a manner similar to European Modernism's appropriation of African and other "non-Western" arts at the beginning of the 20th century? Is the implication that the non-Western work is derivative or lesser than? And what of the localized context specific to the non-Western work? Has that been elucidated throughout the exhibition? If so, who has produced that content?

It is equally problematic that most cross-cultural exhibitions are financed and organized by institutions in the privileged centers—which is to say that an unequal divide is established between the curating culture and the curated cultures. Such scenarios introduce the illusion of a trans-territorial world of multicultural dialogue with currents that flow in all directions, but in actuality, the curators from the centers act like postcolonial explorers scouting out the newest "discovery." In an effort to work against the negative stereotype of the curator-as-explorer, however, curators can instead pursue their goals of mounting a "global" exhibition by positioning themselves as "mediators of cultural exchange," to use Gerardo Mosquera's phrase.[26] In other words, from the outset, curators can and should turn to specialists outside their areas of expertise and admit their own limitations. After all, every curatorial project should begin by being an exercise in modesty. As curators, we must admit that we are not professionally equipped to contextualize work by all artists from across the globe, and must seek the assistance and participation of specialists and/or local advisors from the curated cultures (for instance, scholars, curators, artists, theorists, gallerists, museum directors, collectors, or graduate students) from the moment of conception for a project or exhibition. The regional specialist's understanding of the socio-economic and political contexts, and of the local languages within which the works are being produced, is invaluable and can broaden the sample base of artists from which to choose, often before a curator travels to the region for studio visits. The critical dialogue of exchange that ensues with these advisors will add the necessary breadth to the project as a whole, and allow for an ensemble of perspectives to emerge, enabling the curator to see works anew when they are situated geographically and contextualized culturally.

1989

MAGICIENS DE LA TERRE

Pompidou Center, Paris
Grande Halle de La Villette, Paris

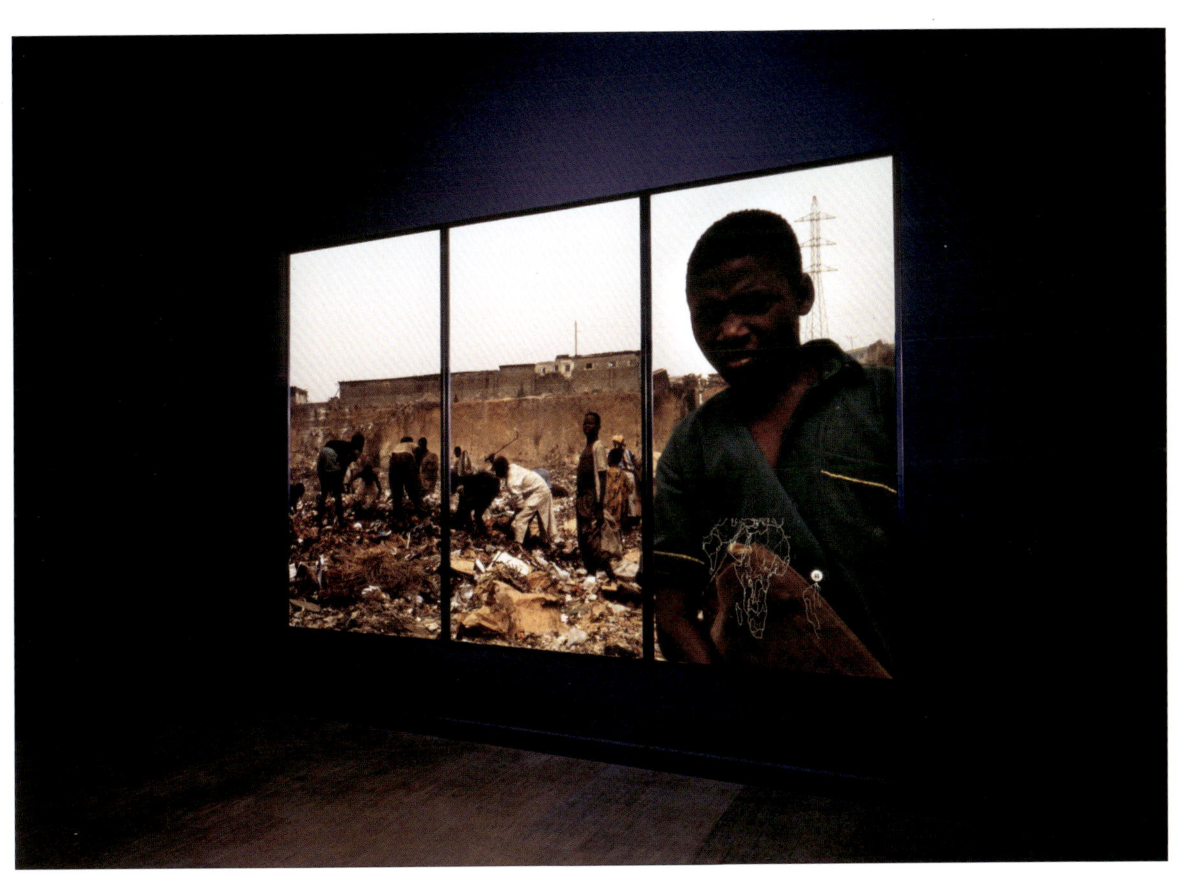

Alfredo Jaar
La Géographie, ça sert d'abord à faire la guerre
1989

Curated by Jean-Hubert Martin and held at the Pompidou Center and the Grande Halle de La Villette in Paris in 1989, *Magiciens de la terre* (*Magicians of the World*) was billed as a "planetary" exhibition of contemporary art. It was the first attempt in museum history to mount a large-scale, postcolonial exhibition that eliminated any sense of hierarchy between the fifty Western and fifty non-Western participants. Unlike the much-criticized exhibition *"Primitivism" in Twentieth-Century Art*, at the Museum of Modern Art (MoMA), New York, in 1984—which valorized Western artistic practice over the "primitive" objects it displayed alongside such "greats" as Picasso and Matisse—*Magiciens* sought to exhibit multiple works by first- and third-world artists together in a non-hierarchical way, and one that would not involve projections about centers and margins and high and low art. The often-cited exception, however, was the much-denounced neighboring of works by the Australian Aboriginal Yuendumu community with a work by Richard Long. Indeed, as Montreal-based art historian and critic Johanne Lamoureux states, the sandpaintings by the Yuendumu were "relegated to a corner like some cast shadow or discarded double, set at the foot of Long's looming mud drawing that dominated an entire room of the Grand Hall." [27]

Magiciens was, nevertheless, organized in direct response to the controversy over *Primitivism*.

Well-established Western artists (such as Anselm Kiefer, Barbara Kruger, Sigmar Polke, Louise Bourgeois, and Francesco Clemente) were featured alongside then-unknown non-Western artists, such as Kane Kwei (Ghana), Patrick Vilaire (Haiti), and Gu Dexing (China), or beside anthropological, religious, and/or ritual objects and artifacts, among them a Benin ceremonial mask and a mandala from Nepal created by three Buddhist monks. [28]

Instead of imposing Western aesthetic criteria on the art and ritual objects, *Magiciens* attempted cross-cultural dialogue via the careful juxtaposition of works from different cultures, allowing each culture to speak for itself rather than relegating it to a footnote in Western art history. In a bid to

Installation view, *Magiciens de la terre*, featuring *On n'a plus besoin de héros* by Barbara Kruger, 1989
Grande Halle de La Villette
1989

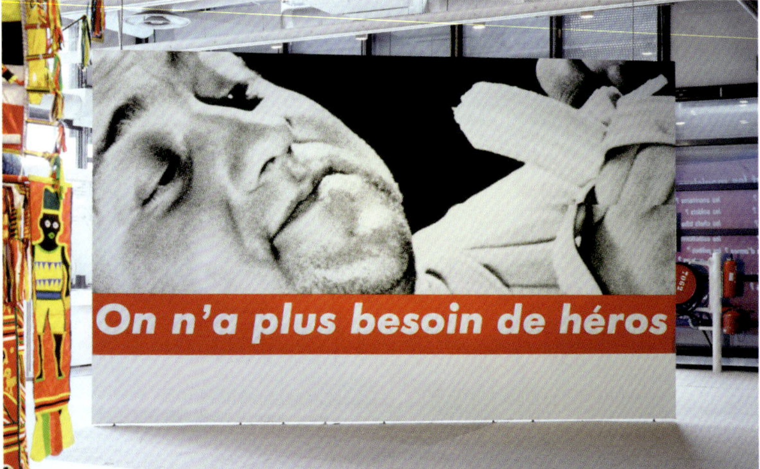

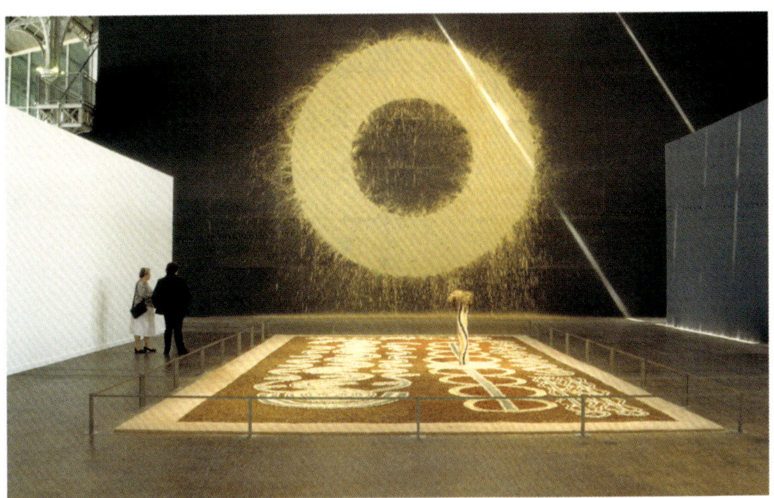

Installation view, *Magiciens de la terre*, featuring *Red Earth Circle* by Richard Long, 1989, and *Yam Dreaming* by Yuendumu Community, 1989
Grande Halle de La Villette
1989

open up the Euro-US art world, the exhibition argued for the universality of the creative impulse and endeavored to offer equal aesthetic experience of contemporary works of art made globally. Except for the central hall of La Villette, where multiple works were featured, each artist was granted a unique space in the galleries. "The works were so different formally from each other that it was crucial to insist on their autonomy," Martin explained.[29] One of the rooms at the Pompidou Center, for example, featured Brazilian artist-priest Mestre Didi, from the Candomblé religion—a religion based on African beliefs that is found mainly in Brazil. Mestre Didi's sculptures, inspired by the emblems of the *orishas* (protector spirits), were made from materials that are considered sacred, including shells, beads, leather, and palm leaves.

Another room was dedicated to the work of Georges Liautaud (Haiti), whose cut-out iron sculptures, created from empty gasoline drums, resembled devils. Throughout the exhibition, visitors also experienced commissioned installations, such as: *Bamboo Corridor* (1989), by Hiroshi Teshigahara (Japan), a coiling bamboo corridor constructed on a terrace at the Pompidou; *Dance Space in a Vodun Temple* (1989), by Wesner Philidor (Haiti), an 86 sq. ft (8 sq. m) floor drawing for ritual dance, compiled from earth and cornflour, that featured religious symbols; *Pediment of the House of Men* (1988), by Nera Jambruk (Papua New Guinea), a massive sculpture rising to the roof of the Grand Hall fabricated from bark and corrugated iron; *Sand Painting* (1989), by Native American artist Joe Ben Junior, which depicted the history of the harvest in Navajo tradition; *House* (1989), by South African tribal painter Esther Mahlangu, showing a house decorated in the tradition of the Ndebele people. Other highlights of the exhibition included *Homeless Vehicle* (1988–89), by Krzysztof Wodiczko (Poland), a vehicle offering mobile solutions for sleeping, designed in collaboration with street dwellers in New York and San Diego; the installation *La Géographie, ça sert d'abord à faire la guerre* (1989), by Chilean-born artist Alfredo Jaar, which examined the horrors of toxic-waste dumping in Nigeria;

and the double-sided billboard, *Qui sont les magiciens de la terre/ On n'a pas plus besoin de héros* (1989), by US artist Barbara Kruger.

Martin's show came under almost immediate attack because of his attempt to depart from the traditional curatorial practices of Euro-US institutions, which continue to grant supremacy to Western art over all other regions of the world. Much was made of the fact, for example, that he included anthropologists and ethnographers on his curatorial team to assist him in discovering contemporary non-Western artists and in understanding the context within which they produced their work.[30] Presented by critics as a curator-explorer, Martin was then accused of fetishizing and decontextualizing the non-Western objects in the exhibition. Indeed, in a pre-exhibition interview with the curator in *Art in America* in May 1989, German art historian Benjamin Buchloch raised questions about the exhibition's approach to the issue of "cultural authenticity" and to its "potential neo-colonialist subtext,"[31] and asked whether Martin's project inevitably "operated like an archeology of the 'other'."[32] In the end, however, even Buchloch had to praise Martin for his "long overdue and courageous attempt to depart from the hegemonic and monocentric cultural perspectives of Western European and American institutions and their exhibition projects."[33]

Eleanor Heartney's post-exhibition review in the same magazine, in July 1989, called *Magiciens* "a problematic but worthwhile attempt to come to terms with Western/non-Western cultural encounters,"[34] but also questioned whether the enterprise smacked of cultural exploitation when coming to terms with such encounters.[35] More recently, Enwezor has stated that the real "flaw" of *Magiciens* is that it "took as part of its reality the fundamental existence of an opposition between the Western center and the non-Western periphery."[36] However, Martin has argued in response that it is idealistic to suggest that the categories of Western and non-Western will vanish any time soon: "As long as the economic power is in the hands of the West, the difference will be impossible to erase."[37]

Questions were also raised by critics about the quality of the works on display, with the implication being that the non-Western objects and artifacts were "primitive," unsophisticated, and therefore paled in comparison with the "high art" objects presented by the Western artists. The term "quality" circled all exhibitions with a multicultural or activist bent in the late 1980s and 1990s. As art critic Michael Brenson explained in the *New York Times,* those in favor of maintaining traditional definitions of the word believed that if

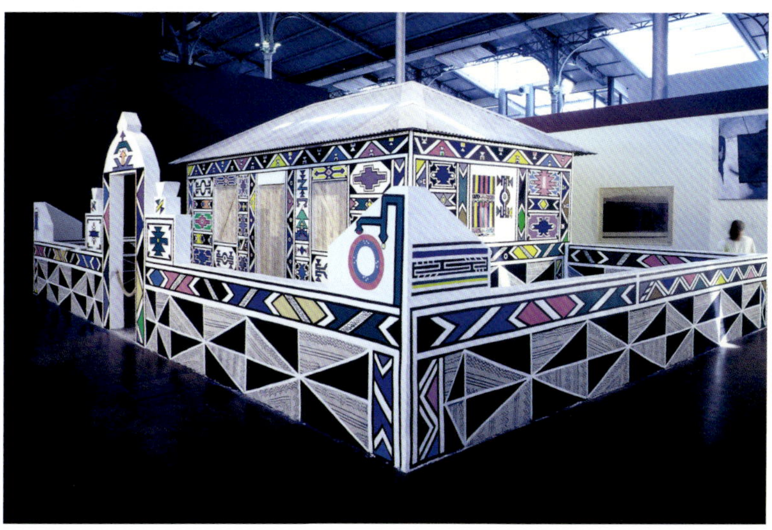

Esther Mahlangu
House
1989

galleries and museums were "to select artists on the basis *not* of quality but of color and sex it would result not in social justice but in second- and third-rate art."[38] Those opposed to the word, however, tended to identify it with formal concerns of the classical, European tradition. Buchloch agreed, stating that the central tool that white, male, Western culture has "traditionally used to exclude or marginalize all other cultural practices is the abstract concept of 'quality'."[39]

Martin responded that he had removed the term from his vocabulary, since there is "no convincing system to establish relative and binding criteria of quality for such a project. We know very well that even the directors of the great Western museums do not have any reliable criteria to establish a consensus on this issue."[40] The word, then, was understood not as a symbol of standards, but as a symbol of exclusion.

Activist/curator Lucy Lippard and cultural theorists Homi Bhabha and Gayatri Spivak were among those who criticized the show for its under-representation of women artists: out of the 100 artists on display, only 10 of them were women.[41] There were no African American artists.

Insofar as it was "the first major exhibition consciously to attempt to discover a postcolonialist way to exhibit objects together," US art critic and scholar Thomas McEvilley understood the show to be "a major event in the social history of art, not in its esthetic history."[42] Indeed, *Magiciens* was a pioneering event in the history of museum exhibitions. Yes, it was flawed, but it initiated endless dialogue, just as Martin had intended.[43] In the 1989 interview with Buchloch (see p. 110), Martin stated that he would like to see the show "operate as a catalyst for future projects and investigations."[44] *Magiciens* has done just that. The exhibition ultimately attempted to challenge a very tired, Eurocentric view of art by prioritizing global discourses and, in so doing, became the established precursor of all global exhibitions of contemporary art.

1990

Curated by
Julia P. Herzberg,
Sharon F. Patton,
Gary Sangster,
and Laura Trippi

THE DECADE SHOW: FRAMEWORKS OF IDENTITY IN THE 1980S

Museum of Contemporary Hispanic Art, New York
New Museum of Contemporary Art, New York
The Studio Museum, Harlem, New York

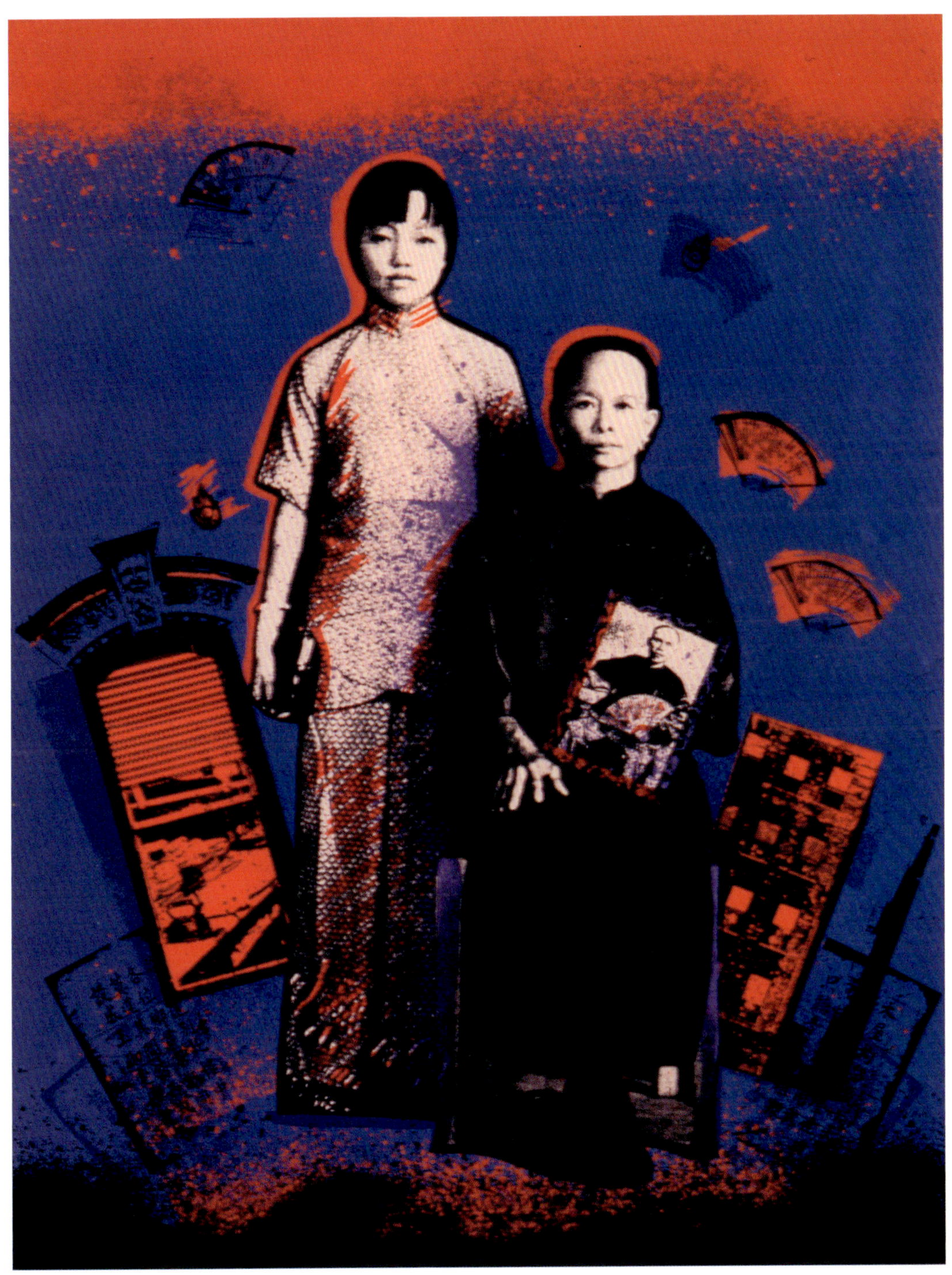

Tomie Arai
Laundryman's Daughter
1989

There were numerous exhibitions in the USA from the late 1980s onward that sought to explore multiculturalism in the visual arts, the most notable of these being *The Decade Show: Frameworks of Identity in the 1980s* (1990) and the 1993 Whitney Biennial. *The Decade Show*—co-organized and presented simultaneously by the Museum of Contemporary Hispanic Art, the New Museum of Contemporary Art, and the Studio Museum in Harlem—featured work by ninety-four artists in a variety of media.[45] The principal goal of the exhibition, as explained by Julia Herzberg, one of its curators, was to give voice to so-called minority artists—defined as Asian, Afro-American, Anglo-European, Native American, Latin American, women, and homosexual artists—most of whom, she argued, have been ignored or overlooked by mainstream museums and art-historical circles.[46]

The exhibition was issues oriented,[47] focusing on key concerns of the 1980s—sexuality, race, religion, age, history, myth, politics, and the environment—as they related to the idea of identity: from the AIDS crisis, homophobia, war, and homelessness to lynching, censorship, and miscegenation. The selection of works was organized around specific themes: at the Studio Museum in Harlem, themes of social practice/cultural criticism and history/memory/artifacts; at the Museum of Contemporary Hispanic Art, themes of biography/autobiography and sexuality/gender; at the New Museum of Contemporary Art, themes of myth/spirituality/nature and discourse/media. While these themes ultimately blurred together and overlapped, with each venue nonetheless offering a different focus and atmosphere, the result was a demonstration of identity as a fluid notion that reflects the diversity of US society. As art critic Elizabeth Hess explained in the *Village Voice*, the show's message was: "rich white male heterosexual rightist Christians, wake up and look at America, because America is not you."[48]

While *The Decade Show* featured a large selection of mainstream artists such as John Coplans, Leon Golub, Cindy Sherman, Bruce Nauman, Dara Birnbaum, Richard Prince, Hans Haacke, Eric Fischl, Barbara Kruger, and others, it also gave visibility to numerous artists with whom museum-goers would probably have been unfamiliar. The exhibition included James Luna's *The Artifact Piece* (1987/1991), a performance-installation, which parodied the ethnographic museum, in which Luna exhibited himself laying in a display case clothed only in a loin cloth. Adjacent to him were two other display cabinets: one contained traditional Native-American treasures, including beaded feathers and decorative pouches and baskets; the other contained traditional US treasures, such as a *Zap* comic, a dog-eared copy of Allen Ginsberg's *Kaddish and Other Poems*, and a "Boycott Grapes" badge.[49]

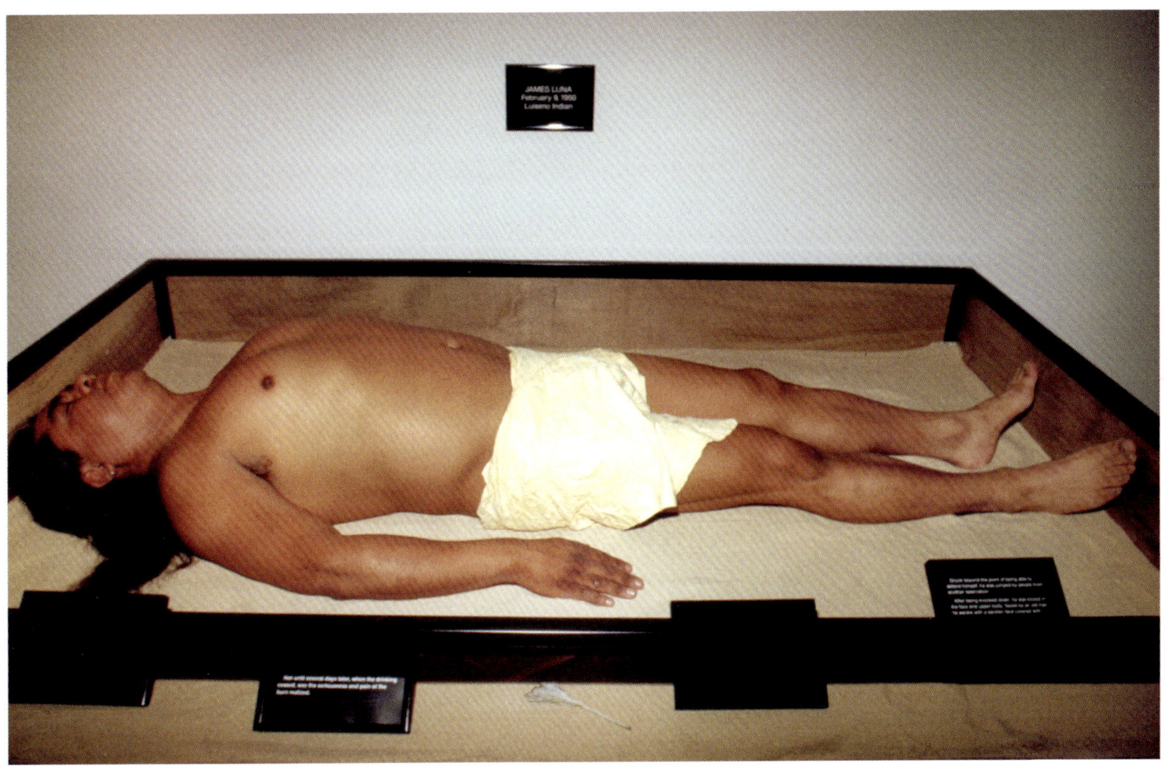

James Luna
The Artifact Piece
1987 and 1991

The Decade Show also featured examples from Melvin Edwards's "Lynch Fragments" series (1963–79), comprised of welded steel scrap and chain contorted into abstract compact sculptures, which referred, in Edwards's mind, to the stories about lynchings that he had heard from his relatives; Adrian Piper's *Ur-Mutter #5* (1989), a photo collage with silkscreen text that challenged the age-old maternal religious symbol of the mother and child by juxtaposing two images—the first an emaciated black woman and child, the other a healthy-looking white woman and son, with "I Read It My Way" written above their heads. The show also included Pat Ward Williams's mixed-media work *Accused/Blowtorch/Padlock* (1986), which featured a *Life* magazine photo from the 1930s of a black man being tortured and lynched, around which the artist had handwritten a diatribe against racism, violence, and journalism, including such lines as: "How can this photograph exist?," "Can you be black and look at this?," "*Life* magazine published this picture," "Oh God, somebody do something."

The exhibition also featured David Wojnarowicz's mixed-media installation in response to the AIDS crisis, *America: Heads of Family, Heads of State* (1989–90), which incorporated macabre images (both from the media and created by Wojnarowicz), his writings, sculpture, found art, and monitor-based videos; Luis Cruz Azaceta's *AIDS Count III* (1988), a large painting depicting a tiny mummy-like figure stretched out horizontally, surrounded by a sea of numerical statistics; and Yolanda López's mixed-media installation *Things I Never Told My Son About Being a Mexican* (1984), and accompanying video, *When You Think of Mexico* (1984), which collectively critiqued the patronizing ethnocentrism encoded in popular imagery of Mexico produced by the USA.[50] Also on view in Times Square, as part of the show, was Alfredo Jaar's video billboard, *A Logo for America* (1987), which opens with an image of the USA, and across it flash the words: "This Is Not America," followed by an image of the US flag, with a second disavowal: "This Is Not America's Flag."

The *Decade Show* received a tremendous amount of press, both good and bad. But, as Hess explained in her review, the exhibition was "bound for glory and controversy."[51] One art critic noted disdainfully, "Multiculturalism is the buzzword among arts groups trying to position themselves for the day when whites of European derivation become a minority in America."[52] Yet, in seeking to include artists outside the Western mainstream, *The Decade Show* was simultaneously accused, by Brenson of the *New York Times* and others, of lacking quality artwork.[53] Roberta Smith was of the opinion that, "Much too often the art in this exhibition nourishes the heart and mind more than the eye...Sincerity, alienation, and just causes," she noted, "don't necessarily make convincing artworks."[54] In short, the show's identity politics and multiculturalism were seen as sacrificing quality for diversity and difference. In retrospect, however, *The Decade Show* has come to be regarded by many as a turning point in the representation of hyphenated artists in the USA and as paving the way for other important multicultural exhibitions.

Yolanda M. López
Things I Never Told My Son About Being a Mexican
1984

Luis Cruz Azaceta
AIDS Count III
1988

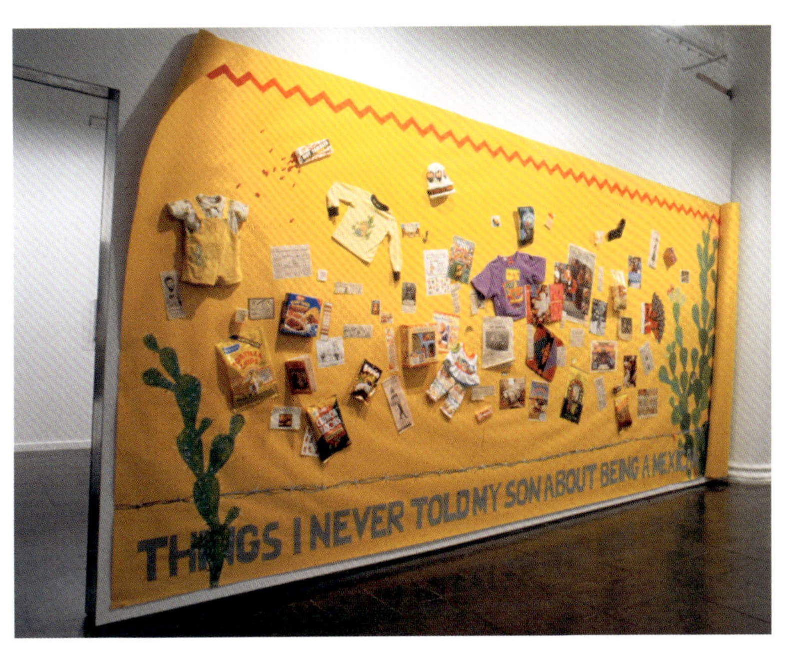
THINGS I NEVER TOLD MY SON ABOUT BEING A MEXICAN

Curated by
Fred Wilson

MINING THE MUSEUM

The Maryland Historical Society, Baltimore, Maryland, USA

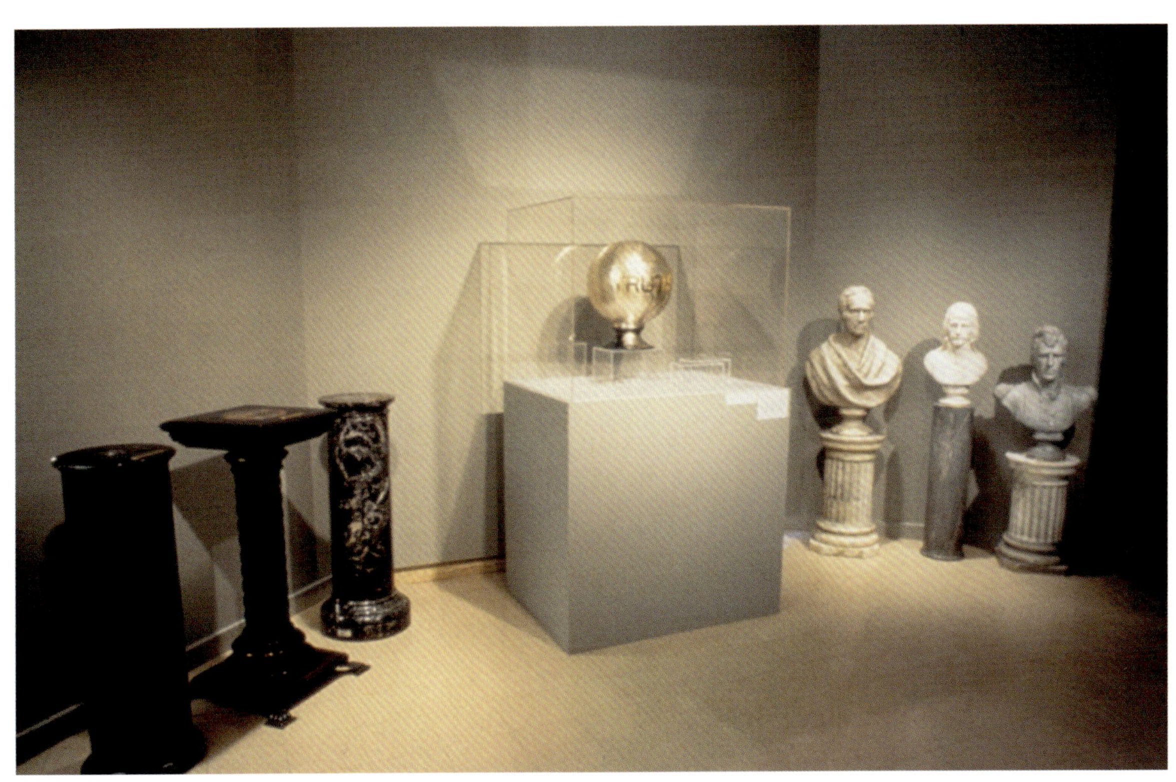

Fred Wilson
The Truth Trophy
1992

Mining the Museum (1992–93) was an exhibition selected and installed by African American artist Fred Wilson, who was commissioned by The Contemporary museum in Baltimore, Maryland, to investigate and interpret the collections of the Maryland Historical Society. [55] Wilson was responsible for all aspects of the Historical Society's exhibition, including arrangement of works, labeling, wall colors, graphics, film projections, educational materials, and audio recordings. He was assisted by The Contemporary's curator, Lisa Corrin, as well as by other artists, community historians, volunteers, and staff from the museum. What Wilson discovered was a displaced or obscured history of African Americans and Native Americans in Maryland. Representations of, or objects owned and made by these peoples were not absent from the museum, but they were consigned to the storerooms and missing from the telling of the institution's story, which tended to focus on country estates, duck hunting, and Maryland's contributions to the American Civil War (1861–65).

Searching through the museum's basement, Wilson found objects that not only clarified his own past but suggested how it had been occluded. His "telling" revealed an alternative historical account from the one narrated by the collection—one that underscored the fact that "history" is necessarily a construction, an act of interpretation that gives rise to such questions as: How is history written?; Whose history is being told?; Whose voice is silenced?; What role does a museum play in confirming hierarchies that value one culture or group over another? "Art and artifact, style and period, high and low, dominant and marginal," Corrin explained, "are the boundaries museums rely on to sustain society's most revered beliefs and values." [56] In this installation of carefully juxtaposed objects, however, Wilson constructed fresh readings and new iconographies, assisting viewers to think critically about hidden meanings and the construction of history.

The first room of the exhibition displayed *The Truth Trophy*—a silver and gold globe that was awarded by the advertising industry in the early 20th century for "truth in advertising." It was flanked on one side by three white pedestals

Fred Wilson
Cabinetmaking 1820–1960
1992

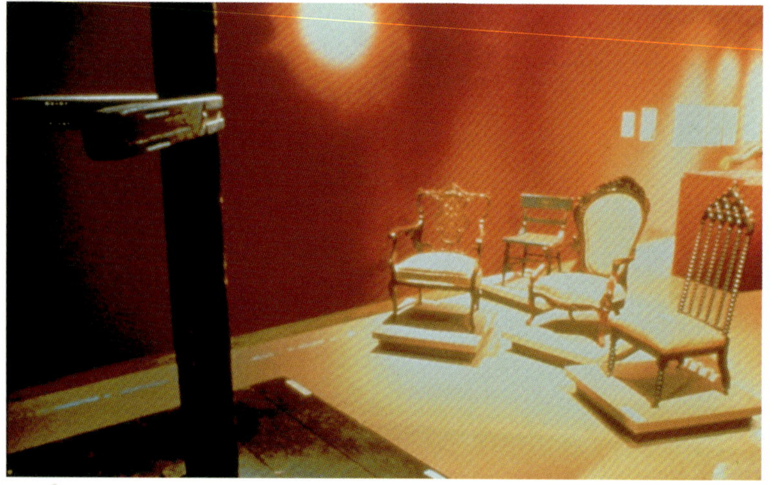

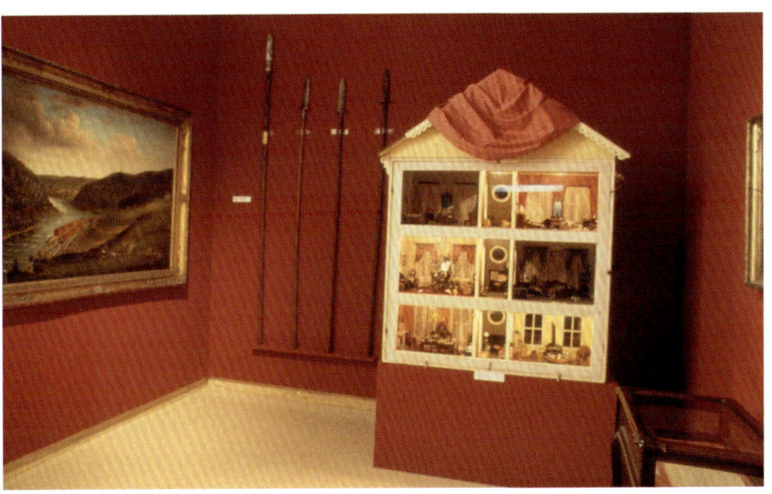

Fred Wilson
Pikes (c. 1859) and *Dollhouse (c. 1904)*
1992

bearing white marble busts of three famous white men—Henry Clay, Napoleon Bonaparte, and Andrew Jackson. On the other side of the globe were three empty black pedestals labeled with the names Benjamin Banneker, Harriet Tubman, and Frederick Douglass—three prominent African American Marylanders who were not represented in the museum's collection. This first exhibit therefore encapsulated the issues at the heart of the show: Whose truth is on exhibit?; Whose history is being told? Wilson thus established from the outset that the installation would explore not what objects mean, but how meaning is produced when "framed" by the museum environment.

In 18th- and 19th-century paintings from the USA, slave children were often shown in the shadows or peeking through partially opened doors. In one exhibit, Wilson highlighted their presence in the artworks by shining spotlights on the figures, and by giving these children a voice, adding audio-tape loops so that as visitors walked past the paintings, they heard the children asking poignant questions, such as "Where did I come from?"; "Where is my mother?"; "Who washes my back?"; "Who combs my hair?"; "Who makes me laugh?" In *Portrait of Henry Darnell III* (*c.* 1710)—by German-born Maryland portrait painter Justus Kühn—Wilson's spotlight illuminated an enslaved child in a dog collar, while on the museum's sound system a child was heard asking, "Am I your brother; Am I your friend?; Am I your pet?" In the case of a group portrait of the children of naval officer Commodore John Daniel Danels (*c.* 1826), Wilson managed to track down the identities of the slaves in the scene and displayed their names prominently on a gallery wall. He also renamed paintings to identify the African Americans represented in them: for example, an oil painting entitled *Country Life*, showing a group of well-dressed white people at a picnic, was renamed *Frederick Serving Fruit* to draw attention to the young African American man who is shown serving them.

Other rooms included works such as: *Model of Baltimore Clipper (Slave Ship After War of 1812)* (1940), which was installed over a case displaying escaped-slave notices; a cast-iron bootjack, entitled

121

Naughty Nellie (c. 1880), in the shape of a black woman on her back with her legs splayed; *Metalwork 1793–1890*, a grouping of silver vessels (pitcher, beer mugs, and goblets) and iron slave shackles with a key, which reminded the visitor that human bondage produced the wealth and leisure symbolized by a silver tea-service; *Modes of Transport 1770–1910*, an Edwardian baby carriage bearing a Ku Klux Klan (KKK) hood placed near a turn-of-the-century photograph that showed black domestics pushing prams that held their infant charges, signifying the irony of African American women raising generations of white supremacists; and *Punt Gun for Chesapeake Bay Hunters*, in which a large shotgun was installed above a case displaying escaped-slave reward posters—the gun was aimed at a nearby display cabinet in which seven duck decoys had been grouped with a wooden dancing doll of a black man in Zouave volunteer uniform (*c.* 1882),[57] while nearby texts on "tolling" and "tracking" spoke of how dogs were used for hunting ducks and runaway slaves.

Portraits of Cigar Store Owners showed five lumbering wooden figures of Native Americans, labeled with names of the merchants who commissioned the objects—the figures had turned their backs on the viewer to gaze at photographs of actual Native Americans. In *Dollhouse (c. 1904)*, Wilson placed a Victorian dollhouse next to a diary opened to a description of a slave revolt. Within the house, the doll furniture was tipped over and the white baby doll, thrown out of a cradle, had been replaced by an African American baby doll; other white dolls were lying on the floor. A huge African American male figure filled the center of another room, his head touching the chandelier. The viewer's approach to the dollhouse triggered two cameras set on moving carousels, which caused names to be projected onto darkened walls: African Americans who resisted slavery (Harriet Tubman and William Parker, for example) and others who had fought with the white abolitionist John Brown at Harper's Ferry in Virginia (now West Virginia) in 1859 in an attempt to initiate a slave revolt—an event that was depicted in a nearby painting at the exhibition.

In one particularly poignant work, Wilson installed a large portrait of a white man in a gilded frame with a gash in the canvas that cut across his face.[58] Through this gash, viewers could see the face of a black man on a video monitor and hear him explaining that he is the son of the white master in the portrait, who had raped one of the slaves. Another exhibit, *Cabinetmaking 1820–1960*, displayed a whipping post from the Baltimore City Jail (*c.* 1850) surrounded by staid Victorian furniture (including one with the logo of Baltimore Equitable Society), which was placed in line, as if for a performance.

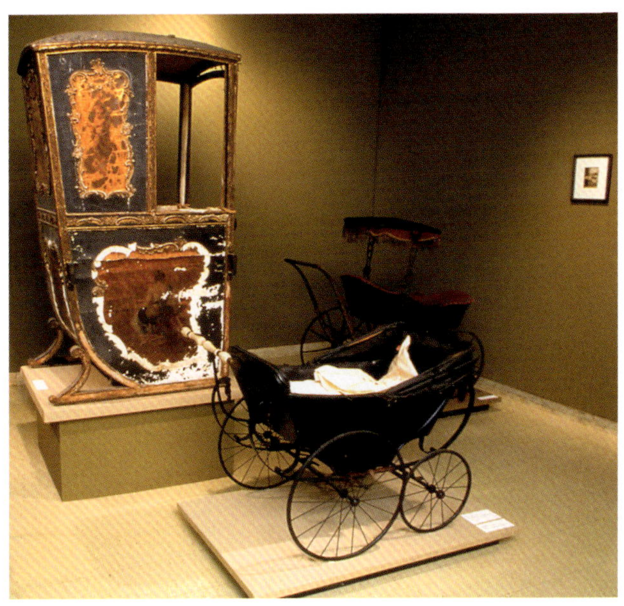

Fred Wilson
Modes of Transport 1770–1910
1992

In the final room, Wilson installed *Benjamin Banneker's Astronomical Journal* (1790–1806), which included a slide projection of Banneker's chart predicting the eclipse of October 18, 1800, as well as a computer showing the night sky of the same day. Banneker (1731–1806) was a self-taught African American mathematician, surveyor, and astronomer, and was born a free man in Baltimore County, Maryland. He was hired by Thomas Jefferson (author of the Declaration of Independence and third president of the USA) to help survey the area that became Washington, DC. The two men corresponded on, among other things, the treatment of blacks and the issue of slavery.

Wilson's exhibition can be situated in the context of other artists who have "intervened" in museums, beginning in 1969 with Andy Warhol's *Raid the Icebox 1*, an exhibition of "forgotten" objects from the art museum of the Rhode Island School of Design, noteworthy for the artist's idiosyncratic choice of objects—including shoes, parasols, chairs, hat boxes, Native American pottery and blankets, wallpaper, even a ginkgo tree growing in the museum's courtyard. Also notable was conceptual artist Joseph Kosuth's *The Play of the Unmentionable* (1990) at the Brooklyn Museum, which (at the height of the controversy over US government funding for "obscene" works of art), juxtaposed works from throughout history that had been deemed politically, religiously, or sexually objectionable, with statements about the role of art in society by figures as diverse as Irish poet and playwright Oscar Wilde, German fascist leader Adolf Hitler, and Swiss-born philosopher Jean-Jacques Rousseau.

Each of these museological interventions was an attempt to redress past representational or structural injustices, and as such constituted a kind of "counter-memory," which curator Brian Wallis has described as "a practice that persistently questions dominant modes of constructing the past while at the same time seeking to recuperate submerged histories or meanings."[59] Unlike the work of his predecessors, however, Wilson's project was a devastating indictment of institutionalized racism.

Curated by
Thelma Golden, John G.
Hanhardt, Lisa Phillips,
Elisabeth Sussman, and
Jeanette Vuocolo

THE WHITNEY BIENNIAL

Whitney Museum of American Art, New York

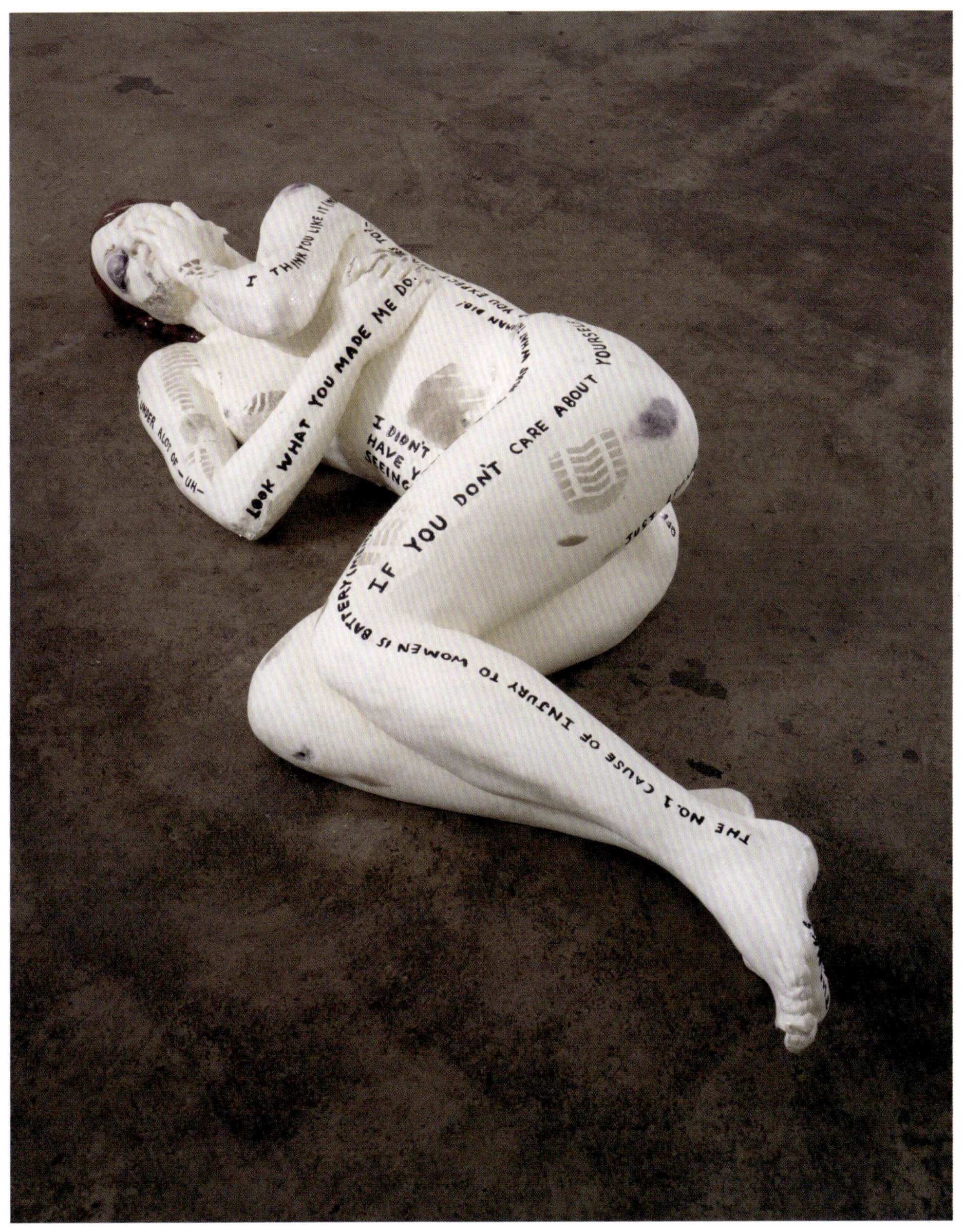

Sue Williams
Irresistible
1992

Along with *The Decade Show*, the Whitney Biennial of 1993 is now regarded as a benchmark in the history of contemporary art exhibitions in the USA insofar as it was one of the first major museum shows to open up the discourse of contemporary art to include voices other than the usual suspects; it introduced to the scene a whole generation of artists that had never shown together before and whose work deserved attention. The exhibition was organized by a team of curators and featured more than eighty artists, most of whom touched on many of the pressing concerns facing the USA at that historical moment, including the AIDS crisis, race, class, gender, imperialism, and poverty. The principal aim of the exhibition, then, was to examine identity politics of the time as well as ever-changing definitions of "Americanness."[60] As Whitney Museum director David Ross explained in the preface to the catalogue, "The '1993 Biennial Exhibition' comes at a moment when problems of identity and the representation of community extend well beyond the art world. We are living in a time when the form and formation of self and community is tested daily. Communities are at war, both with and at their borders. Issues of nation and nationality, ethnic essentialism, cultural diversity, dissolution, and the *politics* of identity hang heavy in the air."[61]

The majority of the work in the exhibition was produced by then unknown artists or relative newcomers (about thirty of the eighty or so artists featured in the museum for the first time). Highlights of the show included: a room-size installation by Pepón Osorio, entitled *Scene of the Crime (Whose Crime?)* (1993), which reconstructed the interior of a Latino family's apartment in which a murder had taken place—a space crammed with objects, from religious relics and icons to family photos, lace, and a shrouded bloody corpse; the video *It Wasn't Love* (1992), by Sadie Benning, in which lesbian lovers are cast in a film-noir road romance; *Gnaw* (1992), a three-part installation by Janine Antoni, comprised of *Chocolate Gnaw* (chocolate chewed by the artist), *Lard Gnaw* (lard chewed by the artist), and *Lipstick Display* (lipstick made with pigment, beeswax, and chewed lard removed from *Lard Gnaw*); an "intervention" by Daniel Joseph Martinez in which the artist replaced the Whitney Museum's color-coded admission buttons, which usually spell WMAA, with fragments of the sentence "I can't/imagine/ever wanting/to be/white," as well as with buttons showing the entire sentence.

The exhibition also featured: Glenn Ligon's *Notes on the Margins of "The Black Book"* (1991–93), which juxtaposed homoerotic photographs of black nudes from Robert Mapplethorpe's *The Black Book* (1986) with excerpts from the words or writings of various critics,

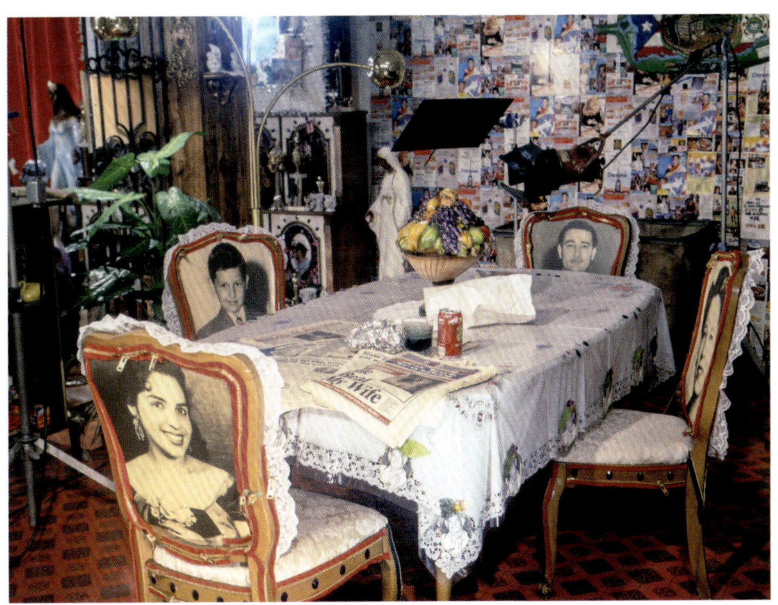

Pepón Osorio
Scene of the Crime (Whose Crime?)
1993

scholars, and politicians (some of which were reactions to Mapplethorpe's images); a series of candid photographs by Nan Goldin from *The Ballad of Sexual Dependency* (1979–86) chronicling the activities and behavior of friends and lovers; Sue Williams's *Irresistible* (1992), a rubber floor-bound sculpture of a battered woman; George Holliday's amateur video of US police beating black motorist Rodney King in 1992 featured in the video section of the exhibition as "art"—this was the first time that live footage of police brutality had appeared in an exhibition, and for this reason it was a hugely significant addition to the show, one that helped redefine the concepts of both media art and documentary art. And in the courtyard performance by Coco Fusco and Guillermo Gómez-Peña, entitled *Two Undiscovered Amerindians Visit the West* (1992–93), the artists enclosed themselves in a cage and performed the role of the cultural Other for museum audiences by presenting themselves as "specimens representative of the Guatinaui people." Gómez-Peña was dressed in an Aztec-style breastplate, complete with a leopard-skin wrestling mask, while Fusco donned a grass skirt, leopard-skin bra, baseball cap, and sneakers. The duo performed "traditional" daily rituals, ranging from sewing voodoo dolls to lifting weights, watching television, and working on laptop computers.

Despite—or indeed, precisely because of—its triumph as a new type of more inclusive curatorial endeavor, the exhibition met with a maelstrom of negative criticism, most of which centered on the buzzphrase "political correctness," implying that, like *The Decade Show*, it had sacrificed quality in favor of multiculturalism.[62] While its defenders (including Roberta Smith, Jennie Klein, and Kay Larsen) lauded the curators for not rounding up predictable contributors from the local commercial galleries, for taking a distinct curatorial position, and for reflecting "the country's diversity by including unusually large numbers of nonwhite artists,"[63] its detractors (including Arthur Danto, Robert Hughes, Michael Kimmelman, Peter Plagens, and Christopher Knight, among others), all white males, were opposed in principle to political art and to the exhibition's confrontational stance. Roger Kimball's response in the *New Criterion*, for example, epitomized the conservative reactions to the Biennial:

> You can see the same loathsome objects and performances in fashionable galleries and on college campuses across the country; you can read the same turgid proclamations in academic journals and museum catalogues everywhere. The wacko feminism, the preening ethnic narcissism, the rejection of artistic standards, the naïve recapitulation of radical clichés about race, gender, class, "power", "the West": it's all here, stuffed in unlovely profusion into every nook and cranny of the Whitney's exhibition space.[64]

In the *New York Times*, Kimmelman wrote, "I hate the show," saying it made him feel "battered by condescension" and that it treated art "as if pleasure were a sin." [65] Peter Schjeldahl of the *Village Voice* agreed, entitling his review "Art + Politics = Biennial. Missing: The Pleasure Principle." [66] Kimmelman was particularly put off by the identity politics on display, describing it as "one sensationalistic image after another of wounded bodies, heaving buttocks, plastic vomit, and genitalia." [67] Writing in *New York* magazine twenty years later, critic Jerry Saltz explained that, in reaction to the Biennial, "People went batshit. Contempt was everywhere." He nevertheless argued in favor of the curatorial premise: given that identity politics was dominating the national conversation, and the country was becoming more diverse, the curators "embraced that new reality in order to move forward; others reacted against it. The Biennial was on the side of the future, and still is." [68]

The 1993 Whitney Biennial was unique in terms of the museum's own exhibition practices. For decades it had included alarmingly few women artists and artists of color in its shows.[69] The 1993 Biennial, however, became renowned as the first one in which white male artists were in the minority.[70] Many have argued that it is for precisely this reason that the 1993 Biennial also became one of the "most reviled and criticized Biennials in recent history." [71] In 1995, however, the Whitney Biennial returned to its previously high percentage of white males and low percentage of artists of color.[72] As a Guerrilla Girls poster succinctly put it, "Traditional Values and Quality Return to the *Whitey* Museum." [73]

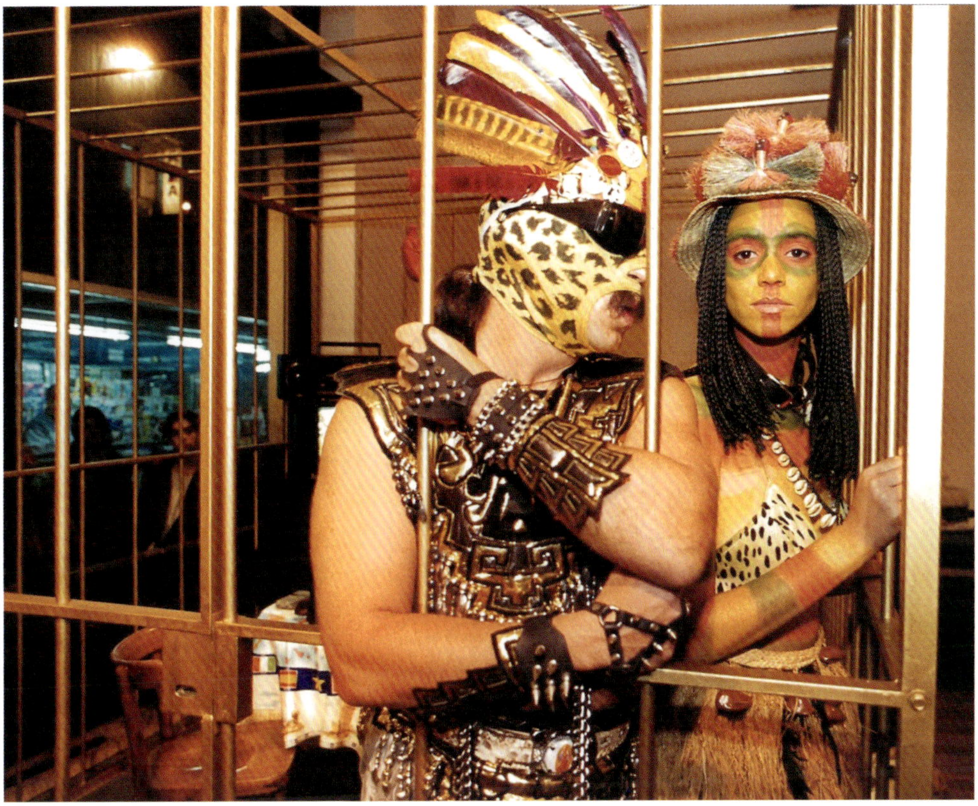

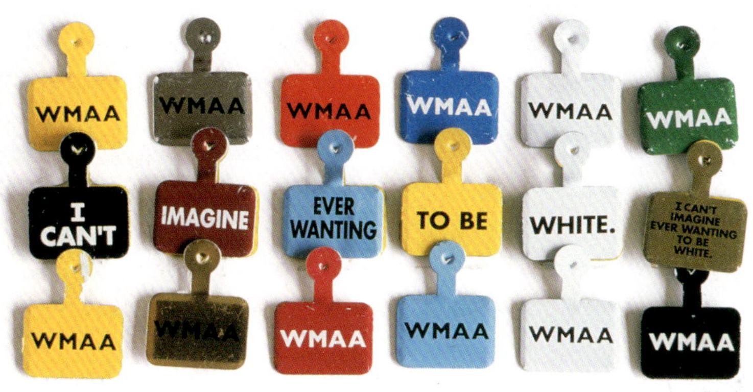

Guillermo Gómez-Peña and Coco Fusco
Two Undiscovered Amerindians Visit the West
1992–93

Daniel Joseph Martinez
Museum Tags: Second Movement (overture); or, Overture con claque (Overture with Hired Audience Members)
1993

Curated by
Serge Fauchereau (Paris); Richard Calvocoressi and Keith Hartley (Vienna); Lutz Becker (Moscow); Michael Asbury and Paulo Venancio Filho (Rio de Janeiro); Okwui Enwezor and Olu Oguibe (Lagos); Reiko Tomii (Tokyo); Donna De Salvo (New York); Emma Dexter (London); Geeta Kapur and Ashish Rajadhyaksha (Bombay/Mumbai)

CENTURY CITY: ART AND CULTURE IN THE MODERN METROPOLIS

Tate Modern, London

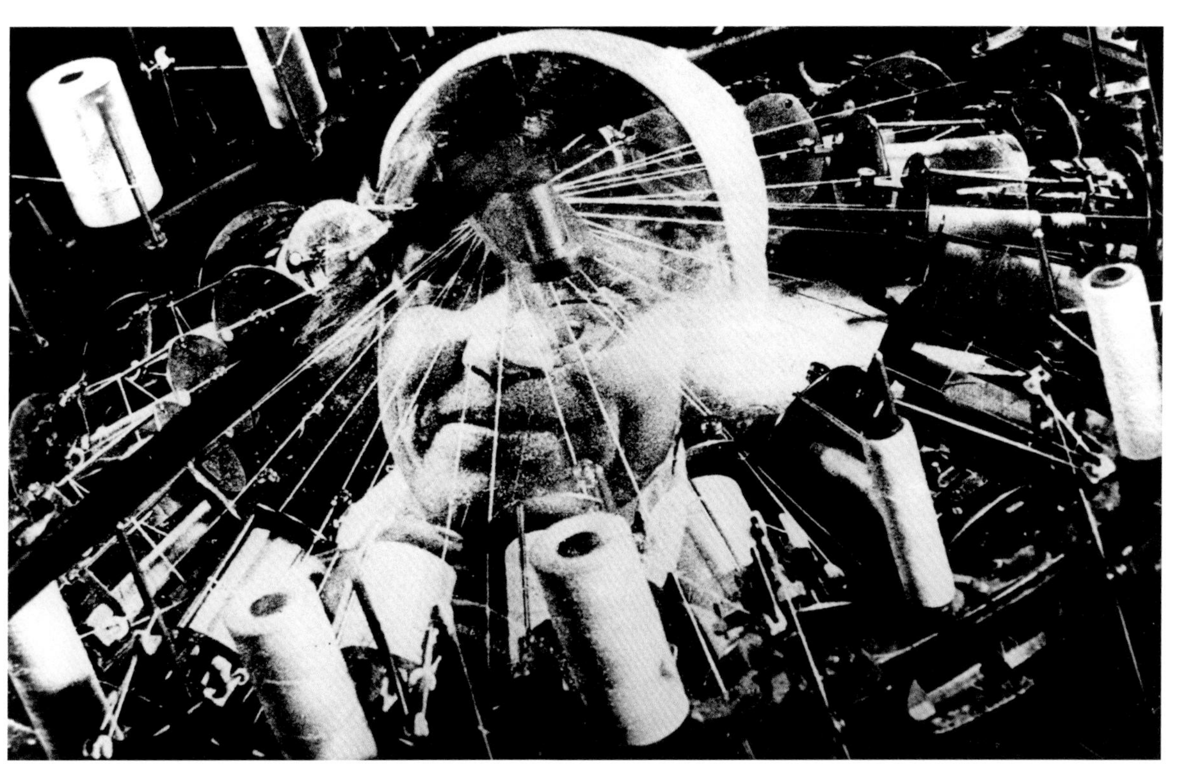

Dziga Vertov
Man with a Movie Camera
1928

Century City: Art and Culture in the Modern Metropolis, Tate Modern's first large thematic exhibition after opening its doors in London in 2001, was a mega-show that focused on nine cities around the world at specific moments, or "creative flashpoints," over the previous one hundred years or so. The exhibition explored the relationship between cultural creativity and the metropolis in Paris (1905–15), Vienna (1908–18), Moscow (1916–30), Rio de Janeiro (1955–69), Lagos (1955–70), Tokyo (1969–73), New York (1969–74), London (1990–2001), and Bombay/Mumbai (1992–2001). Each of these cities had, the exhibition argued, at particular periods, acted as crucibles for innovation, not only in art but in other disciplines—from architecture and dance to film, literature, music, and design. While each of them had generated a distinct artistic culture, they were seen as emblematic of wider global tendencies. Iwona Blazwick, former head of Tate Modern's exhibitions and displays, said it was the first time the gallery was able to "look globally" and represent the four major continents. She explained that there was no single "origin of creativity," and there were "multiple modernisms sparking all over the globe."[74]

The global context of the project and the sheer scale of the exhibition resulted in the museum hiring thirteen curators (see p. 130) to organize the various city components, each with expertise in a geographic region. Some curators selected artworks that explicitly reflected certain conditions of the city in question, while others assembled artifacts to represent the cultural life of the times. The Lagos room (1955–70), for example, was filled with copies of novels and plays by Nigerian authors Chinua Achebe and Wole Soyinka, photographs from family albums, a few black-and-white newsreels, examples of Highlife music (a genre of music and dance originating in late 19th-century Ghana), and editions of the magazines *Nigeria*, *Black Orpheus*, and *Drum*—the sum of which provided a time capsule of a vibrant and optimistic era (before the coups of 1966 and the Biafran War, 1967–70). In the (pre-war) Paris section (1905–15)—beginning with the Fauves, Cubism, and Orphism, and ending with the Ballets Russes and Futurism—the city was revealed as the unrivalled center of the art world at the start of the 20th century, as epitomized in the exhibition with multiple works by Picasso, Braque, Gris, Matisse, Léger, Dufy, and Severini.

London (1990–2001) was presented as a post-industrial metropolis whose recession laid the groundwork for a thriving art scene, one that was linked with the worlds of fashion, music, and design, and marked by the "vernacular, recycled, and humorous," according to curator Emma Dexter.[75] The works explored subjects

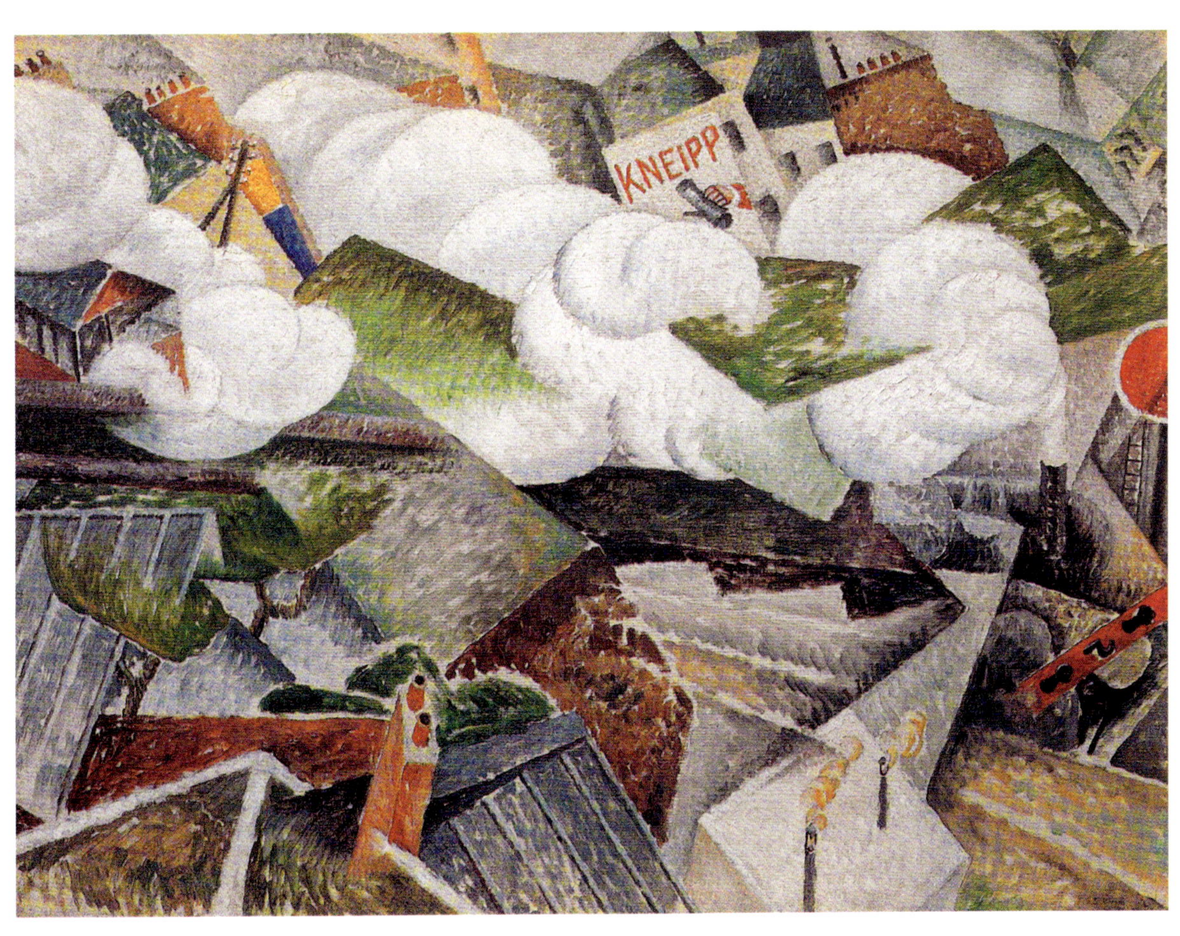

Gino Severini
Train de banlieue arrivant à Paris
(Suburban Train Arriving in Paris)
1915

as varied as homelessness (Janette Parris), rubbish (Runa Islam), chance encounters (Gillian Wearing), architecture (Wolfgang Tillmans and Rachel Whiteread), and the use of everyday materials by artists (Tom Dixon, Tracey Emin, Sarah Lucas, and Chris Ofili).

During the 1990s, Bombay/Mumbai experienced a culture clash between tradition and modernity, epitomized in *Century City* by Atul Dodiya's street images, hand-painted Bollywood billboards, and by Navjot Altaf's installation *Between Memory and History* (2000), which explored the problems of social disruption. Other works in this section addressed the urban anguish of a fast-expanding metropolis (Rummana Hussain), recorded the city's Parsi community (Sooni Taraporevala), or documented violence in the city, as in Vivan Sundaram's sculpture *Memorial* (1993), which used a newspaper image, taken in the midst of the Bombay riots, of a man lying dead in the street—in an elegiac act, the artist placed the photograph in an iron coffin mounted on a gun carriage, as if for a state burial. Another standout work in this section was the four-channel video installation by Nalini Malani, entitled *Hamletmachine* (2000), which examined the then-recent rise of Hindu fundamentalism in South Asia, incorporating texts from the play of the same title by German dramatist Heiner Müller, with fragmented images and sounds from riots in India and Pakistan around that time.

The section examining Tokyo (1969–73) presented the city on the brink of crisis—housing shortages, overpopulation, student revolts, and environmental pollution were among the major concerns.

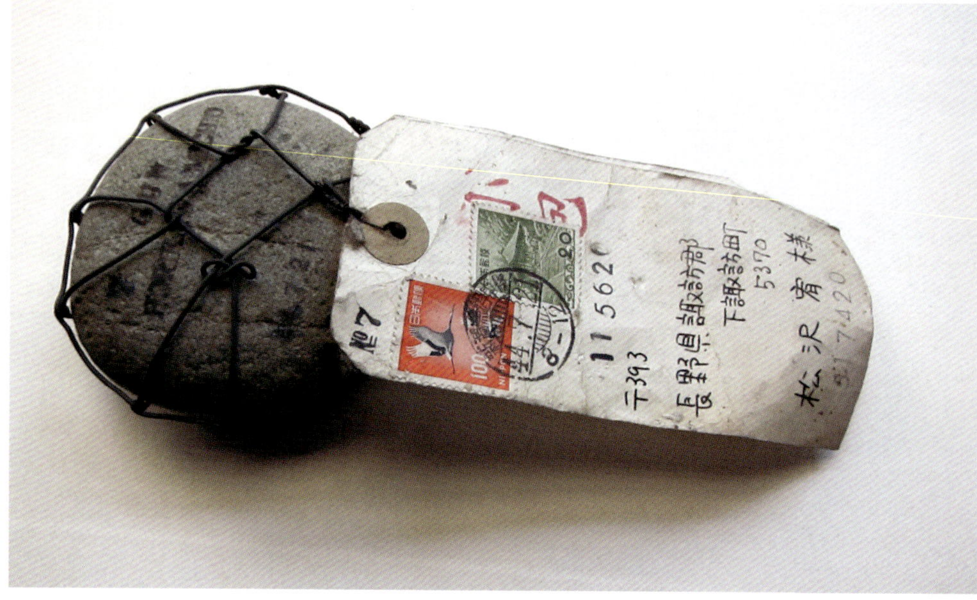

The uncertainty gave rise to anti-art movements, such as Mono-ha, which dominated the art scene at that time, with its founders, Sekine Nobuo and Lee Ufan, advocating for artistic gestures such as digging, moving, or arranging materials. Several works by Sekine and Lee were included in the show, most spectacularly Sekine's *Phase of Nothingness: Oilclay* (1969), which consisted of an immense mound of clay. Other key works in this section included: Matsuzawa Yutaka's *My Own Death* (1970), an imposing sign that hung across the entrance to a gallery, inviting visitors to reflect on questions of time and mortality; Horikawa Michio's *The Shinano River Plan 11* (1969), in which he gathered stones and posted them to eleven luminaries of the art world: his series was conducted at the same time as the Apollo 11 space mission—the artist felt it was more important to gather stones from Earth.

Despite New York's economic stagnation in the early 1970s, the city was a paradise for artists. Many rejected the impersonal and socially disengaged approach of Minimalism, and sought instead to reclaim biographical content, taking their art into the "real" world, and allowing the urban environment to shape it. Performance artist Vito Acconci was shown, for example, in a series of photographs from 1969, following people at random in the streets of New York—the city offered the artist a protective cloak of anonymity and the possibility for chance encounters; and the artist Mary Miss began siting her works, without invitation, in public areas around New York, using the city itself as a backdrop for her impromptu sculptures. Women artists were well represented in this section, including signature works by Hannah Wilke, Lynda Benglis, Adrian Piper, Joan Jonas, Nancy Graves, Mary Beth Edelson, and Eva Hess.

Rio de Janeiro (1955–69) was represented in *Century City* by Neo-Concretist experiments with painting and sculpture that sought to intensify visual expressiveness (Lygia Clark and Hélio Oiticica), by the sounds of the Brazilian music genre Bossa Nova, and by examples of Cinema Novo, a Brazilian genre of film that emerged in the 1960s. Rio was also represented at the exhibition by designs by the architects Le Corbusier, Oscar Niemeyer, Lúcio Costa, and Roberto Burle Marx.

In 1917, Moscow was in a state of revolt as the Bolsheviks seized power and the Romanov dynasty fell to its knees. The new capital of the Soviet Union, Moscow became the center for art, as the avant-garde seized the opportunity to redefine culture and its role in modern society. The Constructivists, for example, led by Vladimir Tatlin, El Lissitzky, and Aleksandr Rodchenko, sought to produce a new,

Horikawa Michio
*The Shinano River Plan 11
(Mail Art by Sending Stones)*
1969

functional art that would be closer to industrial production; while Kazimir Malevich was on a quest for pure, geometric form in his Suprematist compositions, of which several were on view. Dziga Vertov's film *Man with a Movie Camera* (1928) was included as a cross-section montage of urban life in Moscow, which captured the speed and machine rhythms of the new age. Also on view were the extraordinary costume designs of Liubov Popova and Aleksandr Vesnin's theatre set for *The Man Who Was Thursday* (1923), which incorporated platforms, conveyer belts, escalators, film projections, and kinetic light elements to simulate a capitalist metropolis.

Pre-war Vienna (1908–18) was represented in the exhibition by a series of drawings and paintings by Egon Schiele; the couch and chair of the founding father of psychoanalysis, Sigmund Freud; several Expressionist portraits by Oskar Kokoschka; the atonal music of Arnold Schoenberg; architectural drawings of Adolf Loos and Otto Wagner—all these contributions were exemplary of the period in Austria preceding and coinciding with the catastrophic impact of World War I and the consequent disintegration of the Austro-Hungarian Empire.

Century City met with mostly negative reviews. Adrian Searle of *The Guardian* was dismissive of the show, claiming that the curators had neglected to demonstrate the "urgency and vitality" of each period, and as such had "surely done the city, the period and the public a disservice." [76] In *Frieze* magazine, Chris Turner was also disillusioned, arguing that the exhibition had "failed to explore the depth of complexities involved." [77] Blake Gopnik, writing for the *Washington Post*, found the mega-show exhausting and clichéd.[78] However, I would argue for *Century City*'s brilliance. It was, in essence, an exhibition that employed a relational curatorial approach (see pp. 29–33) and that surveyed art from the 20th-century that was global in scope, arranged thematically, that did not assume the "-isms" of the West as the only defining moments globally, but rather as context-specific to one region of the world or another.

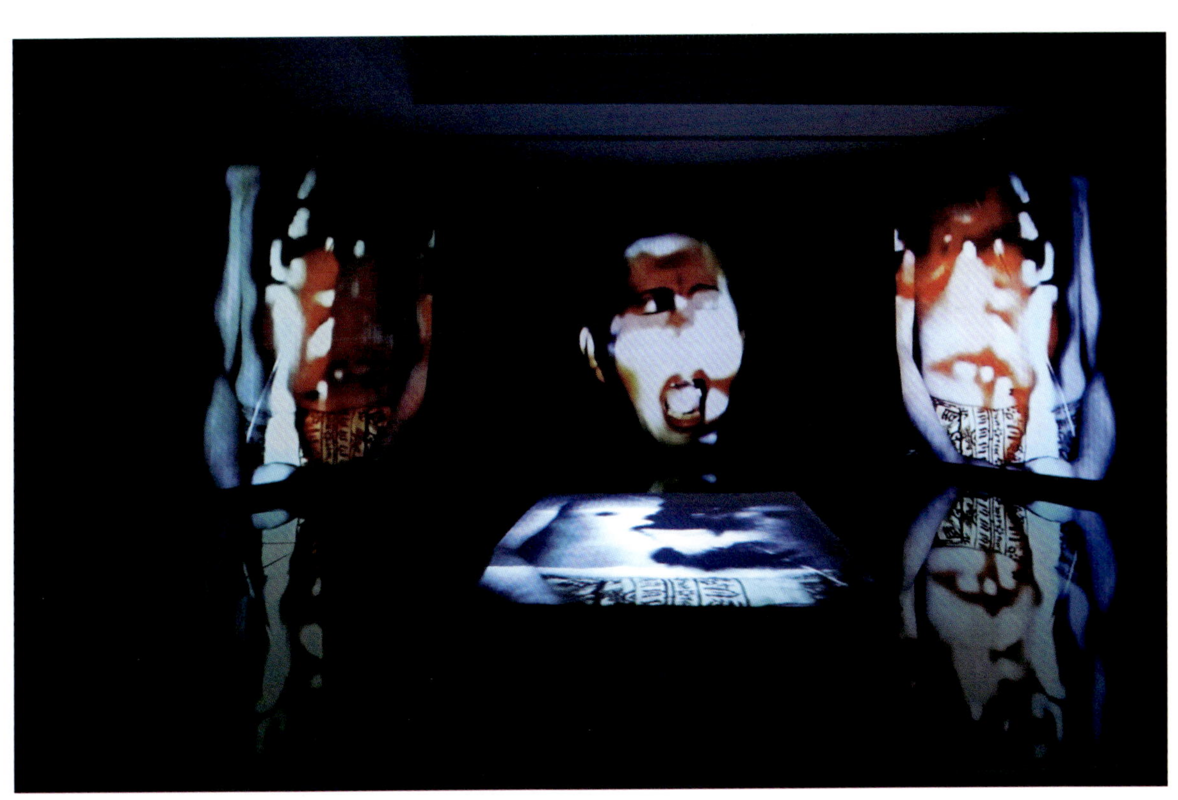

Nalini Malani
Hamletmachine
2000

2002

DOCUMENTA 11

Fridericianum Museum and other venues in Kassel, Germany

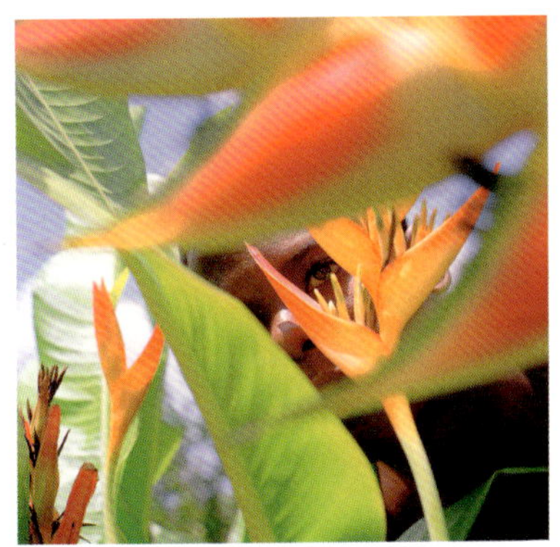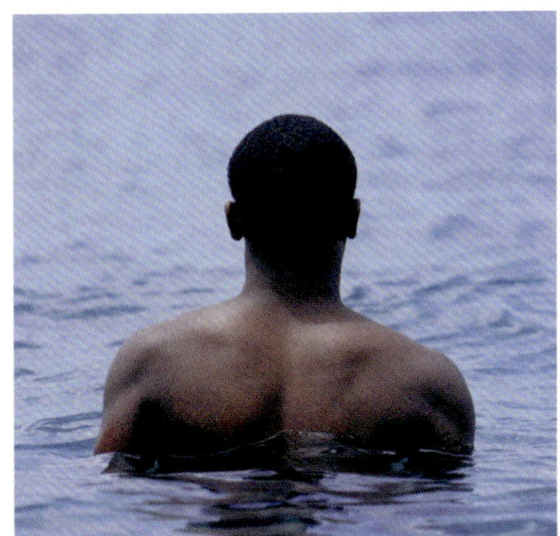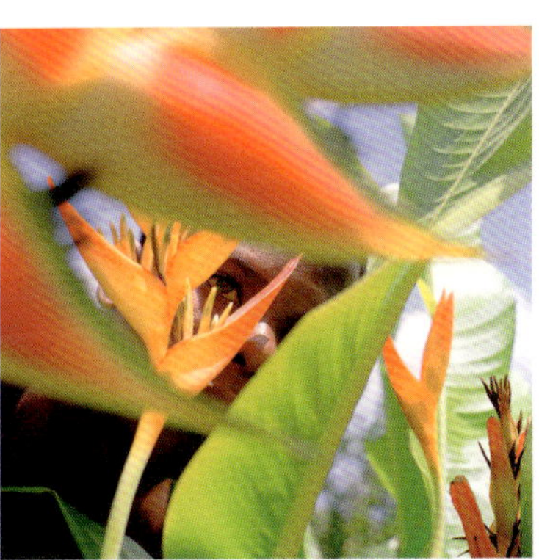

Isaac Julien
Before Paradise
2002

Documenta 11 in 2002 represented a radical departure from the exhibition norm. Not only was it organized for the first time by a non-European, Okwui Enwezor, but it was also the first (and last to-date) *Documenta* to employ a postcolonial curatorial strategy. In the exhibition's catalogue, Enwezor stated his refusal to declare a universal concept for the exhibition, except for "globalization," implying that this was what had underlaid the exclusionary discourses and institutional parameters of Modernism, and instead opted for emphasizing "spectacular differences" in his reflection on "contemporary art in a time of profound historical change and global transformation."[79] Drawing on the work of Michael Hardt and Antonio Negri, Enwezor explains in his catalogue essay that *Documenta 11* aimed to articulate the "anarchic demands of the multitude," or "resistant forces," which have emerged in the wake of Empire. He indicates how, according to Hardt and Negri, "Empire" can be defined as "the domain of actions and activities that have come to replace imperialism."[80]

    Documenta 11's global focus constituted the exhibition's principal organizational framework and its correlating public programs, or platforms, as they were termed, which were devoted to public discussions, conferences, workshops, books, and film and video programs that sought to "mark the location of culture today and the spaces in which culture intersects with the domains of complex global knowledge circuits."[81] The five platforms—hosted in Vienna/Berlin (these two cities shared the same theme), New Delhi, St. Lucia, Lagos, and, finally, Kassel—provided an opportunity for a critical dialogue between curators, scholars, theorists, and artists. The first four platforms also functioned to decenter or deterritorialize *Documenta* from Kassel, its traditional site of operations.[82]

    The exhibition was marked by a constellation of critical issues: intense North-South debates surrounding globalization, racism, the environment, migration, the rise of post-fascism, the increasingly brutal treatment of refugee groups, the Western anti-Islamic hysteria generated by 9/11, an increasingly belligerent US foreign policy, and a critique of

Mona Hatoum
Homebound
2000

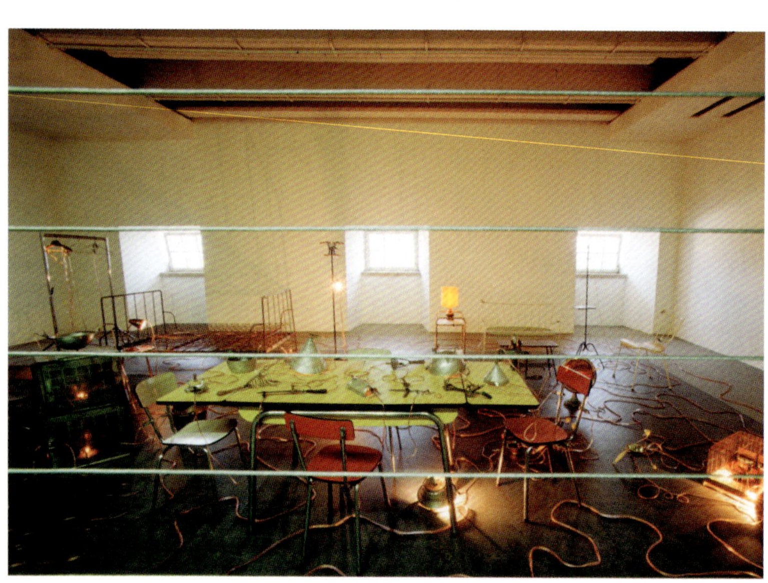

neo-liberalism. Enwezor's curatorial vision reflected this time of "frictions, transitions, transformations, and fissures"[83] by showcasing art that dealt with real inequalities of wealth, justice, and opportunity. Steve McQueen's video *Western Deep* (2002) documented the claustrophobic and exploitative working conditions in a South African gold mine; Kutluğ Ataman's four-channel multi-media installation, *The 4 Seasons of Veronica Read* (2002), recorded the musings of a plant breeder in London whose obsessive quest for perfection was expressed in a language redolent of racism and eugenics; the Italian collective, Multiplicity, presented a multi-screen video installation that described the tragic drowning of a boatload of illegal immigrants in the Mediterranean, featuring interviews and shots of the wreck, filmed by a robot camera; Tania Bruguera's installation *Untitled* (2002) was a gestapo-like chamber with blinding lights and the sound of jackboots and hair-trigger clicks (the sounds came from a live sentry pacing on a catwalk overhead, who loaded his gun repeatedly); Yinka Shonibare's large-scale installation *Gallantry and Criminal Conversation* (2002) parodied the 18th-century Grand Tour (a cultural tour of Europe), with headless white bourgeois travelers in African fabrics shown having sexual intercourse in varying positions; Zarina Bhimji's *Out of Blue* (2002) explored her roots as a Ugandan Asian, featuring haunting footage of President Idi Amin's jails, police cells, and barracks; Doris Salcedo's installation of stainless steel and lead chairs (*Tenebrae, Noviembre 7* and *Noviembre 6*) focused on the "disappeared" and other casualties of political violence in Latin America; and Kendell Geers's photo series *Suburbia* (1999) depicted gated and barbed fences and armed-response warning signs around the residential compounds of wealthy South Africans.

Reviews of *Documenta 11* were mixed. Critics generally judged the exhibition along lines that were political. A number of US-based reviewers expressed reservations, ranging from the charges that it was dour and humorless and overly "documentary," to questions about a perceived prejudice in favor of the Palestinian cause. Peter Plagens of *Newsweek* was particularly dismissive. For him, *Documenta 11* was an "unsurpassable example" of a new convention operating in the art world whereby "exhibitions are a kind of county fair for intellectuals and catalogues resemble UNESCO reports on pressing global problems."[84] "*Documenta* is like a world tour of other people's misery," another critic lamented.[85] Curator and art critic Massimiliano Gioni criticized *Documenta 11* for its clinical and overly aesthetic representation of conflict, which, he argued, turned the spectator into a voyeur and did not provide a blueprint for political action.[86]

Others claimed that the exhibition's focus on non-Western spaces, its transnational scope, "pandered to an ethos of identity politics and multiculturalism."[87] But as Sylvester Okwunodu Ogbechie argued, *Documenta 11* did no such thing: "no evaluation of contemporary culture could ignore the glaring marginalization of large constituencies of non-Western artists that were, under Enwezor's watch, thereby included in a *Documenta* exhibition for the first time."[88] Enwezor's goal, Ogbechie argued, was to construct a new and inclusive discourse for art in an age of globalization, one that could confront the "ethics and limits of occidental power," demand a radical overhaul of contemporary structures of power and privilege, and thereby depart from hegemonic, Euro-US cultural perspectives and their exhibition projects, criticizing the latter's tokenist inclusion of "non-Western" peoples.[89]

Insofar as it comprised a visibly larger number of non-Euro-US artists than did previous *Documenta*s, Enwezor's exhibition can be considered the first truly transnational *Documenta*. A transnational exhibition is different from an international one: the term "transnational" is used purposefully here to designate a new, postcolonial interest in exceeding what Enwezor calls, "the borders of the colonized world…by making empire's former 'other' visible at all times."[90] And as was being advocated simultaneously in postcolonial feminist discourses, the transnational was to be favored over the international insofar as the latter term generally presents not a multiplicity of voices, but a large sampling of Euro-US artists with a limited number of non-Western ones (as with previous *Documenta*s, for example).

The desire to present a truly global or transnational exhibition is what really differentiated Enwezor's curatorial strategy from Jean-Hubert Martin's in *Magiciens de la terre*. In a 2003 *Artforum* roundtable, Enwezor paid tribute to *Magiciens* as "no doubt crucial paradigmatically for the expansion of so-called global exhibitions," but was critical of its "opposition between the Western center and the non-Western periphery."[91] This is why *Documenta 11* has been positioned as a deliberate response and corrective to *Magiciens*.[92]

Kutluğ Ataman
The 4 Seasons of Veronica Read
2002

Yinka Shonibare
Gallantry and Criminal Conversation
2002

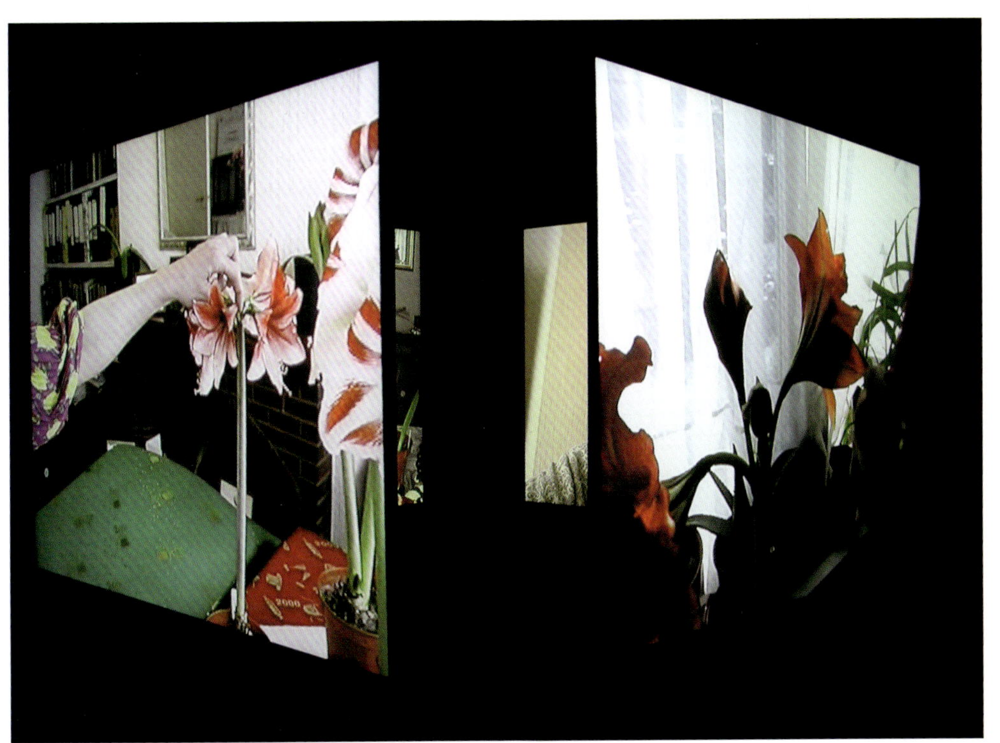

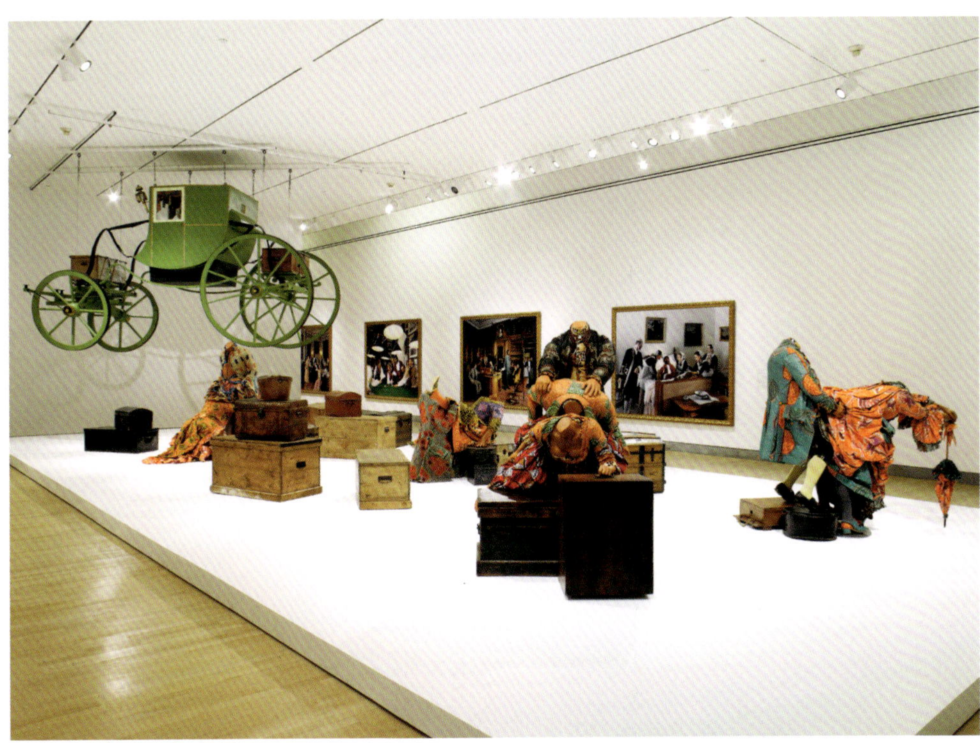

Curated by
Andrea Buddensieg and
Peter Weibel

THE GLOBAL CONTEMPORARY: ART WORLDS AFTER 1989

ZKM/Museum of Contemporary Art, Karlsruhe, Germany

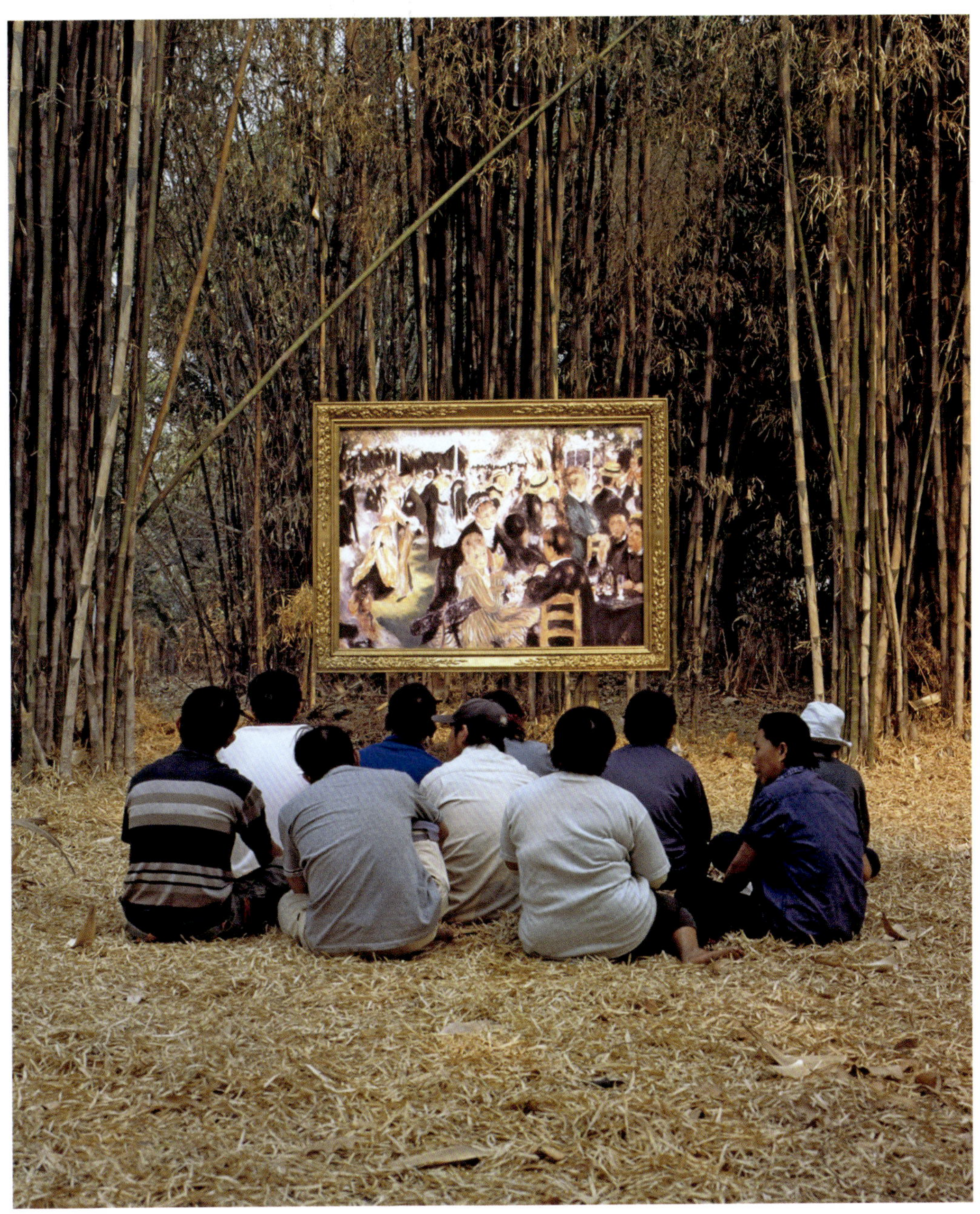

Araya Rasdjarmrearnsook
Still from *Renoir's Ball at the Moulin de la Galette and the Thai Villagers*,
from the series *Dow Song Duang (The Two Planets)*
2008

The Global Contemporary: Art Worlds After 1989 (2011–12), curated by Andrea Buddensieg and Peter Weibel, and organized for the ZKM/ Museum of Contemporary Art, Karlsruhe, Germany, represented one component of the Global Contemporary Project, comprising the exhibition, a book, and ZKM's long-running "Global Art and the Museum" seminar project. The principal aim of the project was to explore today's increasingly post-multicultural understanding of global art, in which, according to Robert Aitken in *Art in America*, "the near-parity of Western and non-Western art—what Weibel has long referred to as the 'included' and the 'excluded'—is symbolized by, and partly the result of, the viral proliferation of biennial exhibitions across the planet." [93] In the exhibition guide, the curators state that "globalization has replaced the concept of an international movement in art under the flag of the West." [94] They prefer the term "global art" to "contemporary art," which, they say, generally refers to art after Modernism. People from regions where Modernism never arrived need to be able to use global art as, in the curators' terms, "a universal forum where artists with diverse origins, and hence with equally diverse perspectives, thematize their working conditions and their personal experiences with the problem of a globalized world." [95] The year 1989 was chosen as the starting point for the exhibition because it represents the year that *Magiciens de la terre* was presented at the Pompidou Center in Paris. It was also a year of transformations: the Berlin Wall fell, having divided Germany since 1961, signaling the end of the Cold War and the beginning of German reunification; and thousands of pro-democracy student-protestors were massacred in Tiananmen Square, Beijing. As Peter Weibel writes in the preface to the exhibition guide: "…the year 1989 signified the end of the Western monopolies. The rise of art from Asia, Africa, South America, etc. in Western institutions is nothing other than the legitimate attempt by other cultures, nations, and civilizations to strip the West of its monopoly on exclusion." [96]

The Global Contemporary was divided into nine "modules." The first of these, "Room of Histories: A Documentation," visualized the chronology and the geographic dissemination of global art production; it contained statistical representations of China's emergence as a gigantic art market and mappings of the spread of far-flung biennial exhibitions, an informal typology of art spaces, including museums operated by private collectors, universities, and governments, as well as a reading room by London-based artist, writer, and curator Rasheed Araeen. The room contained all issues of *Third Text*, the international journal that has functioned since 1987 as a platform for the discourse of art produced by non-Western artists and in non-Western regions. The next module, "World Time: The World as Transit Zone," explored the ways in which successful contemporary artists are dependent on air travel, in a state of permanent jetlag. With his installation *Centro di Permanenza Temporanea* (2007), an abandoned gangway on which asylum seekers are left behind, helpless, Albanian artist Adrian Paci developed— much like German filmmaker Hito Steyerl in her video *In Free Fall* (2010), about an airport cemetery—the topos of the airport as an imaginary, and yet painfully real place of globalization.

In "Life Worlds & Image Worlds," artists presented myriad reactions to the omnipresence of the mass media in the global world, and the ongoing process of rewriting the same images over and over again, including various film cultures (for example, Bani Abidi's video, *...so he starts singing*, 2000, in which a young woman enthusiastically recounts the plots of twenty-six Bollywood films). Here, also, the visitor encountered a harrowing series of silkscreens by Khosrow Hassanzadeh, entitled *Terrorist* (2004), in which the Iranian artist portrayed himself and members of his family as "terrorists"; and a mixed-media installation by Chinese artist Jin Shi, *Retail Business: Karaoke #2* (2009), which included a bejeweled karaoke system shrunk to dimensions transportable by bicycle.

In the next module, "'World Art': The Curiosity Cabinet from a Postcolonial Perspective," the ethnographic museums of the colonial era were shown to have collapsed, and artists presented themselves as "exotic objects" for visual consumption (as in Luna's *The Artifact Piece* (1987/1991, see pp. 114–15), or were critical of the ways in which indigenous iconography and language have been appropriated by "whitefellas" in order to conform to market requirements (as, for example, in Richard Bell's work, *Scientia E Metaphysica (Bell's Theorem)*, 2003).

Works in the section "Boundary Matters: The Concept of Art in Modernity" exposed art history as fiction, mocked Western institutions that claim to know what art is, and revealed a clash of cultures. For example, in the video series *Dow Song Duang (The Two Planets)*, 2008, by Thai artist Araya Rasdjarmrearnsook, a group of villagers in different rural locations in Thailand are shown viewing 19th-century painted masterpieces by Jean-François Millet, Auguste Renoir, Edouard Manet, and Vincent van Gogh; and in *Moments of Glory* (2011) Iranian artist Leila Pazooki parodied the art market by quoting phrases taken from online art magazines, comparing non-Western artists with Euro-US icons of Western art in colorful neon lights with the inscriptions "Indian Damien Hirst," "Cindy Sherman of Asia," "Dali of Bali," and "Renoir of South Africa," mocking the need of the global art market to use recognizable names to make a non-Euro-US art scene visible.

The module "Networks and Systems: Globalization as Subject" featured artist collectives and collaborations whose subject was globalization, including Pinky Show, RYBN.ORG, and Ghana Think Tank, and the The Xijing Men collective who proclaim a fictional artists' state with Olympic flags in their work *Welcome to Xijing—Xijing Olympics* (2008), and Slovenian artist Tadej Pogačar's *MonApoly, A Human Trade Game* (2004) in which the viewer becomes a "player" in an abstract planning game on the subject of human trafficking. The module "Art as Commodity: The New Economy and the Art Markets" included works that reflected on the current condition of the art market. Beijing-based artist and curator Liu Ding invited viewers to discuss the value system represented by art with his *Store* (2008, ongoing), and undermined the exhibition by offering "unfinished paintings" for sale; while in German artist Christian Jankowski's video *Kunstmarkt TV* (2008) art objects were praised by a team of salespeople on a home-shopping program, with the telephone numbers of order hotlines appearing on screen; and Thai painter Navin Rawanchaikul's *SUPER CHINA!* (2009) depicted famous representatives of the Chinese art scene disguised as superstars, engaged in activities ranging from archery and motorcycling to bathing or eating fast food.

The module "Lost in Translation: New Biographies of Artists" argued that artists have moved away from self-representation in the traditional sense in favor of the adoption of fictional identities and performative roles, as in Israeli artist Tamy Ben-Tor's video works in which she parodied her own encounters with the international art world; in *Drop the Monkey* (2009), Israeli video artist Guy Ben-Ner interviewed himself by telephone; and South African-born artist Moshekwa Langa presented a diary with a long list of names in *Ohne Titel* (2003). The final module in the exhibition was the "Artist-in-Residence Program," to which the curators invited international artists, or "global players," to participate.[97]

The Global Contemporary received mixed reviews. Kerstin Winking of *Third Text* was pleasantly surprised: "Since [the] accent on inclusiveness seems to have been the dominant criterion for selection, the resulting exhibition was overstuffed, superficial and anachronistic—and in this paradoxically succeeded in illustrating the notion of global art."[98] Writing for *Art in America*, Robert Aitken

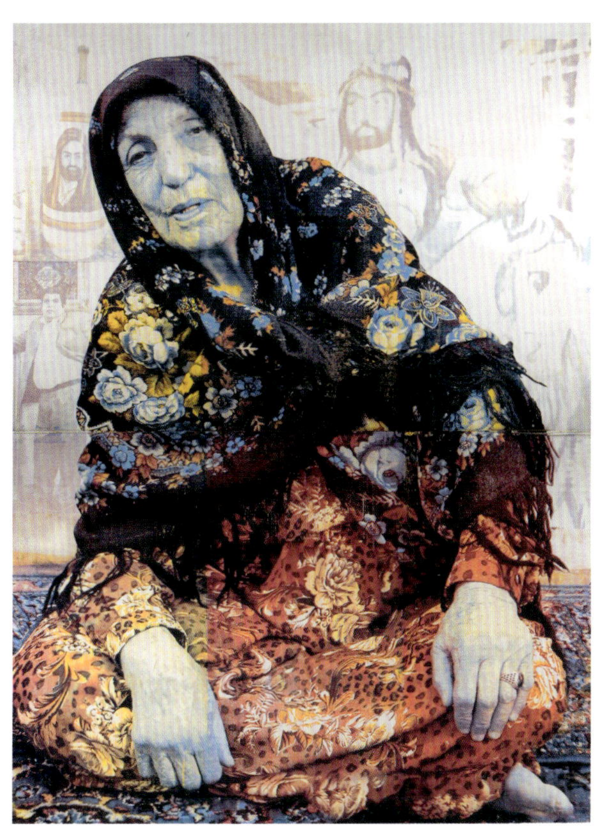

praised the curators for the large pool of exhibited artists, which, he argued, had "the salutary effect of deemphasizing the role of celebrity artists and the importance of the market."[99] He was disappointed, however, that despite the project's focus on the 21st-century art world, the age of digital media was unaccounted for, and the proliferation and primacy of art fairs were overlooked, as was the effect of economic pressure on artists to be international players.[100]

Pat Binder and Gerhard Haupt, editors of *Universes in Universe*, were befuddled by the overall curatorial premise, and asked why 1989 was chosen as the geopolitical turn for the exhibition, calling it an "extension of the Eurocentric perspective": "For in many of the world regions that the artists come from, this date does not play such a key role at all."[101] Writing for *ArtReview*, JJ Charlesworth was outright dismissive of the show's curatorial premise, calling it "a ponderous reiteration of current orthodox liberal thinking about cultural identity and art's purpose in the era after Western colonial dominance, revealing the depth of confusion about how to privilege the politics of difference when the critique of Eurocentrism, faced with the shift of economic and political power to the East and South, is fast becoming an irrelevance."[102] In short, he was critical of the exhibition's postcolonialist orthodoxy, which he saw as the norm for critics and curators steeped in the all-too-Western critique of Western universalism. The privileging of cultural difference in the exhibition (and catalog) was seen as suppressing the progressive potential of global art (the internationalizing and universalizing of cultural forms and audiences).

Khosrow Hassanzadeh
Reyhan Hassanzadeh,
from the series *Terrorist*
2004

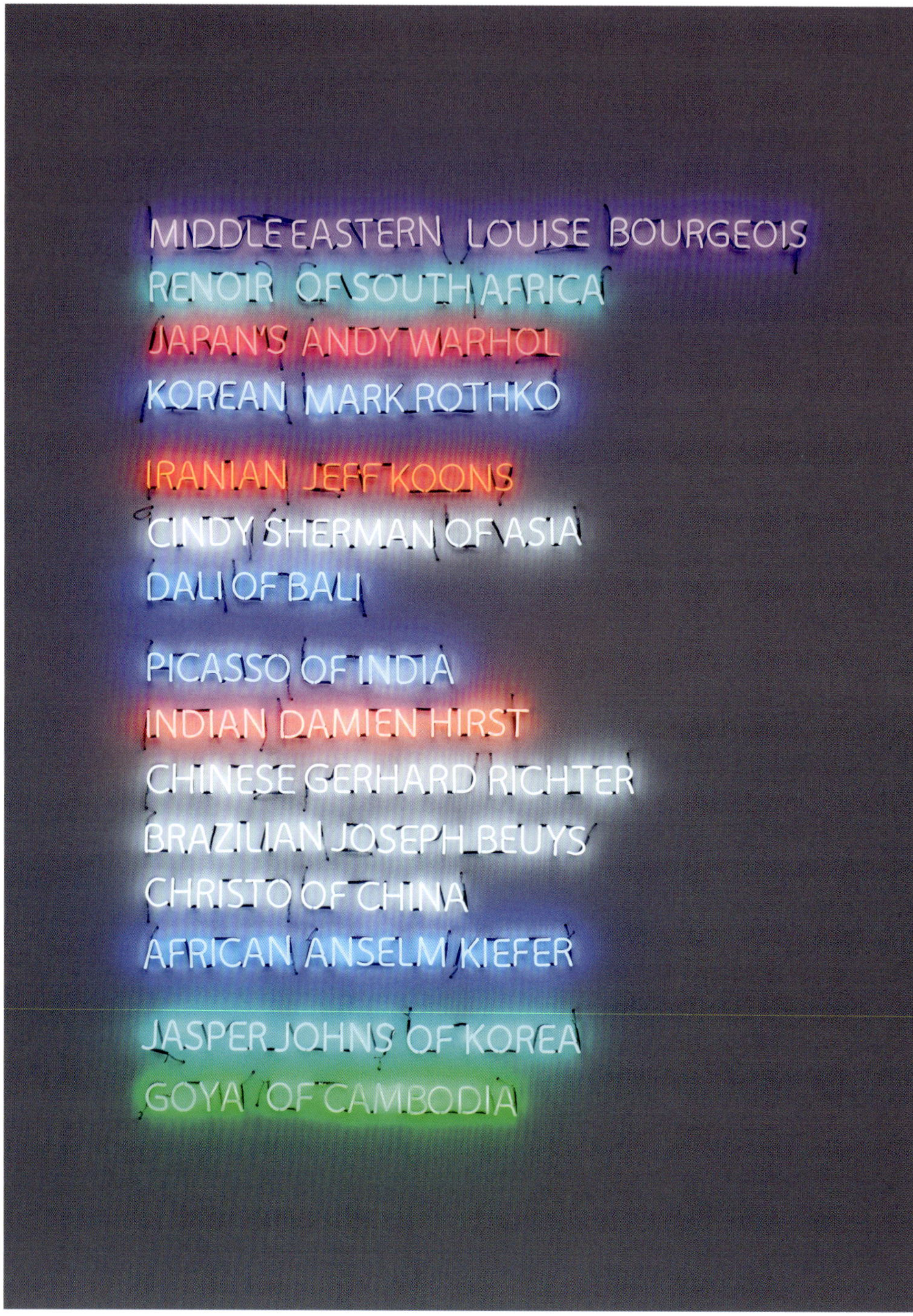

Leila Pazooki
Moments of Glory
2011

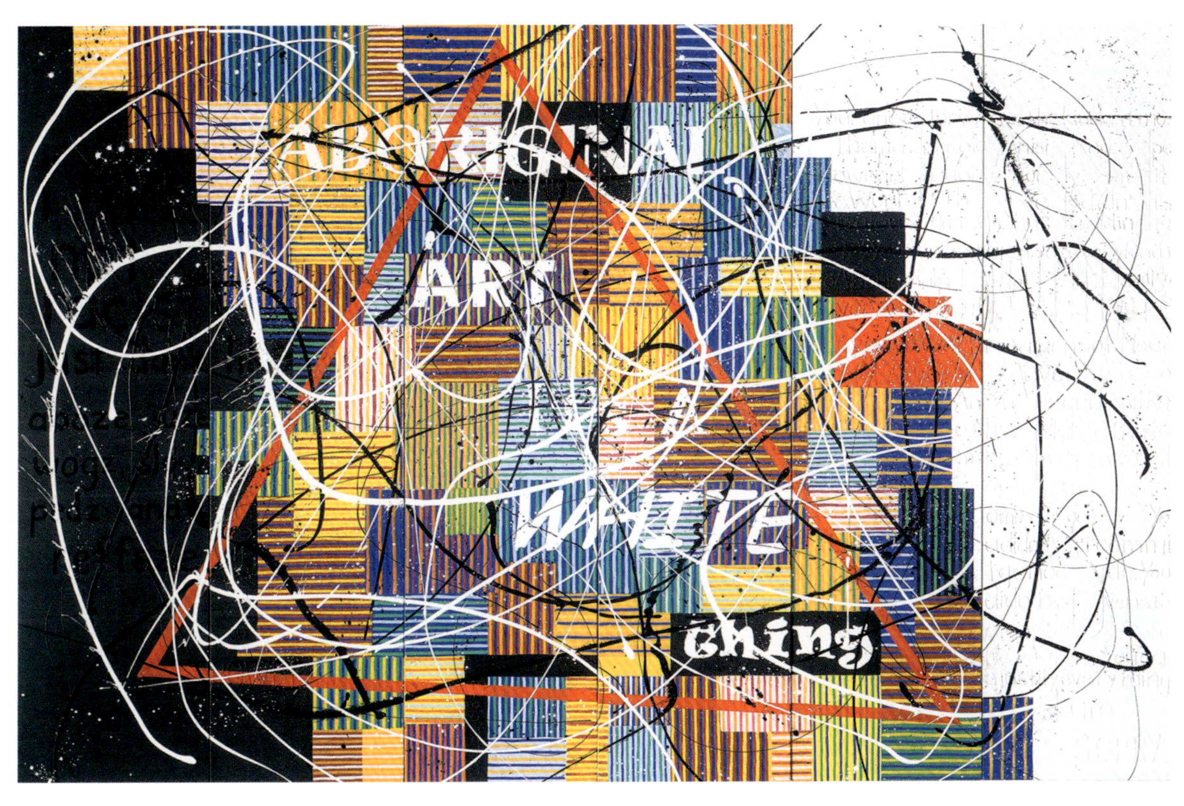

Richard Bell
Scientia E Metaphysica (Bell's Theorem)
2003

VENICE BIENNALE 2015: ALL THE WORLD'S FUTURES

Italian Pavilion and the Arsenale, Venice, Italy

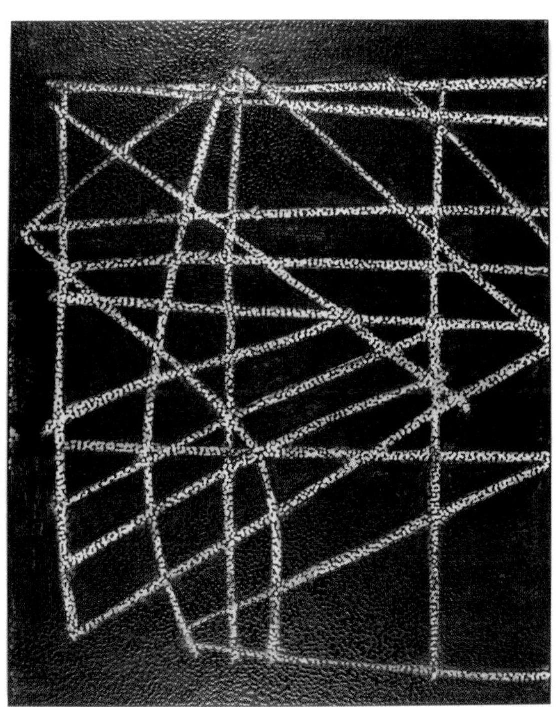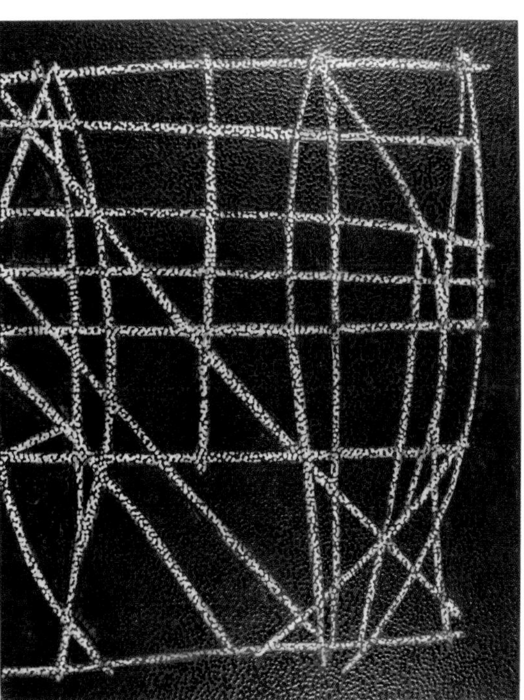

Daniel Boyd
Untitled (TI1)
2015

Like his *Documenta 11*, Okwui Enwezor's Venice Biennale (2015), entitled *All the World's Futures*, was equally transnational in scope. While there were strong contingents from every continent, for the first time in the Biennale's history, African artists were a major presence, comprising 14% of the artists in the exhibition.[103] Of the 136 artists from 53 countries only 22% were from North America (most of whom were African American), which is far lower than in earlier Biennales, where European- and US-based artists tended to make up the majority. While the injection of cultural diversity into the exhibition was not a central aim, Enwezor did want to attend to frequent blind spots on the part of more mainstream curators.

In a curatorial statement, Enwezor explained that the exhibition's premise was rooted in the upheaval and disquiet of our time, stating that:

> The global landscape lies shattered and in disarray, scarred by violent turmoil, panicked by specters of economic crisis and viral pandemonium, secessionist politics and a humanitarian catastrophe on the high seas, deserts, and borderlands, as immigrants, refugees, and desperate peoples seek refuge in seemingly calmer and prosperous lands. Everywhere one turns new crisis, uncertainty, and deepening insecurity across all regions of the world seem to leap into view…How can the current disquiet of our time be properly grasped, made comprehensible, examined, and articulated?[104]

The works on display throughout the Biennale therefore examined the then-current state of things—from global starvation, industrial pollution, and the atrocious conditions of garment workers in developing countries to ecology and the arms trade. Rather than one overarching theme that encapsulated these various responses to the "disquiet" into one unified field of vision, the Biennale was instead informed by a layer of intersecting filters, or sub-chapters, defined by Enwezor as "Liveness," "Garden of Disorder," and "Capital."

Only a few of the critical reviews of the exhibition appreciated its preoccupation with socio-political concerns. Roberta Smith of the *New York Times*, for example, commended Enwezor's clarity and purpose: "There is something admirable and even heroic about [his] morality-based approach."[105] Moreover, she agreed with Enwezor that "The world is a mass of intractable ills on which art must shed light."[106] She continued: "*All the World's Futures* brings out into the open a central preoccupation of the moment, namely the belief that

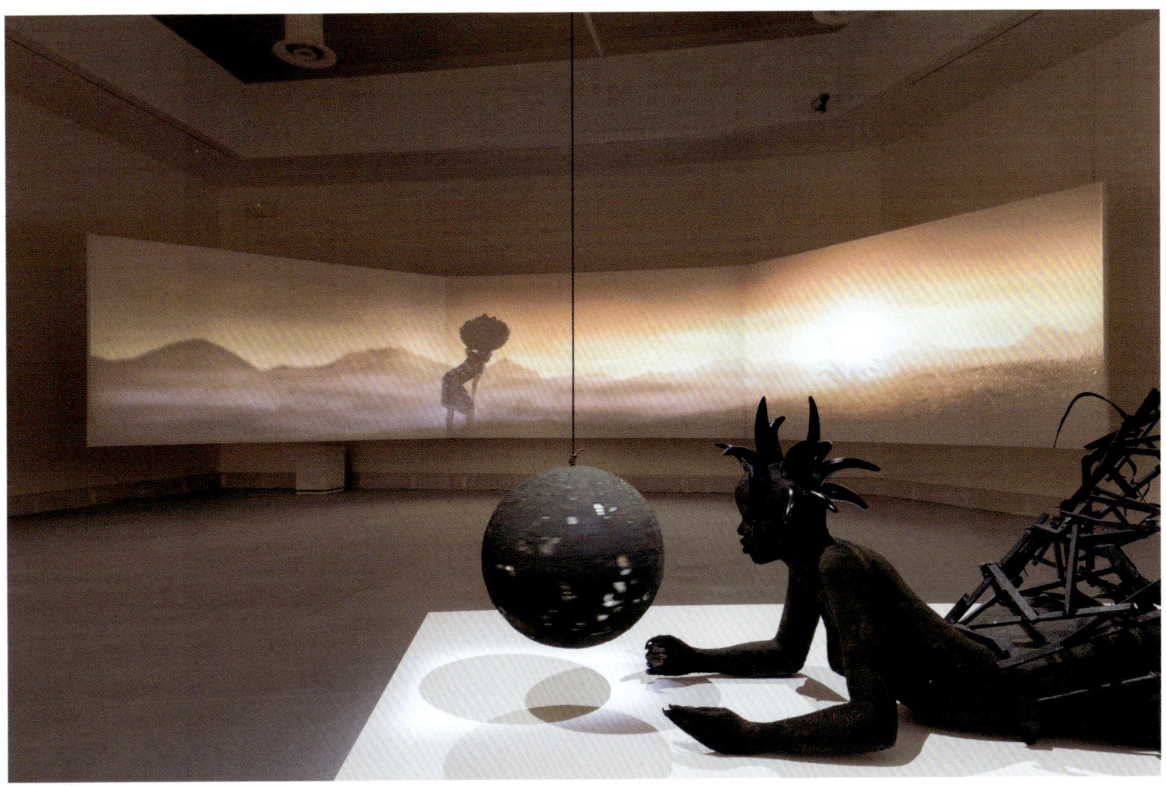

Wangechi Mutu
The End of Carrying All
2015

art is not doing its job unless it has loud and clear social concerns."[107] Other reviews—such as those by Laura Cumming, Juliana Engberg, and Martin Gayford—were damning, calling the exhibition "grim," "gloomy," and lacking in "visual power, originality, wit or bravado."[108] As Cumming explained, "It feels more like a glum trudge than the usual exhilarating adventure."[109] Some argued that the works were simply politically correct agitprop; others highlighted the contradiction between political correctness and the fact that "outside the yachts of billionaire collectors are moored in a long line on the fondamenta."[110] What these critics failed to recognize is that it was precisely this contradiction that Enwezor sought to highlight.

The most controversial aspect of the exhibition was the Arena auditorium, designed by Ghanaian-British architect David Adjaye, dedicated to Karl Marx's *Capital: A Critique of Political Economy* (1867), which Enwezor deemed an "utterly contemporary" work, calling the Arena itself "the Biennale's central nervous system."[111] During the course of the almost seven-month exhibition, the auditorium was utilized by actors (directed by London-based installation artist and filmmaker Isaac Julien), who read all four volumes of Marx's book, including footnotes. After the reading, the Arena's program expanded into recitals of work songs, librettos, readings of scripts, discussions, plenaries, and film screenings devoted to diverse theories and explorations of *Capital*—most of which were works produced specifically for the Biennale.

Given that Marx's *Capital* was a critique of the effects of the Industrial Revolution and its reliance on exploitation of workers, much of the art on view at the Biennale addressed issues of labor, with colonialism as a visible subtext. Enwezor's curatorial decision concerning *Capital* was obviously intended to highlight extreme income disparity. However, as critic Gregory Volk made clear in his review of the exhibition for *Art in America*, "[M]any people (especially Eastern Europeans who grew up under Communist governments) will recall that Joseph Stalin, emboldened by his understanding of Marx, slaughtered some 34 million to 49 million people; that Chairman Mao, likewise emboldened by Marx, was responsible for the deaths of about 45 million; and that all sorts of authoritarian regimes, including the former East Germany with its notorious state security apparatus the Stasi, derived their abysmal power from Marxist ideology." [112]

So, while Enwezor's Arena was not the most popular component of the exhibition, its presence as a curatorial intervention was a triumph insofar as it was a continuously unfolding live event that changed daily and, as Enwezor explained, allowed for the Biennale to be "relentlessly incomplete," [113] and "a total cacophony." [114] As such, Enwezor employed a relational or dialogic curatorial approach (exhibition-as-polylogue, see pp. 29–33), in which the destructive center-periphery binary collapses in favor of multiplicity and multivocality.

Ibrahim Mahama
Out of Bounds
2014–15

Mika Rottenberg
No Nose Knows
2015

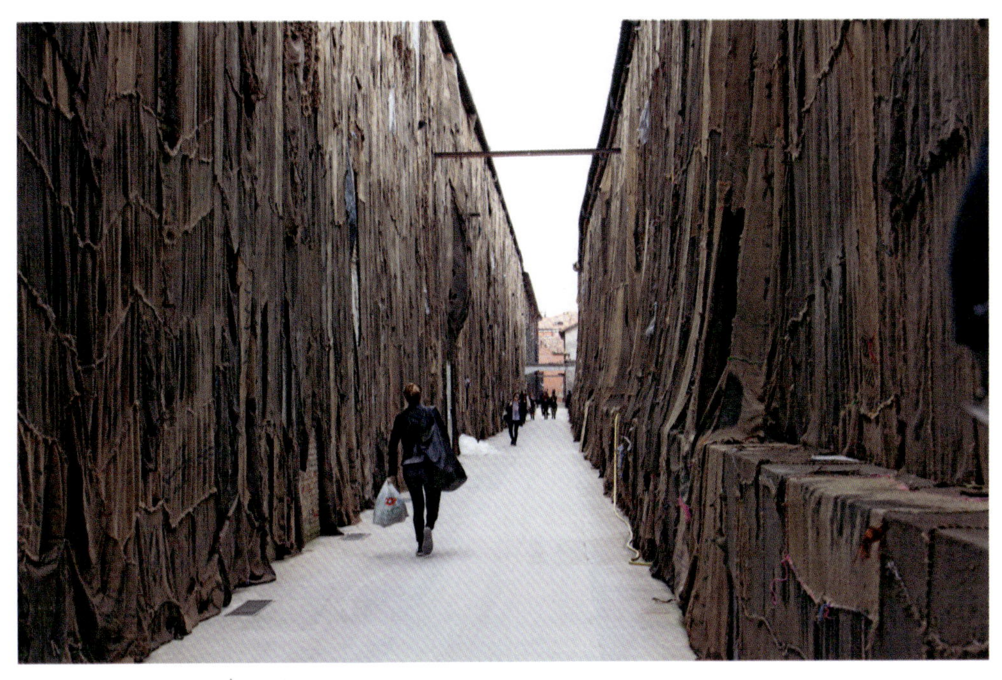

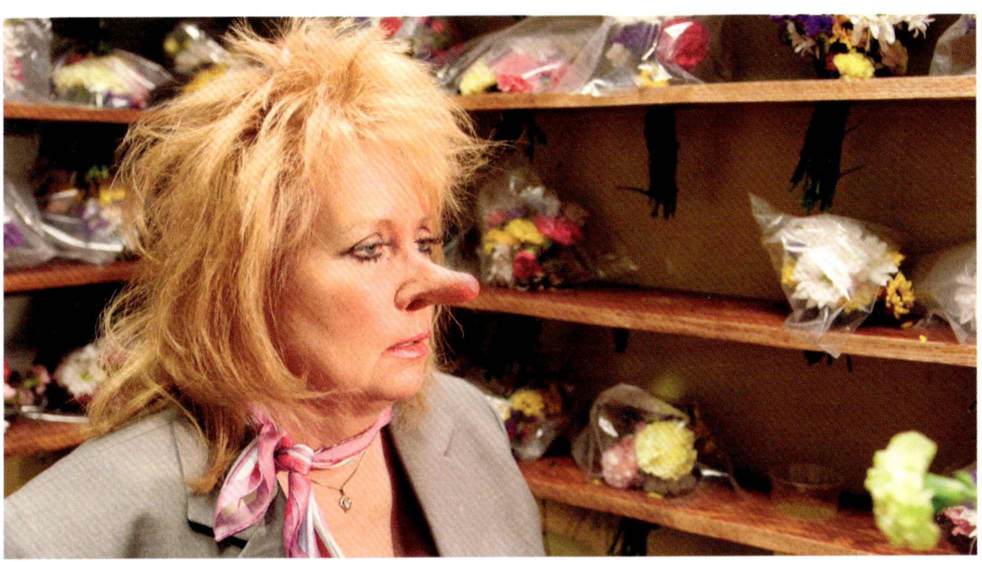

4. CHALLENGING HETEROCENTRISM AND LESBO-HOMOPHOBIA

"The discipline of art history (and the academy as a whole) still takes gay and lesbian/queer studies as a minor area of expertise, a queer endeavor." [1]

Jonathan Weinberg

In 1978, the US artist and writer Harmony Hammond organized an exhibition entitled *A Lesbian Show* at 112 Greene Street Workshop in New York, which featured the work of eighteen artists. [2] Her aim in the exhibition was not to discover or define a lesbian sensibility, but to present works with a broad range of aesthetic and shared thematic concerns, including "issues of anger, guilt, hiding, secrecy, coming out, personal violence and political trust, self-empowerment, and the struggle to make oneself whole." [3] Indeed, according to Hammond, only a few of the works referenced lesbian sexuality, and the majority of them did not engage directly with lesbian identity or experience. The only uniting factor was that the artists were willing to be "out" in this context. This was a courageous act, since most lesbians did not want to be identified solely on the basis of their sexual orientation at that time. As a result, most of the works—those by Mary Ann King and Maxine Fine, for example—dealt with "notions of camouflage or hiding," and none was erotic in content because, as Hammond explained, the "artists were wary of the ever-present male gaze." [4]

In her *Village Voice* review of the exhibition, Kay Larson noted that the show would have been disappointing for anyone looking for "definitions." The fact that the exhibition happened at all is what made it important, she argued, for it forced everyone to consider "what an art based on sexual politics might look like."[5] Larson understood that lesbian art would need time and a sympathetic environment in which to develop, and discussed the exhibition in terms of marginalization, the representation of difference, and the problems of self-ghettoization.

ESSENCE AND SENSIBILITY

The case of *A Lesbian Show* raises key issues relating to LGBTQ exhibitions. First is the concept of a "sensibility" specific to sexual orientation? As with "women's art" or "Latino art," what is "lesbian art"? What is "gay art"? Does it look different from art produced by non-LGBTQ artists? And if there is a sensibility, how does it manifest itself in the work? These and similar questions have arisen repeatedly in the historiography of LGBTQ exhibitions—from *Great American Lesbian Art Show* (GALAS, 1980) and *Extended Sensibilities: Homosexual Presence in Contemporary Art* (1982) to *In a Different Light: Visual Culture, Sexual Identity, Queer Practice* (1995), and *Queer British Art 1861–1967* (2017)—in the same way as the idea of a "feminine sensibility" had dominated women's art production and exhibitions in the 1970s and 1980s. As early as 1977, art historians Arlene Raven and Ruth Iskin argued that lesbian sensibility was not based in sexual orientation, but flourished in women-identified communities.[6] They claimed that when an artist was surrounded and inspired by women, she would undergo a "radical transformation of self, her muse would be female, and the sensibility her art embodied would be lesbian."[7] It was, they insisted, a revolutionary rather than an aesthetic mode of thinking that was transformative and creative.[8] They also argued that heterosexual, bisexual, and celibate women were capable of producing art with a lesbian sensibility, and that lesbian artists did not always do so.[9]

In a brochure from the 1980 GALAS exhibition encouraging artists to submit work (see p. 168), the organizers defined lesbian art as "art made by lesbians; art which explores lesbian content; art which is woman-identified. There's no strict definition—if you feel your creative work is lesbian in form or content, please join us!"[10] Only "out" lesbians were invited to this "Invitational" section of the exhibition since the organizers believed that their work deliberately articulated their lesbian identity, although it was sometimes unclear how this was made manifest. In an attempt to address the ambiguity, the GALAS organizers asked each artist to include a statement explaining why their work embodied a lesbian sensibility.

Dan Cameron, curator of *Extended Sensibilities*, also believed wholeheartedly in an identifiable gay sensibility. In his catalogue essay "Sensibility as Content," he explained how he had attempted to broaden the scope of the exhibition beyond what he defined (and exhibited) as "homosexual subject matter" or "ghetto content," which consisted of figurative, sometimes overt, representations of gay and lesbian life and sexuality.[11] By contrast, Lawrence Rinder, co-curator of *In a Different Light*, insisted there was no such thing as a gay sensibility, but went on to argue, contradictorily, that "the phenomenon of 'camp' had long before entered the mainstream academic discourse as the token legitimate aesthetic sensibility identified with homosexuality..."[12] Indeed, many critics claimed that *In a Different Light* offered up an example of a "queer sensibility" in that the curatorial approach functioned as a sort of curatorial "outing" of certain modern and contemporary artworks. The show's curators chose to use the word "queer" rather than "gay" and "lesbian" because they believed that it was fast "becoming a term that subverts or confuses group definition rather than fostering it...queer identity is spontaneous, mutable, and inherently political."[13] It is for these reasons—its mutability and political/activist associations—that since the early 1990s, "queer" has been the chosen term of self-identification for many LGBTQ people. "Queering" has also become a common curatorial practice, as was certainly the case with the exhibition *Ars Homo Erotica*, curated by Paweł Leszkowicz in 2010, which involved a radical re-visioning of Poland's National Museum permanent collection from a "queer" perspective.

"OUTING," CENSORSHIP, AND SINS OF OMISSION

Another issue raised by Hammond's *A Lesbian Show* in 1978, as well as by the GALAS project in 1980, was the artists' willingness to "come out" publicly. Since sexuality is not generally physically manifest—as is usually the case with sex and race—it requires disclosure, a self-outing. For many this is liberating; for others, terrifying. Fear of being "outed" can be so intense that some artists have resorted to coded iconographies, as in the work of Jasper Johns, Robert Rauschenberg, and Marsden Hartley. The gay liberation movement of the 1960s and 1970s certainly changed that for some. As gays and lesbians became increasingly public, less closeted, they gained confidence and self-outing became less of an issue.

But what if artists are not "out" publicly, as was the case with Johns and Rauschenberg: should a curator "out" an artist, even if the artist had intended not to "out" him- or herself? In 2013, the Museum of Modern Art (MoMA) presented an exhibition of the work of Johns and Rauschenberg from the mid to late 1950s that made no mention of the fact that the two artists were lovers for six years during this period of artistic triumph, when they were moving away from Abstract Expressionism toward Pop art. Instead, the introductory placard described them as "friends" who were "in dialogue with one another" during this period. (MoMA's profile of gay icon Andy Warhol also fails to mention he was homosexual.) Given that Johns and Rauschenberg were closeted, does this represent homophobia and/or censorship on the part of the museum? Mark Joseph Stern, writing for *Slate*, argues that "museums have a responsibility to acknowledge and consider the sexuality of artists in their collections when it is relevant to the work they are displaying...In the case of Johns and Rauschenberg, ignoring orientation amounts to curatorial malpractice."[14] For Stern, then, the museum's actions were censorious. The oversight was particularly egregious, he argued, because Pop art, the movement the two artists helped to establish, was "built upon rejection of societal norms, including hyper-masculinity and heteronormativity. Its gay dimension was present from its genesis, yet a casual visitor to Johns and Rauschenberg might think Pop art merely sprung out of two buddies' wacky experiments."[15] MoMA's censorship—or "curatorial malpractice"—also called into question how thoroughly the curators Ann Temkin and Christophe Cherix had researched the abundant academic writing on the subject, including the now-canonical essay by Ken Silver, "Modes of Disclosure: The Construction of Gay Identity and the Rise of Pop Art" (1992), which argued convincingly that the artists' homosexuality, however coded, was evident in many of their works from the 1950s.[16]

It was also a curatorial oversight not to call attention to the artists' relationship in that three years earlier, in 2010, the exhibition *Hide/Seek* at the Smithsonian's National Portrait Gallery, Washington DC, had broken the silence on Johns and Rauschenberg, openly exploring the artists' sexuality as it intersected with their work. According to Jonathan Katz, Rauschenberg's guilt and turmoil over their relationship are explored in works such as *Canto XIV* (1959–60); and Johns's *In Memory of My Feelings—Frank O'Hara* (1961) is an obvious eulogy for the relationship.[17]

As early as 1978, in a now-canonical essay entitled "Closets in the Museum: Homophobia and Art History," James Saslow criticized the discipline of art history for the official practice of suppressing issues of homosexuality in art and exhibitions.[18] He proposed that the history of gay art be written anew, openly, as had been done with the history of women artists by feminist scholars. Saslow railed against traditional museology for hiding homoerotic materials in closets and avoiding or marginalizing them in permanent collections—if not outright censoring of the material.

LGBTQ exhibitions were censored by the US government in 1989, beginning with the cancellation of a Robert Mapplethorpe exhibition at the Corcoran Gallery of Art, Washington, DC, in June of that year, on the grounds of "obscenity"—a crusade led by Senator Jesse Helms, then head of the National Endowment for the Arts (NEA). A few months later, in November 1989, there was another case of US government intervention: the exhibition *Witnesses: Against Our Vanishing*, which presented works about the AIDS crisis, curated by Nan Goldin for Artists Space in New York City, had its NEA funding revoked. The controversy was ignited by the essay "Post Cards from America: X-Rays from Hell," written by the artist David Wojnarowicz in the exhibition catalogue, which denounced Senator Helms, Representative William Dannemeyer, Cardinal John Joseph O'Connor, and other right-wing policy-makers for their support of legislation that, Wojnarowicz argued, would further the spread of AIDS by discouraging education on safe-sex practices.[19] The exhibition's grant was partially restored, but not before there was significant national press coverage of the story (see p. 180). What is notable in this case is that it was not an artwork that was considered inflammatory, but rather an artist's text, and one that had clearly been leaked before the show's opening.

The issue of censorship in gay and lesbian representation also reared its head in 2007, when Catholic politicians in Milan banned an exhibition on the history of homosexuality, amid concerns about whether the works on display would offend Catholics and were suitable for children. City officials insisted they withdraw the censored works from the exhibition; instead, the organizers decided to move it to a different city. Thus the exhibition *Art and Homosexuality—From Von Gloeden to Pierre et Gilles* opened at Palazzina Reale in Florence, uncensored, albeit without the official blessing of the city council. (Although the exhibition surveyed more than one hundred years of art, it included only twenty women artists and even fewer artists of color.)

In 2010 there was another highly publicized case of censorship by conservative politicians. During *Hide/Seek*'s run at the National

Portrait Gallery (see p. 206), congressional Republicans threatened to cut the museum's funding due to the depiction of male nudity and, in particular, to a gay-themed, allegedly blasphemous, work of art by Wojnarowicz, featuring an eleven-second sequence of ants crawling over a crucifix, which was viewed by the Republicans as an attack on Christianity.[20] The museum quickly removed the offending piece.

Related to the issue of censorship is the fact that many exhibitions that claim to examine LGBTQ issues and histories often omit transgender artists (and also lesbian artists, who are more often than not excluded from *group shows*, particularly those curated *by* men). This is certainly the case with most of the exhibitions discussed in this chapter. So, what of the "T" in LGBTQ—where are the transgender artists? There are far more images of transgendered individuals in exhibitions than images by transgendered artists. Images of drag queens by artists like Goldin and Catherine Opie, or photographs of Warhol in drag, or portraits of the US filmmaker Jack Smith are somehow meant to represent an entire population; but rarely are works by transgendered artists—such as Del LaGrace Volcano, Amos Mac, Juliana Huxtable, Vaginal Davis, Zackary Drucker, Patrick Staff, Candy Darling, Loren Cameron, among many others—included in major exhibitions. Exceptions include *neoqueer* (2004), presented at the Center on Contemporary Art, Seattle; and *Citizen Queer* (2004) at the Shedhalle in Zurich; and *Trigger: Gender as a Tool and a Weapon* (2017) at the New Museum of Contemporary Art in New York—all of which included transgender artists.[21]

Although transgender artists still have a long way to go to achieve full inclusion in the historiography of LGBTQ exhibitions, gay and lesbian artists have made great strides since the late 1970s, beginning with Hammond's *A Lesbian Show*. Since then, art-history textbooks and courses have begun to examine LGBTQ art history, and exhibitions abound. However, while queer theory has allowed art historians and critics to incorporate artists' sexuality into interpretation of their works, orientation is rarely noted in museums. Activist exhibitions such as *Ars Homo Erotica* and *Hide/Seek* have certainly addressed "sins of omission" by "outing" historical objects, as have new art museums dedicated to LGBTQ art, including the Schwules Museum in Berlin and the Leslie-Lohman Museum of Gay and Lesbian Art in New York, founded in 1985 and 1987, respectively.

Despite these gains, many mainstream (non-LGBTQ) art-world professionals are dismissive of exhibitions with selection criteria based on sexual orientation—they are considered tokenist and essentialist, and therefore no longer necessary in a post-identity world. But, as this book reiterates, there is still a pressing need for further curatorial activism that focuses exclusively on work by artists who are not white, heterosexual, Western males. There is also a need, as is evident in the pages that follow, for curators of LGBTQ exhibitions to be more self-critical of their inclusion and exclusion criteria: the majority of these shows demonstrate a dearth of women artists, artists of color, and artists from non-Western countries, thus confirming the perpetuation of lesbo-phobic, sexist, and racist curatorial practices within the LGBTQ art community.

1980

Curated by
Terry Wolverton,
Tyaga, Jody Hoeninger,
Bia Lowe, Louise Moore,
and Barbara Stopha

GREAT AMERICAN LESBIAN ART SHOW (GALAS)

The Women's Building, Los Angeles, California, USA (Invitational exhibition)
GALAS also held more than two hundred exhibitions
simultaneously in different locations throughout the USA and Canada

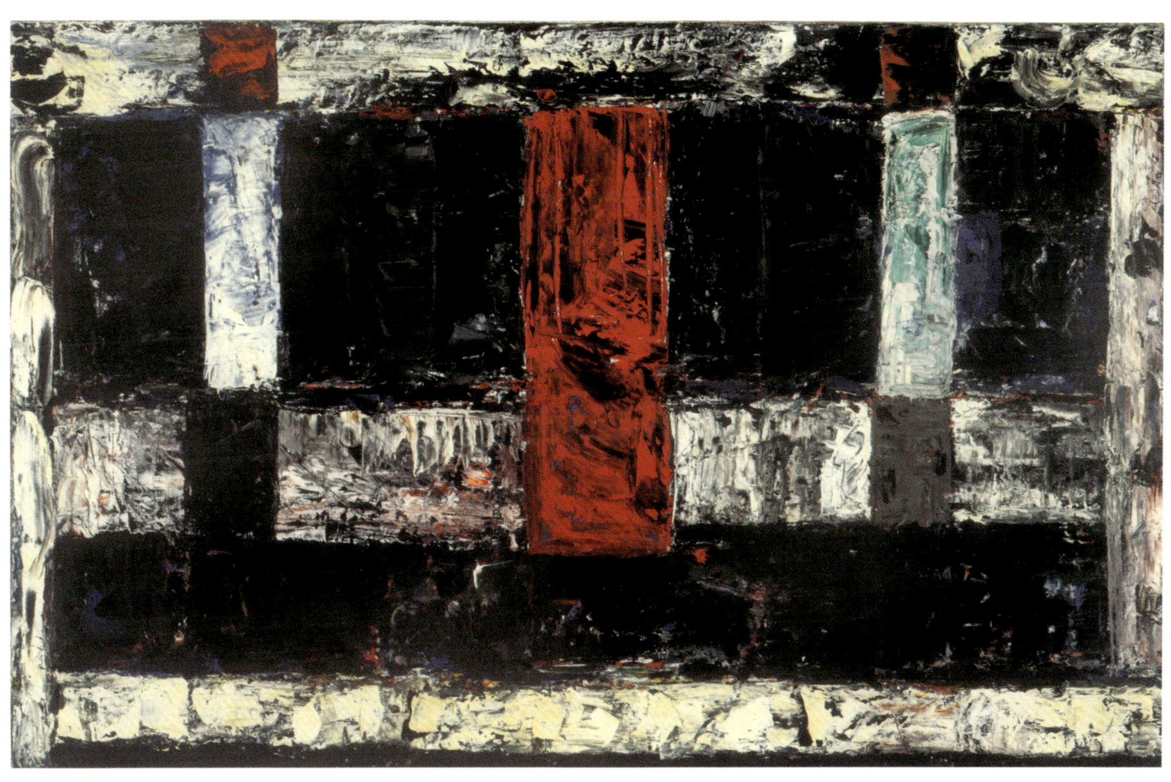

Louise Fishman
Ashkenazi
1978

In spring 1980, a collective of artists associated with the Woman's Building in Los Angeles (Terry Wolverton, Tyaga, Jody Hoeninger, Bia Lowe, Louise Moore, and Barbara Stopha) organized the Great American Lesbian Art Show (GALAS), a three-part initiative that sought to increase visibility for lesbian artists.[22] As Wolverton has explained, "The milieu that gave rise to GALAS was lesbian feminist, separatist, essentialist. Lesbians in general, and lesbian art in particular, existed almost entirely outside the boundaries of mainstream culture…When lesbian artists began, in the mid 70s, to seek out predecessors, they did not seem to exist."[23] The purpose of the GALAS project, then, was "to claim territory."[24] It was inspired by the Lesbian Art Project (LAP), an initiative at the Woman's Building from 1977 to 1979, founded by Wolverton and Arlene Raven, which had given a platform to lesbian perspectives through performance, art making, salons, workshops, and writing. In addition to an Invitational exhibition at the Woman's Building, the GALAS project included more than two hundred "sister" events and exhibitions in different parts of the USA and Canada, as well as the establishment of the GALAS archives.

The "Invitational," the first part of the initiative, curated by Bia Lowe, was an exhibition featuring works by ten "out" lesbian artists: Lula Mae Blocton, Tee Corinne, Betsy Damon, Louise Fishman, Nancy Fried, Harmony Hammond, Debbie Jones, Lili Lakich, Gloria Longval, and Kate Millett. According to the *GALAS Brochure*, the Invitational aimed to "honor and thank ten women, who, through their vision and visibility, have been role models for the Collective, as lesbian artists."[25] The artists included a variety of work, ranging from abstract to figurative. Artists' statements on wall panels accompanied each of the works. Hammond contributed two abstract sculptures—*Adelphi* and *Durango*, both dated 1979—which, the artist explained, aimed to invoke "lesbian places," and referred to "sensuous times and spaces between women…Specifically they are places where my lover and I met, and touched."[26] Corinne and Millett contributed erotic photographs. Corinne presented a series of solarized photographs of nude women alone or engaged in sexual activities with partners; some were arranged in mandala shapes, which she hoped would obscure the identities of her models, and invite viewers to move closer to comprehend the lesbian content of the images. Millett included a series of photographic diptychs of models (her lovers) that incorporated handwritten calligraphic texts—for example, *Hindsight* (1979), a photograph of a woman's vagina framed by buttocks and upper thighs. Lakich presented some neon drawings, including an

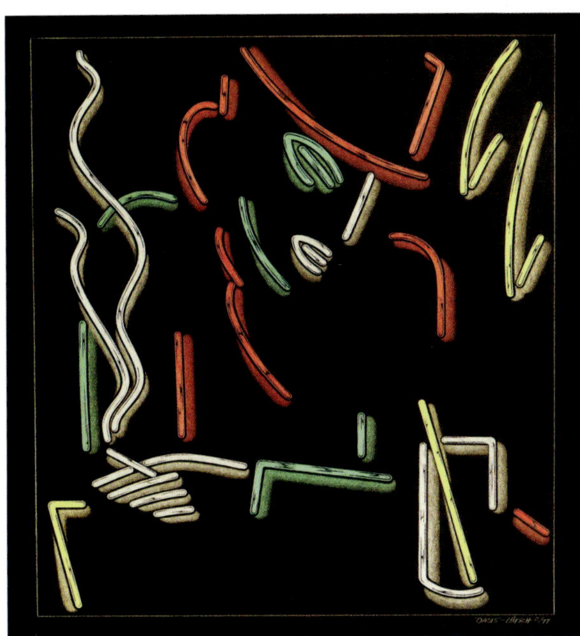

Lili Lakich
OASIS: Portrait of Djuna Barnes (Red)
1977

abstract portrait of the pioneering lesbian author Djuna Barnes, and another, entitled *The Warrior* (1979), depicting Robin Tyler, "an active lesbian feminist, a crusader," according to Lakich.[27]

Also in the Invitational section, Fried's bas-relief tablets made of painted dough consisted of narrative scenes of lesbian couples in domestic settings, which the artist insisted were personal, and "only incidentally (and unintentionally) had a broad appeal to a lesbian audience."[28] The hanging sculpture *Goddess: Self Portrait* (1979), by Jones, was made from wood, feathers, raffia, bone, and shell inlay and represented a large, abstract vagina, which the artist hoped would inspire viewers to reach "into the cavity," "instinctively and without embarrassment."[29] Longval contributed three paintings to this section, one of which was a softly rendered, triple-image portrait of the English writer Virginia Woolf. At the opening reception, to an audience of five hundred, Damon organized a performance entitled *What Do You Think About Knives?* (1980), in which participants used knives to act out aggressions—for example, one performer acted as a nun stabbing meat; another, naked, threw knives at a wall. (Throughout the run of the exhibition, a trace of the performance was represented in the galleries by a mound of dirt with stones and sacks of sand.) Blocton, who in her artist statement articulated the complex relationship between racial and sexual identity, presented a series of colored pencil drawings of unfurled ribbon. Fishman contributed an abstract painting entitled *Ashkenazi* (1978), referencing her Jewish heritage, accompanied by the words: "The hardest part is the guilt."[30] Straight women were welcomed at the Invitational exhibition, while men (whether gay or straight) were excluded at certain times so that the art could be viewed in a woman-only environment.

In the second component of the GALAS initiative, the collective called for a celebration of lesbian culture to be organized by women in their own communities, to raise awareness of "the power of lesbian vision and sensibility."[31] To encourage participation, the collective designed a poster, placed announcements in lesbian publications, distributed an *Inform-Hers Packet*—which explained how to organize a GALAS event, including tips on fundraising, public relations, and documentation—and also distributed a brochure entitled "What Is Lesbian Art?" (see p. 160). In response to this call for participation, eighteen separate shows were held in Los Angeles, and exhibitions, poetry readings, performances, and film screenings took place in various cities, including New York, Chicago, Minneapolis, Miami Beach, San Francisco, and Honolulu, as well as in smaller communities such as Flint, Michigan, and Woodstock. In the USA, more than three hundred artists in at least twenty-five states participated by organizing events in their own communities.

The third and final component of the GALAS initiative comprised an extensive archive. In the hope that the show would kick-start a beginning that others could build upon, and committed to preserving this initiative for the future, the collective compiled a slide archive of the work exhibited in the GALAS national network. This archive was then duplicated and a set was donated to the Lesbian Herstory Archives, the National Gay Archives, and the Woman's Building.[32]

The GALAS Invitational received mainstream recognition in the press—a first for a lesbian art show in the USA. The *Los Angeles Times* critic Diane Elvenstar applauded the exhibition as one that "blasted myths and provided models," while the *Gay Community News* placed the exhibition in the context of lesbian invisibility, and praised

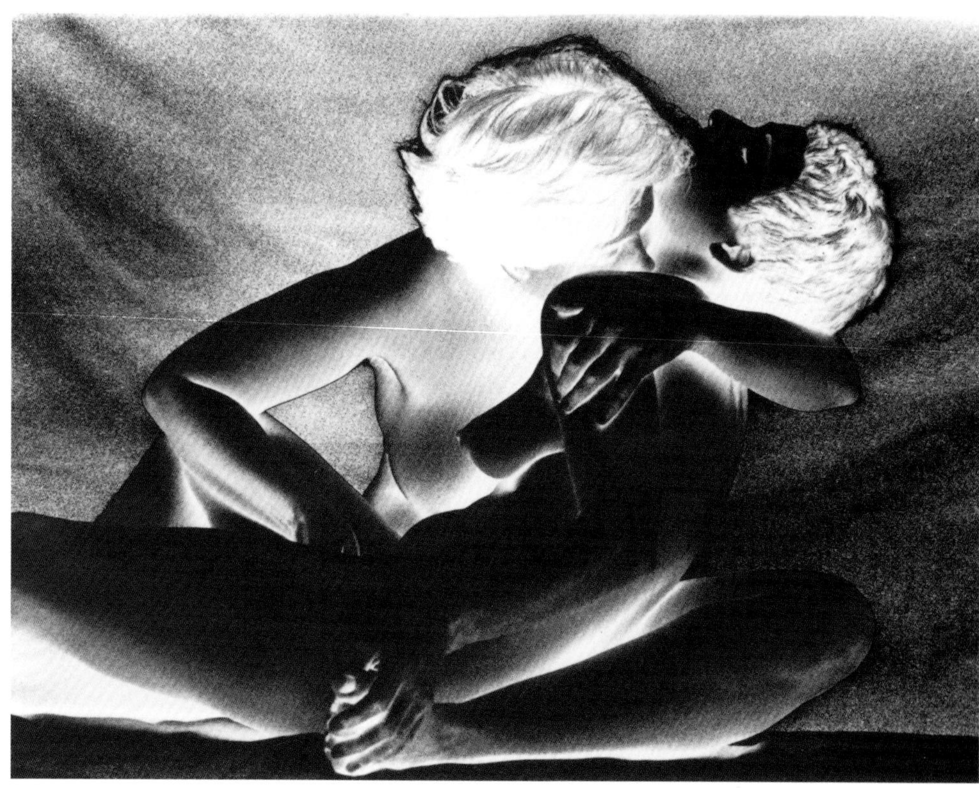

Harmony Hammond
Durango
1979

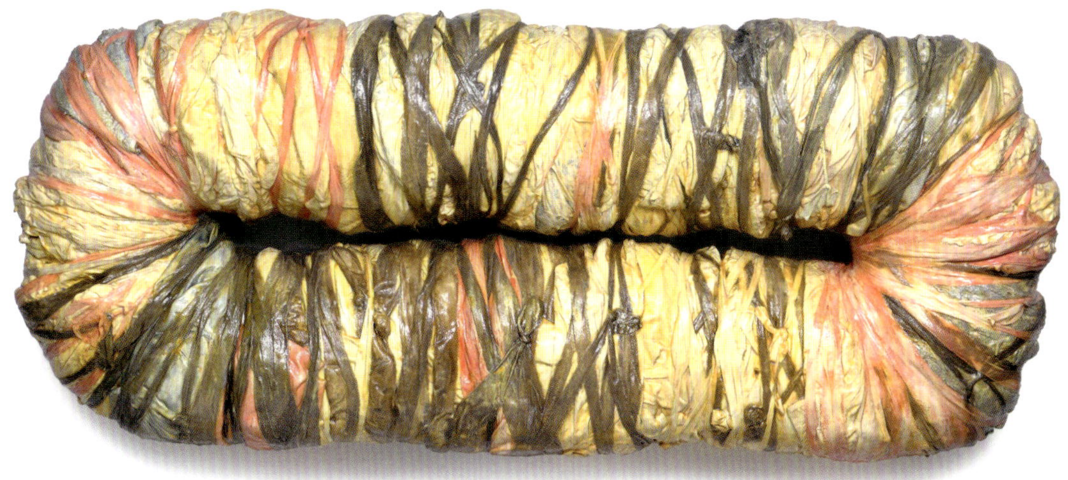

it as a statement of pride and self-affirmation.[33] After first dismissing
GALAS as a "special interest" exhibition, and certain works as
"poorly crafted" and "vulgarly exhibitionist," the critic from *Artweek*
commended it as "a celebration of lesbian artists who have produced
authentic works of art which make a non-apologetic, positive
and determined statement."[34] Suzanne Muchnic, writing for the
Los Angeles Times, called the Invitational disappointing, and
the criteria for choosing participants "contrived." She described
Hammond's sculptures as "insipid," while Millett's and Corinne's
representations of "women loving women" were "sophomore design
projects."[35] In all cases, the critics objected to the selection of artists
on the basis of their sexuality and commitment to lesbian visibility,
rather than to the quality of their work.

Tee Corinne
Untitled photograph
1977

EXTENDED SENSIBILITIES: HOMOSEXUAL PRESENCE IN CONTEMPORARY ART

New Museum of Contemporary Art, New York

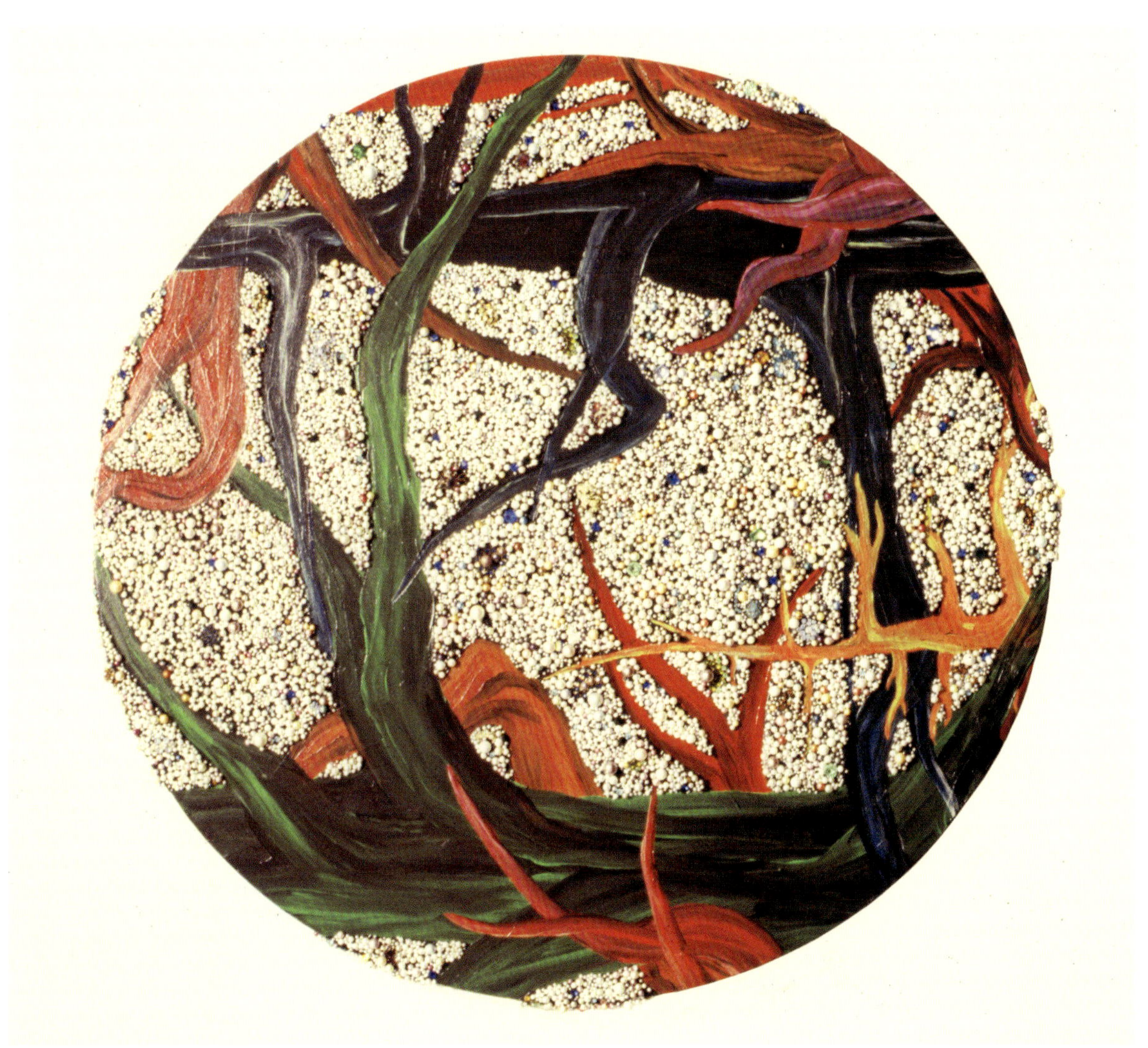

Arch Connelly
Lens
c. 1982

Curator Dan Cameron organized *Extended Sensibilities: Homosexual Presence in Contemporary Art* at the New Museum of Contemporary Art in New York in 1982. The exhibition was proclaimed by the then-director of the museum, Marcia Tucker, as the first attempt by a US museum to reflect the concerns of the homosexual community.[36] It was also the first exhibition to bring together work by gays and lesbians: eleven men and eight women artists were chosen as "carriers," to use the curator's term, of a "homosexual sensibility."[37] It is significant that the word "homosexual" was thought to encompass "lesbian" identity, despite the fact that it is a term that eclipses women and does not account for lesbianism. As Luce Irigaray has discussed, the word "homosexual" is etymologically derived from the Latin *homo*, meaning "man," and the Greek *homo*, meaning "same."[38] The term "gay" is also typically used to describe male homosexuals.

In his introductory essay, "Sensibility as Content," Cameron explained how he had attempted to broaden the scope of the exhibition (see p. 161). He wanted to expand the concept of "gay art" by also showcasing "sensibility content"—works that he believed emerged from "the personal experience of homosexuality, which need not have anything to do with sexuality or even lifestyle."[39] The sensibility artist, he said, "manipulates images and materials that serve as an outward extension of his/her feelings of personal, cultural, and aesthetic identity."[40] Cameron's underlying assumption was that if an artist identified as gay/lesbian then this would symbolically, metaphorically, or explicitly be manifest in the work. This "sensibility content" may or may not come across as "homosexual" to those who view the art, he asserted, "but it does represent a breakthrough in its attempts and successes to speak gay thoughts which are also about other things as well."[41] Cameron noted that many of the artists in the exhibition had been reluctant to participate, not having "come out" yet, and were fearful of repercussions to their careers, so the "homosexual content" in the work was often repressed, not overt.[42]

Rather than including predictable contributors—such as Robert Mapplethorpe and Keith Haring—Cameron thought it more interesting to exhibit a mix of well- and lesser-known artists, and to spotlight those "whose sexuality had not been discussed in relation to their work."[43] Highlights of the exhibition included a series of photostat images by a jokey transvestite team known as Les Petites Bonbons; John Henninger's *Lying Man* (1978–82), a life-size, sewn-cloth sculpture of a man (donning only a white G-string and black combat books) reclining seductively in a Turkish bath; Lee Gordon's series of painted self-portraits from 1981, including *Self-Portrait in Slip*; Charley Brown's

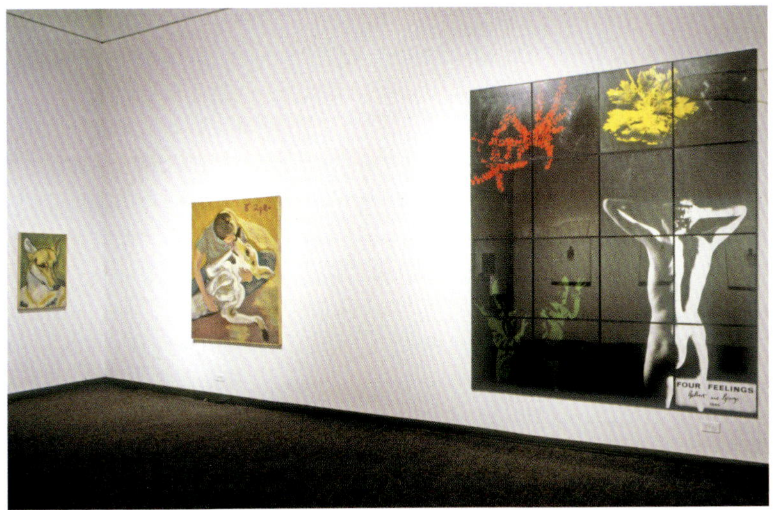

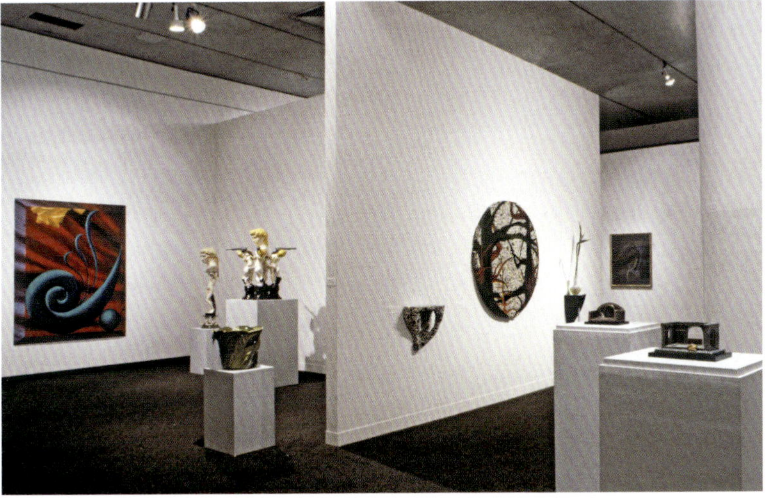

Installation views, *Extended Sensibilities: Homosexual Presence in Contemporary Art*
New Museum of Contemporary Art
1982
Curated by Dan Cameron

cardboard glamorizations of his transvestite friend Bi, including *Bi Untitled* (1980); Gilbert & George's *Four Feelings* (1980), a photo-sculpture glorifying adolescent males; Harmony Hammond's *Grasping Affection* (1981–82), described by one critic as a "big, assertive wall sculpture of proboscis-like forms built up of mummy-like wrappings"; [44] Carla Tardi's *Spring Again* (1981), an abstract canvas that Cameron argued metaphorically embodied a "gay sensibility"; [45] In Fran Winant's *Cindy* (1976), a dog stands-in for a former lover; and Arch Connelly's *Lens* (*c.* 1982) is a campy assemblage involving acrylic and costume jewelry on canvas.

Extended Sensibilities received mostly negative reviews—although it was consistently praised for legitimizing homosexuality as a subject of aesthetic inquiry, and for generating a much-needed debate about gay and lesbian representation in art. [46] Most commentators criticized the exhibition as too "apolitical, asexual, and safe"; [47] others considered the quality of the works on view as "embarrassingly amateur," "generally uninspiring," [48] and "second-rate." [49] Writing in the *Village Voice*, Jeff Weinstein dismissed the exhibition as lacking in liberationist politics, but acknowledged it as an important crossover show because it had attracted an audience of gays and lesbians from outside the art world. [50] (Indeed, *Extended Sensibilities* became the best-attended show to that date at the New Museum.) James Saslow, writing for *The Advocate*, was particularly dismissive. He was disappointed that the exhibition and its catalogue did little to extend awareness of gay sensibilities and at times tended to "reinforce existing ignorance and stereotypes." While he delighted in Cameron's sensitivity to "the campy iconoclasm of drag, glitter and outrageousness"—best demonstrated by Gordon's self-portraits and Brown's portraits of his friend Bi—Saslow was puzzled by the inclusion of works by artists such as Tardi, querying the inclusion of her abstract oils. [51] Above all, he was disdainful that the exhibition "will tell the world at large precious little about who we really are," and that "it challenges few myths, proposes no new ones and overlooks whatever might upset the established aesthetic and social apple-cart." [52]

Richard Flood, writing for *Artforum*, was puzzled by the exhibition, describing it as without a thesis, and as primarily "a vehicle for social and sexual confrontation." He nevertheless praised it as an "ambitious attempt to address sexuality as both creative determinant and political strategy." [53] The *New York Times* critic Grace Glueck considered the appearance of the exhibition to be "inevitable" now that homosexuals were enjoying greater social visibility and figurative art was (at the time she was writing) once more at the fore of public attention. She took issue with Cameron's definition of "sensibility content," arguing that it didn't work within the context of the show and that although there were many excellent works in the exhibition with "outright homosexual themes," there were also many other works by artists who "speak gay thoughts"—these, she noted, were "indistinguishable from those done by heterosexual artists or by homosexual artists who don't label themselves as such," and cited entries by Fried, Hammond, and Damon, among others. [54]

Charley Brown
Bi Untitled
1980

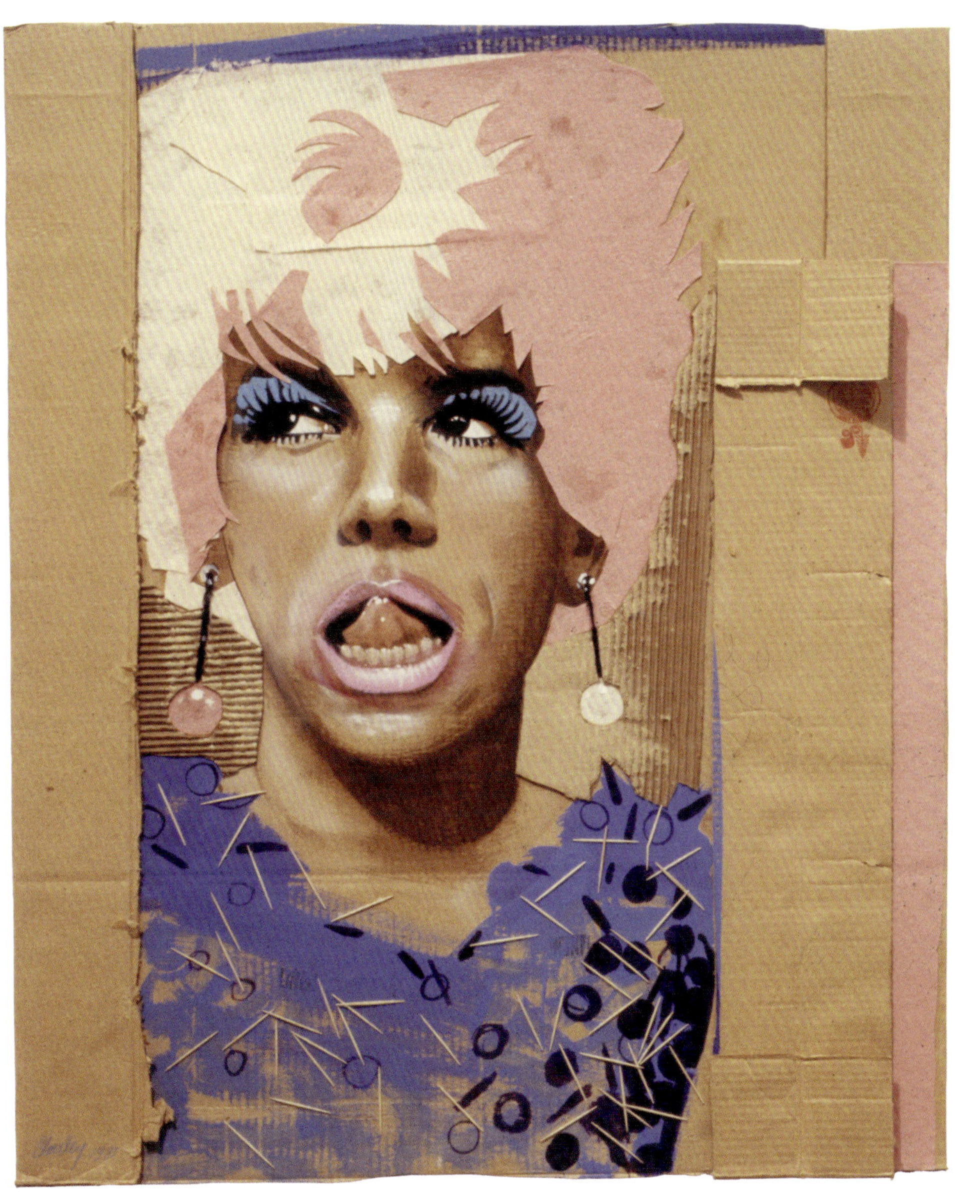

WITNESSES: AGAINST OUR VANISHING

Curated by Artists Space, New York

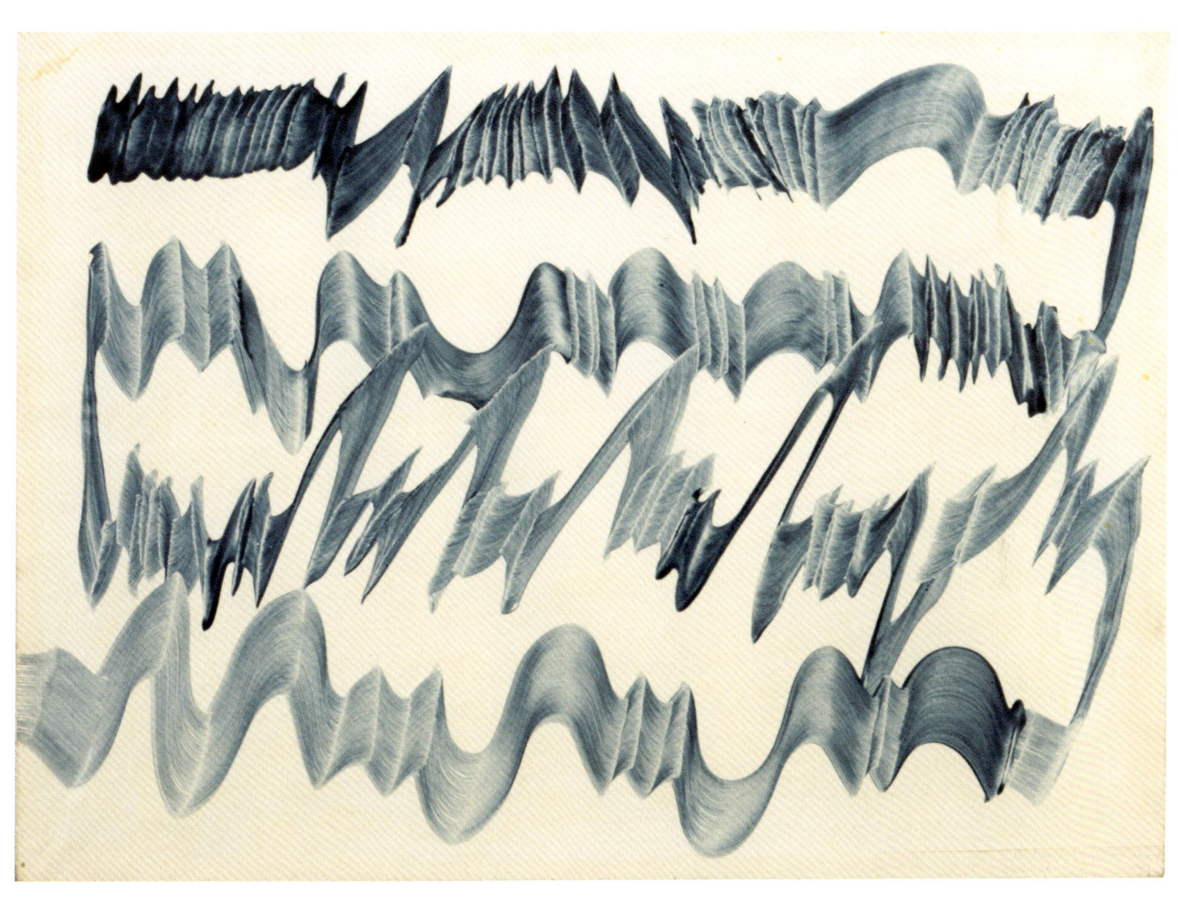

James Nares
Heartbeats
1988

In the autumn of 1989, artist Nan Goldin organized a highly controversial exhibition at Artists Space in New York entitled *Witnesses: Against Our Vanishing*, which focused on the response of New York artists to the AIDS crisis. Goldin selected twenty-two of her artist-friends—some already dead, some HIV-positive, many in mourning—who were then living and working on the Lower East Side of the city, and whose work addressed the AIDS epidemic in a variety of ways.[55] In her catalogue essay, "In the Valley of the Shadow," Goldin said she did not consider the exhibition to be a definitive statement about the state of art in the era of AIDS, but "a vehicle to explore the effects of the plague on one group of artists in a way that hopefully will speak to all survivors of this crisis."[56] Her aim was to produce a show by, for, and about her community of friends and to exhibit work that dealt overtly with sex and sexuality. "I want to empower others," she explained, "by providing them a forum to voice their grief and anger in the hope that this public ritual of mourning can be cathartic in the process of recovery, both for those among us who are now ill and those survivors who are left behind." She was concerned, she said, with art "as outcry, and as a mechanism of survival."[57]

However, even before the exhibition opened in November, it was catapulted into the national spotlight by the controversy surrounding Wojnarowicz's essay in the exhibition catalogue, which particularly offended recently elected chairman of the NEA John Frohnmayer, leading the government to withdraw its $10,000 funding of the show (see p. 163).[58] Artists Space director Susan Wyatt contacted the NEA about the decision: after much debate, and amid anti-government protests, the grant was partially restored—it was specified that the money should be used to fund the exhibition but not the catalogue.[59] Goldin reported that there were, " 15,000 people at the opening because of the anger at the government's response."[60]

The exhibition included works conveying both the rage of those suffering from AIDS and the psychic pain of those who care for them during their agonizing physical decline. Philip-Lorca diCorcia's photographic portrait, *Vittorio* (1989), for example, depicts an emaciated AIDS patient in a hospital, surrounded by balloons, his head disappearing into rays of ethereal light from a nearby window. The portrait is of artist Vittorio Scarpati, who also contributed works to the exhibition—these consisted of a series of extraordinary black-and-white line drawings, carried out during the months of his final hospitalization in 1989, before the show's opening. Despite his anguish, the series possesses a free-running sardonic humor. For example, in the drawing *Who's fallen asleep in his soup for the 20th time*

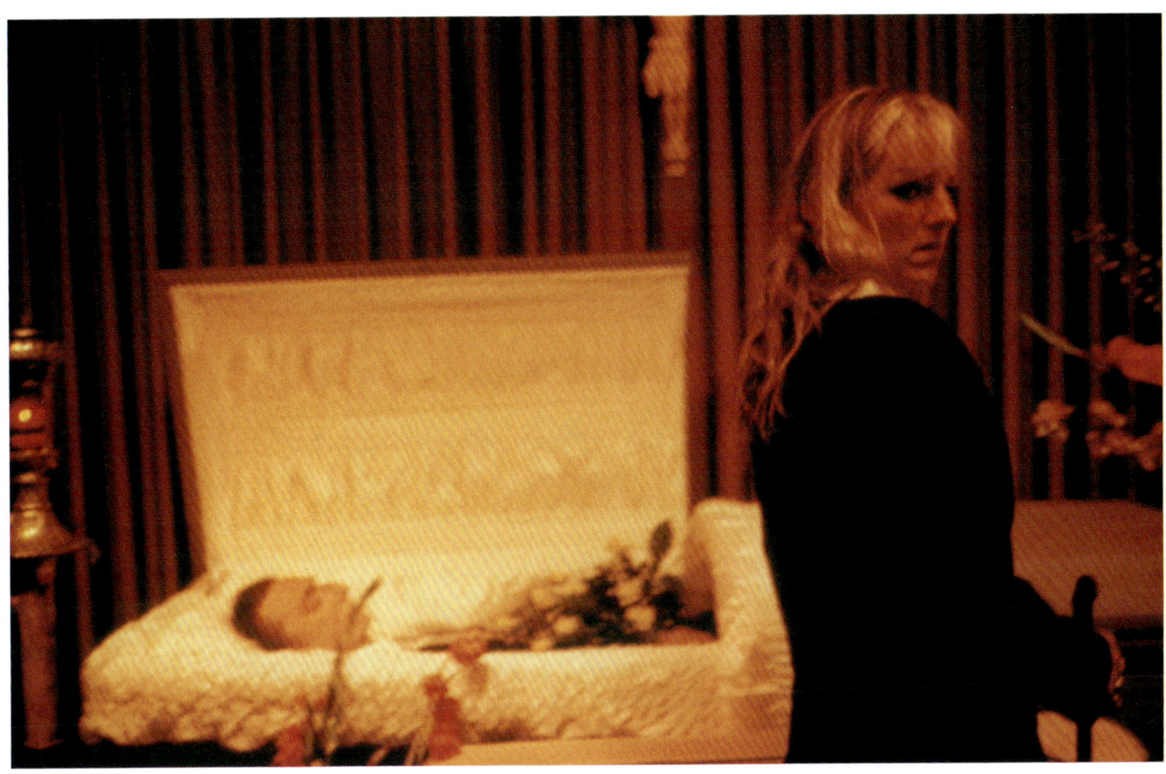

Nan Goldin
*Cookie at Vittorio's Casket, NYC,
September 16, 1989*
1989

(1989), Calvin Reid notes that Scarpati depicts himself "surrounded by intravenous tubes, hearts, lungs, arteries—the deteriorating components of a body racked with disease but still suffused with personal memories and a vivid sensibility. Scarpati's work is at once innocently humorous and frightfully knowing; it reveals him as far more coherent in the face of the general incoherence surrounding AIDS than most of us could hope to be in the same situation."[61] Greer Lankton's life-sized sculptural work, *Freddy and Ellen* (1985), depicting the couple in skeletal format, was equally powerful, as was James Nares's *Heartbeats* (1988), in which the artist charted the beats of the heart as wavy ribbons of pigment on canvas. Other key works included a Peter Hujar photograph, *Self-Portrait, Lying Down* (1976); Mark Morrisroe's *In the Home of a Rubber Fetishist* (1982); David Armstrong's black-and-white photographs *Kevin at St. Luke's Place, NYC, 1977* and *Kevin at Avenue B, NYC, 1983* depict a man before and after sickness has entered his life; and a photographic installation by Dorit Cypis, *Yield (The Body)* (1989) reasserted the physicality of bodies unmarked by disease, and was comprised of a series of twenty-eight small photographic portraits of the artist's nude body—by the photographers Linda Brooks, Ann Marsden, Lyn Hambrick, and Nan Goldin—set on four shelves, shown below a far larger photographic self-portrait.

Another powerful contribution that demonstrated the sense of immense loneliness the disease leaves among the bereft was a series of color photographs by Shellburne Thurber depicting empty, mundane bedrooms. In Kiki Smith's *All Our Sisters* (1989), a banner covered with silk-screened images of women and children emphasized that no one is exempt from the ravages of AIDS; from the ceiling, above the banner, Smith suspended a paper sculpture in the shape of a woman's body—a symbol of the body's former wholeness, as well as a reminder of what the artist called the absent "souls of my community dead from AIDS, alive in me."[62] (Smith's sister, Bibi, died of AIDS in 1988.) Also included in the show were works from Wojnarowicz's *The Sex Series* (1988–89), a series of six photomontages, printed as negatives, made up of underlying mundane images (including a speeding train, a plane disgorging parachutes, a house next to a water tower), over which the artists had pasted circular cameos containing explicit homoerotic scenes.

Witnesses received broad attention in the national press, although most of it focused on the pre-opening censorship debate, with sensationalist titles, such as "Offensive Art Exhibit" and "Art for AIDS sake has feds trying to yank gallery's grant."[63] Writing for the *New York Times*, John Russell, while dismissive of the "questionable taste" of some of the works, described the show as "neither gratuitous nor merely sensational"; "Nor," he asserted "is it defeatist."[64] Kay Larson of *New York* magazine agreed, arguing that the exhibition was "a melancholy memorial not an inflammatory broadside."[65]

Philip-Lorca diCorcia
Vittorio
1989

Kiki Smith
All Our Sisters
1989

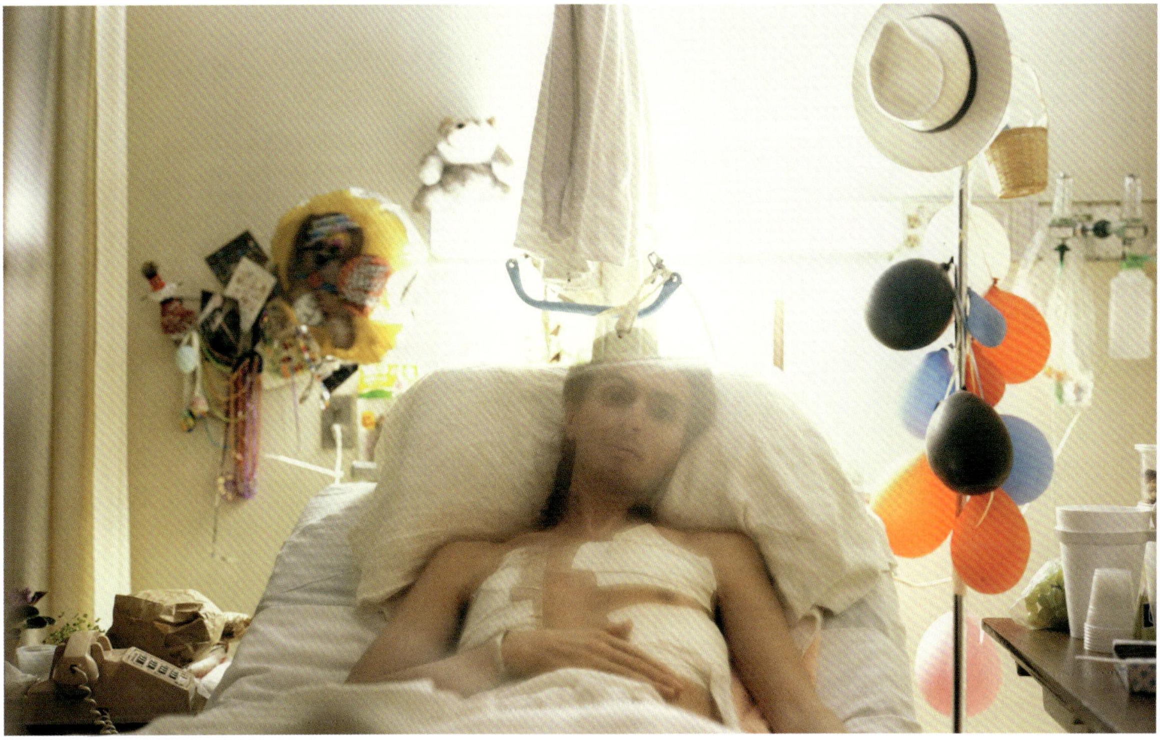

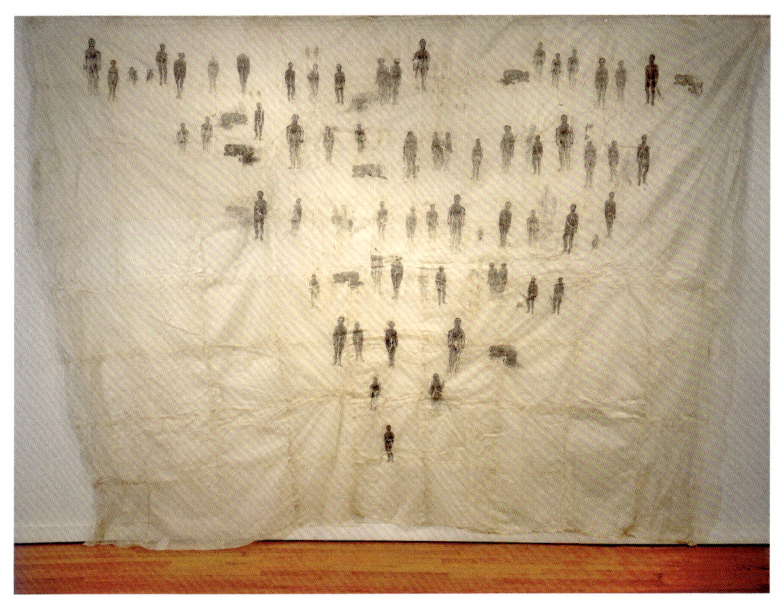

1995

Curated by
Nayland Blake and
Lawrence Rinder

IN A DIFFERENT LIGHT: VISUAL CULTURE, SEXUAL IDENTITY, QUEER PRACTICE

Art Museum and Pacific Film Archive at the University of California, Berkeley, USA

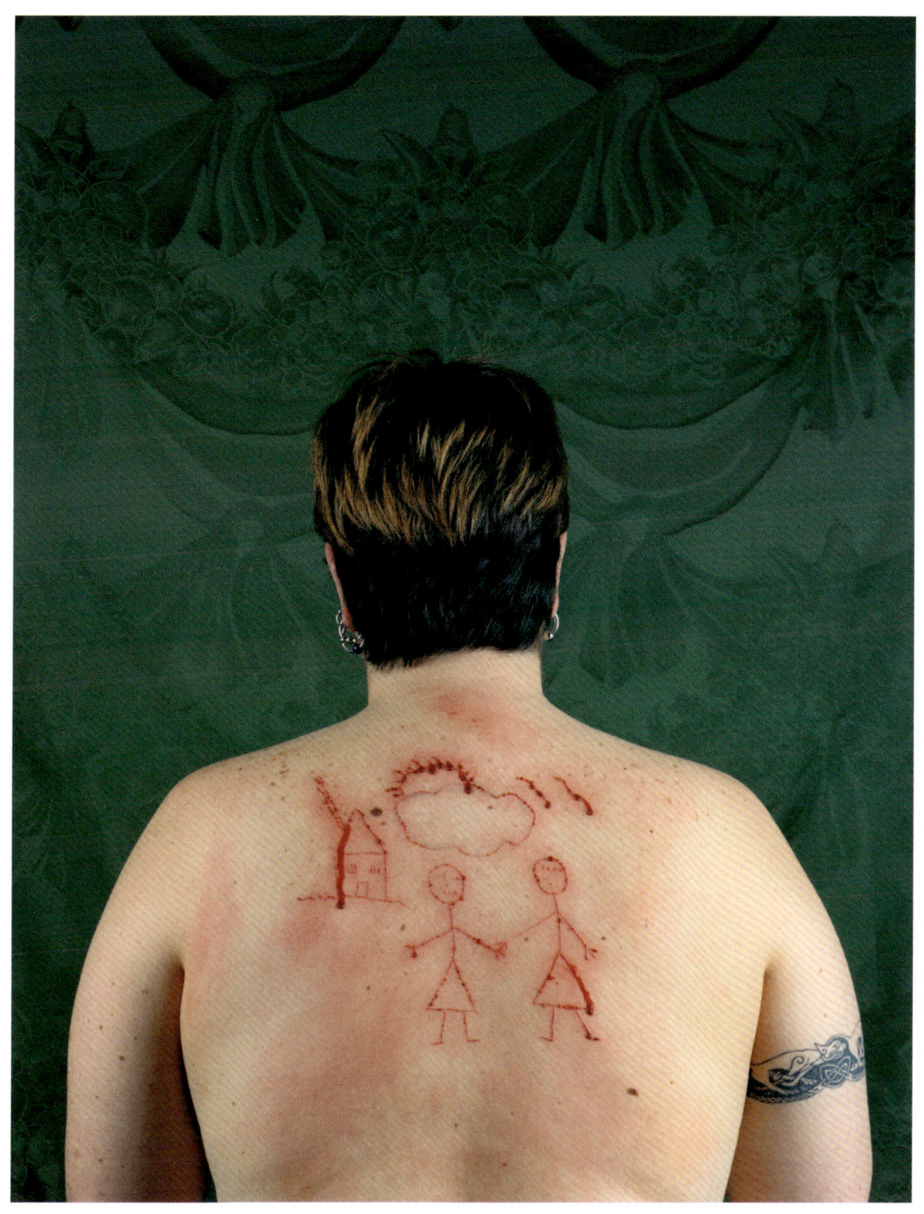

Catherine Opie
Self-Portrait/Cutting
1993

In a Different Light: Visual Culture, Sexual Identity, Queer Practice, curated by Nayland Blake and Lawrence Rinder, was presented in 1995 at the Art Museum and Pacific Film Archive at the University of California, Berkeley. The exhibition explored "the resonance of gay and lesbian experience in 20th-century American art" and featured over two hundred objects by more than one hundred artists (mostly US, mostly male), as well as ephemera such as 'zines, magazines, and record covers.[66] It did not claim to be a definitive survey of gay and lesbian art, but "a gathering of images and objects which shed new light on our collective history," with a selection of works that conveyed gay and lesbian views of the world rather than one that "represented gay and lesbian lives."[67] Instead of asking "What does gay art look like?" the curators asked, "What do queer artists do?" In so doing, they attempted to steer away from "the identification of queer as a noun or adjective and towards using it as a verb."[68] The decision to use the word "queer" rather than gay and lesbian allowed the curators to include heterosexual artists, in addition to gay and lesbian artists, arguing that straight artists also create artworks that "contribute to the cultural dialogue of both the gay and lesbian communities and of the culture as a whole."[69] They hoped that viewers would begin to view gay and lesbian culture as being less "tied to sexual behavior and more as a mutable cultural phenomenon with issues that can be taken up by anyone."[70] For example, they argued that drag is not exclusive to gay culture, citing cases of heterosexual cross-dressing by artists such as Vito Acconci, Lynda Benglis, Cindy Sherman, and Marcel Duchamp. By including heterosexual artists and a wide array of works with no single theme and little overtly "gay" content (which Blake dubbed as "retrograde"), the curators rejected the essentialist notion of a gay or lesbian "sensibility" (unlike Cameron, who had argued for "Sensibility as Content"; see p. 161).[71] As Rinder explained, "If there are such things that can be called gay or lesbian sensibilities—aesthetic or otherwise—these are highly amorphous phenomena within US culture and are not attached exclusively to people who have sex with people of the same sex."[72] In sum, *In a Different Light* was not a show of gay and lesbian images, but instead a mapping of queer practice in the visual arts over the past thirty years, with some historical precedents sprinkled throughout.

The exhibition was organized into nine sections, moving from emptiness ("Void"), identity ("Self"), and self as other ("Drag") through personal and social connections ("Other," "Couple," "Family") to an engagement with the world ("Orgy," "World," "Utopia"). Included in "Void" were images by artists who had developed personal

iconographies to describe emotional states, particularly feelings
of mournful emptiness in the wake of AIDS, as evident in Michael
Jenkins's *Snowflakes* (1990), in which white felt dots refer both to snow
and to lesions caused by the cancer Kaposi sarcoma (KS, which is often
associated with AIDS): according to Blake, they formed, "a freezing
blizzard of infection in contrast to the woolen blankets they rest
on." The section entitled "Self" presented a series of self-portraits,
including a "fabulously tasteless," [73] faux-jewel encrusted self-portrait
by Arch Connelly from 1982; Catherine Opie's photograph *Self-
Portrait/Cutting* (1993), in which the artist's back is tattooed with an
image of lesbian suburban bliss; Mapplethorpe's photograph *Self-
Portrait with Whip* (1978), which shows the artist self-pleasuring with
a whip up his anus. The "Drag" category was divided into two sections:
first, drag as a parody of gender norms, as in Acconci's *Conversions
Part III* (1971); second, the younger artists' approach to drag, which
often involved them in adopting other personas and voices, as in

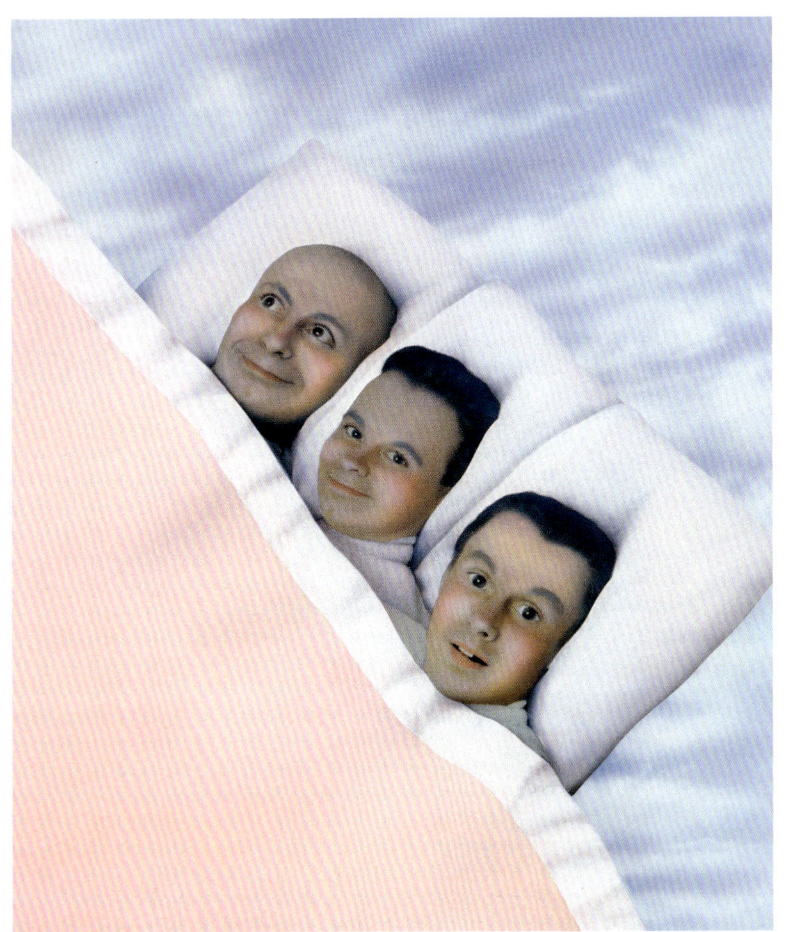

General Idea
Baby Makes 3
1984/1989

Deb Kass's *Altered Image* (1994),
in which the artist cross-dresses
as Warhol in drag, and *Artist's
Conception: Miss General Idea
1971* (1971) by the Canadian
Art Collective, General Idea,
which represents a glamorous
drag queen.

In the "Other" section,
artists expressed the longing
of unrequited love. Romaine
Brooks's painting *Peter, a Young
English Girl* (1923–24), for
example, is a portrait of the
artist's lover; Donald Moffett's
You, You, You (1990)—a light box
showing a still photograph of
a reclining male nude jacking
off—"provided one of the few
literal erections or vaginas on
view";[74] and Millie Wilson's
Daytona Death Angel (1994),
a 5-ft (1.5-m) synthetic-hair wig,
with braiding that resembles
pubic contours, was intended
as an abstract representation

of the female serial killer Aileen Wuornos. The section "Couple" included pairings of same-sex couples, as in *Two Friends at Home, N.Y.C.*, by Diane Arbus (1965), and Nan Goldin's *Siobhan and I: sex (black bra), NYC* (1990). The "Family" group presented works by queer artists exploring homosexuality in relation to the heterosexual nuclear family, as in General Idea's *Baby Makes 3* (1984/1989), showing three men in bed together, floating in the clouds—ridiculing the idea of the "happy family." The works in the "Orgy" section explored sexual pleasure and freedom, such as a series of erotic photographs by Tee Corinne from *Yantras of Womanlove* (1982) and the photo-collage *The Hitchhiker* (1982) by David Hockney. The "World" section focused on attempts by queer artists to envision interaction with the society-at-large, such as Marlene McCarty's matchbook piece, *Crossfire* (1992), featuring the double-edged slogan "Lick Me I'm Sick," encouraging the viewer to play with fire. The works in "Utopia" presented utopian musings—bold and dreamy imaginings of an ideal world, as in Jack Pierson's wall sculpture *Heaven* (1992).

The exhibition received mixed reviews. Writing for *New Art Examiner*, Cecilia Dougherty deemed it "horribly flawed" in that it presented artists and artworks out of context, situating them into a "queer" setting, one based on style and suggestion rather than on histories, intentions, or dialogues. She was particularly critical of the fact that "work by women, especially by lesbians, was the most misrepresented, under-represented, and misinterpreted in the exhibit," and that when work by lesbians was shown, it was only "in gay male terms."[75] For example, she cited specific works by lesbian artists Amy Adler and Monica Majoli, who contributed a drawing of a nude male torso (*After Sherrie Levine*, 1994), and a painting of a gay male sex scene (*Untitled*, 1990). Dougherty also criticized an

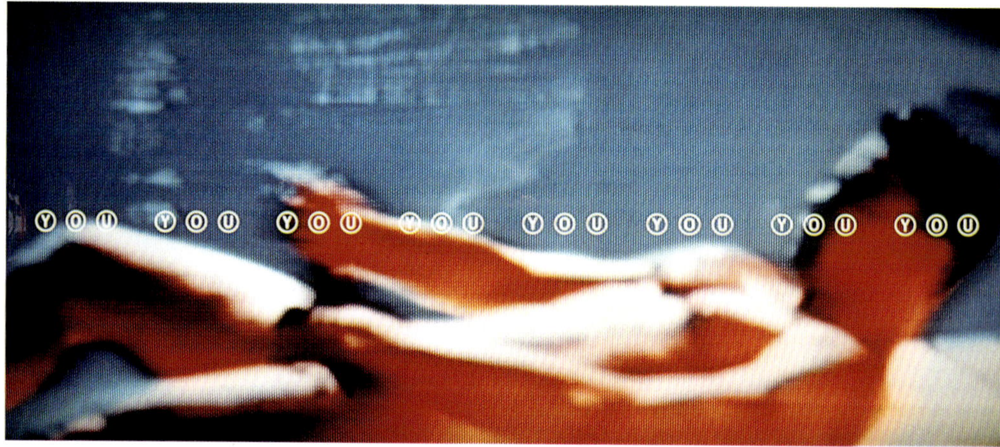

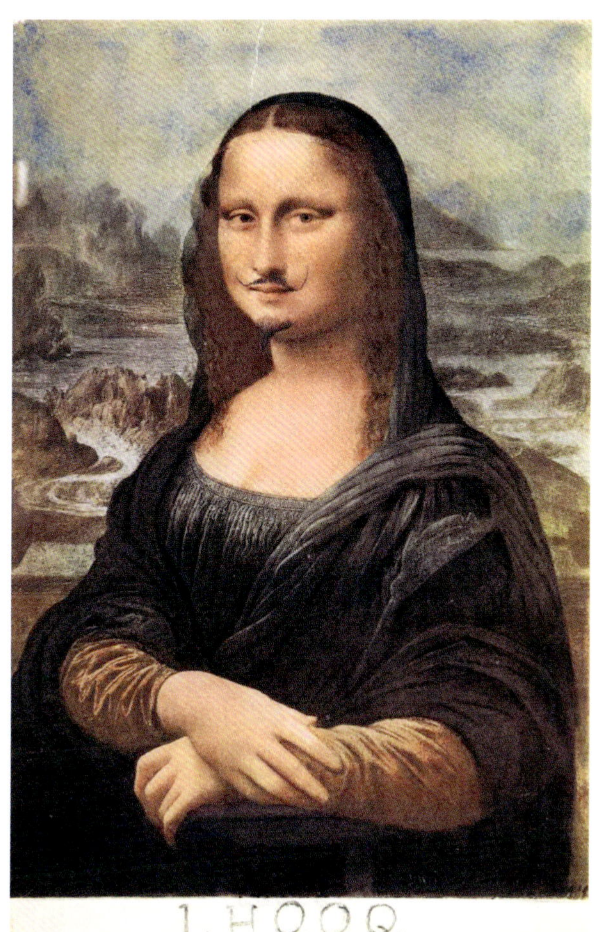

Marcel Duchamp
L.H.O.O.Q.
1919

Donald Moffett
You, You, You
1990

installation in which the works of Judie Bamber, Judy Chicago, and Zoe Leonard were hung on wallpaper, designed by Rex Ray, depicting cum stains (*Untitled*, 1993–94), concluding that, "The work by [these] women is literally placed in the context of the male jerking off. The aggressive intrusion of male sexuality into everything female on the wall subverts a feminist, or female-oriented, reading of the work."[76] In short, Dougherty was perturbed by the way in which lesbian expression became a subcategory of gay male expression, and straight feminism the historical precedent for lesbian work.

Robert Atkins was equally dismissive of the exhibition, but for different reasons. Calling it "apolitical and over-aestheticized," he took issue with the curators' rejection of gay identity as too-politicized or "politically correct" an organizational scheme for an exhibition. He was perplexed that "the stridency of gay libbers (absolutely necessary in a homophobic world far-too-unimaginable to twenty-somethings)" had been replaced by "perversely dandyish apoliticism."[77] *Los Angeles Times* critic Christopher Knight, however, considered the show a resounding success, principally because it presented gay identity as "a living, open-ended question, rather than a deadened, proscribed answer," which meant "you find yourself looking at art in ways you otherwise wouldn't."[78] (He asked, for example, whether Jasper Johns intended his *Ale Cans*, 1964, to be a sublimated queer couple.) David Bonetti of the *San Francisco Chronicle* was equally impressed, calling the show "groundbreaking" and commending it for its capturing of a "queer sensibility" at a moment of profound change, with the advent of the AIDS epidemic and the rise of a newly politicized generation of queer artists.[79]

Incidentally, of the non-ephemera works in the exhibition, eighty-two were by male artists, fifty were by women artists, and less than ten were by non-white artists.

Curated by
Juan Vicente Aliaga

EVERYWHERE: SEXUAL DIVERSITY POLICIES IN ART (EN TODAS PARTES: POLÍTICAS DE LA DIVERSIDAD SEXUEL EN EL ARTE)

Centro Galego de Arte Contemporánea, Santiago de Compostela, Spain

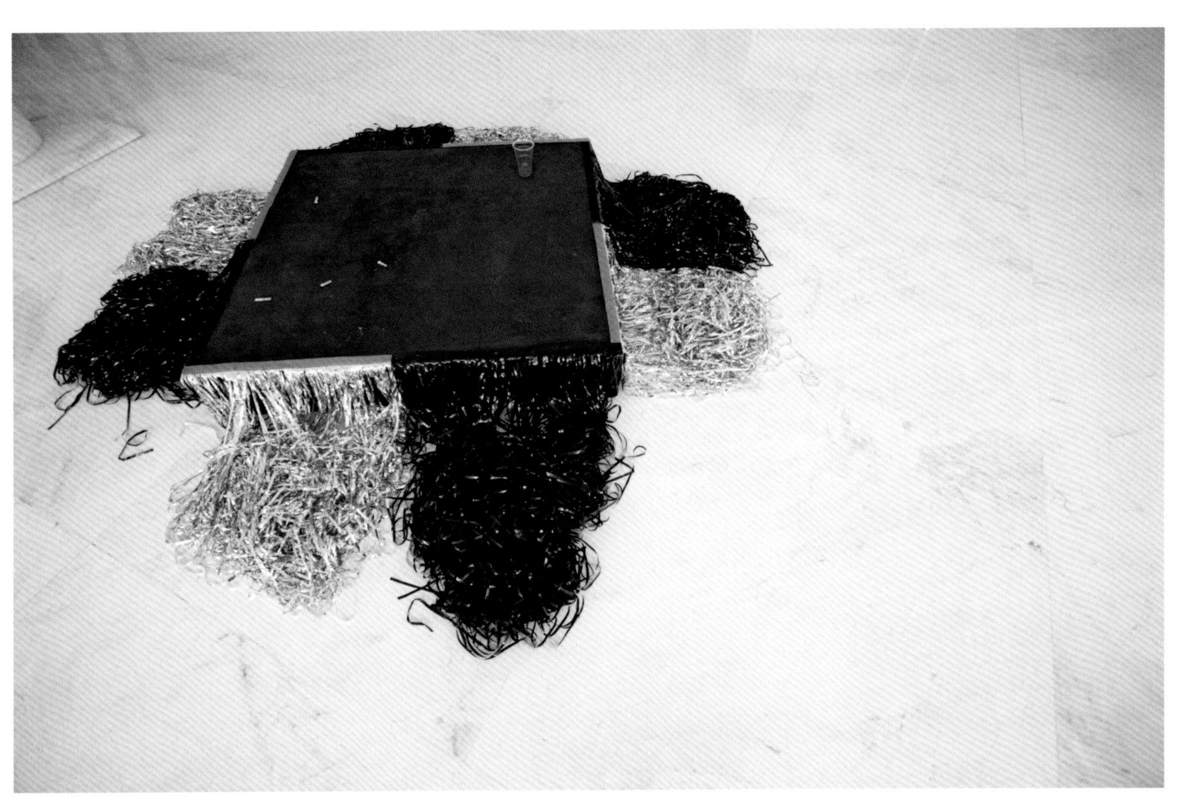

Jack Pierson
Black Jackie
1991

Everywhere: Sexual Diversity Policies in Art (*En Todas Partes: políticas de la diversidad sexuel en el arte*) was a large-scale exhibition curated by Juan Vicente Aliaga and held at the Centro Gallego de Arte Contemporánea (CGAC) in Santiago de Compostela, Spain, in 2009. It presented an international compendium of objects by seventy-five artists (only a quarter of whom were women), all of which had some relationship to sexual diversity or dissidence.[80] All the artists were LGBTQ-identified and all the works were post-1969—the year the curator used to mark the beginning of the gay liberation movement, when the Stonewall Riots took place in New York City. Aliaga's aim was that the show should examine the multifarious ways in which sexual diversity is visually manifest.

Everywhere (*En Todas Partes*) was divided into four sections. The first section, "A sexual paradise? Myth and reality in the sixties and seventies," comprised historical works from the early days of gay and lesbian activism and artistic production, including works by Robert Mapplethorpe, Luciano Castelli, Jack Smith, Andy Warhol, José Pérez Ocaña, Tee Corinne, and Barbara Hammer, with a special focus on camp, hyper-masculinity, body worship, and androgyny. The second section, "The stigma of AIDS and the birth of a new consciousness," focused on the 1980s, with the beginnings of the AIDS crisis, and included activist works by fierce pussy, the AIDS Coalition to Unleash Power (ACT UP), David Wojnarowicz, Isaac Julien, Keith Haring, and Pepe Espaliú, among others. Section three, "Between queer thought and the politics of normalization: from the nineties until today," concentrated on the impact of queer theory (by Judith Butler and Eve Kosofsky Sedgwick, in particular) on sexual identity politics in the 1990s, which influenced concepts of "gender performativity" at the same time as it dismantled strict correlations between sex and gender.[81] This section was divided into six subcategories: "The attraction (and necessity) of transformation" explored the possibilities of gender transformation in the drag-king works of Catherine Opie and Del LaGrace Volcano, as well as notions of intersexuality (with German artist, Ins Kromminga); "Heterodox sexualization in the occupation of public space" examined works that depicted public spaces (parks and urinals, for instance) as sites for sexual exploration, and included contributions by Jesús Martínez Oliva, Tom Burr, and Zoe Leonard; "Communities, families, couples, friendships, relationships" brought together works that resist heterosexist norms of community, by artists such as Sunil Gupta, Pierre et Gilles, Mark Raidpere, Félix González-Torres; the subsection "The transgressive permanence of desire" argued that despite the greater visibility given to homosexuality in

Western countries, there are ongoing prohibitions, against which artists continue to protest, as evident in the work of Monica Majoli, Elmgreen & Dragset, Nicole Eisenman, LSD, and Dias & Riedweg; "Lights and shadows of mass culture seen from the LGBTQ perspective" was comprised of works from various mass-media arenas (music, fashion, design, television, advertising), which the curator associated with sexual dissidence (including works by Leigh Bowery, Azucena Vieites, Jack Pierson, and by the art collective Cabello/Carceller); the sixth subsection, "The historiographical impulse: exploring the past with queer eyes," was based on the curator's premise that "The history of culture has been male, heterosexual, white and misogynist,"[82] and included artists who have pushed back against that oppression by generating images of power (Renate Lorenz & Pauline Boudry), dignity (Henrik Olesen), and demystification (Yeguas del Apocalipsis, Juan Davila).

The final, fourth, section of the exhibition, "Sexual diversity in a global world," included images by artists from non-Western countries (Iran, India, Palestine, and Turkey, among others), where, in some cases, homosexuality is considered a criminal act and discrimination is carried out on a daily basis; artists in this section included Tejal Shah, Akram Zaatari, and Ahlam Shibli. Of particular note was a collage by Tariq Alvi, *The Importance of Hanging* (2008), which shows two boys, with nooses around their necks, who are about to be executed for homosexuality by the two hangmen standing in front of them—a reference to an actual event that took place in Iran in 2006.

Everywhere (En Todas Partes) received multiple reviews in the Spanish press, with one critic in particular taking aim at the overt homosexual content. José Luis Jiménez, writing for *ABC.es*, reported that the museum had received complaints from visitors about "offensive" content, referring to images displaying anal penetration and sadomasochist scenes.[83] Aliaga defended the exhibition at the press conference, arguing simply that "public space is heterosexual," and that he had "sexualized it" with images that already exist in culture.[84] Another issue raised in the media was that the CGAC was a museum funded almost entirely by the Ministry of Culture of the government of Galicia, and one that was frequented by local schoolchildren—who, it was claimed, would now be susceptible to "homosexual practices."[85] Other critics praised the exhibition for its inclusion of artists from non-Western countries, making it clear that "any reflection on art related to these matters will be incomplete if Muslim, African and Far East countries are left out."[86]

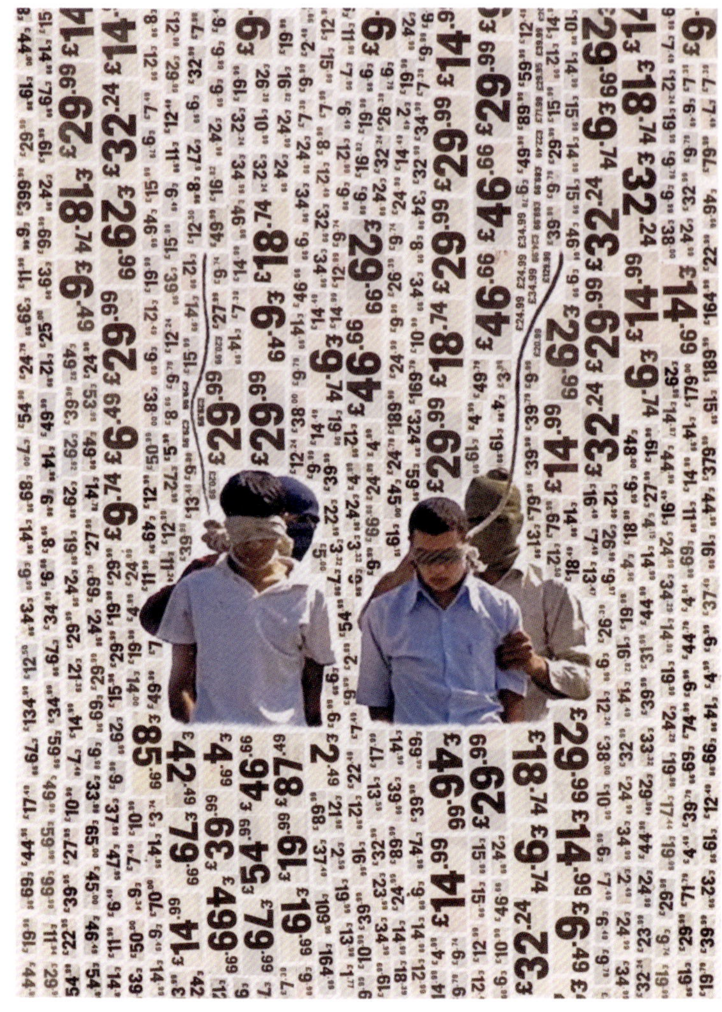

Tariq Alvi
The Importance of Hanging
2008

Nicole Eisenman
Betty Gets It
1992

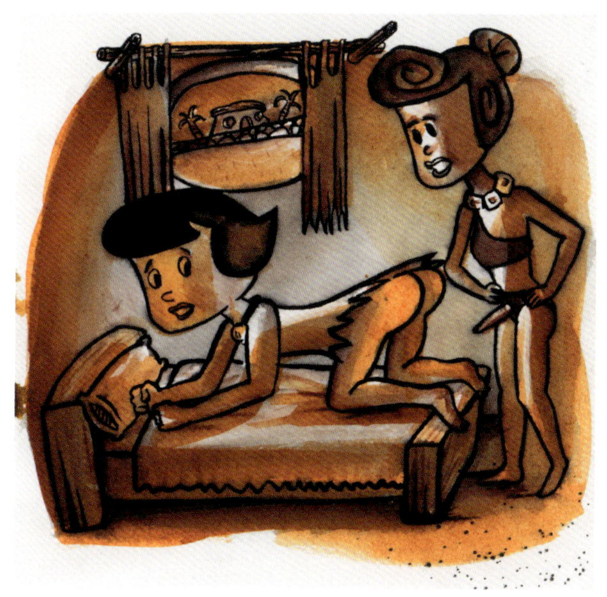

Installation view, *En Todas Partes:
políticas de la diversidad sexuel en el arte*
Centro Galego de Arte Contemporánea,
Santiago de Compostela, 2009
Curated by Juan Vicente Aliaga

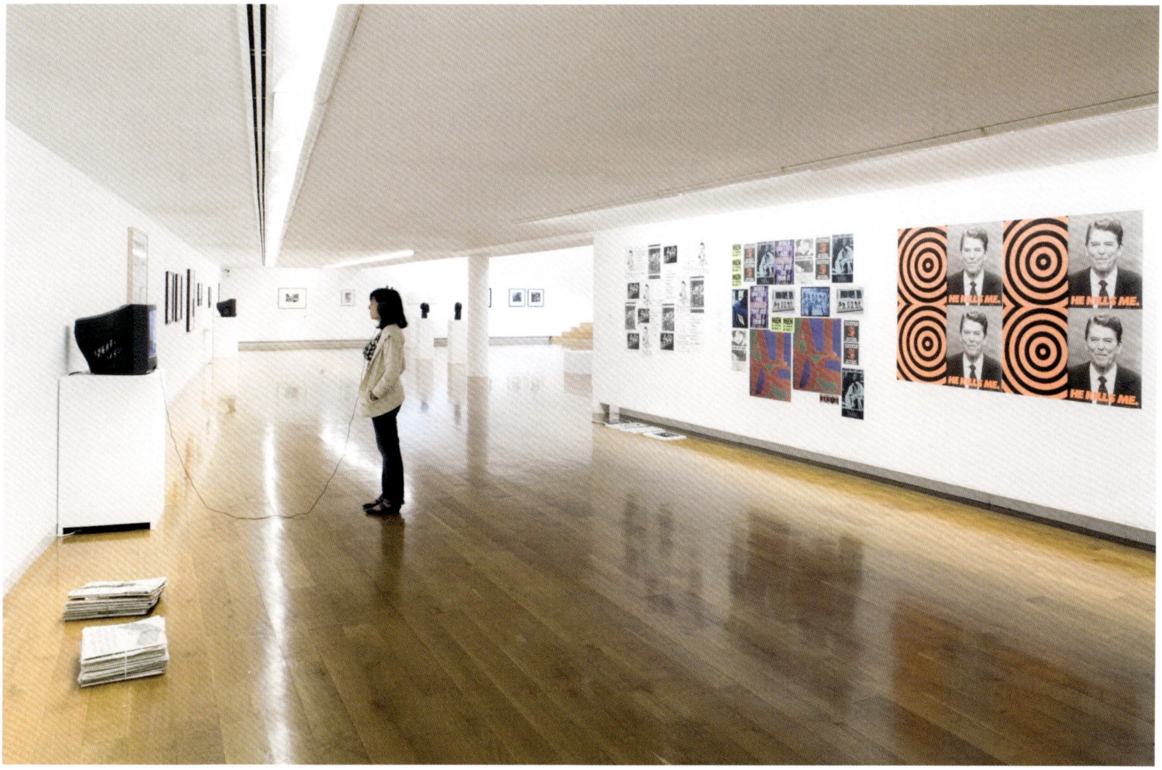

Curated by
Paweł Leszkowicz

ARS HOMO EROTICA

The National Museum in Warsaw (NMW), Poland

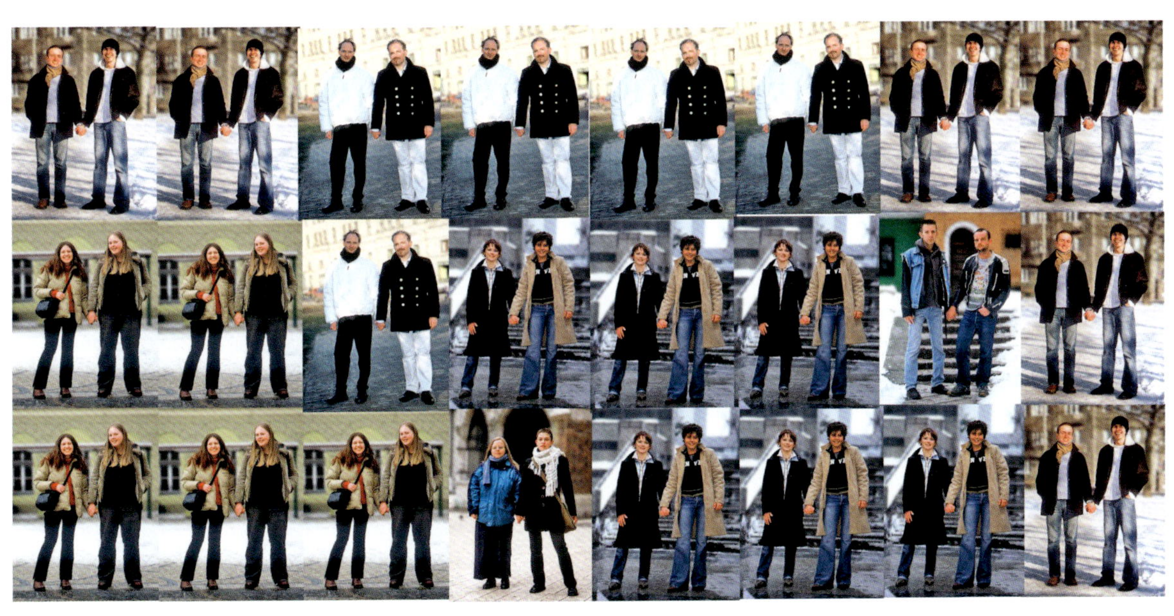

Karolina Breguła
Let Them See Us
2003

Ars Homo Erotica curated by Paweł Leszkowicz and presented in 2010 at the National Museum in Warsaw (NMW), Poland, was an exhibition of over two hundred artworks that traced the theme of homoerotic desire from antiquity to the present (most of which dealt with gay male subjects, with very little focus on lesbian imagery). The majority of works were culled from the museum's permanent collection (only historical works were displayed), while others, by contemporary artists, were curated into the show. It was not an exhibition of gay and lesbian art, but rather a survey of works by homosexual and heterosexual artists that demonstrated the presence of homoerotic motifs throughout the history of art.

The exhibition had multiple aims. The first was a curatorial "outing" of works in the museum's permanent collection, most of which had been forgotten or relegated to storage rooms, or whose erotic content, when exhibited, had been obscured by museum labels. The second aim was a presentation of contemporary homoerotic works, mostly by artists from Central and Eastern Europe (with a few contributions from US artists), which were scattered throughout the galleries and juxtaposed with historical works. By setting the recent work into historical context, Leszkowicz sought to validate and legitimize contemporary LGBTQ art practice. A third aim was to "challenge the heteronormative visual canon" by highlighting alternative erotic narratives and different canons of art and love.[87] Another expressed aim of the exhibition was to "reinvent the National Museum and turn it into an active agent of cultural and political debate and change in the region."[88] As Leszkowicz explained, "An exhibition about homoeroticism radically subverted any kind of nationalist concept, because the notion of nation and nationality is always connected with the heteronormative, patriarchal ideology." He continued, "This was a chance to rethink the authoritarian concept of the museum and the collection. What is in, what is out, bringing outside what is hidden, suppressed, breaking the heteronormative filter imposed on the cultural institution, but also on the concepts of personal and national identity..."[89] He also used the venerable hosting museum as a platform from which to advocate for equality for the LGBTQ community in Poland: he hoped the exhibition would function as a protest against the persistent inequalities faced by gays and lesbians in the country, and that it would help to promote widespread tolerance of sexual difference.

The show ignited controversy in a country in which the Catholic Church plays a major role in public life. Far-right politicians and intellectuals had protested ferociously when, in the autumn of

2009, the museum announced its plans to stage a show on art and homosexuality. In a special letter to the Minister of Culture, politicians demanded a stop to the project, and members of the ultra-conservative Law and Justice party attacked the exhibition in parliament, as well as in the media. For example, an MP for the Law and Justice Party, declared that, just as pedophilic and zoophilic art does not exist, neither does homosexual art exist, while another MP declared, "The Polish culture minister should ban this obscene exhibition, which is a waste of taxpayers' money. The National Museum should focus on wholesome, patriotic topics." [90] However, when the show opened as planned on June 11, 2010, it was received peacefully, and there were no protests or attacks throughout its three-month run. Indeed, it attracted not only forty-four thousand visitors, but also tremendous international attention, with hundreds of articles and mentions in global media—more than any previous exhibition at the NMW.

Ars Homo Erotica was divided into nine sections. The exhibition opened in the museum's main hall with "A Time of Struggle," a section devoted to the current political conflicts around LGBTQ rights in Central and Eastern Europe, with examples that included *Struggle* (1911) by Edward Wittig—a bronze statue depicting three nude men wrestling—as well as more contemporary works by artists such as the collective Blue Noses, whose photograph *Kissing Policemen* (2005) showed two policemen kissing in a Siberian forest; and Karolina Breguła's series of photographs *Let Them See Us* (2003), which offered straightforward portrayals of same-sex couples holding hands (the photographs first appeared on billboards in Poland several years earlier, and were censored).

The section "Homoerotic Classicism" focused on heroic and sensual male nudes from the classical and contemporary periods, ranging from ancient sculptures of Greek gods and satyrs (male nature spirits, half-man and half-goat) to Egyptian pottery with homoerotic scenes and a plastic cast of a male nude by Krzysztof Malec from 1994. In the third section, the "Male Nude" was presented as a foundational homoerotic subject (just as the female nude forms the foundation of heterosexual art)—a subject that was frequently censored as pornographic in

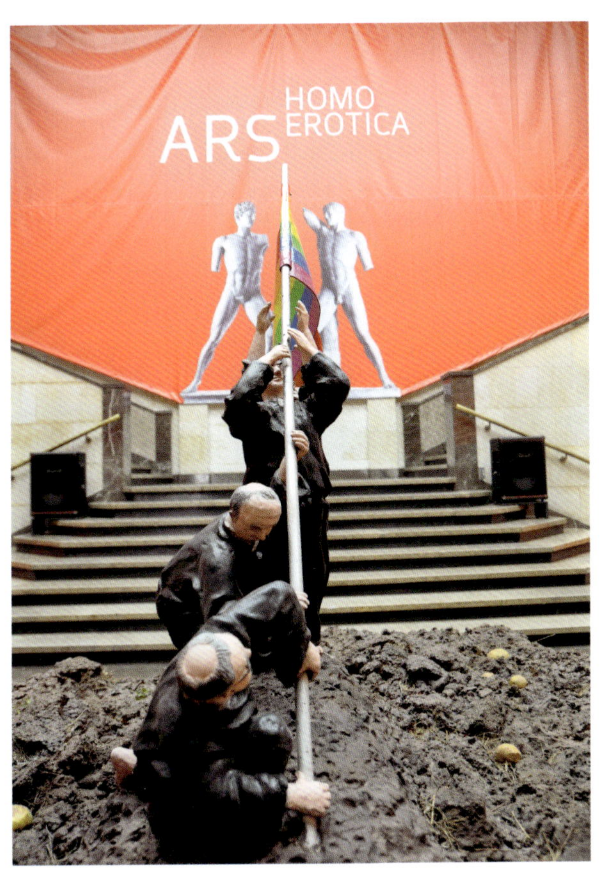

Installation view, *Ars Homo Erotica*
National Museum in Warsaw
2010
Curated by Paweł Leszkowicz

Communist Poland, only to return triumphantly, without censorship, in the 1990s. This section included a plethora of academic nude sketches and paintings from the mid- to late 19th century, as well as late-19th-century photographs of nude boys by German photographer Wilhelm van Gloeden, and recent works by artists Adám Dallos and Katarzyna Kozyra.

The section "Iconography of Male Couples in Mythology" presented works depicting man-to-man physical contact, including representations of gods and heroes from ancient mythology, such as Zeus and Ganymede, Apollo and Hyacinth, Achilles and Patrocles, Hercules and Antheus, David and Goliath; these appeared alongside contemporary art depicting amorous pairings of male bodies by Lukasz Stoklosa and Krysztof Jung, among others. The section "Ganymede" was explained by the curator: "In medieval court and monastic culture, the word 'Ganymede' had the same meaning as 'gay' today and explicitly referred to homosexual circles." [91] This section included recent images of the historic figure (including one by Barbara Falender, *Ganymede II*, 1987, in marble), 18th- and 19th-century watercolors and etchings, as well as examples from the first century BCE in white marble.

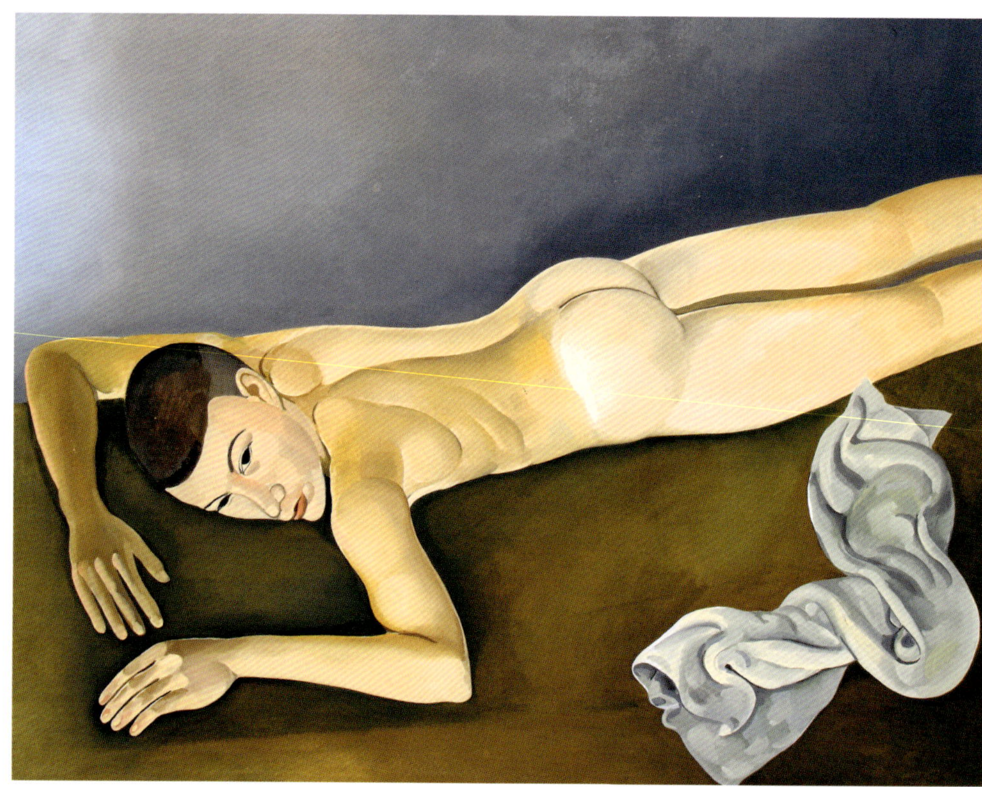

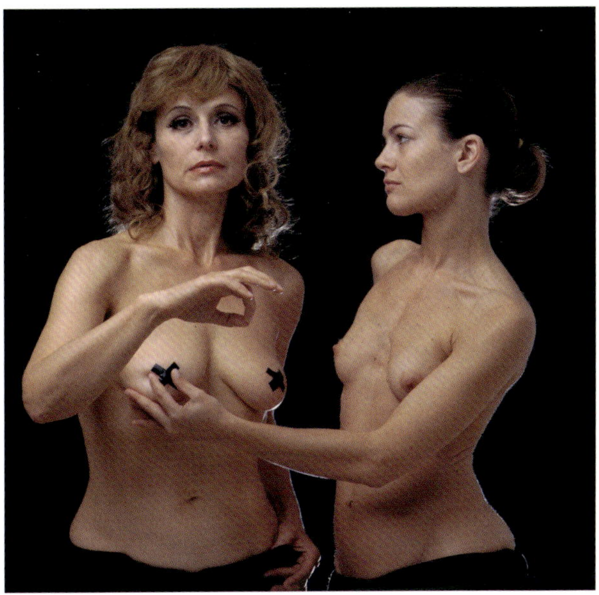

Tanja Ostojić and Marina Gržinić
*Politics of Queer Curatorial Positions:
After Rosa von Praunheim, Fassbinder
and Bridge Markland*
2003

The section devoted to Saint Sebastian, the early Christian saint and martyr most frequently associated with homoerotic iconography—whose representation allows for depictions of the ecstatic and penetrated male body—included 16th- and 17th-century paintings, as well as a recent photograph by Stasys Eidrigevičius and a video by Karol Radziszewski. The seventh section, "Lesbian Imaginarium," featured historical and mythical subjects with lesbian themes (such as the ancient Greek poet Sappho, the Roman goddess Diana, and nymphs), 19th-century portraits of romantic friendships, juxtaposed with contemporary lesbian photography and video by various artists, including Tanja Ostojić and Marina Gržinić, Catherine Opie, and Hanna Jarzabek; the *Da Boyz* series of photos (2009–10) by Jarzabek about the everyday life of lesbians in Poland was particularly strong. The "Transgender" section presented works related to the act of moving beyond and between genders, as well as images of androgynous figures, such as the *Genderqueer* series (2008) by the art collective KKJR, and George Grosz's watercolor *Carnival* (1930–32). The final section was devoted to the "Archive," and included film and theater materials related to postmodern LGBTQ culture.

Ars Homo Erotica received mixed reviews. Polish art critic Marek Bartelik wrote in *Artforum* that the exhibition was "a subversive event, exposing intolerance, speaking directly about complex aspects of sexuality, raising public awareness about the presence of LGBTQ people in Poland, and mobilizing them to act as a community." [92] Julia Michalska announced in the *Art Newspaper*: "Poland's National Museum champions gay rights," [93] and the influential media outlet *Deutsche Welle* observed that "Parts of the show are addressed to young gay visitors who are still grappling with their identity." [94]

Tomasz Karabowicz
Lying
2009

2010 – 2012

Curated by
Jonathan Katz and
David Ward

HIDE/SEEK: DIFFERENCE AND DESIRE IN AMERICAN PORTRAITURE

— National Portrait Gallery, Smithsonian Institution, Washington, DC, 2010–2011
— Brooklyn Museum, New York, 2011–2012
— Tacoma Art Museum, Tacoma, Washington, USA, 2012

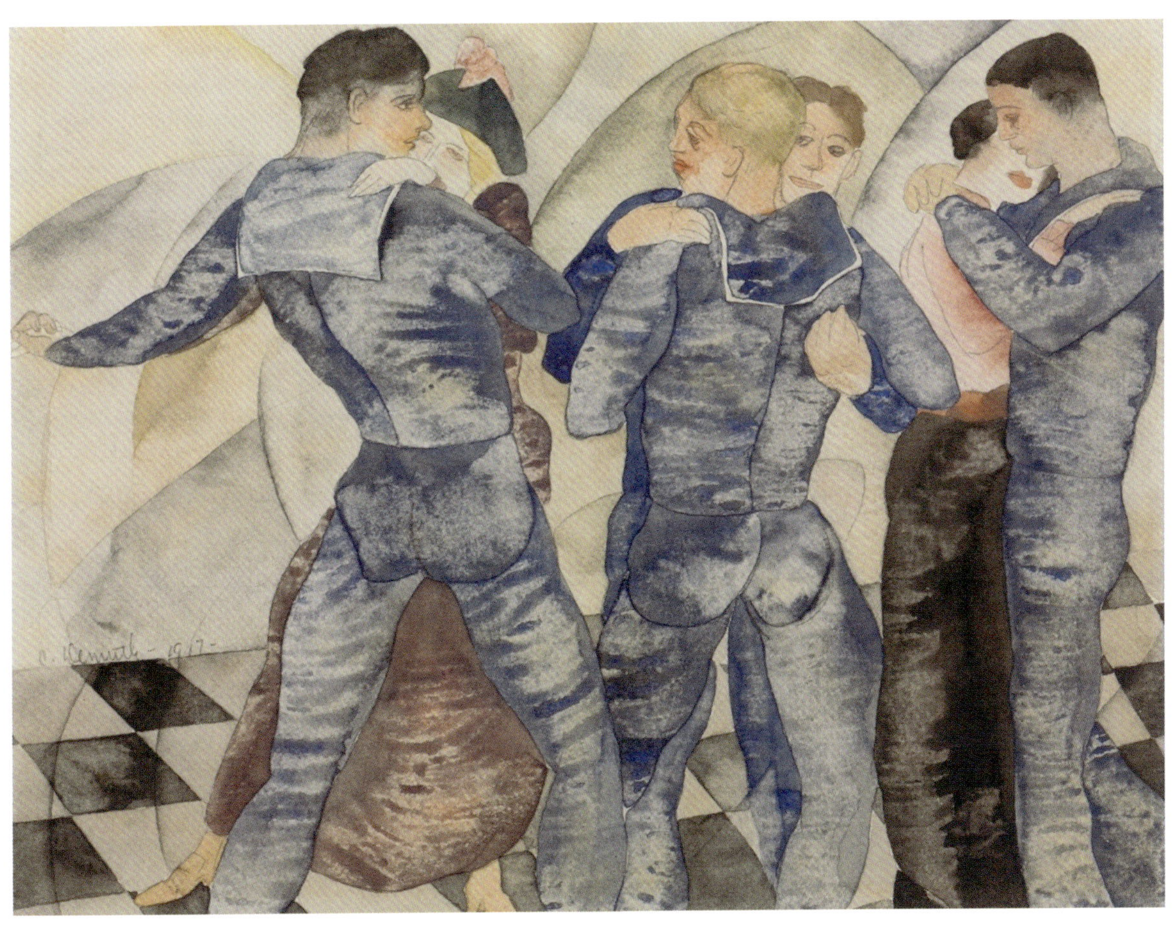

Charles Demuth
Dancing Sailors
1917

Curated by Jonathan Katz and David Ward, the exhibition *Hide/Seek: Difference and Desire in American Portraiture* traveled to three venues in the USA between 2010 and 2012. It was the first major show to trace both the impact of same-sex desire and the defining presence of gay and lesbian artists in the making of modern US portraiture. It examined more than a century of art, and a variety of sexual identities, bringing together over one hundred works in a wide variety of media. The exhibition highlighted the contributions of gay and lesbian artists, many of whom developed strategies to code and disguise their own as well as their subjects' sexual identities. It included gay and straight artists depicting gay and straight subjects, and its focus on famous artists demonstrated how thoroughly sexuality permeated the 20th-century and early 21st-century canon of art.

The exhibition was divided into seven sections. "Before Difference, 1870–1918" included works produced before the division of sexes into "normal" and "deviant," via implementation of the legal codification "homosexual." Thomas Eakins's painting, *Salutat* (1898)—which depicts a boxer post-bout, presented as an object of admiration by a male audience—was posited as a prime example of a covert representation; by contrast, George Bellows's lithograph *The Shower-Bath* (1917) is an erotically-charged image showing a thin, effeminate man looking seductively over his shoulder at a man standing behind him—classically masculine and beefy of build—who is returning his gaze. The "Modernism" section focused on the gay subcultures in cities such as New York, predominantly during World War I (1914–18)—a time when abstraction trumped representation, and artists coded, disguised, and sublimated identities that were regarded as taboo. In *Painting No. 47, Berlin* (1914–15), for example, Marsden Hartley camouflaged his mourning for a beloved Prussian officer with a pattern of flags, uniforms, and emblems; Fred Holland Day cloaked his nude boys in Greek mythology and veiled them in pictorial blur. Other artists were overt in their representation of sexual nonconformity, as in Charles Demuth's *Dancing Sailors* (1917), an erotic watercolor depicting soldiers in close embrace; or in the series of photographic portraits by Berenice Abbott depicting women in masculine attire, including *Djuna Barnes* (1925) and *Janet Flanner* (1927).

The section "1930s and After" explored the many contributions gay and lesbian artists made to US Modernism of the 1930s, including Hartley's *Eight Bells Folly: Memorial for Hart Crane* (1933), an abstract painting in honor of the gay poet Hart Crane. The codes were not always as abstract, however. In Carl Van Vechten's double portrait of the choreographer Antony Tudor and the ballet dancer Hugh Laing

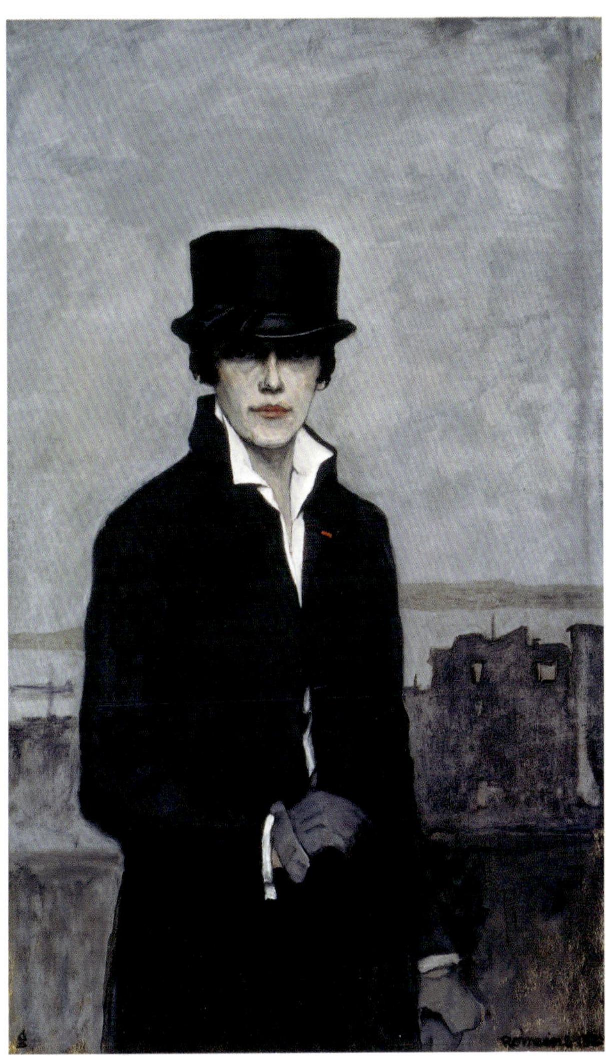

Romaine Brooks
Self-Portrait
1923

(1940), for example, the two handsome, urbane men nestle close together, almost imperceptibly holding hands behind an accommodating elbow. Grant Wood's painting *Arnold Comes of Age* (1930) quietly references, according to the curators, "a gay presence in the [American] heartland." The section "Consensus and Conflict" examined work produced in the 1950s and early 1960s, a time of social and cultural conflict, as well as one in which the US government was obsessed with "subversion" (also known as the "Lavender Scare"), prompting artists to suppress or code gay and lesbian content for fear of exposure: Robert Rauschenberg's lithograph *Canto XIV* (1959–60) and Jasper Johns's *In Memory of My Feelings—Frank O'Hara* (1961) were used as prime examples.

The section "Stonewall and After" focused on work produced from the 1960s to the early 21st century, which grew out of the gay liberation movement sparked by the Stonewall Riots of 1969. The period produced an artistic breakthrough for many, and enabled artists to "come out" publicly. There were several works of art that embodied this newfound sense of liberation, as evident in the self-portraits of Robert Mapplethorpe and Andy Warhol, Peter Hujar's portrait of Susan Sontag (1975), and Warhol's *Camouflage Self-Portrait* (1986). In the "AIDS" section, viewers encountered works that dealt directly with the AIDS crisis in the USA (or the "gay plague," as it was also called). Artistic responses to the crisis featured elegiac, moving works and memorials, including an unfinished painting by Keith Haring (1989); Félix González-Torres's candy spill, *Untitled (Portrait of Ross in L.A.)* (1991)—a 175-lb (80-kg) pile of candies with multi-colored wrappers, from which visitors were encouraged to take samples, so that as the pile diminished it mirrored how the artist's late partner, Ross Laycock, had wasted away until he eventually died of complications from AIDS; David Wojnarowicz's *Untitled (Face in Dirt)* (1993), a photograph of a face partially buried in dirt; AA Bronson's lacquer on vinyl portrait of Felix Partz on his deathbed, *Felix, June 5, 1994* (1994/1999)—the artist photographed Partz three hours after his death, then some five years later worked from that initial image to produce the portrait; and Jerome Caja's portrait of a friend, *Charles Devouring Himself* (1991), painted with a mixture of nail polish and cremation ashes. The final section, "New Beginnings," covered the postmodern period, from the 1990s to the early 21st century, with key examples including Cass Bird's photograph of a transgender individual, *I Look Just Like My Daddy* (2003), and a series of images from Catherine Opie's *Being and Having (Papa Bear, Chief, Jake, & Chicken)*, representing androgynous women sporting dark moustaches (1991).

Hide/Seek ignited a public controversy during its run at the Smithsonian's National Portrait Gallery in Washington, DC, when Catholic League and conservative congressmen publicized their objections to an edited version of a film by Wojnarowicz, *A Fire in My Belly*, from 1987 (produced in response to a lover's death and after the artist himself discovered that he too had contracted HIV), and specifically to the sequence of ants crawling over a crucifix (see p. 164). Congress demanded the removal of the video, and the Smithsonian yielded to political pressure. It didn't stop there. That same month, November 2010, Georgia congressman Jack Kingston railed against the gallery's depictions of male nudity and of US television star Ellen DeGeneres grabbing her breasts, and called for a congressional review of the Smithsonian's funding.[95]

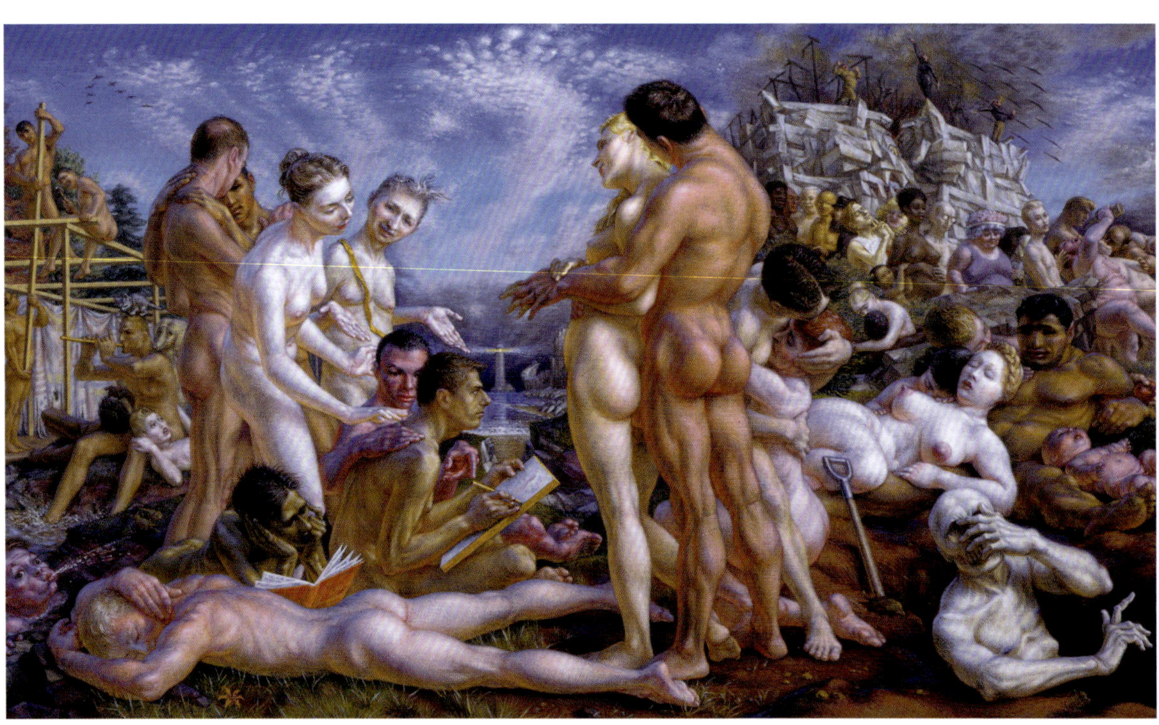

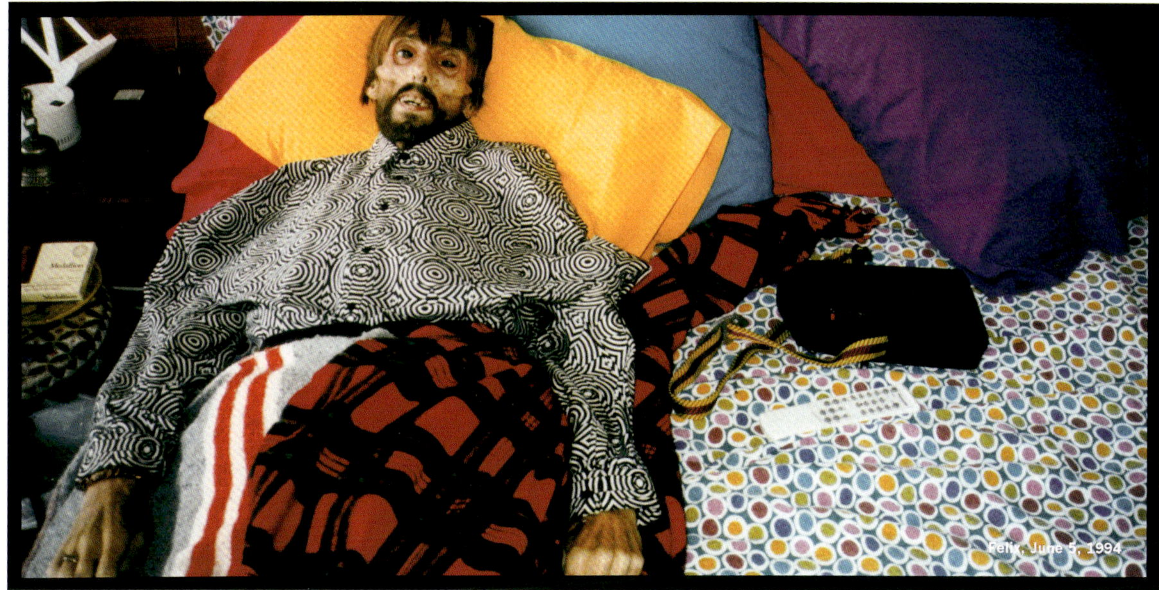

AA Bronson
Felix, June 5, 1994
1994/1999

The exhibition received mostly positive reviews. Roberta Smith of the *New York Times* hailed it as a historic event. Holland Cotter was less generous, calling it a "let-down," and its emphasis on art stars "an exercise in Hall of Fame building, rather than like an effort to chip away at the very idea of hierarchy and exclusion." [96] Ariella Budick, writing for the *Financial Times*, claimed that "Not everything in the exhibition shines, but the collective impact is stunning." [97] Intriguingly, none of the media criticized the exhibition for its dearth of female artists and artists of color: of more than one hundred works in the exhibition, just twenty-one were by women, and only four were by artists of color (all male); nor did they criticize it for the fact that, when women artists were included, it was generally for their portraits of males (Miller, Neel, Brooks, Stettheimer), or because their images were of "masculine" women (Brooks, Bird, Opie, Kass, Abbott).

Paul Cadmus
What I Believe
1947–48

2015 – 2017

ART AIDS AMERICA

Tacoma Art Museum, Tacoma, Washington, USA, 2015–2016
The Bronx Museum of the Arts, New York, 2016
Zuckerman Museum of Art, Kennesaw, Georgia, USA, 2016
Alphawood Gallery, Chicago, Illinois, USA, 2016–2017

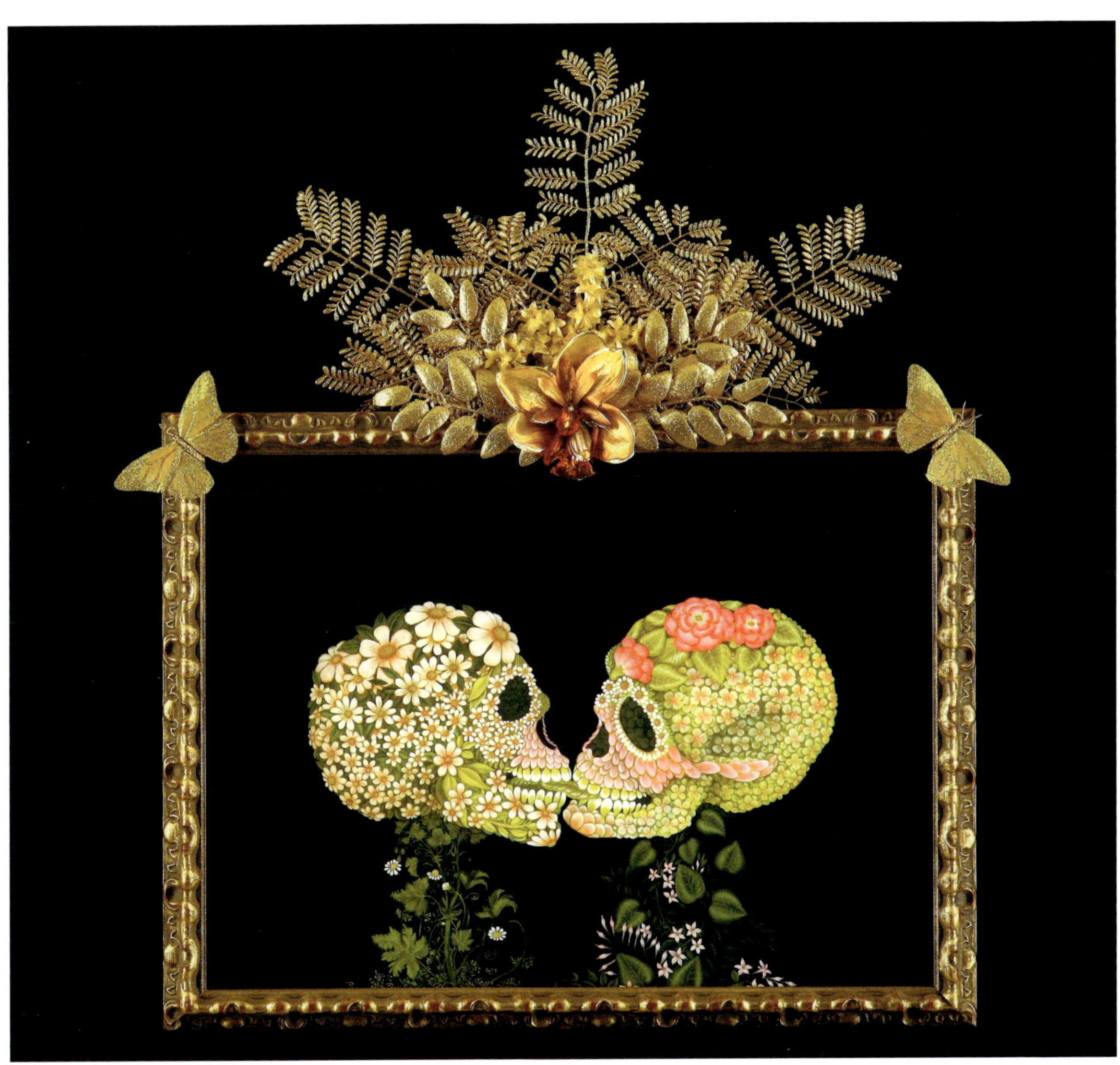

Tino Rodríguez
Eternal Lovers
2010

The exhibition *Art AIDS America*, curated by Jonathan Katz and Rock Hushka, traveled to four venues in the USA between 2015 and 2017. Its main premise was that since the early 1980s, AIDS has been the great, albeit repressed influence shaping art, politics, medicine, and popular culture in the USA. With some 125 objects by around 100 artists (mostly white males), the exhibition introduced and explored a wide spectrum of artistic responses to AIDS, from the politically outspoken and covert to the quietly mournful. (Of the artists featured in the exhibition—76 male, 21 female, and 1 trans—33 self-identified as HIV positive, while 23 had died of HIV-related causes.) By way of its inclusion of recent works by artists living with AIDS, the show also demonstrated that HIV is by no means over: the Centers for Disease Control and Prevention reported in 2015 that 1.2 million Americans are HIV positive, with some 50,000 new cases reported each year.[98] The exhibition included Robert Farber's audio piece *Every Ten Minutes*, in which a bell rang throughout the galleries every ten minutes to signal another death from AIDS—a continual reminder to visitors of the horrifying persistence of the disease.

One of the principal aims of the exhibition, Katz explained, was to ask "why so much art about AIDS doesn't look like art about AIDS,"[99] and, in response, to present the myriad ways AIDS can figure in visual art, from literal to abstract, from explicit to interpreted. AIDS art should not be considered synonymous with AIDS activist art, the curators argued. Many artists responded to the crisis by "carefully and strategically" positioning their works within the art world "in order to operate, as it were, at a subterranean level, so as to avoid censure."[100] Katz is referring here to the fact that during the 1980s and 1990s, any US museum that received federal funding was forbidden to display work that made explicit reference to homosexuality or AIDS due to a legal statute authored by then-North Carolina Republican senator Jesse Helms. The desire to express one's politics covertly also related to what Katz described as the policing coming from "postmodernist criticism at the moment, which decried authorial or expressive work."[101]

The exhibition was divided into four categories—"Body," "Spirit," "Activism," and "Camouflage"—which were a nod to the disease's physical, emotional, and spiritual effects on the people diagnosed, as well as to the impact on lovers, friends, and families of those living with HIV/AIDS, or of those who have simply had to navigate the world and the possibility of infection. The first section, "Body," concentrated on the devastating effects AIDS has on the human body, presenting works such as Ross Bleckner's painting *Brain Rust* (2013), which evoked a foggy scan of a brain, weakened

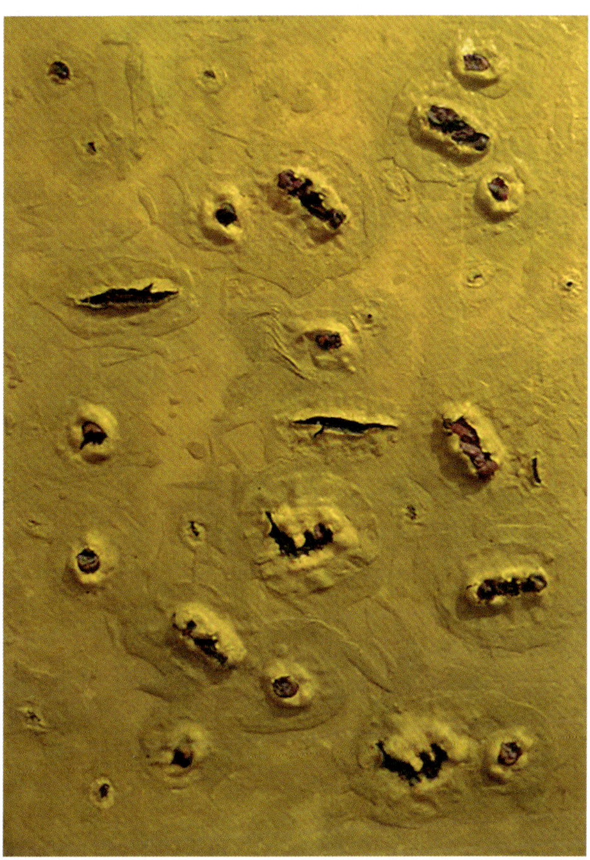

Izhar Patkin
Unveiling of a Modern Chastity
1981

by the ravages of HIV or the experimental medicines used to treat it; a photographic self-portrait by David Lebe, *Morning Ritual 29* (1994), depicting the artist injecting his morning medicine; and Keith Haring's bronze sculpture, *Altarpiece* (1990)—the artist's last work before succumbing to AIDS—which resembled a church altarpiece, and featured an image of a crying mother holding an infant, whose tears fall onto crowds below. "Spirit," the show's second section, featured the first AIDS work (according to Katz) —a painting by Izhar Patkin, entitled *Unveiling of a Modern Chastity* (1981), a large yellow canvas with huge, gaping rust-colored "wounds" referring to AIDS-related Kaposi sarcoma (KS) lesions. This section also presented, among other works, Shimon Attie's *Untitled Memory (Projection of Axel H.)* (1998), a photograph of a bed with the ghostly projected image of Axel H., a friend of the artist who had died of AIDS; Tino Rodríguez's *Eternal Lovers* (2010), an oil on wood painting depicting two colorful skulls kissing; Martin Wong's painting *Iglesia Pentecostal Mansion de Luz* (1985), in which the shadowy facade of a Pentecostal church is painted in blood red and shuttered with locks; and a famous Mapplethorpe photograph, *Untitled (Flowers)* (1983), taken a year after AIDS had been given a name, which shows a monstrously enlarged shadow of wilting lilies looming like an ominous specter.

The largest and strongest section of the exhibition, "Activism," denoted works that were overtly political—including the ACT UP/Gran Fury collective's famous 1987 window installation at the New Museum of Contemporary Art, New York, *Let the Record Show*, which was re-created in the exhibition with the same pink triangle and the words "Silence = Death" in neon;[102] a display cabinet full of objects from Visual AIDS—a New York-based organization that supports HIV-positive artists and uses art to fight AIDS—which included tote bags, stickers, pins, broadsides, among other objects; Kiki Smith's *Red Spill* (1996), a memorial to her sister who died of AIDS in 1988, which took the form of dozens of blood platelet-like glass discs strewn across the floor; Karen Finley's interactive work *Written in Sand* (1992), an open, sand-filled steamer trunk with instructions for viewers to write the name of someone they have lost to AIDS in the sand, then gently erase it. This section also presented a suite of self-portraits by Kia Labeija, the only female HIV-positive artist of color in the show; Charles LeDray's *Untitled* (1991), featuring a teddy bear dressed in a white funeral suit, lying in a tiny, silk-lined coffin; and Robert Sherer's *Sweet Williams* (2013), a delicate painting of cut flowers, painted using HIV-negative and HIV-positive blood, and named in memory of all the Bills, Wills, and Williams the artist had known who died of the disease.

The smallest and weakest section in the show, "Camouflage," featured artists such as Ray Navarro and Julie Tolentino who, according to the wall text, "bury references to AIDS or sexuality so thoroughly that they often claimed that their work had no personal or expressive meanings at all." In *Untitled (Buffalo)* (1988–89), for example, David Wojnarowicz photographed a diorama of buffalo being herded off a cliff. On the surface, it does not appear to be about AIDS. But for the artist, who succumbed to the disease in 1992, the image served as "a chilling metaphor of the politics of AIDS in the US in the late 1980s" and as an expression of his "rage, desperation and helplessness," the label explained.

Art AIDS America garnered both praise and criticism. The *Seattle Times* called the Tacoma Art Museum's version of the exhibition "a moving new show," and Seattle's alternative arts and culture newspaper *The Stranger* designated it "an epic and a national treasure"—a "masterpiece," albeit "messy" and "not perfect." [103] However, the Tacoma edition also sparked public protests about the lack of racial diversity in the exhibition (of the 107 artists on display only 5 were African American). While subsequent presentations of the exhibition attempted to address this omission by featuring additional black artists, the controversy continued throughout the show's run. For instance, Jared Quinton, writing for *Art21 Magazine*, criticized the Bronx Museum's version for its "whitewashing," but went on to praise it overall for having "reveal[ed] a community that harnessed the power of art to tell untold stories and to fight, even in small ways, for the dignity, exposure, and basic services it was denied." [104] Deborah Solomon of WNYC radio called the Bronx Museum's version of *Art AIDS America* "a landmark show...a big, bold courageous show [that] deserves enormous attention," and one that "alters art history." [105] The *Atlanta Journal– Constitution* called the Zuckerman Museum of Art's edition "a powerful, harrowing survey" that was "unapologetically raw, sexually provocative and not for the pearl-clutching prone." [106] Yet protests persisted—in this instance, however, it related to the exhibition's content, when State Representative Earl Ehrhart claimed, for example, that "a fully loaded porta-potty would be better artistic expression," and State Senator Lindsey Tippins called the art "trash." [107] For Chicago's Alphawood Gallery, the exhibition was renamed *Art AIDS America Chicago* and was praised by the *Chicago Reader* as "astonishing in its breadth" and for its display of the physiological horror of AIDS as "unflinching and honest"; [108] others criticized it as "didactic," [109] and asked "Where are the women of color? Or the women? Or the people of color?" [110] *New Art Examiner* argued that by concentrating mostly on the experiences of white gay males, the exhibition "under-represented the comprehensive damage inflicted by this disease." [111]

Installation view, *Art AIDS America*
2015–17
Curated by Jonathan Katz and Rock Hushka, ACT UP/Gran Fury collective

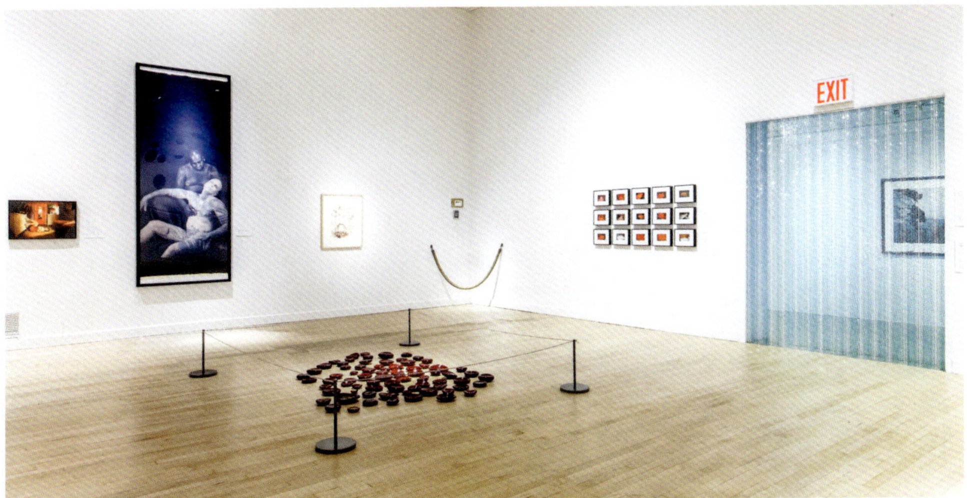

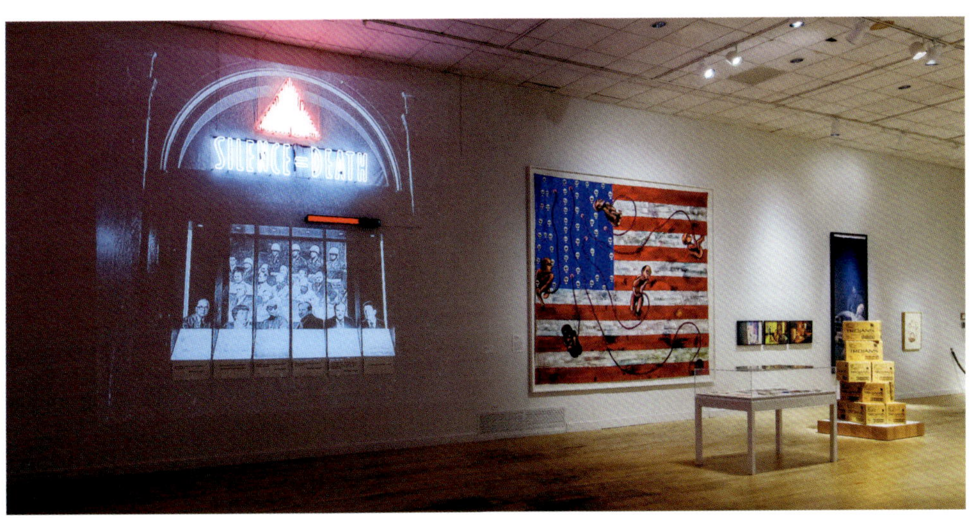

5. A CALL TO ARMS: STRATEGIES FOR CHANGE

"As the feminist critic and philosopher Gayatri Spivak constantly reminds us, we must always acknowledge not only who we are, but *where* we are, that is, where we are positioned in relation to hierarchies, and to questions of authority and privilege."[1]

Marcia Tucker

This book is, in part, a celebration of curatorial activists, and of the stellar exhibitions they have held to address the sexism, racism, homo-/lesbo-phobia, and Western-centrism that is endemic in the art world. As is evident in the preceding pages, many curators are working tirelessly to develop strategies to counter the persistent under-representation, silencing, and erasure of numerous artists throughout the world. Theirs is not affirmative-action curating, it is *smart* curating. Theirs is a practice rooted in ethics, and, as such, their exhibitions function as curatorial correctives to the exclusion of Other artists from the master narratives of art history and the contemporary art scene itself. These curators have taken immense strides forward in challenging hierarchies and assumptions, initiating debate, and circulating new knowledge.

All of this offers up not only hope but also new opportunities. However, the art world remains dominated and defined by straight, white men—the legacy of authority and privilege has not been laid to rest. This book contributes not only to an understanding of how that legacy has unfolded in the past, but also of how it can be perpetuated in the future—unless initiatives are taken to halt its progress. The decision to participate in such initiatives is, in essence, a political act. The second decade of the 21st century ushered in an era of overtly reactionary ideology in the West, in which a number of progressive policies were undermined, threatened, and dismantled. In the USA in particular, the Trump administration brought with it an alt-right conservative agenda rooted in racist, xenophobic, gynophobic ideology. We need now—perhaps more than ever—to be reminded of the dangers of white, male supremacy, its insidiousness, and to develop tactics for combatting it at every turn. We must deploy strategies to ensure that Other artists are acknowledged as major contributors to our civilization and that they take their rightful place alongside the "greats" of art history.

CURATORIAL RESPONSIBILITY

Curators must be encouraged to build on the historiography of the activist exhibitions from the 1970s to the present, many of which are discussed within this book. They should also make every attempt to ensure that the work of non-white, non-male, non-heterosexual artists is accessible and readily available to those scholars, gallerists, and curators who construct history and influence the marketplace. There is simply no excuse not to include Other artists in group shows. As Russell Storer, senior curator at the National Gallery in Singapore, suggests, curators need to do more research and stop being lazy: "In order to address these serious disparities, curators need to work much harder, and become much more informed, especially when examining art from other contexts that you are not familiar with or not living in. Curators need to become aware of what all artists are doing, how they are working, the kind of ideas and interests they are dealing with, and that can be quite different to what white male artists are doing."[2]

Those who are perpetuating discriminatory practices should be held accountable, and curatorial misconduct criticized, to the point where it becomes acknowledged as unacceptable. And instead of reinstalling permanent collections at museums that simply reconfigure hegemonic narratives—as was the case when MoMA reopened its galleries in 2004—we need to offer new perspectives on old stories.[3] As Oscar Wilde famously declared, "The one duty we owe to history is to re-write it."[4] Museum curators should insist on more diverse exhibition schedules. How difficult would that be?

It is disheartening that so many art professionals who have the power to institute change often do nothing to counter overt discrimination against Other artists, especially when suitable work by them is readily available. In an era that postdates the women's, gay, and civil-rights movements, curators continue to organize international contemporary art exhibitions that include almost exclusively male artists from the USA and Europe. One of the classic and most glaring examples of such misrepresentation was an exhibition held in 1984 at MoMA entitled *An International Survey of Recent Painting and Sculpture*, curated by Kynaston McShine.

The show marketed itself as an up-to-date summary of the most significant contemporary art in the world.[5] However, of the 169 artists featured, only 13 were women. It was this exhibition—and a sexist comment by McShine ("any artist who wasn't in the show should rethink his career")[6]—that inspired the formation of the art-activist group, the Guerrilla Girls, in 1985.[7]

These are not just issues from the past—discriminatory practices persist today in most mainstream museums, gallery rosters, and auction price differentials. Writing for *Time Out London*, for example, art editor Eddy Frankel noted that virtually all the major exhibitions in London in autumn 2016 were by men—"and that," he said, "is total bullshit." He suggested that museums and galleries should feel "seriously ashamed" that they had "collectively completely ignored female artists for a whole season"[8] and called on them to take note of that omission. What he failed to point out was that of the fourteen major solo shows in London, only one featured an artist of color, Wilfredo Lam.

Even though the *New York Times* indicated in 2016 that there has been an increase in women-only shows at major museums, this openness does not seem to have trickled down into mainstream (non-activist) curatorial practice.[9] Moreover, one wonders the extent to which the mere existence of women-only shows unintentionally absolves major institutions of their social responsibility to women. Given decades of feminist, anti-racist, and postcolonial theorizing, we should surely expect contemporary exhibitions to be more inclusive of Other artists and, at the very least, curators to be more self-conscious about their exclusions and inclusions.

KEY QUESTIONS

However, as this book makes clear, all is not lost in this rigged system—there are many curators around the world who are battling for equality. And if we don't join their ranks as fellow curatorial activists, then what can the rest of us do? How can each of us act to guarantee that more voices are included? How can we re-envision the historical definition of "greatness," to include all Other artists? As Spivak has indicated, we must always be mindful of where we are positioned in relation to discourses of power, authority, and privilege.[10]

If we cannot help others to see the structural and systemic problems that exist, then we cannot even begin to fix them. How can we elicit sympathy to the point of action? How can we go about educating disbelievers who contend—because there are signs of improvement—that the battle has been won? How do we fight against cognitive dissonance when people's instinct is often to rationalize or ignore concepts they don't agree with? If we present empirical evidence that works against people's core beliefs, how can we guarantee that this evidence is accepted? How do we denaturalize what is perceived as natural? And in so doing, do we run the risk of encountering a backlash—anger, denial or, worse, dismissal? How can we get those in power to loosen their grip? Will women, non-whites, and LGBTQ artists ever achieve parity in the art world, and is "parity" even our ultimate ambition?

With respect to women artists, it is utopian to think that their professional position will cease to be problematic when we live in a world in which women are oppressed and discriminated against on a daily basis—from campus rape, domestic violence, street harassment, abortion restrictions, unequal pay, access to childcare, and so on. Abuse against women is as endemic as it is tolerated and ignored. As Nochlin argued in 1971: "It is certainly not realistic to hope that the majority of men, in the arts, or in any other field, will soon see the light of day and find that it is in their own self-interest to grant complete equality to women." She continued, "Most men... are reluctant to give up this 'natural' order of things in which their advantages are so great," and "those who have privileges inevitably hold on to them, and hold tight." [11] Her words resonate today.

A similar argument could be made with respect to non-white artists. The Black Lives Matter movement in the USA has made clear that people of color are far from equal in a white-suprematist culture rooted in centuries-old systemic racism. Most mainstream (non-activist) curators tend to reproduce a whitewashed art world, offering little more than lip service to the concept of racial inclusion. But as Maurice Berger explored in his seminal article "Are Art Museums Racist?": "Not until the white people, who now hold the power in the art world, scrutinize their own motives and attitudes toward people of color, will it be possible *to unlearn racism*." [12]

We must unlearn both racism and sexism. To do so, is to ask another series of difficult questions: Who are the collectors of art and the museum board members?; Who is the audience?; Who is asked to make fundamental policy decisions?; Who sets the priorities?; Who holds the power? Which artists succeed, and why? Success in the art world necessitates gallery representation, inclusion in solo and group shows, exhibition reviews and press coverage, a collector base, and (eventually) museum exposure. If the art system is predisposed toward white male artists, then the success rate for Other artists is comparatively lower.

GALLERY REPRESENTATION
AND ART COLLECTORS

Galleries can start changing this by being more proactive about supporting and promoting Other artists. In recent years, some of the statistics generated by surveys on gender and racial discrimination in galleries in the UK and the USA have been deplorable. But by reporting on discriminatory practices and disseminating these types of statistics in magazines, exhibitions, and at art fairs, the Guerrilla Girls, Gallery Tally, East London Fawcett (ELF), and Pussy Galore, among others, are holding the offending galleries accountable.

Art collectors should also demand a more equitable variety of artworks from which to choose. They have the power (read $) to demand a broader selection than is currently offered by most gallerists. If galleries were more proactive about supporting and promoting Other artists, then their percentage of sales would increase exponentially. However, as Nochlin warns, there are many collectors who "out of habit, laziness, or even misogyny—simply don't bother with women...I mean, who wouldn't think of collecting Louise Bourgeois. You'd be crazy if you didn't."[13]

There have been numerous private collections presented as special exhibitions in museums of late—most of them demonstrate gender and racial biases. For example, *Embracing the Contemporary: the Keith L. and Katherine Sachs Collection* at the Philadelphia Museum of Art in 2016 featured fifty-one artists: three were women and one was an artist of color. Critic Ken Johnson, writing for the *New York Times*, was dismayed: "Considering how hugely active and influential female artists have been in many different genres during the time the couple has been collecting, why does the show focus almost exclusively on white, male artists in its embrace of the contemporary?"[14] The Sachses are not alone. Four years earlier, the Art Gallery of New South Wales in Sydney hosted an exhibition of John Kaldor's art collection: of the more than two hundred works, only four were by women and two were by non-white artists.[15] More alarmingly, not a single critic made mention of the racism and sexism embedded in Kaldor's collecting practices. He was not held publicly accountable.

The Guerrilla Girls have come up with an effective and humorous way to address such discrimination: when they encounter a private collection with few women in it, they send a Guerrilla Girls' *"Dearest Art Collector"* (2007) postcard, which reads, "It has come to our attention that your collection, like most, does not contain enough art by women. We know that you feel terrible about this and will rectify the situation immediately."

Real progress is evident in some areas, however—especially with respect to philanthropic initiatives that support female artists, such as the Barbara Lee Foundation, which funds exhibitions; or Valeria Napoleone XX, which provides gifts and funds new work; or Elisabeth Murdoch's prize for female artists; or Elizabeth Sackler's Center for Feminist Art at the Brooklyn Museum. These initiatives can and will make a difference for female artists.

MEDIA REPRESENTATION

Work by Other artists is consistently held in comparatively low esteem by the art press, as well, judging by the amount of coverage allotted to them in magazines and periodicals. Critics and arts writers need to pay more attention to who they are supporting, promoting, and writing about in magazines, journals, books, and monographs. Publishers should be more self-aware and curb overt declarations of sexism/racism in their pages. In 2008, for example, *The Independent*'s art critic Brian Sewell famously declared that the art world is not sexist, that Bridget Riley and Louise Bourgeois are second-rate artists, and that, "Only men are capable of aesthetic greatness...[Women artists] fade away in their late 20s or 30s. Maybe it's something to do with bearing children." [16] Should *The Independent* be printing such overtly sexist statements?

Similarly, in 2014, *The Guardian*'s Jonathan Jones wrote, "The reason there are no great female artists is, in short, because of men like me. Art criticism defines the lofty peaks of the canon and it is, let's say, a macho trade. I'd go further. I think to feel a passion for an artist—a real passion like the enthusiasm that made John Ruskin write five volumes of sprawling prose to prove the greatness of JMW Turner—involves a kind of deep identification, a sense of meeting your double, the artist who speaks for you." [17] By Jones's logic, it is the "macho trade" of the arts that makes it impossible for a woman artist to be ranked among the great. Put simply, men cannot identify with their artwork: "At certain points of my life I loved both Jackson Pollock and Damien Hirst like the brother I never had. Their art spoke to me, man. And you can't imagine artists more male than those." [18] (To which Madeleine Dore from *ArtsHub* retorted, "Who knew Jackson Pollock's *Blue Poles* could only truly move the male viewer, that embedded in the canvas was a secret camaraderie invisible to all women.") [19] Jones's analysis is fascinating, and raises two important points: first, if he is correct, then we need more women critics who can break into that old-boy network; second (a bigger issue, discussed by Nochlin), what is "greatness," other than a set of standards made by men for men —a paradigm that must be dismantled before we can move forward.

Provocations like those from Sewell and Jones should not be tolerated. But, as ever, there is hope in resistance. In the USA and the UK, a number of art writers are actively promoting women artists and artists of color and calling out institutions, galleries, the press, and the auction houses for white suprematist practices—notably, Eddy Frankel, Katy Deepwell, Adrian Searle, Eleanor Heartney, Jerry Saltz, Holland Cotter, Alex Greenberger, and Ben Davis, among others.

ART AND MONEY

The availability of works by Other artists at galleries and in auction houses has a tremendous impact on the amount of press coverage and the interest they receive from collectors, museums, and so on. This, in turn, directly affects their market and monetary values. It is within this arena that women artists and artists of color are particularly discriminated against. In the *New York Times* article "X-Factor: Is the Art Market Rational or Biased?," Greg Allen explains that if a woman artist is represented by a prominent, "blue-chip" gallery, or shows in prestigious museums, or is sought by prominent collectors, her work will always be priced considerably lower than that of her male colleagues simply because it is made by a woman.[20]

Sociologist Sarah Thornton, author of *Seven Days in the Art World*, argues that "One would expect the art world to be more egalitarian…At the top end of the market, the people who can afford to spend a lot are entrepreneurial [white] men. And they buy entrepreneurial [white] artists—Warhol, Hirst, Koons—artists they perhaps identify with."[21] Saltz agrees. In an article in the *Village Voice* entitled "The Battle for Babylon," he attempts to explain the reason for the deplorable ratios in the art market, contending that the art system "knows art is a good investment and is traditionally made by men so more men show and sell while fewer women sell at all…Thus the discourse is being driven from a place that suppresses difference."[22] More recently, Saltz has confessed that he just doesn't "get this auction thing": "What's so interesting about a handful of very, very rich people with penises buying the work of a handful of artists with penises for very, very high prices in public, in front of other people with penises and some very tall thin blond people with great shoes and no penises?"[23] Artist Deborah Kass insists that things have become even worse since art became an asset class, and hedge-fund managers began buying artwork as an investment, paying extremely high prices for mostly white male artists, driving market prices up, and ultimately devaluing women artists.[24]

To address these and similar issues, we must work to create an art world in which high quality, rather than high prices, are consistently reinforced as the touchstones of success—for all artists, equally. As Josh Spero humorously suggests, the true sign of equality will be "when art by women is just as unaffordable to most as art by men."[25]

BOARDS, DIRECTORS, AND CURATORS

Museum directors can have a direct impact in the battle against sexism and racism—by, for example, diversifying boards, demanding broader representation in exhibitions, hiring non-white and female curators and staff, and so on. Unfortunately, however, most museums aim to preserve the narrow interests of their mostly white male, upper-class patrons and donors—who, as discussed, tend to gravitate to artwork by white male artists. Art that demonstrates its difference from the mainstream, or that challenges dominant values and ideologies, is rarely acceptable to white male patrons, curators, and administrators.

Museums should be making a far more concerted effort to diversify their programming. Curator Helen Molesworth recently revealed in the *Art Newpaper* that the real burden is on the curators and directors: "When you look at your [exhibition] schedule and you see that you have mostly men, you actually have to push hard against that. You have to insist internally that you are going to put women on the schedule."[26] Interviewer Julie Halperin asked her why it was so hard to accomplish in practice, and whether this was due to "curatorial laziness," and/or "lack of funding or incentive to look beyond the obvious." Molesworth responded:

> The only way you get diversity is to actually do it. That means that certain men don't get shows. There are only X number of slots every year on the calendar and the number of artists always exceeds the number of slots. If you are going to be equitable, some of the dudes don't get shows that year. That's what's hard about it. Most museums still maintain a commitment to an idea of the best, or quality, or genius. And I'm not saying I don't agree with those as values.

But I think those values have been created over hundreds of years to favor white men. One of the things you have to say as a curator is "We are not going to present the value that already exists; we are going to do the work to create value around these woman artists and artists of color that would just come 'naturally' to the white male artist".[27]

In other words, since curatorial selections are generally based on arbitrary, Eurocentric standards of "taste" and "quality"—the code words of sexual/racial indifference and exclusion—which have always favored white males, we need to change those values or work hard to create new or different values around Other artists. We can do that quite simply by making more concerted efforts to exhibit, acquire, and promote them.

Tate Modern has done a good job in this regard, despite its hugely disappointing representation of women and non-white artists in the re-hang of the permanent collection in 2016. But Frances Morris, the museum's first female director, has been keen to point out that when the institution first opened in 2000, only a small proportion of the art on display was by women; by 2016, half of the solo rooms at the new Tate Modern were exhibiting works by women. When asked why she was making efforts to support women artists, she stated, simply, "Institutional bias, unconscious bias. It is still a boys' club, no question in my mind."[28] It is no coincidence that Georgia O'Keeffe and Mona Hatoum both had major retrospectives at the museum in 2016.

Tate Modern is also making progress with respect to diversity: of the works in the 2016 re-hang of the permanent collection, there are eight hundred works by three hundred artists from more than fifty countries. Seventy-five percent of the work on view has been purchased since 2000, which demonstrates a major institutional initiative toward inclusivity, a movement away from the established canon toward a global and more gender-balanced vision of modern and contemporary art. The museum's recalibration of its collection to more accurately reflect the world we live in is in many ways unmatched by other mainstream institutions. Nonetheless, its programming and exhibition checklists must continue to be monitored.

Acquisition into a collection is too frequently an uphill battle for Other artists. Most museum boards have Acquisition Committees to whom curators present objects for possible purchase. It is these boards that often approve the works that will be accessioned into the museum's collection. The majority of boards are composed of white men, which makes the curators' task all the more difficult if s/he is presenting work by Other artists for consideration. The imbalance in acquisitions could be addressed more effectively if museum collection policies were modified to attend specifically to gender and race discrepancies.

In order to address exclusionary collection practices, and despite the risk of ghettoizing the work of Other artists, I believe we need more museums like the Studio Museum in Harlem, Manhattan. Founded in 1968 to fill a void left by mainstream institutions, its mission was to support the "study, documentation, collection, preservation, and exhibition of art and artifacts of Black America and the African diaspora." [29] Until there is equality, there is still a pressing need for such specialized museums. Rather than stifling Other artists via segregation, museums that cater to Other art—such as the Studio Museum, the National Museum of Women in the Arts, and the Leslie-Lohman Museum of Gay and Lesbian Art—allow that art to flourish despite the dominant culture's ostensible lack of interest. If mainstream curators can be encouraged to visit these alternative spaces, new knowledge can be gained, and inclusion will become a more likely possibility.[30]

TALKING BACK

To reiterate: curators and other art-world professionals should be amenable to self-critique and, as cultural critic bell hooks asserts, producing work "that opposes structures of domination, that presents possibilities for a transformed future by willingly interrogating their own work on aesthetic or political grounds. This interrogation itself becomes an act of critical intervention, fundamentally fostering an attitude of vigilance rather than denial." [31] Learning how to listen to others is not enough in itself: we must first listen to ourselves. Curators must begin by asking themselves: What are my biases?; Am I excluding large constituencies of people in my selections?; Have I favored male artists over female, white over black—if so, why?

And Other artists must learn to make trouble, to speak up, even if it runs the risk of being deemed a complainer. bell hooks emphasizes the importance of marginalized peoples standing their ground, and urges all writers from oppressed groups to speak, *to talk back*—a term that she defines as the movement from object to subject. "Speaking," she says, "is not solely an expression of creative power; it is an act of resistance, a political gesture that challenges politics of domination that would render us nameless and voiceless.

As such, it is a courageous act—as such, it represents a threat." [32]
To talk back is to liberate one's voice. [33]

Don't just sit and wait for change to come: be proactive. Take affirmative action. Call out institutions, critics, curators, collectors, and gallerists for their sexist and racist practices. And, yes, we need to keep crunching the numbers and churning out the stats. Counting is, after all, a feminist strategy. [34] This data must be disseminated publicly, and shared. By drawing attention to disparities—as the Guerrilla Girls, Gallery Tally, ELF, Pussy Galore, and others are doing—arts' professionals will be under greater pressure to take more notice of who they are supporting, promoting, writing about, and publishing. Let us hope that the state of false consciousness that "all is well" in the art world can be undermined, that the myth of equality can be debunked via the dissemination of these statistics, and that individuals—men and women alike— can be called out for their discriminatory practices. [35]

Now is the time for us to work together to change what is an abhorrent situation for Other artists. Instead of making excuses, denying statistics, or shying away from inequalities of gender, race, and sexuality, we must face these issues head-on in order to come up with strategies and solutions that will guarantee equal opportunity and exposure. With a little more energy and action, the creation of a just art world does not have to be a pipe dream.

NOTES

Full bibliographic information for the short-form citations is given in the Bibliography.

Preface

1 Griselda Pollock, *Vision and Difference*, p. 72.
2 Holland Cotter, "At MoMA."
3 Cheryl Donegan in Jerry Saltz, "Jerry Saltz meeting with MoMA."

Introduction

1 Lucy R. Lippard, *From the Center.*
2 Sonnet Stanfill, "Taking on the Boys' Club."
3 In Susanna Rustin, "Health, education and arts."
4 Lippard, *Mixed Blessings.*

1. WHAT IS CURATORIAL ACTIVISM?

1 Linda Nochlin, in an interview with the author, May 2015.
2 This heading draws from text featured in Richard Bell's painting *Bell's Theorem* (2002), which reads: "Aboriginal art: it's a white thing," a reference to the exploitation of Aboriginal artists by white dealers and businessmen.
3 Of the 300 artists represented, just 32% were women and 29% were non-white (statistics compiled by the author).
4 Of the 600 works, 31% were by women and 23% were by non-white artists (statistics compiled by the author).
5 Of the works on display in the permanent collection, 21% were by women and 14% by non-white artists. The statistics in this paragraph were compiled by the author.
6 On April 1, 2014, ArtSlant reported: "To mark the 30-year anniversary of the first Guerrilla Girls protest at MoMA, Director Glenn D. Lowry announced yesterday plans to give the museum over exclusively to women artists for the entire year of 2015." See ArtSlant, "MoMA Plans Only Female Art." Accessed: July 2017.
7 The statistics in this paragraph were compiled by the author.
8 The statistics in this paragraph were compiled by the author.
9 In 2008, the Guerrilla Girls teamed up with art activists the Brainstormers to produce a "Mad Libs" postcard: on the address side, it listed dozens of galleries with shockingly uneven representation of male versus female artists; on the other side, it provided a letter with blanks that could be filled in and posted to the sender's "favorite" culprit.
10 The statistics in this paragraph are from Maura Reilly, "Taking the Measure of Sexism." Accessed: April 2017.
11 Hebron, in a phone interview with the author, May 2015.
12 In 2013, East London Fawcett (ELF) examined the artists represented by 134 commercial galleries in London and found that less than a third were women.
13 In 2015, Natalie Hegert reported in "The Rounds of A Rumour" (accessed April 2017) that women tend to outnumber men by three to one in terms of numbers of students enrolled in studio art and art history programs, for example: the School of the Art Institute of Chicago was 70% female; Rhode Island School of Design was 67% female; Maryland Institute College of Art was 71% female; and the Courtauld Institute of Art, London, is a whopping 80% female. More than a decade earlier, Roberta Smith had also noted higher numbers of women art students, in a panel she moderated entitled "'Feminisms' in Four Generations," held on Saturday, January 7, 2006, at the CUNY Graduate Center in New York City, as part of the 5th Annual New York Times Arts and Leisure Weekend.
14 These statistics are taken from a poster entitled "2016 Manhattan Boycott Guide," created by the Pussy Galore collective (see illustration, p. 19).
15 For the information in this paragraph, see artnet News, "Who Are the Top 100?" Accessed: April 2017.
16 Nochlin, "Why Have There Been No Great Women Artists?," p. 46.
17 See Griselda Pollock in *Differencing the Canon.*
18 Adrienne Rich, *On Lies*, p. 35.
19 See Elaine Showalter, "Feminist Criticism," p. 183. In the beginning, the revisionary imperative was "righteous, angry, and admonitory," according to Showalter. In 1970, Kate Millett rocked the foundations of the literary canon with her book *Sexual Politics*, in which she castigated time-honored classics—from Henry Miller's *Black Spring* and D. H. Lawrence's *Lady Chatterley's Lover* to Norman Mailer's *The Naked and the Dead*—for their use of sex to degrade and undermine women. Millett's revisionist strategy revealed patriarchy to be a socially conditioned belief system masquerading as a natural phenomenon—her theories were considered incendiary.
20 Showalter, "Feminist Criticism," p. 183.
21 Ibid.
22 Susan Hardy Aiken, "Canonicity," p. 298.
23 Pollock, *Differencing the Canon*, p. 24.
24 Ibid.
25 Ibid.
26 For example, in speaking about his position as an indigenous art curator at the Gallery of Modern Art in Brisbane, Australia, Bruce McLean explained his role as "trying to create a space within white institutions to help audiences understand Aboriginal art and culture from a radically different point of view." This quote is from the author's notes, taken during a panel at the Cairns Indigenous Art Fair (CIAF), Cairns, Australia, in August 2011, where McLean was speaking.
27 As quoted in the letter Rattemeyer sent to the guest curators.
28 Lucy R. Lippard, *From the Center*, p. 38.
29 Adrian Searle, "Queer British Art."
30 Janet Street-Porter, "The Tate Gallery is wrong."
31 See Matilda Battersby, "Queer British Art."
32 See Gayatri Spivak, *In Other Worlds*. Spivak has, however, at various times mentioned that she has been unhappy with the way the concept of strategic essentialism has been taken up and used. In some interviews, she has even disavowed the term, although she seems not to have completely deserted the concept. See, for example, Sara Danius and Stefan Jonsson, "An Interview with Gayatri Chakravorty Spivak," pp. 24–50.
33 See Ella Shohat, "Area Studies," pp. 1269–72.
34 As in the concept of time conveyed by the lyrics "Is time long or is it wide?," from the Laurie Anderson song "Same Time Tomorrow," in the album *Bright Red*, 1994.
35 Aiken, "Canonicity," p. 298.
36 "Act of survival," in Adrienne Rich, *On Lies*, p. 35; "perpetual regeneration" in Aiken, "Canonicity," p. 298.
37 Pollock, *Differencing the Canon*, p.11.
38 Roland Barthes, "The Death of the Author," p. 146.
39 Chandra Talpade Mohanty, *Feminisms Without Borders*, p. 244.
40 Ibid.
41 See Jean-Hubert Martin, Carlo Severi, and Julien Bonhomme, "Jean-Hubert Martin et la pensée visuelle." Accessed: April 2017.
42 See Dina Morin, "Carambolages."
43 Roland Barthes, "The Death of the Author," p. 159.
44 Martin, quoted in "Paris Diary by Laure: 'Listen with your eyes: Jean-Hubert Martin'." Accessed: April 2017.
45 Martin, in Roxana Azimi, "'Carambolages,'" author's translation.

2. RESISTING MASCULINISM AND SEXISM

1 Louise Bourgeois, in Camille Guichard (dir.), *Arte Video*, a documentary about Bourgeois.
2 Nochlin's essay "Why Have There Been No Great Women Artists?" was first published in 1971 in Vivian Gornick and Barbara Moran (eds.), *Woman in Sexist Society*. References to the essay in this book are from the edition published in Maura Reilly (ed.), *Women Artists*, pp. 42–68.
3 The actual figure was 43%, which is a huge improvement on the 1996 Biennale, when just 8% of the artists were women. In the 2005 Venice Biennale, group exhibitions curated by de Corral and Martínez, women artists represented 38% of the artists included. Statistics compiled by the author.
4 Nochlin, "Why Have There Been No Great Women Artists?," p. 67.
5 Ibid.
6 Deborah Solomon, "Art Talk."
7 These exhibitions included: *26 Contemporary Women Artists* (1971), *Womanhouse* (1972), *c. 7,500* (1973–74), *Women Artists: 1550–1950* (1976–77), *Feministische Kunst International* (1979), *Issue: Social Strategies by Women Artists* (1980), *Art et féminisme* (1982), *The Revolutionary Power of Women's Laughter* (1983–85), *La Femme et l'art* (1983), *Feminisme in het Medium* (1984), *Difference: On Representation and Sexuality* (1985), *Making Their Mark: Women Artists Move into the Mainstream, 1970–85* (1989), among others.
8 These exhibitions included: *Mujeres artistas: protagonistas de los ochenta* (1990), *Parler femme* (1991), *Regards de femmes* (1993), *Bad Girls* (1993 and 1994), *Back Talk: Women's Voices in the 90s* (1993), *Dialogue with the Other* (1994), *Inside the Visible: An Elliptical Traverse of 20th Century Art in, of, and from the Feminine* (1994–97), *Laughter Ten Years After* (1995), *Division of Labor: "Women's Work" in Contemporary Art* (1995), *Gender Beyond Memory: The Works of Contemporary Women Artists* (1996), *Sexual Politics: Judy Chicago's "Dinner Party" in Feminist Art History* (1996), *Vraiment: feminisme et Art* (1997), *5th Istanbul Biennial: On Life, Beauty, Translations and Other Difficulties* (1997).

9 These exhibitions included: *Personal and Political: The Women's Art Movement, 1969–1975* (2002), *Gloria: Another Look at Feminist Art in the 1970s* (2002), *Fusion Cuisine* (2002), *Post\Feministiche Positionen der neunziger Jahre aus der Sammlung Goetz* (2002), *51st Venice Biennale* (2005), *It's Time for Action* (2006), *Konstfeminism: Strategies and Consequences in Sweden from the 1970s to the present* (2006–07), *Gender Battle\Global Feminisms* (2007), *WACK! Art and the Feminist Revolution* (2007–09), *Kiss Kiss Bang Bang* (2007), *Gender Battle: The Impact of Feminism in the Art of the 1970s* (2007), *The Furious Gaze* (2008), *Gender Check* (2009), *En Todas Partes: políticas de la diversidad sexual en el arte* (2009), *Rebelle: kunst en feminisme 1969–2009* (2009), *Burning Down the House* (2009), *Elles@centrepompidou* (2009–11), *Donna: Avanguardia femminista negli anni '70* (2010), *re.act.feminism #2* (2011–13), *Women In-Between: Asian Women Artists 1984–2012* (2012–13), *Future Feminism* (2014), *Feminismen* (2015), *Women of Abstract Expressionism* (2016), *Revolution in the Making* (2016), among many others.

10 In addition to the exhibitions listed in Note 9, see also, for example: *Art/Women/California, 1950–2000: Parallels and Intersections* (2002), *Girls Night Out* (2004), *It's Time for Action* (2006), *Claiming Space: Some American Feminist Originators* (2007), *The Furious Gaze* (2008), among many others.

11 See Phoebe Hoban, "We're Finally Infiltrating."

12 The TFAP website, developed and administered by the Institute for Women and Art at Rutgers University, New Jersey, lists and archives all these diverse feminist art activities.

13 Graham Bowley, "Institute of Contemporary Art."

14 In Mark Brown, "Frances Morris."

15 Cited in Hilarie Sheets, "Female Artists."

16 The first museum exhibition in the USA to address the omission of women artists from the traditional canon of art history was *Old Mistresses: Women Artists of the Past*, held from April 17 to June 18, 1972, at Walters Art Gallery in Baltimore, and curated by Ann Gabhart and Elizabeth Broun. The exhibition featured thirty women artists, including Sofonisba Anguissola, Lavinia Fontana, Susanne de Court, Artemisia Gentileschi, Elisabetta Sirani, Rachel Ruysch, Angelica Kauffman, Anne Vallayer-Coster, Adélaïde Labille-Guiard, Elisabeth Louise Vigée Le Brun, Marguerite Gérard, Sarah Miriam Peale, Jane Stuart, Lily Martin Spencer, Rosa Bonheur, Mary Cassatt, Cecilia Beaux, Romaine Brooks, among others. Note: The Baltimore Museum of Art concurrently exhibited 20th-century works by women selected from its own collections.

17 Robert Hughes, "Rediscovered."

18 See Grace Glueck, "The Woman as Artist," p. 50.

19 Other works had been horribly neglected. One painting on wood by Judith Leyster was found with a bad case of worms, "discovered only when the Dutch museum that owned it responded to a request for its loan." See Glueck, "The Woman as Artist," p. 50.

20 Ibid.

21 Ibid., p. 56.

22 Ann Sutherland Harris, *Women Artists*, pp. 21–26.

23 John Perrault, "Women Artists," p. 40.

24 Cheryl Smith, "Bad Girls," p. 12.

25 Ibid., i.

26 Ibid.

27 Ibid., ii.

28 D. J. Fontana, *What's On In London*.

29 Brian Sewell, *Bad Girls* exhibition review, *London Evening Standard*.

30 Katy Deepwell, "Feminist Curatorial Strategies."

31 Iwona Blazwick, "Who's Bad?" Accessed: April 2017.

32 Laura Cottingham, "Who's Bad?" Accessed: April 2017.

33 Ekow Eshun, "Bad Girls!," pp. 152–53.

34 Tanner, email to author, September 2015.

35 Ibid.

36 Marcia Tanner in *Bad Girls* (exhibition catalogue).

37 Ibid., p. 42.

38 Ibid., p. 49.

39 Ibid., p. 4.

40 Ibid., p. 10.

41 Helen Chadwick, "Who's Bad?" Accessed: April 2017.

42 Blazwick and Cottingham, "Who's Bad?" Accessed: April 2017.

43 Blazwick, "Who's Bad?" Accessed: April 2017.

44 Jan Avgikos, "Bad Girl Blues," p. 86.

45 Ibid.

46 B. Ruby Rich, "Who's Bad?" Accessed: April 2017.

47 Nicola Tyson, "Who's Bad?" Accessed: April 2017.

48 Benjamin Weissman in Avgikos, "Bad Girl Blues," p. 86.

49 Roberta Smith, "A Raucous Caucus."

50 As quoted on the MIT Press website. Accessed: August 2015.

51 Elizabeth Hess, "And Everything Nice."

52 The more famous artists included Louise Bourgeois, Hannah Höch, Sophie Taeuber-Arp, Ana Mendieta, Eva Hesse, Claude Cahun, Yayoi Kusama, Agnes Martin, Mona Hatoum, Lygia Clark, Charlotte Salomon, and Francesca Woodman, among others.

53 Catherine de Zegher, "Introduction," p. 20.

54 Ibid., pp. 20–23.

55 Cited in Jo Ann Lewis, "The Feminine Century."

56 Sue Malvern, "Virtuous and Vulgar Feminisms," p. 488.

57 Catherine de Zegher in an email to the author, September 2015.

58 Katy Deepwell, "Interview with Catherine de Zegher," p. 64.

59 Ibid., p. 74.

60 Ibid.

61 Amelia Jones, "Feminist Subjects," p. 11.

62 Adrian Searle, "Unworthy of Great Women."

63 Ibid. Searle explains, "One section of the show is titled 'Enjambment', a literary idea concerning the way lines of a poem run into and over one another, and it is an apt description of the exhibition as a whole, of the fractured, splintered grating of one thing against another, of overlaps and discords."

64 Maureen Turman, "Review: Inside the Visible," p. 59.

65 Ibid. Searle, in "Unworthy of Great Women," agreed: "As long on explication and language-mangling density as it is short on overall readability, the catalogue, like the show, contains great moments alongside second-rate, tedious and indulgent *longueurs*. It is a faulty but necessary map, and without it we're likely to get lost."

66 Deepwell, "Interview with Catherine de Zegher,", p. 73.

67 Ruth Wallen, "Review of Sexual Politics," p. 341.

68 Julie Springer, "Review of Sexual Politics," p. 53.

69 Amelia Jones, *Sexual Politics*, p. 37.

70 Jones, email to author, September 2015.

71 Amelia Jones and Cornelia H. Butler, "History Makers."

72 Jones, *Sexual Politics*, p. 23.

73 Christopher Knight, "More Famine Than Feast."

74 Gary Kornblau, "The Best and Worst," p. 96: "Director Henry T. Hopkins is the newest serpent in our garden—offering megabuck exhibition funds in exchange for featuring (again) Judy Chicago's 1979 *The Dinner Party*—and curator/art historian Amelia Jones swallowed the tainted fruit whole. Blockbuster lust met academic ambition. However well-intentioned, the reactionary use of feminist theory to make Chicago's kitsch extravaganza look good succeeded only in making the rest of feminist art look bad, setting us back thirty years. The very idea of Hannah Wilke, Lynda Benglis, Eleanor Antin, Cindy Sherman, Judie Bamber, and other major artists as spear-carriers to a Chicago diva in the museum's opera is obscene. The sight of it really sucked." Another negative review of the exhibitions was M. A. Greenstein's, "And You Thought Feminism Was Dead," pp. 17–18.

75 Donald Preziosi, "'Sexual Politics." Other positive feedback included two letters to the editor of *Los Angeles Times* by James Griffith and Carolyn Wolf, collected under the title "Dinner Party: Emotional Moving Feast."

76 David Joselit, "Identity Politics," pp. 36–39.

77 Of the total works on display, 38% were by women and most were by feminist artists, many of whom are well-known, such as Barbara Kruger, Jenny Holzer, Ghada Amer, Louise Bourgeois, and Mona Hatoum; others were relative newcomers to the scene, including Runa Islam, Regina José Galindo, Lida Abdul, Valeska Soares, and Joana Vasconcelos.

78 Alison Gingeras, "Stealing the show," pp. 265ff.

79 Marcia E. Vetrocq, "Be Careful What You Wish For," p. 108ff.

80 Adrian Searle, "Filth, blasphemy and big, big stars."

81 Christopher Knight, "Fueled by politics."

82 Jennifer Allen, "Women on the Verge," p. 82; Linda Nochlin, "What befits a woman?"

83 The exhibition was at the Davis Museum and Cultural Center at Wellesley College in Wellesley, Massachusetts, from September to December 2007.

84 Donna Haraway, "A Cyborg Manifesto," p. 155.

85 This robust section presented works by artists such as Cass Bird, Tracey Rose, Oreet Ashery, Tracey Emin, Lisa Reihana, Dayanita Singh, Wangechi Mutu, Ingrid Mwangi, Jenny Saville, among others.

86 Carol Armstrong, "Review: Global Feminisms and Wack!," p. 360; Peter Schjeldahl, "Women's Work"; Roberta Smith, "They Are Artists Who Are Women."

87 Helena Reckitt, in "Unusual suspects," pp. 34–42.

88 Dena Muller, "Review: *Global Feminisms*," p. 471.

89 In addition to leading figures such as Eleanor Antin, Lynda Benglis, Louise Bourgeois, Judy

Chicago, Mary Beth Edelson, Eva Hesse, Mary Kelly, Ana Mendieta, Annette Messager, Yoko Ono, Adrian Piper, Martha Rosler, Miriam Schapiro, Carolee Schneemann, Mierle Laderman Ukeles, and Hannah Wilke, there were dozens of less familiar artists, among them: Indian-born Nasreen Mohamedi, New Zealand-born Alexis Hunter, Zarina Hashmi, Sanja Iveković, a conceptual photographer based in Croatia, the social activist Mónica Mayer from Mexico City, the British performance artist Rose English; the German filmmaker Ulrike Ottinger, the Danish pioneer of body art, Kirsten Justesen.

90 Carol Armstrong, "Review: Global Feminisms and Wack!" p. 362. Armstrong also notes that, "The themes…operate in multiple paradigms, flowing in and out of given scholarly taxonomies, proliferating the intertextual dialogue between the artworks. Mixing and matching some of the old categories with new ones, and paying attention to artistic intention as well as posthumous critical interpretations, the exhibition is more a showcase of possibilities than a strict academic argument. Gone are the divisions between expressive and conceptual models; absent is the notion that subjectivity is inherently regressive; missing is the classification of an essentialist 1970s contrasted with a theoretical 1980s; nowhere to be found are the misconceptions of an anti-formal feminism or a lack of feminist painting." Ibid.

91 See Harper Montgomery, "Wack!" Accessed: April 2017.

92 The six artists were: Senga Nengudi, Howardena Pindell, Faith Ringgold, Betye Saar, Camille Billops, and Lorraine O'Grady.

93 Butler, "Art and Feminism," p. 15.

94 See Peggy Phelan, "Survey," p. 18.

95 Butler, "Art and Feminism,", p. 21. As Butler also explained in "History Makers," "I think framing this [feminist] work, bringing it back and re-contextualising it, will actually enliven the discourse surrounding it and raise more questions about the history of feminist art than it will answer."

96 Holland Cotter, "The Art of Feminism."

97 Karen Kurczynski, "Book Review: Wack!," pp. 50–53.

98 Doug Harvey, "Upside Yo Head."

99 Cotter, "The Art of Feminism."

100 Ingrid Rowland, "Women Artists Win!"

101 Mike Sperlinger, "Wack!," p. 22.

102 The curatorial team for *Elles* included Camille Morineau, Emma Lavigne, Quentin Bajac, Cécile Debray, and Valérie Guillaume.

103 Morineau in an email to the author, May 2012.

104 Cited in Phoebe Hoban, "The Feminist Evolution."

105 Morineau left the institution to pursue independent curating and has since organized a large and highly-acclaimed exhibition dedicated to Niki de Saint Phalle, one of France's most famous feminist artists, which premiered in September 2014 at the Grand Palais in Paris. The statistics in this paragraph are from an email from Morineau to the author in May 2012.

106 Morineau, email to the author, May 2012.

107 See Okwui Enwezor, in *Artforum International*, p. 201.

108 See Nicole Salez, "elles@centrepompidou: Interview de Camille Morineau."

109 See, for example, Christine Frérot, "elles@centrepompidou," p. 136; and Suzanne

Muchnic, "At Paris's Pompidou Center." Accessed: April 2017.

110 See Emmanuelle Lequeux, *Le Monde*.

111 Catherine Gonnard, "Intersecting Views," p. 152.

112 Germaine Greer, "Why the world doesn't need an Annie Warhol or a Francine Bacon."

113 Jonathan Jones, "Mistresspieces."

114 Alfred Pacquement, "Preface," p. 13.

115 Amelia Jones, "Feminist Subjects," p. 12.

116 *Re.act.feminism*, n.d., "The Programme." See also Bettina Knaup and Beatrice E. Stammer (eds.), *re.act.feminism—a performing archive*.

117 Deepwell, "re.act.feminism," p. 81.

118 Bettina Knaup, cited in Deepwell, "re.act. feminism," p. 81.

119 Ibid. Such themes were explored in the works of Regina José Galindo (*Perra*, 2005), Tanja Ostojić (*Integration Project*, 2000–11), Ewa Partum (*Selbstidentifikation*, 1980), Orlan (*MesuRage de la Place Saint-Lambert*, 1980), and Raeda Saadeh (*Vacuum*, 2007).

120 Irmgard Berner, *Berliner Zeitung*, July 2, 2013.

121 See *Das Kunstmagazin*, "Five Tips of the Week," June 28, 2013. re.act.feminism was one of the five shows the editorial team was recommending to see in Berlin.

122 See Kathrin Bettina Müller, "Find Your Own Path".

3. TACKLING WHITE PRIVILEGE AND WESTERN-CENTRISM

1 Judith Wilson, "Art," p. 7.

2 Okwui Enwezor, "The Black Box," p. 45.

3 See Martin Gayford, "More Marx," p. 50.

4 Eunsong Kim and Maya Isabella Mackrandilal, "The Whitney Biennial."

5 See Whitney Museum website, "Whitney Biennial 2014." Accessed: May 2015. Ironically, the 1993 Whitney Biennial was one of the most multi-cultural exhibitions in US history, and was renowned as the first one in which white male artists were in the minority.

6 See Ben Davis, "The Yams."

7 See Felicia R. Lee, "Racially Themed Work."

8 See the press release by the collective #StopErasingBlackPeople. Accessed: April 2017.

9 Artist Chris Jordan has argued that African Americans have suffered 41% of all AIDS deaths in the USA and account for 44% of all new HIV infections in the USA: quoted in Rosemary Ponnekanti, "Tacoma Art Museum." Similarly, the Centers for Disease Control and Prevention website states that, "African Americans are the racial/ethnic group most affected by HIV in the United States." Accessed: April 2016.

10 Richard Brody, "The Oscar Whiteness Machine."

11 Parul Sehgal, "Fighting Erasure."

12 Kymberly Pinder, "Black Representation," p. 533.

13 Ibid.

14 Stuart Hall, "New Ethnicities," p. 442.

15 Beryl Wright, quoted in Maurice Berger, "Are Art Museums Racist?" p. 72.

16 See Chimamanda Ngozi Adichie, "The Danger of a Single Story." Accessed: April 2016.

17 See BFAMFAPHD website. Accessed: May 2015. The collective's analysis is drawn from the US Census Bureau's 2010–12 "American Community Survey," from which they created their own Census Report that looks specifically at the demographics and lives of artists

in New York City. Unsurprisingly, the situation was also dire in the late 1980s: a 1989 study of "art-world racism" in New York by the artist Howardena Pindell demonstrated that white-identified galleries and museums have little interest in enfranchising African Americans and other people of color. Based on her statistical overview of the demographics of mainstream art exhibitions, Pindell concluded that "black, Hispanic, Asian, and Native American artists are…with a few, very few, exceptions systematically excluded." See Howardena Pindell, "Art World Racism," p. 32.

18 Olu Oguibe, *The Culture Game*, xiii.

19 Ibid.

20 Gerardo Mosquera, "The Marco Polo Syndrome," p. 223.

21 Olu Oguibe, *The Culture Game*, p. 10.

22 Ibid., xiii.

23 Mosquera, "The Marco Polo Syndrome," pp. 221–22.

24 Mosquera, "Some Problems," p. 135.

25 See Kobena Mercer, "Black art," pp. 61–78.

26 Gerardo Mosquera, as cited in Mari Carmen Ramírez, "Beyond 'The Fantastic'," p. 243.

27 Johanne Lamoureux, "From Form to Platform," p. 71.

28 Ibid.

29 Chelsea Haines, "The Whole Earth Show Revisited," p. 130.

30 Benjamin H. D. Buchloch, "The Whole Earth Show," p. 153.

31 Ibid., p. 151.

32 Ibid., p. 155.

33 Ibid., p. 151.

34 Eleanor Heartney, "The Whole Earth Show, Part II," p. 90.

35 Ibid., pp. 91–92.

36 See Tim Griffin, "Global tendencies," p. 152ff.

37 See Haines "The Whole Earth Show Revisited," p. 129.

38 Michael Brenson, "Is 'Quality' An Idea?"

39 Buchloch, "The Whole Earth Show," p. 158.

40 Martin quoted in Buchloch, "The Whole Earth Show," p. 158.

41 See Lucy R. Lippard, in *Mixed Blessings*, who lists the ten women artists as Marina Abramović, Louise Bourgeois, Bowa Devi, Coosje van Bruggen, Seni Camara, Rebecca Horn, Shirazeh Houshiary, Barbara Kruger, Esther Mahlangu, and Nancy Spero.

42 Thomas McEvilley, "The Global Issue," p. 157.

43 Buchloch, "The Whole Earth Show," p. 155.

44 Ibid., p. 213.

45 The four curators were Sharon F. Patton, Julia P. Herzberg, Laura Trippi, and Gary Sangster.

46 Julia Herzberg, "Re-Membering Identity," p. 37. Brenson notes that Lowery Stokes Sims wrote in her catalog essay about the "long struggle of 'women, gays, and hyphenated Americans of African, Latin, Asian and native descent' to have their cultural values recognized by an establishment that upholds Western culture as a 'sole criterion by which to judge such qualifiers as 'quality', 'beauty', and, yes, even 'truth'," see Brenson, "Is 'Quality' An Idea?"

47 As mentioned in a general press release issued by New Museum of Contemporary Art in 1990.

48 Elizabeth Hess, "The Decade Show," p. 87.

49 First performed in 1987 at the Museum of Man in Balboa Park, San Diego, this was Luna's second re-enactment. As he explained: "I had long looked at representation of our peoples in museums and they all dwelled in the past. They were one-sided. We were

simply objects among bones, bones among objects, and then signed and sealed with a date. In *The Artifact Piece* I became the Indian and lied in state as an exhibit along with my personal objects. That hit a nerve and spoke loud both in Indian country, the art world and the frontier of anthropology. The installation took objects that were representational of a modern Indian, which happened to be me, collecting my memorabilia such as my degree, my divorce papers, photos, record albums, cassettes, college mementos. It told a story about a man who was in college in the 60s, but this man happened to be native, and that was the twist on it." See Kenneth R. Fletcher, "James Luna."

50 See Julio V. Blanc, "When You Think of Mexico," p. 17.

51 Hess, "The Decade Show." And as Eunice Lipton pointed out, "At the very least such an exhibit—because of its multicultural interests, its physical location in different demographic enclaves in the city, the equal involvement of culturally different institutions and networks—calls ethnocentrism into question. This is not a patronizing exhibit of the art of 'exotica' put together by the philanthropic goodwill and high-art-world curiosity of a few white curators. It is an exhibit attempting to construct a multivocal art world. It begins to suggest that the notion of a 'center' and a 'margin' is anachronistic and that maintaining such a model represents a desire to wield exclusive power and control." See Lipton, "Here Today," p. 20.

52 See Kay Larson, "Three's Company."

53 Curator Lowery Stokes Sims sent a letter to Michael Brenson in which she attempted to further elucidate the importance of recognizing "difference" in regard to artists of color who addressed questions of identity from different perspectives from white American artists.

54 Roberta Smith, "Three Museums."

55 The Contemporary museum is a "nomad" museum that does not hold collections—so although the exhibition was commissioned by The Contemporary, it was held at The Maryland Historical Society.

56 Lisa Corrin, "Do museums perpetuate cultural bias?"

57 Zouaves were French infantry units (*c.* 1830–62)—often composed of Algerian recruits—noted for their resilience, precision drilling, and distinctive uniforms.

58 By choosing to display this damaged picture, Wilson violates another museum taboo: "Damaged goods are an institutional shame hidden in the recesses of vaults, discreetly out of public view. The exposure of this private shame functions as a metaphor for the hidden shame of the animated figure whose torn white surface can no longer conceal the black face within." See Lisa Corrin, "Mining the Museum," p. 14.

59 Brian Wallis, "A Forum, Not a Temple," p. 620.

60 David Ross, "Preface: Know Thy Self," p. 9.

61 Ibid.

62 Elisabeth Sussman, "Then and Now," p. 75.

63 Smith, "At the Whitney."

64 Roger Kimball, "Of Chocolate," p. 55.

65 Michael Kimmelman, "At the Whitney."

66 Peter Schjeldahl, "Art + Politics," p. 34.

67 Kimmelman, "At the Whitney."

68 Jerry Saltz, "'93 in Art."

69 The statistics for the representation of female versus male artists in the Whitney Biennials from 1973 to 1993 can be found in Carrie Rickey's "Illustrated Time Line," pp. 304–308. On average, the figure was 28% women artists.

70 Of the artists included in the 1993 Whitney Biennial, 36.4% were white males, 29.5% were white females, 22.75% were males of color and 11.4% were females of color. These statistics are taken from a 1995 poster by the Guerrilla Girls entitled "Traditional Values and Quality Return to the Whitey Museum." On their website, the caption to the poster reads: "The Whitney Museum Gets a New Name: The 1993 Whitney Biennial was the first ever to have a minority of white male artists...In 1995 the museum returned to previous miniscule percentages of artists of color. That's why when we tried to typeset the word Whitney, we just couldn't find the letter 'n.'" Accessed: May 2017.

71 Ibid.

72 Ibid. The website states that from 1993 to 1995, the percentage of white males at the Whitney Biennial increased from 36.4% to 55.5%.

73 Ibid.

74 In *Xinhua News Agency*, "Britain's Tate Modern," p. 1.

75 See Emma Dexter, "Century City." Accessed: March 2017.

76 Adrian Searle, "Urban Sprawl."

77 Chris Turner, "Century City."

78 Blake Gopnik, "Century City Sprawl," G.8.

79 Enwezor, "The Black Box," p. 42.

80 Ibid., p. 45. In their book *Empire*, p. xv, Michael Hardt and Antonio Negri describe the "multitude" as a "resistance force, opposed to the power of the Empire." See Hardt and Negri, *Empire*, p. xv.

81 Enwezor, "The Black Box," p. 40.

82 Ibid.

83 Enwezor, as quoted in Moira Jeffrey, "Tall Order," p. 23.

84 Peter Plagens, "A Country Fair," p. 58.

85 Jeffrey, "Tall Order," p. 23.

86 See Thomas McEvilley, "*Documenta 11*."

87 Sylvester Okwunodu Ogbechie, "Ordering the Universe," p. 82.

88 Ibid.

89 Ibid. However, despite his support of Enwezor's curatorial aim, Ogbechie was concerned that the focus on non-Western art might simply be answering global capitalism's persistent need for new commodities, and that by bringing these artists from margin to center, Enwezor was now making them available for easy consumption. He argued: "the exhibition may be constructing the conditions for a new appropriation of the 'other' by the West, in a manner similar to modernism's appropriation of African and other 'non-Western' arts at the beginning of the twentieth century." Ibid.

90 Enwezor, "The Black Box," p. 45.

91 Enwezor, quoted in Tim Griffin, "Global Tendencies," p. 154. The participants in the roundtable included Enwezor, Yinka Shonibare, James Meyer, Francesco Bonami, Martha Rosler, Catherine David, and Hans-Ulrich Obrist. Incidentally, Yinka Shonibare also defended *Magiciens* when he placed it within a history of exhibitions, along with *Documenta* 10 and 11, that "created a necessary forum for giving visibility to the non-Western artist"; see Griffin, "Global Tendencies," pp. 152–63, especially pp. 154, 206, 212 (the article was continued at the back of the magazine).

92 Lamoureux, "From Form to Platform," p. 82. Incidentally, Katy Deepwell notes (in "Women Artists," p. 44) that 37% of the artists in Enwezor's exhibition were women. (To put this in perspective: the 12th edition of *Documenta*, curated by Roger Buergel, included 57 women out of 109 artists—a promising 52%. Carolyn Christov-Bakargiev's ratios from 2012 weren't much better than Enwezor's, however—in her exhibition, only 38% of the artists in the exhibition were women. Nonetheless that is an improvement on Catherine David's exhibition in 1997: the first female director included less than 2% women. Statistics compiled by the author.)

93 See Robert Atkins, "Everybody's Art."

94 *The Global Contemporary After 1989* [exhibition guide], p. 6.

95 Ibid.

96 Peter Weibel, "Globalization and Contemporary Art," p. 21.

97 These artists included Anetta Mona Chişa & Lucia Tkáčová, Minerva Cuevas, Ala Ebtekar, Yara El-Sherbini, Brendan Fernandes, Will Kwan, Pooneh Maghazehe, Karen Mirza & Brad Butler, Eko Nugroho, Ruth Sacks, and Tintin Wulia.

98 Kerstin Winking, "The Global Contemporary," p. 622.

99 Atkins, "Everybody's Art."

100 Ibid. "Participation [in art fairs] has become mandatory for major-league galleries, forcing out less well-financed rivals, ensuring consolidation within the art industry and making fairs the place where dealers close an ever-larger percentage of their private sales."

101 Pat Binder and Gerhard Haupt, "The Global Contemporary." Accessed: May 2016.

102 JJ Charlesworth, "The Global Contemporary."

103 The figure of 14% is roughly in line with the African continent's portion of the world's population. There were also strong contingents from all the other continents, although European artists were the largest group—about one-third was born in Europe and nearly 44% lived and worked there. North America and Asia followed in the number two and three spots, accounting for about 22% and 15%, respectively. See *ArtNews*, "How Geographically Diverse is the 2015 Venice Biennale?"

104 See Okwui Enwezor, "All the World's Futures" (curatorial statement). Accessed: May 2016.

105 Roberta Smith, "Art for the Planet's Sake."

106 Ibid.

107 Ibid.

108 Laura Cumming, "56th Venice Biennale," p. 30; Gayford, "More Marx"; Juliana Engberg, "Theatre of Labour," pp. 58–63.

109 Cumming, "56th Venice Biennale."

110 Gayford, "More Marx," p. 50.

111 Enwezor quoted in Michelle Kuo, "Global Entry," p. 86.

112 Gregory Volk, "All the World's Futures." Accessed: March 2017.

113 From Enwezor's curatorial statement, "All the World's Futures." Accessed: May 2016.

114 Enwezor, cited in Kuo "Global Entry." Enwezor noted in the same interview that he didn't fear the fact that it may prove a total cacophony. He continued, "As Public Enemy said, 'Bring the noise.' I want an enlivening setting for this Biennale. I am interested in not simply having dead time, where things are sitting there waiting for the public to come, but in presenting experiences that are current, with daily and different iterations,

different textures. So you see these works happening before you—it's not post-production. And I want to see if it's possible to inject some kind of previsual moment into the exhibition. That's why I wanted to bring in works that have to do with the voice, with orality, with speaking. And with words—words that are said, sung, recited, written, projected, sculpted, drawn, or painted."

4. CHALLENGING HETEROCENTRISM AND LESBO-HOMOPHOBIA

1 Jonathan Weinberg, "Things Are Queer," p. 12.
2 The artists were: Harmony Hammond, Louise Fishman, Kate Millett, Fran Winant, Barbara Asch, Suzanne Bevier, Betsy Damon, Maxine Fine, Jessie Falstein, Mary Ann King, Gloria Klein, Dona Nelson, Flavia Rando, Sandra de Sando, Amy Sillman, Ellen Turner, Janey Washburn, and Ann Wilson (with Amy Scarola, Etana Dreamer, and Yvonne Lindsay adding their work to the walls during the exhibition).
3 Harmony Hammond, "A Lesbian Show," p. 45.
4 Ibid., p. 44.
5 Kay Larson, "Lesbian Art," p. 67.
6 Arlene Raven and Ruth Iskin, "Through the Peephole," pp. 20–21. See also Margo Hobbs Thompson, "DIY Identity Kit," pp. 260–82.
7 Raven and Iskin, "Through the Peephole," pp. 20–21, 24.
8 Ibid., p. 28.
9 Ibid., p. 23.
10 From the *GALAS Brochure* (unpaginated, unbound, multi-page photocopy).
11 Dan Cameron, "Sensibility as Content," pp. 6–9.
12 Lawrence Rinder, "An Introduction to *In a Different Light*." Accessed: May 2017.
13 Ibid.
14 Mark Joseph Stern, "Putting Artists Back in the Closet?" Accessed: May 2013.
15 Ibid.
16 Ken Silver, "Modes of Disclosure," pp. 179–203.
17 Jonathan Katz, "Hide/Seek: Difference and Desire," pp. 44–45.
18 James Saslow, "Closets and the Museum," pp. 215–27.
19 David Wojnarowicz, "Post Cards," pp. 6–11.
20 Brian Logan, "Hide/Seek."
21 Maura Reilly co-curated *neoqueer* with Craig Houser and co-curated *Citizen Queer* with Frederikke Hansen.
22 The Woman's Building, founded in Los Angeles in 1973, housed the Feminist Studio Workshop, The Center for Feminist Art Historical Studies (run by Arlene Raven and Ruth Iskin), the Women's Graphic Center, Womanspace (a gallery), Gallery 707, and two more galleries, a bookstore, a press, and an improvisational-theater group.
23 Terry Wolverton, "Great American Lesbian Art Show," p. 50.
24 Wolverton, *Insurgent Muse*, p. 92.
25 From the *GALAS Brochure*.
26 Hammond, GALAS Guidebook.
27 See Diane Elvenstar, "Art from Closet to Gallery," pp. G1–G2.
28 Thompson, *Sex and Sensibilities*, p. 301.
29 Quoted in Neal Menzies, "Sexual Identity."
30 Thompson, "DIY Identity Kit,' p. 264.
31 In GALAS *Inform-Hers Packet:* "[GALAS] is a national series of exhibits and events honoring lesbian creativity... [T]he goals of GALAS are: to celebrate lesbian art by making it public, visible, and accessible; to build a national network of lesbian artists and a permanent

slide collection of lesbian art...We are asking women to organize exhibits of lesbian art in your own communities. These shows will occur at the same time all across the United States!" From the *GALAS Brochure*.
32 Wolverton, "Great American Lesbian Art Show," p. 52.
33 Elvenstar, "Art from Closet to Gallery," pp. G1–G2; *Gay Community News* [anon.], "National network honors lesbian artists."
34 Menzies, "Sexual Identity and Anonymity," p. 4.
35 Suzanne Muchnic, "Art Review," Sec. VI, p. 1.
36 Marcia Tucker, *Extended Sensibilities*, p. IV: "It is the first museum exhibition in the United States to address an important question: in what way and to what extent has some of the most interesting contemporary art addressed and reflected the concerns of the homosexual community, which has substantially increased its visibility in the past few years."
37 The nineteen artists were Charley Brown, Scott Burton, Craig Carver, Arch Connelly, Janet Cooling, Betsy Damon, Nancy Fried, Jedd Garet, Gilbert & George, Lee Gordon, Harmony Hammond, John Henninger, Jerry Janosco, Lili Lakich, Les Petites Bonbons, Ross Paxton, Jody Pinto, Carla Tardi, and Fran Winant.
38 Luce Irigaray, *Speculum*, p. 101.
39 Cameron, "Sensibility as Content," p. 8.
40 Ibid. The "sensibility content" category was further sub-divided into three types: "the homosexual self," the "homosexual other," and "the world transformed," pp. 7–8.
41 Ibid., p. 6.
42 Cameron, "Extended Sensibilities," p. 54.
43 Ibid.
44 Grace Glueck, "Botanical Bronzes," C22.
45 See Cameron, "Sensibility as Content," pp. 37–38.
46 See, for example, James Saslow, "New York's 'Extended Sensibilities'," pp. 48–51.
47 See, for example, Hammond, "A Lesbian Show," p. 57.
48 See Saslow, "New York's 'Extended Sensibilities',": "generally uninspiring," p. 51; "embarrassingly amateur," p. 48.
49 Richard Flood, "Review: *Extended Sensibilities*," p. 72.
50 Jeff Weinstein, "Gay or Not," p. 10.
51 Saslow, "New York's 'Extended Sensibilities'," p. 48: "campy iconoclasm...etc"; re. Tardi: p. 51: "Sadder still is the tendency of the catalogue to bury all discussion of subject matter under an avalanche of formalist art-critical jargon. I am not at all sure what Carla Tardi's abstract oils on wood panels have to do with gay sensibility, and my puzzlement is not resolved by being told about 'an imagery that emulates the direction and movement, but metamorphoses the tactility and form, of nature herself'."
52 Ibid., p. 51.
53 Flood, "Review: *Extended Sensibilities*," p. 73.
54 Glueck, "Botanical Bronzes," C22.
55 The twenty-two artists were: David Armstrong, Tom Chesley, Dorit Cypris, Philip-Lorca diCorcia, Jane Dickson, Darrel Ellis, Allen Frame, Peter Hujar, Greer Lankton, Siobhan Liddel, James Nares, Perico Pastor, Margo Pelletier, Clarence Elie Rivera, Vittorio Scarpati, Jo Shane, Kiki Smith, Janet Stein, Stephen Tashjian, Shellburne Thurber, Ken Tisa, David Wojnarowicz.
56 Nan Goldin, "In the Valley," pp. 4–5.

57 Ibid., p. 5. The show was also intended, according to Susan Wyatt (executive director of Artists Space), as "a kind of testimony of survival, of keeping the faith, despite the insidious nature of the disease and the prejudice surrounding it"; Susan Wyatt, quoted in John Russell, "Images of Grief and Rage." In her catalog essay, Linda Yablonsky described the show as making the "forbidden visible": "In shows like this one, we can review our triumphs, air our grief, lay ourselves bare, heal, shiver"; Yablonsky in *Witnesses*, pp. 12–13. In the end, it was less a show about AIDS, and more of "a collective memorial," according to Goldin in "In the Valley."
58 As Larson explains, Wojnarowicz "lashes out at the disease that is ruining his life, the desperate plight of the HIV poor, and the callousness of the establishment. He speaks from an afflicted heart: 'Rage', he writes, 'may be one of the few things that binds or connects me to you.' The punishments he would like to inflict on Helms, Dannemeyer, and others who have actively blocked safe-sex instruction are what have landed him in trouble with the NEA. (He wants to throw Dannemeyer from the Empire State Building and douse Helms with gasoline.) Yet he explicitly says these are fantasies." Kay Larson, "Days of Rage," p. 79.
59 Few perceived the partial reversal as a victory. Wojnarowicz, in particular, was outraged by Wyatt's decision to accept the partially restored grant, and even refused to attend the opening: "I don't feel that civil or constitutional rights are a worthy trade for money." As quoted on the Artists Space website in "Witnesses: Against Our Vanishing." Accessed: May 2016.
60 See Goldin, "20 years: AIDS & Photography." Accessed: April 2016.
61 Calvin Reid, "Beyond Mourning," pp. 51–56.
62 Kiki Smith, quoted in Artists Space (eds.), *Witnesses*, p. 28.
63 See Artists Space, "Press Release." Accessed: May 2017.
64 Russell, "Images of Grief and Rage."
65 Larson, "Days of Rage," p. 79.
66 Rinder, "An Introduction to *In a Different Light*," p. 1.
67 Ibid.
68 Nayland Blake, "Curating *In a Different Light*," p. 11.
69 Rinder, "An Introduction to *In a Different Light*," p. 6.
70 Kevin Killian, "The Secret Histories," p. 23.
71 Blake, "Curating In a Different Light," p. 23.
72 Rinder, "An Introduction to *In a Different Light*," p. 7.
73 See David Bonetti, "Looking at Art."
74 See Robert Atkins, "Goodbye," pp. 80–85.
75 Cecilia Dougherty, "Identity Crisis," p. 29ff.
76 Ibid.
77 Atkins, "Goodbye," pp. 80–85.
78 Christopher Knight, "Shining a 'Different Light'."
79 Bonetti, "Looking at art."
80 See Juan Vicente Aliaga, "Un mapa infinito" ["An Infinite Map"], pp. 282–306. The artists in *En Todas Partes* included: ACT UP and Gran Fury, Tariq Alvi, Xoán Anleo / Uqui Permui, Alexander Apóstol, Kutluğ Ataman, Ron Athey, Charles Atlas, Leigh Bowery, Kaucyila Brooke, Bruce LaBruce, Tom Burr, Cabello / Carceller, Loren Cameron, Giuseppe Campuzano, Luciano Castelli, Tee Corinne, Juan Davila, Del LaGrace Volcano, Dias &

Riedweg, George Dureau, Nicole Eisenman, Michael Elmgreen & Ingar Dragset, Pepe Espaliú, Fierce Pussy, Samuel Fosso, Annette Frick, Carmela García, Robert Gober, Roberto González-Fernández, Félix González-Torres, Nancy Grossman, Hervé Guibert, Sunil Gupta, Barbara Hammer, Keith Haring, Lyle Ashton Harris, David Hockney, Ins A Kromminga, Derek Jarman, Isaac Julien, Zoe Leonard, Lenilson, Renate Lorenz & Pauline Boudry, LSD (Fefa Vila), Monica Majoli, Robert Mapplethorpe, Jesús Martínez Oliva, Pepe Miralles, Donald Moffett, Ocaña, Marcel Odenbach, Elisabeth Ohlson, Henrik Olesen, Catherine Opie, Ulrike Ottinger, Pablo Pérez-Mínguez, Pierre & Gilles, Jack Pierson, Mark Raidpere, Catherine Saalfield, Tejal Sham, Ahlam Shibli, Jack Smith, Annie Sprinkle / Les Nichols, Wolfgang Tillmans, Herbert Tobias, Tom of Finland, Monika Treut, Video-Nou, Azucena Vieites, Andy Warhol, David Wojnarowicz, Yeguas del Apocalipsis, and Akram Zaatari.

81 In *Gender Trouble*, Judith Butler challenged the concept of a stable gender identity and maintained that it is the *repetition* of "gender acts"—including, how we dress, our language and choice of sexual partner, our manner-isms and affectations—that determines our gender. She considered cross-dressing and drag to be examples of the various ways in which "performativity of gender" can be used to subvert the norms of gender identity and thereby to destabilize traditional notions of masculinity and femininity.

82 Aliaga in an email to the author, August 2016.

83 See José Luis Jiménez, "Denuncian al CGAC." See also Xosé Manuel Lens, "Arte y Diversidad Sexual"; and "En Todas Partes" (anon.).

84 See Jiménez, "Denuncian al CGAC."

85 Ibid.

86 See Javier Montes, "Review: En Todas Partes".

87 Paweł Leszkowicz, *Ars Homo Erotica*, pp. 8–16.

88 Leszkowicz, "The Power of Queer Curating," pp. 118–52.

89 Ibid.

90 On the controversy surrounding the exhibi-tion, see Julia Michalska, "Poland's National Museum."

91 Leszkowicz, *Ars Homo Erotica*, p. 162.

92 Marek Bartelik, "Ars Homo Erotica."

93 Michalska, "Poland's National Museum."

94 Rafal Kiepuszewski, "Warsaw's exhibition."

95 Logan, "Too Shocking for America."

96 Roberta Smith, "This Gay American Life," C.23; Holland Cotter, "Sexuality in Modernism."

97 Ariella Budick, "Hide/Seek: Difference and Desire."

98 See the Centers for Disease Control and Prevention website. Accessed: August 2016.

99 Quoted in Stan Ziv, "Exhibit at Bronx Museum."

100 Katz quoted in Sarah Douglas, "Is this the first AIDS artwork?"

101 Ibid.

102 The New Museum of Contemporary Art had invited ACT UP (AIDS Coalition to Unleash Power) to raise AIDS awareness. "The tri-angle was from the Nazi prison camps and it was inverted. This was about activating a new kind of power...It was 1987 and 40,000 people had already died. And Reagan (the president at the time) was saying nothing. This is where the conversation of AIDS was directly inserted into the museum." Rock Hushka, chief curator of Tacoma Art Museum (TAM), as quoted in Florangela Davila, "TAM's new exhibit."

103 Michael Upchurch, "How AIDS changed American art"; and Jen Graves, "Tacoma Art Museum's *Art AIDS America*."

104 Jared Quinton, "Two Exhibitions." Accessed: August 2016.

105 Deborah Solomon, "Review: A Brave Show on Art and AIDS," WNYC Radio, July 29, 2016.

106 Felicia Feaster, "Powerful Zuckerman survey show."

107 On the controversy surrounding the exhibi-tion, see Ziv, "Exhibit at Bronx Museum."

108 Tal Rosenberg, "A former bank in Lincoln Park."

109 Robin Dluzen, "Art AIDS America Chicago."

110 Tempestt Hazel, "When the End is the Beginning."

111 Thomas Feldhacker, "Under-Representing an American Tragedy," p. 30.

5. A CALL TO ARMS: STRATEGIES FOR CHANGE

1 Marcia Tucker in Ella Shohat, *Talking Visions*, p. xii.

2 Russell Storer in an interview with the author, September 2015, Brisbane, Australia.

3 In her installation of the collection at Tate Modern in London in 2000, Iwona Blazwick arranged the works into four overarching themes instead of according to a chronologi-cal, linear interpretation that adhered to a strict art-historical canon. Sadly, the instal-lation received terrible press, and by 2004 the museum had returned to the master, synchronic narrative.

4 Oscar Wilde, "The Critic as Artist," p. 979.

5 Other examples of major exhibitions over the past few decades that display a surprising gender and race disparity include *Documenta 8* (1987), organized by Manfred Schneckenburger; *Objects of Desire: The Modern Still Life* (1997) at MoMA, New York, organized by Margit Rowell, which presented only three white women and one artist of color out of a total of seventy-one artists; *Manifesta 5* (2004), in San Sebastian, Spain, which was approximately 80% male; and *Discrete Energies* (2005), a fifty-year-anniversary exhi-bition of *Documenta* held at the Fridericianum in Kassel, Germany, curated by Michael Glasmeier, which included eleven (white) women out of eighty-three artists.

6 Quoted by Käthe Kollwitz in a Guerrilla Girls online interview, "Confessions of the Guerrilla Girls." Accessed: April 2017.

7 Another excellent example of gender and race disparity in exhibition practice is one curated by Christine Macel at the Pompidou Center, Paris, in spring 2005, entitled *Dionysiac: Art in Flux*. The show, which took the Greek god Dionysus as a source of inspiration and explored themes of intoxication, ecstasy, wild revelry, and music, featured commissioned installations by fourteen international art-ists—all white males. "You got to admit, that takes balls," Max Henry exclaimed in a review of the show; see Max Henry, "Dionysus in Paris." Accessed: April 4, 2017.

8 Eddy Frankel, "Almost every major art exhibition."

9 Hilarie Sheets, "Female Artists."

10 See Marcia Tucker on Gayatri Spivak in Shohat, *Talking Visions*, p. xii.

11 Linda Nochlin, "Why Have There Been No Great Women Artists?," p. 47.

12 Maurice Berger, "Are Art Museums Racist?," p. 74 [author's italics].

13 Nochlin quoted in Barbara A. MacAdam, "Where the Great Women Artists Are Now."

14 Ken Johnson, "51 Contemporary Artists."

15 These Other artists included: Paul Chan, Nam June Paik, Saskia Olde Wolbers, Vanessa Beecroft, Hilla and Bernd Becher, Jennifer Allora and Guillermo Calzadilla.

16 Brian Sewell, quoted in Andrew Johnson, "There's Never Been a Great Woman Artist."

17 Jonathan Jones, "The $44m for Georgia O'Keeffe."

18 Ibid.

19 Madeleine Dore, "Where Are the Women?"

20 Greg Allen, "X-Factor," section 2, p. 1.

21 Quoted in Andrew Johnson, "There's never been."

22 Jerry Saltz, "The Battle for Babylon."

23 Saltz, Facebook post, November 11, 2012.

24 Deborah Kass, in a phone conversation with the author, May 2015.

25 Josh Spero, "Portrait of inequality."

26 Julia Halperin, "Creating value."

27 Ibid.

28 Morris, quoted in Andrew Taylor, "Tate Modern director."

29 See Berger, "Are Art Museums Racist?"

30 Similarly, participation in feminist curatorial initiatives such as "If I Can't Dance, I Don't Want To Be Part of Your Revolution," a curato-rial group from Amsterdam, Holland, founded in 2005 by curators Frédérique Bergholtz, Annie Fletcher, and Tanja Elstgeest, moves academic feminism into the public sphere. Along with collectives such as the Feminist Curators United (fCU), an initiative that I started in 2015 with Helena Reckitt at Goldsmiths, University of London, and Lara Perry at University of Brighton, England, we can create a critically necessary "old girl's" network for curators.

31 bell hooks, "Expertease," p. 20.

32 bell hooks, *Talking Back*, pp. 8–9.

33 See Chimamanda Ngozi Adichie, "We Should All Be Feminists, " TED talk. However, as Sarah Ahmed cautions, to "speak out" or "call out" an injustice is to run the risk of being deemed a "feminist killjoy," and a com-plainer. In her TED talk, Adichie responded to such accusations by declaring herself a "Happy Feminist." Accessed: May 2017.

34 For example, in 2013, the *New York Times Book Review* responded to data showing it infrequently featured female authors when it appointed Pamela Paul as its new editor and made a public commitment to righting the balance. See Mallary Jean Tenore, "New York Times Book Review editor." Accessed: May 2015.

35 For example, the December 2014 issue of *Vanity Fair* featured an article by Ingrid Sischy entitled "Prima Galleristas," (aka "The Top 14 Female Art Dealers"), which was accompanied by a photograph by Annie Leibovitz—a re-creation of a famous 1982 photograph by Hans Namuth, which featured a nearly all-male portrait of art-world power-houses. While the "update" was a stunning portrait of an iconic group of powerful art-world women, what was left unsaid was how few of these "galleristas" actually support women artists. Indeed, all but one of them—Jeanne Greenberg Rohatyn—represented women less than 33% of the time. In effect, these women gallerists collude in practices against their own sex.

BIBLIOGRAPHY

Adichie, Chimamanda Ngozi, "The Danger of a Single Story," TED Talk, 2009. Available at: www.ted.com/talks/chimamanda_adichie_the_danger_of_a_single_story.

— , "We Should All Be Feminists," TED Talk, 2012. Available at: www.ted.com/talks/chimamanda_ngozi_adichie_we_should_all_be_feminists; and reproduced in Chimamanda Ngozi Adichie, *We Should All Be Feminists*, London: Vintage Books, 2014.

Aiken, Susan Hardy, "Women and the Question of Canonicity," *College English*, Vol. 48, No. 3, March, 1986.

Aliaga, Juan Vicente, "Un mapa infinito. Acerca de las representaciones de la diversidad sexual en el arte desde los sesenta hasta la actualidad," ["An Infinite Map: On the Representations of Sexual Diversity in Art from the Sixties to the Present"] *En Todas Partes: Políticas de la diversidad sexual en el arte* [exhibition catalogue], Santiago de Compostela: CGAC, 2009.

Allen, Greg, "X-Factor: Is the Art Market Rational or Biased?" *New York Times*, May 1, 2005, section 2.

Allen, Jennifer, "Women on the Verge," *Artforum International*, 43.3, November 1, 2004.

Armstrong, Carol, "Review: Global Feminisms and Wack!" *Artforum*, May 2007.

Artists Space, "Press Release: Witnesses: Against Our Vanishing," n.d. Available at: s3.amazonaws.com/asmedia/57d1215edd94b1d11d664c3a451c7dc3/r7SSvfP_Vy.pdf.

Artists Space (eds.), *Witnesses: Against Our Vanishing* [exhibition catalogue], New York: Artists Space, 1989.

artnet News, "Who are the Top 100 Most Collectible Living Artists?," May 26, 2016. Available at: news.artnet.com/market/top-100-collectible-living-artists-504059.

ArtNews, "How Geographically Diverse is the 2015 Venice Biennale?," March 6, 2015.

ArtSlant, "MoMA Plans Only Female Art for 2015," April 1, 2014. Available at: www.artslant.com/ny/articles/show/39142-bnews-moma-announces-2015-focus-on-women-artists-gagosian-to-open-yet-another-gallery-jemima-kirke-quits-girls-and-putin-reveals-his-first-solo-exhibition.

Atkins, Robert, "Goodbye Lesbian/Gay History, Hello 'Queer Sensibility': Meditating on Curatorial Practice," *College Art Association Journal*, winter 1996.

— , "Everybody's Art," *Art in America*, March 2014.

Avgikos, Jan, Michael Corris, and Benjamin Weissman, "Bad Girl Blues," *Artforum*, 32.9, May 1994.

Azimi, Roxana, "'Carambolages', un melting-pot d'oeuvres d'art au Grand Palais," *Le Monde*, March 7, 2016.

Bartelik, Marek, "Ars Homo Erotica," *Artforum*, October 2010.

Barthes, Roland, "The Death of the Author," *Image-Music-Text*, New York: Hill and Wang, 1977.

Battersby, Matilda, "Queer British Art at Tate Britain: Is it wrong to group together LGBT art?," *The Independent*, April 6, 2017.

Berger, Maurice, "Are Art Museums Racist?," *Art in America*, September 1990.

Berner, Irmgard, *Berliner Zeitung*, July 2, 2013.

BFAMFAPHD website, available at: bfamfaphd.com.

Binder, Pat, and Gerhard Haupt, "The Global Contemporary." Available at: u-in-u.com/en/specials/2011/global-contemporary/.

Blake, Nayland, "Curating *In a Different Light*," *In a Different Light: Visual Culture, Sexual Identity, Queer Practice*, San Francisco: City Lights Publishers, 1995.

Blanc, Julio V., "When You Think of Mexico: Latin American Women in the Decade Show," *Arts Magazine*, April 1990.

Blazwick, Iwona, and Laura Cottingham, "Who's Bad?: A Mixed Response to a Season of Bad Girls," *Frieze*, March 6, 1994. Available at: frieze.com/article/whos-bad.

Bonetti, David, "Looking at art 'In a Different Light'," *San Francisco Chronicle*, January 11, 1995.

Bowley, Graham, "Institute of Contemporary Art in Boston Gets Gift of Works by Women," *New York Times*, December 9, 2015.

Brenson, Michael, "Is 'Quality' An Idea Whose Time Has Gone?," *New York Times*, July 22, 1990.

Brody, Richard, "The Oscar Whiteness Machine," *New Yorker*, January 21, 2016.

Brown, Mark, "Frances Morris to Become New Tate Modern Chief," *The Guardi an*, January 15, 2016.

Buchloch, Benjamin H. D., "The Whole Earth Show: An Interview with Jean-Hubert Martin," *Art in America*, 77, May 1989.

Budick, Ariella, "Hide/Seek: Difference and Desire in American Portraiture," Brooklyn Museum, New York. *Financial Times*, December 7, 2011.

Butler, Cornelia H., "Art and Feminism: An Ideology of Shifting Criteria," *WACK! Art and the Feminist Revolution*, Cambridge, Mass., & London: MIT Press, 2007.

— , and Amelia Jones, "History Makers," *Frieze*, April 3, 2007.

Butler, Judith, *Gender Trouble: Feminism and the Subversion of Identity*, London & New York: Routledge, 1990.

Cameron, Dan, "Sensibility as Content," in *Extended Sensibilities: Homosexual Presence in Contemporary Art*, New York: New Museum of Contemporary Art, 1982.

— , "Extended Sensibilities," *In a Different Light: Visual Culture, Sexual Identity, Queer Practice*, San Francisco: City Lights Publishers, 1995.

Centers for Disease Control and Prevention. Available at: www.cdc.gov/hiv/group/racial-ethnic/africanamericans/index.html.

Chadwick, Helen, "Who's Bad?: A Mixed Response to a Season of Bad Girls," *Frieze*, March 6, 1994. Available at: frieze.com/article/whos-bad.

Charlesworth, JJ, "The Global Contemporary," *ArtReview*, summer 2013.

Corrin, Lisa, "Do museums perpetuate cultural bias?" *Chronicle of Higher Education*, June 15, 1994.

— , "Mining the Museum," *Mining the Museum*, New York: New Press, 1994.

Cotter, Holland, "Sexuality in Modernism: The (Partial) History," *New York Times*, December 10, 2010.

— , "The Art of Feminism as it First Took Shape," *New York Times*, March 9, 2007.

— , "At MoMA, Women at Play in the Fields of Abstraction," *New York Times*, April 13, 2017.

Cottingham, Laura, "Who's Bad?: A Mixed Response to a Season of Bad Girls," *Frieze*, March 6, 1994. Available at: frieze.com/article/whos-bad.

Cumming, Laura, "56th Venice Biennale," *The Observer*, May 10, 2015.

Danius, Sara, and Stefan Jonsson, "An Interview with Gayatri Chakravorty Spivak," *Boundary 2*, Vol. 20, No. 2, summer 1993.

Davila, Florangela, "TAM's new exhibit looks at the scourge of AIDS on people and art," *Crosscut*, October 14, 2015.

Davis, Ben, "The Yams, On the Whitney and White Supremacy," *Artnet*, May 30, 2014.

Deepwell, Katy, "Interview with Catherine de Zegher," *n.paradoxa*, December 1996.

— , "Women Artists at Manifesta 4 and Documenta 11," *n.paradoxa* 10, July 2002.

— , "Feminist Curatorial Strategies and Practices Since the 1970s," in Janet Marstine (ed.), *New Museum Theory and Practice: An Introduction*, Massachusetts, USA; Oxford, UK; and Victoria, Australia: Blackwell Publishing, 2006.

— , "re.act.feminism: feminist, gender-critical and trans-gender performance art: Katie Deepwell Interviews Bettina Knaup and Beatrice Stammer," *n.paradoxa*, Vol. 30, July 2012.

Dexter, Emma, "Century City: London, 1990–2001." Available at: www.tate.org.uk/whats-on/tate-modern/exhibition/century-city/century-city-london-1990-2001.

Dluzen, Robin, "'Art AIDS America Chicago' at Alphawood Gallery Chicago," art ltd., February 23, 2017.

Dore, Madeleine, "Where Are the Women?," *ArtsHub Australia*, December 12, 2014.

Dougherty, Cecilia, "Identity Crisis," *New Art Examiner*, September 1995.

Douglas, Sarah, "Is this the first AIDS artwork?" *ArtNews*, September 18, 2015.

Elvenstar, Diane, "Art from Closet to Gallery," *Los Angeles Times*, May 27, 1980.

Engberg, Juliana, "Theatre of Labour: The 56th Venice Biennale," *Art Monthly Australia*, No. 282, August 2015.

Enwezor, Okwui, "The Black Box," *Documenta 11_Platform 5*, Stuttgart: Hatje Cantz Verlag, 2002.

— , *Artforum International*, Vol. 49, No. 4, December 2010.

— , "All the World's Futures" (curatorial statement, 56th Venice Biennale, 2015),

October 2014. Available at: u-in-u.com/en/venice-biennale/2015/curatorial-statement/.

Eshun, Ekow, "Bad Girls!," *Elle* (UK), December 1993.

Feaster, Felicia, "Review: Powerful Zuckerman survey show tackles AIDS crisis in art," *Atlanta Journal-Constitution*, February 23, 2016.

Feldhacker, Thomas, "Under-Representing an American Tragedy," *New Art Examiner*, Vol. 31, No. 5.

Fisher, Jean, "The Other Story and the Past Imperfect," *Tate Papers*, No. 12, autumn 2009.

Fletcher, Kenneth R., "James Luna," *Smithsonian Magazine*, April 2008.

Flood, Richard, "Review: *Extended Sensibilities*," *Artforum*, March 1983.

Fontana, D. J., *What's On In London*, November 1993.

Frankel, Eddy, "Almost every major art exhibition this autumn in London is by a man," *Time Out* (London), August 10, 2016. Available at: www.timeout.com/london/blog/almost-every-major-art-exhibition-this-autumn-in-london-is-by-a-man-and-that-is-total-bullshit-says-art-editor-eddy-frankel-081016.

Frérot, Christine, "elles@centrepompidou," *ArtNews*, November 2009.

GALAS Brochure (unpaginated, unbound), accessed from: GALAS Archive, Lesbian Herstory Archives of the Lesbian Herstory Educational Foundation, Inc., Brooklyn, New York, 1980.

Gay Community News, "National network honors lesbian artists" [anon.], 7.38, April 12, 1980: 2.

Gayford, Martin, "More Marx than Dante," *The Spectator*, May 16, 2015.

Gingeras, Alison, "Stealing the show," *Artforum International*, Vol. 44, No. 1, 2005.

Glueck, Grace, "The Woman as Artist: Rediscovering 400 Years of Masterworks," *New York Times Magazine*, September 25, 1977.

— , "Botanical Bronzes from Nancy Graves," *New York Times*, October 22, 1982.

Goldin, Nan, "In the Valley of the Shadow," *Witnesses: Against Our Vanishing*, New York: Artists Space, 1989.

— , "20 years: AIDS & Photography," n.d. Available at: digitaljournalist.org/issue0106/voices_goldin.htm.

Gonnard, Catherine, with Nathalie Ernoult, "Intersecting Views on the Exhibition 'elles@centrepompidou'," *Diogenes*, No. 225, Vol. 57, Issue 1, February 2010.

Gopnik, Blake, "Century City Sprawl," *Washington Post*, March 18, 2001.

Gornick, Vivian, and Barbara Moran (eds.), *Woman in Sexist Society: Studies in Power and Powerlessness*, New York: Basic Books, 1971.

Graves, Jen, "Tacoma Art Museum's *Art AIDS America* Is a Messy Masterpiece That Reframes the Past 40 Years of American Art," *The Stranger*, October 7, 2015.

Greenstein, M. A., "And You Thought Feminism Was Dead: Judy Chicago's 'Dinner Party' in Feminist Art History," *Artweek*, Issue 27, July 1996.

Greer, Germaine, "Why the world doesn't need an Annie Warhol or a Francine Bacon," *The Guardian*, January 17, 2010.

Griffin, Tim, "Global Tendencies: Globalism and the Large-Scale Exhibition," *Artforum* 42.3, November 2003.

Griffith, James, and Carolyn Wolf, "Dinner Party: Emotional Moving Feast," *Los Angeles Times*, May 11, 1996.

Guerrilla Girls, "Confessions of the Guerrilla Girls," n.d. Available at: www.guerrillagirls.com/confessions_interview/.

— , "Traditional Values and Quality Return to the Whitey Museum," 1995. Available at: www.guerrillagirls.com/19951999projects/d2zpc6t87mawj66c99wrrc726jr1pj.

Guichard, Camille, (dir.), *Arte Video*, Paris: Terra Luna Films, Georges Pompidou Center, 2008.

Haines, Chelsea, "The Whole Earth Show Revisited," *Mousse Magazine*, 44, June 2014.

Hall, Stuart, "New Ethnicities," in David Morley and Kuan-Hsing Chen (eds.), *Stuart Hall: Critical Dialogues in Cultural Studies*, London: Routledge, 1996.

Halperin, Julia, "Creating value around women artists: the chief curator's view," *Art Newspaper*, May 3, 2016.

Hammond, Harmony, *GALAS Guidebook*, accessed from: The Lesbian Herstory Archives of the Lesbian Herstory Educational Foundation, Inc. Brooklyn, New York, 1980.

— , "A Lesbian Show at 112 Greene Street Workshop, January 21–February 11, 1978," *In a Different Light: Visual Culture, Sexual Identity, Queer Practice*, San Francisco: City Lights Publishers, 1995.

Haraway, Donna, "A Cyborg Manifesto: Science, Technology, and Socialist-Feminism in the Late Twentieth Century" (1985), in Donna Haraway, *Simians, Cyborgs, and Women: The Reinvention of Nature*, New York: Routledge, 1991.

Hardt, Michael, and Antonio Negri, *Empire*, Cambridge, Mass.: Harvard University Press, 2001.

Harvey, Doug, "Upside Yo Head," *Los Angeles Weekly*, March 12, 2007.

Hazel, Tempestt, "When the End is the Beginning: Art AIDS America," *Sixty Inches from Center*, March 28, 2017.

Heartney, Eleanor, "The Whole Earth Show, Part II," *Art in America*, 77, July 1989.

Hegert, Natalie, "The Rounds of A Rumour," ArtSlant, 2015. Available at: www.artslant.com/ny/articles/show/39451-the-rounds-of-a-rumor-womenmoma2015.

Henry, Max, "Dionysus in Paris," *artnet.com*, March 9, 2005. Available at: www.artnet.com/Magazine/features/henry/henry3-9-05.asp.

Herzberg, Julia, "Re-Membering Identity: Vision of Connections," *The Decade Show: Frameworks of Identity in the 1980s*, New York: Museum of Contemporary Hispanic Art, 1990.

Hess, Elizabeth, "The Decade Show: Breaking and Entering," *Village Voice*, June 5, 1990.

— , "And Everything Nice," *Village Voice*, February 1, 1994.

Hoban, Phoebe, "We're Finally Infiltrating," *ArtNews*, February, 2007.

— , "The Feminist Evolution," *ArtNews*, December, 2009.

hooks, bell, "Expertease," *Artforum*, Vol. 27, No. 9, May 1989.

— , *Talking Back*, Boston: South End Press, 1989.

Hughes, Robert, "Rediscovered: Women Painters," *Time*, January 10, 1977.

Irigaray, Luce, *Speculum of the Other Woman* [1974], trans. Gillian C. Gill, Ithaca: Cornell University Press, 1985.

Jeffrey, Moira, "This One's a Bit of a Tall Order," *The Herald*, September 13, 2002.

Jiménez, José Luis, "Denuncian al CGAC por el contenido pornográfico de su última exposición," *ABC.es*, May 20, 2009.

Johnson, Andrew, "There's Never Been a Great Woman Artist," *The Independent*, July 6, 2008.

Johnson, Ken, "51 Contemporary Artists, But Just Three Women," *New York Times*, August 25, 2016.

Jones, Amelia, *Sexual Politics: Judy Chicago's Dinner Party in Feminist Art History*, California: University of California Press, 1996.

— , and Cornelia H. Butler, "History Makers," *Frieze*, April 3, 2007.

— , "Feminist Subjects versus Feminist Effects: The Curating of Feminist Art (or Is It the Feminist Curating of Art?)," in Elke Krasny, Lara Perry, and Dorothee Richter (eds.), *On Curating*, Issue 29 (special issue), "Curating in Feminist Thought," Zürich: 2016.

Jones, Jonathan, "Mistresspieces: Why switching art by men and women doesn't work," *The Guardian*, October 25, 2012.

— , "The $44m for Georgia O'Keeffe's work shows how little female artists are valued," *The Guardian*, November 21, 2014.

Joselit, David, "Identity Politics: Exhibiting Gender," *Art in America* 85, January 1997.

Katz, Jonathan, "Hide/Seek: Difference and Desire in American Portraiture," in Jonathan Katz and David C. Ward (eds.), *Hide/Seek: Difference and Desire in American Portraiture*, Washington, DC: Smithsonian Books, 2010.

Kiepuszewski, Rafal, "Warsaw's exhibition of homoerotic art stirs protest," *Deutsche Welle*, August 1, 2010.

Killian, Kevin, "The Secret Histories," *Artforum International*, Vol. 33, No. 6, February 1995.

Kim, Eunsong, and Maya Isabella Mackrandilal, "The Whitney Biennial for Angry Women," *New Inquiry*, April 4, 2014.

Kimball, Roger, "Of Chocolate, Lard and Politics," *National Review*, April 26, 1993.

Kimmelman, Michael, "At the Whitney, Sound, Fury, and Not Much Else," *New York Times*, April 25, 1993.

Knaup, Bettina, and Beatrice E. Stammer (eds.), *re.act.feminism—a performing archive*, Berlin and London: Verlag fuer Moderne Kunst/Live Art Development Agency, 2014.

Knight, Christopher, "Shining a 'Different Light' on both artist and viewer," *Los Angeles Times*, February 4, 1995.

— , "More Famine Than Feast; Focusing on the Flawed 'Dinner Party' Undermines 'Sexual Politics'," *Los Angeles Times*, May 2, 1996.

— , "Fueled by politics," *Los Angeles Times*, June 21, 2005.

Kornblau, Gary, "The Best and Worst Exhibitions of 1996," *Artforum* 35, December 1996.

Das Kunstmagazin editorial team, "Five Tips of the Week,"*Das Kunstmagazin*, June 28, 2013.

Kuo, Michelle, "Global Entry," *Artforum*, May 2015.

Kurczynski, Karen, "Review: Wack!" *Women's Art Journal*, Vol. 29, No. 2, autumn–winter 2008.

Lamoureux, Johanne, "From Form to Platform: The Politics of Representation and the Representation of Politics," *Art Journal* 64, spring 2005.

Larson, Kay, "Lesbian Art: The Colonized Self," *Village Voice*, Vol. 23, Issue 6, March 6, 1978.

— , "Days of Rage," *New York* magazine, November 27, 1989.

— , "Three's Company," *New York* magazine, June 11, 1990.

Lee, Felicia R., "Racially Themed Work Stirs Conflict at the Whitney Biennial," *New York Times*, May 16, 2014.

Lens, Xosé Manuel, "Arte y Diversidad Sexual: Crónica de la exposition 'En Todas Partes'," *El Pais*, June 6, 2009.

Lequeux, Emmanuelle, *Le Monde*, May 28, 2009.

Leszkowicz, Paweł, *Ars Homo Erotica*, Warsaw: CePed, 2010.

— , "The Power of Queer Curating in Central Eastern Europe," in Katrin Kivimaa (ed.), *Working with Feminism: Curating and Exhibitions in Eastern Europe*, Estonia: Tallinn University Press, 2012.

Lewis, Jo Ann, "The Feminine Century," *Washington Post*, June 23, 1996, G.06.

Lippard, Lucy R., *From the Center: Feminist Essays on Women's Art*, New York: E. P. Dutton & Co., 1976.

— , *Mixed Blessings: New Art in a Multicultural America*, New York: Pantheon, 1990.

Lipton, Eunice, "Here Today. Gone Tomorrow? Some Plots for a Dismantling," *The Decade Show: Frameworks of Identities in the 1980s*, New York: New Museum of Contemporary Art/ Studio Museum Harlem, 1990.

Logan, Brian, "Hide/Seek: Too Shocking for America," *The Guardian*, December 5, 2010.

MacAdam, Barbara A., "Where the Great Women Artists Are Now," *ArtNews*, February 2007.

Malvern, Sue, "Virtuous and Vulgar Feminisms," *Art History*, Vol. 20, Issue 3, September 1997.

Martin, Jean-Hubert, Carlo Severi, and Julien Bonhomme, "Jean-Hubert Martin et la pensée visuelle," *Gradivha*, 13/2011. Available at: gradhiva.revues.org/2120.

— , "Paris Diary by Laure: 'Listen with your eyes: Jean-Hubert Martin'," n.d., Available at: parisdiarybylaure.com/ listen-eyes-jean-hubert-martin/.

McEvilley, Thomas, "The Global Issue," *Art and Otherness: Crisis in Cultural Identity*, Kingston, New York: Documentext/ McPherson, 1992.

— , "Documenta 11," *Flash Art*, September 10, 2002.

Menzies, Neal, "Sexual Identity and Anonymity," *Artweek: the national voice of West Coast contemporary art*, May 24, 1980, Vol. 11, Number 20.

Mercer, Kobena, "Black art and the burden of representation," *Third Text*, Vol. 4, Issue 10, 1990.

Michalska, Julia, "Poland's National Museum champions gay rights," *Art Newspaper*, Issue 214, July/August 2010.

Millett, Kate, *Sexual Politics*, New York: Doubleday & Co., 1970.

Mohanty, Chandra Talpade, *Feminisms Without Borders*, North Carolina: Duke University Press, 2003.

Montes, Javier, "Review: En Todas Partes," *ABC de las Artes*, May 30, 2009.

Montgomery, Harper, "Wack! Art and the Feminist Revolution," *Art Nexus* 7, No. 69, June–August 2008. Available at: www.artnexus.com/Notice_View. aspx?DocumentID=19462.

Morin, Dina, "Carambolages, ou l'art en dérapage contrôlé!" *Aleteia*, June 24, 2016.

Mosquera, Gerardo, "Some Problems in Transcultural Curating," in Jean Fisher (ed.), *Global Visions: Towards a New Internationalism in the Visual Arts*, London: Third Text Publications, 1994.

— , "The Marco Polo Syndrome," in Zoya Kocur and Simon Leung (eds.), *Theory in Contemporary Art Since 1985*, London: Blackwell Publishing, 2012.

Muchnic, Suzanne, "Art Review: Exhibition of Lesbian Artworks," *Los Angeles Times*, May 27, 1980.

— , "At Paris's Pompidou Center, the year of the women," latimes.com, May 24, 2009. Available at: articles.latimes.com/2009/ may/24/entertainment/ca-elles24.

Muller, Dena, "Review: *Global Feminisms*," *SIGNS*, winter 2008.

Müller, Kathrin Bettina, "Find Your Own Path," *Die Tageszeitung*, August 2, 2013.

Nochlin, Linda, "What befits a woman?," *Art in America*, September, 2005.

— , "Why Have There Been No Great Women Artists?" [1971], in Maura Reilly (ed.), *Women Artists: The Linda Nochlin Reader*, New York and London: Thames & Hudson, 2015.

Ogbechie, Sylvester Okwunodu, "Ordering the Universe: Documenta 11 and the Apotheosis of the Occidental Gaze," *Art Journal* 64, spring 2005.

Oguibe, Olu, *The Culture Game*, Minnesota: University of Minnesota Press, 2004.

Pacquement, Alfred, "Preface," *Elles@centre-pompidou*, Paris: Centre Pompidou, 2009.

Perrault, John, "Women Artists," *SoHo Weekly News*, October 13, 1977.

Phelan, Peggy, "Survey" in Helena Reckitt (ed.), *Art and Feminism*, London and New York: Phaidon, 2012.

Pindell, Howardena, "Art World Racism: A Documentation," *New Art Examiner*, Vol. 16, No. 7, March 1989.

Pinder, Kymberly, "Black Representation and Western Survey Textbooks," *Art Bulletin*, September 1999, Vol. LXXXI, No. 3.

Plagens, Peter, "A Country Fair for Intellectuals," *Newsweek*, June 17, 2002.

Pollock, Griselda, *Vision and Difference: Feminism, femininity and the histories of art*, London and New York: Routledge, 1988.

— , *Differencing the Canon: Feminist Desire and the Writing of Art's Histories*, London and New York: Routledge, 1999.

Ponnekanti, Rosemary, "Tacoma Art Museum faces protest over lack of diversity in 'Art AIDS America'," *News Tribune*, December 20, 2015.

Preziosi, Donald, "'Sexual Politics' an Important Show," *Los Angeles Times*, May 13, 1996.

Quinton, Jared, "Two Exhibitions Show Artists Grappling with the Ravages of AIDS," *Art21 Magazine*, August 12, 2016. Available at: magazine.art21.org/2016/08/12/two-exhibitions-show-artists-grappling-with-the-ravages-of-aids/#.WOBR9lKZPjE

Ramírez, Mari Carmen, "Beyond 'The Fantastic': Framing Identity in US Exhibitions of Latin American Art," *Beyond the Fantastic: Contemporary Art Criticism from Latin America*, ed. Gerardo Mosquera, Cambridge, MA: MIT Press, 1996.

Raven, Arlene, and Ruth Iskin, "Through the Peephole: Toward a Lesbian Sensibility in Art," *Chrysalis*, 4, 1977.

Re.act.feminism, "The Programme," n.d.

Reckitt, Helena, "Unusual suspects: *Global Feminisms* and *WACK! Art and the Feminist Revolution*," in *n.paradoxa*, Vol. 18, July 2006.

Reid, Calvin, "Beyond Mourning," *Art in America*, April 1990.

Reilly, Maura, "Taking the Measure of Sexism: Facts, Figures, and Fixes," *ArtNews*, May 26, 2015. Available at: www.artnews. com/2015/05/26/taking-the-measure-of-sexism-facts-figures-and-fixes/.

— , (ed.), *Women Artists: The Linda Nochlin Reader*, New York and London: Thames & Hudson, 2015.

Rich, Adrienne, *On Lies, Secrets and Silence*, London: W. W. Norton & Co, 1980.

Rich, Ruby B., "Who's Bad?: A Mixed Response to a Season of Bad Girls," *Frieze*, March 6, 1994. Available at: frieze.com/article/ whos-bad.

Rickey, Carrie, "Illustrated Time Line: A Highly Selective Chronology," in Norma Broude and Mary D. Garrard (eds.), *The Power of Feminist Art: The American Movement of the 1970s, History and Impact*, New York: Harry N. Abrams, 1996.

Rinder, Lawrence, "An Introduction to *In a Different Light*," *In a Different Light: Visual Culture, Sexual Identity, Queer Practice*, San Francisco: City Lights Publishers, 1995. Available at: archive.bampfa.berkeley.edu/ex-hibition/InaDifferentLight/An_Introduction_ to_In_a_Different_Light_by_Lawrence_Rinder. pdf.

Rosenberg, Tal, "A former bank in Lincoln Park is housing an incredible exhibit about AIDS," *Chicago Reader*, December 15, 2016.

Ross, David, "Preface: Know Thy Self (Know Your Place)," in *1993 Biennial Exhibition*, New York: Whitney Museum of Art, 1993.

Rowland, Ingrid, "Women Artists Win!" *New York Review of Books*, May 29, 2008.

Russell, John, "Images of Grief and Rage in Exhibition on AIDS," *New York Times*, November 16, 1989.

Rustin, Susanna, "Health, education and arts should be sacrosanct says Southbank's Jude Kelly," *The Guardian*, March 12, 2016.

Salez, Nicole, "elles@centrepompidou: Interview de Camille Morineau," *Tout Pour Les Femmes*, June 5, 2009.

Saltz, Jerry, "The Battle for Babylon," *Village Voice*, September 16, 2005.

— , "Jerry Saltz meeting with MoMA's Chief Curator of Painting and Sculpture, Ann Temkin," post on Saltz's Facebook page, June 29, 2009.

— , "'93 in Art," *New York* magazine, February 3, 2013.

Saslow, James, "Closets and the Museum: Homophobia and Art History," in Karla Jay and Allen Young (eds.), *Lavender Culture*, New York: New York University Press, 1978.

— , "New York's 'Extended Sensibilities': A Dog on Two Legs," *Advocate*, December 9, 1982.

Schjeldahl, Peter, "Art + Politics = Biennial. Missing: The Pleasure Principle," *Village Voice*, March 16, 1993.

— , "Women's Work: Feminist Art at the Brooklyn Museum," *New Yorker*, April 9, 2007.

Searle, Adrian, "Unworthy of Great Women," *The Guardian*, October 15, 1996.

— , "Urban Sprawl," *The Guardian*, February 1, 2001.

— , "Filth, blasphemy and big, big stars," *The Guardian*, June 14, 2005.

— , "Queer British Art, 1861–1967 review: strange, sexy, heart-wrenching," *The Guardian*, April 3, 2017.

Sehgal, Parul, "Fighting Erasure," *New York Times* (online), February 2, 2016.

Sewell, Brian, *London Evening Standard*, November 12, 1993.

Sheets, Hilarie, "Female Artists Are (Finally) Getting Their Turn," *New York Times*, March 29, 2016.

Shohat, Ella, "Area Studies, Transnationalism, and the Feminist Production of Knowledge," *SIGNS*, Vol. 26, No. 4, summer 2001.

— , (ed.), *Talking Visions: Multicultural Feminism in a Transnational Age*, Cambridge, Mass., & London: MIT Press, 2001 (Foreword by Marcia Tucker).

Showalter, Elaine, "Feminist Criticism in the Wilderness," *Critical Inquiry*, Vol. 8, No. 2, 1970.

Silver, Ken, "Modes of Disclosure: The Construction of Gay Identity and the Rise of Pop Art," *Hand Painted Pop: American Art in Transition, 1955–62*, Los Angeles: Museum of Contemporary Art, 1992.

Sischy, Ingrid, "Prima Galleristas," *Vanity Fair*, December 2014.

Smith, Cheryl, "Bad Girls," in Laura Cottingham and Cheryl Smith (eds.), *Bad Girls*, London: ICA Editions, 1996.

Smith, Roberta, "Three Museums Collaborate to Sum Up a Decade," *New York Times*, May 25, 1990.

— , "At the Whitney: A Biennial with a Social Conscience," *New York Times*, March 5, 1993.

— , "A Raucous Caucus of Feminists Being Bad," *New York Times*, January 21, 1994.

— , "They Are Artists Who Are Women; Hear Them Roar," *New York Times*, March 23, 2007.

— , "This Gay American Life, In Code or in Your Face," *New York Times*, November 18, 2011.

— , "Art for the Planet's Sake at the Venice Biennale," *New York Times*, May 15, 2015.

Solomon, Deborah, "Art Talk: What's Hot in the Fall Art Season? White Men," WNYC Radio, September 9, 2013.

— , "Review: A Brave Show on Art and AIDS," WNYC Radio, July 29, 2016.

Sperlinger, Mike, "Wack!" *Art Monthly*, Issue 307, June 2007.

Spero, Josh, "Portrait of inequality: why women in the art world earn less than men," *London Evening Standard*, December 10, 2014.

Spivak, Gayatri, *In Other Worlds: Essays in Cultural Politics*, New York and London: Routledge, 1987.

Springer, Julie, "Review of Sexual Politics," *Woman's Art Journal*, Vol. 20, No. 1, spring–summer 1999.

Stanfill, Sonnett, "Taking on the Boys' Club at the Art Museum," *New York Times*, October 19, 2016.

Stern, Mark Joseph, "Is MoMA Putting Artists Back in the Closet?," *Slate*, February 26, 2013. Available at: www.slate.com/blogs/browbeat/2013/02/26/moma_closets_jasper_johns_and_robert_rauschenberg_why.html.

#StopErasingBlackPeople. Available at: stoperasingblackpeoplenow.tumblr.com.

Street-Porter, Janet, "The Tate Gallery is wrong to put on a 'queer' art exhibition," *The Independent*, April 22, 2016.

Sussman, Elisabeth, "Then and Now: Whitney Biennial 1993," *Art Journal*, Vol. 64, No. 1, spring, 2005.

Sutherland Harris, Ann, *Women Artists: 1550–1950* [exhibition catalogue], Los Angeles: Los Angeles County Museum of Art, 1976.

Tanner, Marcia, *Bad Girls* [exhibition catalogue], New York: New Museum of Contemporary Art, and Cambridge, MA: MIT Press, 1994.

Taylor, Andrew, "Tate Modern director Frances Morris on why the art world is still a boys' club," *Sydney Morning Herald*, August 30, 2016.

Tenore, Mallary Jean, "New York Times Book Review editor: Featuring diversity of authors is 'extremely important'," Poynter, April 11, 2013. Available at: www.poynter.org/2013/new-york-times-book-review-editor-featuring-diversity-of-authors-is-extremely-important/209920/.

"En Todas Partes" [anon.], *Artecontexto*, July 9, 2009.

Thompson, Margo Hobbs, *Sex and Sensibilities: The Aesthetic and Political Struggles over Women's Representations of the Female Body*, Ph.D dissertation, Northwestern University, 1998.

— , "DIY Identity Kit: The Great American Lesbian Art Show," *Journal of Lesbian Studies*, Vol. 14, 2010, Issue 2–3.

Tucker, Marcia, *Extended Sensibilities: Homosexual Presence in Contemporary Art*, New York: New Museum of Contemporary Art, 1982.

— , in Ella Shohat (ed.), *Talking Visions: Multicultural Feminism in a Transnational Age*, Cambridge, Mass., & London: MIT Press, 2001 (Foreword by Marcia Tucker).

Turman, Maureen, "Inside the Visible," *Art Documentation: Bulletin of the Art Libraries Society of North America*, Fall 1996, Vol. 15, Issue 2.

Turner, Chris, "Century City," *Frieze*, Issue 60, June–August 2001.

Tyson, Nicola, "Who's Bad?: A Mixed Response to a Season of Bad Girls," *Frieze*, March 6, 1994. Available at: frieze.com/article/whos-bad.

Upchurch, Michael, "How AIDS changed American art: Tacoma Art Museum show charts responses to the HIV crisis," *Seattle Times*, October 19, 2015.

Vetrocq, Marcia E., "Venice Biennale: Be Careful What You Wish For," *Art in America*, Vol. 93, September, 2005.

Volk, Gregory, "All the World's Futures, Trials and Tribulations at the Venice Biennale," *Art in America*, May 8, 2015. Available at: www.artinamericamagazine.com/news-features/previews/all-the-worlds-futures-trials-and-tribulations-at-the-venice-biennale/.

Wallen, Ruth, "Review of Sexual Politics," *Women's Studies*, 1999, Vol. 28.

Wallis, Brian, "A Forum, Not a Temple: Notes on the Return of Iconography to the Museum," *American Literary History*, Vol. 9, No. 3, autumn 1997.

Weibel, Peter, *The Global Contemporary After 1989* [exhibition guide], ZKM/Museum of Contemporary Art, 2011–12.

— , "Globalization and Contemporary Art," in Hans Belting, Andrea Buddensieg, and Peter Weibel (eds.), *The Global Contemporary and the Rise of New Art Worlds*, Cambridge Mass.: MIT Press, 2013.

Weinberg, Jonathan, "Things Are Queer," *Art Journal*, Vol. 55, No. 4, "We're Here: Gay and Lesbian Presence in Art and Art History," winter 1996.

Weinstein, Jeff, "Gay or Not," *Village Voice*, November 2, 1982.

Whitney Museum website, "Whitney Biennial 2014." Available at: whitney.org/Exhibitions/2014Biennial

Wilde, Oscar, "The Critic as Artist" [1891], *The Collected Works of Oscar Wilde*, London: Wordsworth Editions, 2007.

Wilson, Judith, "Art," in Donald Bogle (ed.), *Black Arts Annual 1987/88*, New York: Garland, 1989.

Winking, Kerstin, "The Global Contemporary," *Third Text*, Vol. 26, Issue 5, 2012, p. 622.

Wojnarowicz, David, "Post Cards from America: X-Rays from Hell," *Witnesses: Against Our Vanishing*, New York: Artists Space, 1989.

Wolverton, Terry, *Insurgent Muse: Life and Art at the Women's Building*, San Francisco: City Lights Publishers, 1992.

— , "Great American Lesbian Art Show," *In a Different Light: Visual Culture, Sexual Identity, Queer Practice*, San Francisco: City Lights Publishers, 1995.

Xinhua News Agency, "Britain's Tate Modern Hosts Century City Show" [anon.], *Xinhua News Agency*, January 30, 2001.

Yablonsky, Linda, in *Witnesses: Against Our Vanishing*, New York: Artists Space, 1989.

Zegher, Catherine de, "Introduction," *Inside the Visible: An Elliptical Traverse of 20th-Century Art in, of, and from the Feminine*, Cambridge, Mass., and London: MIT Press, 1996.

Ziv, Stan, "Exhibit at Bronx Museum Explores the Influence of HIV/AIDS On American Art," *Newsweek*, July 16, 2016.

PICTURE CREDITS

Dimensions of works are given in centimeters and inches, height before width before depth.

a=above, b=below

18 Guerrilla Girls, 1986 Report Card, 1986. Screenprint on paper, 56 × 43 (22 × 16⅞). Next to Pussy Galore, 2015 Report Card, 2015. Courtesy guerrillagirls.com. © Guerrilla Girls

19 Pussy Galore, Manhattan Boycott Guide, 2016. © Pussy Galore

32 Courtesy Jean-Hubert Martin

43 Suzanne Valadon, *The Blue Room*, 1923. Oil on canvas, 90 × 116 (35⅜ × 45⅝). Centre Georges Pompidou, Paris

45 Elisabeth Louise Vigée Le Brun, *Varvara Ivanovna Ladomirskaïa*, 1800. Oil on canvas, 63.5 × 55.2 (25 × 21¾). Columbus Museum of Art, Ohio. Derby Purchase Fund, inv. 1963.019.

46 Brooklyn Museum Archives. Records of the Department of Photography: Exhibitions. Installation view, "Women Artists: 1550–1950," 1977

47 Anne Vallayer-Coster, *Vase of Flowers with a Bust of Flora*, 1774. Oil on canvas, 154 × 130 (60⅝ × 51⅛). Private Collection

49 Kathe Burkhart, *Fuck You: From the Liz Taylor Series (Cleopatra)*, 1984. Acrylic, composition leaf on canvas, 182.9 × 121.9 (72 × 48). Permanent Collection, Art Institute of Chicago

52 Lutz Bacher, *Playboys (Feminist Movement)*, 1993. Acrylic and screenprint on canvas, 112.4 × 91.8 (44¼ × 36⅛). Purchase, with funds from the Painting and Sculpture Committee 2012.87. Whitney Museum of American Art, New York. Courtesy Lutz Bacher, Greene Naftali; New York and Galerie Bucholz, Köln/ Berlin/New York

55a Portia Munson, *Pink Project: Table*, 1994. Mixed media, 76.2 × 243.8 × 426.7 (30 × 96 × 168). Image courtesy New Museum, Brooklyn. © Portia Munson

55b Photograph Fred Scruton, 1994. Courtesy New Museum, Brooklyn

57 Hannah Höch, *Mutter*, c. 1930. Watercolour and photo collage on paper, 25.6 × 20 (10⅛ × 7⅞). © DACS 2018

58 Nancy Spero, Panel X of *Torture for Women* (detail), 1976. Cut-and-pasted typed text, painted paper, gouache, and handprinting on paper, 14 panels. 51 × 3810 (20 × 1500) overall. Courtesy Galerie Lelong & Co. © The Nancy Spero and Leon Golub Foundation for the Arts/DACS, London/VAGA, New York 2018

61a Charlotte Salomon, From the series *Life? or Theater?*, 1940–42. Gouache, 25.1 × 32.4 (9⅞ × 12¾). Collection Jewish Historical Museum, Amsterdam. © Charlotte Salomon Foundation, Charlotte Salomon®, www.jck.nl

61b Yayoi Kusama, *Baby Carriage*, 1964, repainted c. 1966. Baby carriage, cloth, stuffing, silver metallic paint, 96.5 × 59 × 101.6 (38 × 23¼ × 40). Allen Memorial Art Museum, Oberlin College, Ohio. Gift of Mr. and Mrs. Harry L. Tepper, 1974. © Yayoi Kusama

63 Cindy Sherman, *Untitled Film Still #35*, 1979. Gelatin silver photograph, 24 × 16.7 (9⁷⁄₁₆ × 6⁹⁄₁₆). Museum of Modern Art, New York. Horace W. Goldsmith Fund through Robert B. Menschel. Courtesy the artist and Metro Pictures, New York

65 Judy Chicago, *The Dinner Party*, 1979. Ceramic, porcelain, textile, 1463 × 1463 (576 × 576). Brooklyn Museum, New York. Gift of the Elizabeth A. Sackler Foundation, 2002.10. © Judy Chicago, ARS/NY, © ARS, NY, London 2018

67a Mary Kelly, *Post-Partum Document: Introduction*, 1973. Perspex units, white card, wool vests, pencil, ink, 1 of 4 units, 20 × 25.5 (7⅞ × 10) each. Collection Eileen Norton, Santa Monica

67b Yoko Ono, Yoko Ono performing *Cut Piece*, Sogetsu Art Center, Tokyo, Japan, 1964. Photograph by Hirata. © Yoko Ono

69 Photo Maura Reilly

70 Pipilotti Rist, *Homo Sapiens Sapiens*, 2005. Video installation, duration 5:50. Courtesy the artist, Luhring Augustine, New York and Hauser & Wirth. © Pipilotti Rist

72 Mariko Mori, *Wave UFO*, 1999–2003. Brainwave interface, vision dome, projector, computer system, fiberglass, Technogel®, acrylic, carbon fiber, aluminum, magnesium, 493 × 1134 × 528 (194⅛ × 446½ × 207⅞). Image courtesy Shiraishi Contemporary Art, Inc., Tokyo, and Deitch Projects, New York. © Mariko Mori, Member Artists Rights Society (ARS), New York /DACS 2018

73 Shahzia Sikander, *SpiNN*, 2003. Digital animation with sound, 6:38 minutes. Music by David Abir. Courtesy the artist

75 Miwa Yanagi, *Yuka*, 2000. From *My Grandmother* series. C-Print, Plexiglas, dibon, 160 × 160 (63 × 63). Courtesy Almine Rech Gallery. © Miwa Yanagi

78 Tania Bruguera, *The Burden of Guilt*, 1997–99. Re-enactment of a historical event, decapitated lamb, rope, water, salt, Cuban soil, dimensions variable. Photograph courtesy Studio Bruguera

79a Brooklyn Museum Digital Collections and Services. Records of the Department of Digital Collections and Services: Exhibitions. Installation view, "Global Feminisms," 2007

79b Ghada Amer, *Encyclopedia of Pleasure*, 2001. Canvas, gold thread on a cardboard frame, dimensions variable. Courtesy Cheim & Read, New York

81 Faith Ringgold, *Freedom Woman Now*, 1971. Cut-and-pasted coloured paper on board, 76.2 × 50.8 (30 × 20). Museum of Modern Art, New York. The Abby Aldrich Rockefeller Endowment for Prints. Digital image 2017, The Museum of Modern Art, New York/Scala, Florence. © Faith Ringgold/ARS, NY and DACS, London 2018

84a Eleanor Antin, *Plaisir d'Amour (after Couture)*, 2007. Chromogenic print, 154.9 × 235 (61 × 92½). Courtesy the artist and Ronald Feldman Fine Arts, New York

84b Howardena Pindell, *Free, White, and 21*, 1980. Video: colour, sound. Inv# PINNM001. Courtesy the artist, Garth Greenan Gallery, and The Kitchen, New York

85 Installation view, "WACK! Art and the Feminist Revolution," March 4–July 6, 2007. The Geffen Contemporary, The Museum of Contemporary Art, Los Angeles. Photograph Brian Forrest. Courtesy The Museum of Contemporary Art, Los Angeles

87 Frida Kahlo, *The Frame*, 1938. Oil on aluminum, 28.5 × 20.7 (11¼ × 8⅛). Centre Georges Pompidou, Paris. © Banco de México Diego Rivera Frida Kahlo Museums Trust, Mexico, D.F./DACS 2018

90 Niki de Saint Phalle, *Crucifixion*, c. 1965. Various objects on wire mesh, 245 × 160 × 50 (96½ × 63 × 19⅝). Photograph Centre Pompidou, MNAM-CCI, Dist. RMN-Grand Palais/Georges Meguerditchian. © Niki de Saint Phalle Charitable Art Foundation/ ADAGP, Paris and DACS, London 2018

91a Véronique Ellena, *Les Dimanches*, in *Les Calanques (Sundays)* series, 1997. Photograph Courtesy @ Galerie Alain Gutharc, Paris. © Véronique Ellena

91b Lee Bontecou, *Untitled*, 1966. Welded steel, canvas, epoxy, leather, wire and light, 199.4 × 302.3 × 78.7 (78½ × 119 × 31). Museum of Contemporary Art, Chicago. Gift of Robert B. Mayer Family Collection, 1991.85. Photograph MCA Chicago. Copyright Lee Bontecou

93 Oreet Ashery, *Hairoism*, 2009–11. 5 photographs, 4 posters, video: colour, sound, duration 20:00 min. Courtesy the artist

94 Photo Anne Quirynen. Courtesy cross links e.V.

97a Lilibeth Rasmussen, *Never Mind Pollock*, 2009. Performance duration 40–50 minutes, performed during Re.act feminism, Berlin. Photograph Andreas Rosforth

97b Ewa Partum, *Selbstidentifikation (Selfidentification)*, 1980. 10 black and white photomontages and 2 performance photos. From exhibition and performance in 1980 at Galeria Mala in Warsaw, which consisted of three elements: a photographic exhibition, a film projection and a performance. Motif 1 of 12. Unique. 50 × 73 (19⅝ × 28¾) each. Courtesy the Artist and BROADWAY 1602 HARLEM.© Ewa Partum

107 Alfredo Jaar, *La Géographie, ça sert d'abord à faire la guerre*, 1989. Mixed-media installation, overall dimensions variable. Courtesy the artist, New York

108 Barbara Kruger, *On n'a plus besoin de héros*, 1989. Installation view, "Magiciens de la terre," 1989. La Grande Halle de la Villette. Photo Centre Pompidou, MNAM-CCI Bibliothèque Kandinsky, Dist. RMN-Grand Palais/Béatrice Hatala/Konstantinos Ignatiadis

109 Installation view, "Magiciens de la terre," 1989. La Grande Halle de la Villette. Photo Centre Pompidou, MNAM-CCI Bibliothèque Kandinsky, Dist. RMN-Grand Palais/Béatrice Hatala/Konstantinos Ignatiadis. Featuring Richard Long, *Red Earth Circle*, 1989. © Richard Long. All Rights Reserved, DACS 2017. Featuring Yuendumu Community, *Yam Dreaming*, 1989. Courtesy Warlukurlangu Artists Aboriginal Corporation

111 Esther Mahlangu, *House*, 1989. Mixed media, dimensions variable. Installation view, "Magiciens de la Terre," 1989. La Grande Halle de la Villette. Photo Centre Pompidou, MNAM-CCI Bibliothèque Kandinsky, Dist. RMN-Grand Palais/Béatrice Hatala/ Konstantinos Ignatiadis

113 Tomie Arai, *Laundryman's Daughter*, 1989. Silkscreen, printed on BFK Rives, 76.2 × 55.9 (30 × 22) (print). Edition of 25. © Tomie Arai, 1989

115 James Luna, *The Artifact Piece*, 1987 & 1991. Courtesy the artist and New Museum, New York

117a Yolanda M. López, *Things I Never Told My Son About Being a Mexican*, 1984. Mixed-media installation, 1984. Installation view from "The Decade Show: Frameworks of

Identity in the 1980s", The New Museum of Contemporary Art, New York, 1990. Photograph Fred Scruton. Courtesy the artist and New Museum, Brooklyn

117b Luis Cruz Azaceta, *AIDS Count III*, 1988. Acrylic on canvas, 195.6 × 449.6 (77 × 177). Photograph Dylan Cruz Azaceta. Courtesy the artist & Arthur Roger Gallery, New Orleans

119 Fred Wilson, *The Truth Trophy*, 1992. Left to right: empty pedestals, labeled Harriet Tubman, Frederick Douglass and Benjamin Banneker; globe, *c.* 1913; Shobal Vail Clevenger, *Henry Clay*, *c.* 1870; artist unknown, *Napoleon Bonaparte*, *c.* 1850; C. Hennecke & Co, *Andrew Jackson*, *c.* 1870. Photograph courtesy Maryland Historical Society. © Fred Wilson, courtesy Pace Gallery

120 Fred Wilson, *Cabinetmaking 1820–1960*, 1992. From left: whipping post, date and maker unknown; armchair, *c.* 1896, maker unknown; side chair with logo of Baltimore Equitable Society, *c.* 1820–40, maker unknown; armchair, *c.* 1855, by J. H. Belter; side chair, *c.* 1840–60, maker unknown. Photograph courtesy Maryland Historical Society. © Fred Wilson, courtesy Pace Gallery

121 Fred Wilson, *Dollhouse (c. 1904)*, 1992. From left: artist unknown, *Gap at Harper's Ferry*, before 1933, oil on canvas; pikes used in John Brown's raid on Harper's Ferry, October 1859; dollhouse, *c.* 1904, painted wood, fabric, dolls, and dollhouse furniture. Photograph courtesy Maryland Historical Society. © Fred Wilson, courtesy Pace Gallery

123 Fred Wilson, *Modes of Transport 1770–1910*, 1992. Installation view, "Mining the Museum: An Installation by Fred Wilson," Maryland Historical Society, 1992–93. Photograph Maryland Historical Society. © Fred Wilson, courtesy Pace Gallery

125 Sue Williams, *Irresistible*, 1992. Rubber mixed with pigment, 30.5 × 144.8 × 61 (12 × 57 × 24). Courtesy 303 Gallery, New York. © Sue Williams

127 Pepón Osorio, *Scene of the Crime (Whose Crime?)*, 1993. Mixed-media installation at Whitney Biennial. Whitney Museum of American Art, New York. Courtesy Ronald Feldman Fine Arts, New York. © Pepón Osorio

129a Guillermo Gómez-Peña and Coco Fusco, *Two Undiscovered Amerindians Visit the West*, 1992–93. Performance piece. Photograph Nancy Lytle. Courtesy Coco Fusco

129b Daniel Joseph Martinez, *Museum Tags: Second Movement (overture); or, Overture con claque (Overture with Hired Audience Members)*, 1993. Paint and enamel on metal, dimensions variable. From the 1993 Whitney Biennial, Whitney Museum of American Art, New York. Courtesy the artist and Roberts & Tilton, Culver City, California

131 Vufku/REX/Shutterstock

133 Gino Severini, *Train de banlieue arrivant à Paris (Suburban Train Arriving in Paris)*, 1915. Oil on canvas, 886 × 1156 (348⅞ × 455⅛). Tate, London. © ADAGP, Paris and DACS, London 2018

134 Horikawa Michio, *The Shinano River Plan 11 (Mail Art by Sending Stones)*, 1969. Stone, wire, mail tags (mailed to Matsuzawa Yutaka). Collection of Matsuzawa Kumiko. Photograph Reiko Tomii

137 Nalini Malani, *Hamletmachine*, 2000. Four channel Videoplay, with three screens and a bed of salt, 20 minutes. Performer Harada Nabuo. Produced during the Fukuoka Asian Art Museum Residency Program 1999–2000. Courtesy Nalini Malani

139 Isaac Julien, *Before Paradise*, 2002. Pigment ink print. Printed at Hare & Hound Press, San Antonio, Texas. Three panels, 100 × 100 (39⅜ × 39⅜) each. Courtesy the artist and Victoria Miro, London. © Isaac Julien

140 Mona Hatoum, *Homebound*, 2000. Kitchen utensils, furniture, electric wire, light bulbs, computerized dimmer unit, amplifier and speakers, dimensions variable. Photograph © documenta archiv/Ryszard Kasiewicz. © Mona Hatoum

143a Kutluğ Ataman, *The 4 Seasons of Veronica Read*, 2002. Four screen video installation. Courtesy the artist

143b Yinka Shonibare, *Gallantry and Criminal Conversation*, 2002. 11 life-size mannequins, metal and wood cases, Dutch wax-printed cotton, leather, wood, steel, dimensions variable. Brooklyn Museum Digital Collections and Services. Records of the Department of Digital Collections and Services: Exhibitions. Installation view "Yinka Shonibare" 2009. © Yinka Shonibare MBE. All Rights Reserved, DACS 2018

145 Araya Rasdjarmrearnsook, *Renoir's Ball at the Moulin de la Galette and the Thai Villagers*, 2008. From *Dow Song Duang (The Two Planets)* series. Video duration 10:52. Courtesy the artist and Tyler Rollins Fine Art, New York

149 Khosrow Hassanzadeh, *Reyhan Hassanzadeh*, 2004. From the *Terrorist* series. Silkscreen and acrylic on canvas, 200 × 320 (78¾ × 126). Coll.no. TM-6269-3. Nationaal Museum van Wereldculturen, Leiden

150 Leila Pazooki, *Moments of Glory*, 2011. Neon light sculpture, dimensions variable. Courtesy Nadour Collection, Paris/Düsseldorf

151 Richard Bell, *Scientia E Metaphysica (Bell's Theorem)*, 2003. Synthetic polymer, paint on canvas, 240 × 360 (94½ × 141¾). Image courtesy the artist and Milani Gallery, Brisbane

153 Daniel Boyd, *Untitled (TI1)*, 2015. Diptych, oil and archival glue on linen, 213 × 334 (83⅞ × 131½) overall, 213 × 167 (83⅞ × 65¾) each. Photograph Jessica Maurer. Courtesy the artist and Roslyn Oxley9 Gallery, Sydney

155 Installation view, Venice Biennale, 2015, Maura Reilly

157a Ibrahim Mahama, *Out of Bounds*, 2014–15. Coal sacks, metal tags and jute ropes on coal sacks, dimensions variable. Site-specific installation, 56th Venice Biennale. Courtesy the artist and APALAZZOGALLERY

157b Mika Rottenberg, *No Nose Knows*, 2015. Film still from video, duration approximately 22 minutes. Courtesy Andrea Rosen Gallery, New York. © Mika Rottenberg

167 Louise Fishman, *Ashkenazi*, 1978. Oil on linen, 81.3 × 121.9 (32 × 48). Courtesy Cheim & Read, New York

169 Lili Lakich, *OASIS: Portrait of Djuna Barnes (Red)*, 1977. Prismacolor pencil on black board, 61 × 91.4 (24 × 36). © Lili Lakich 1977

170 Tee Corinne, untitled solarized photograph, dimensions unknown. Published on the cover of *Sinister Wisdom*, spring 1977. Tee A. Corinne Papers, Coll 263. Special Collections and University Archives, University of Oregon Libraries, Eugene, Oregon

171 Harmony Hammond, *Durango*, 1979. Fabric, wood, latex and foam rubber, gesso and rhoplex, 76.2 × 43.2 × 45.7 (30 × 17 × 18). Art Institute of Chicago. Gift of Judith Daner, 1986.985. Courtesy Alexander Gray Associates, New York, NY. © Harmony Hammond /DACS, London/VAGA, NY 2018

173 Arch Connelly, *Lens*, *c.* 1982. Mixed media, dimensions unknown. Courtesy New Museum, Brooklyn

175a Installation view, "Extended Sensibilities: Homosexual Presence in Contemporary Art," New Museum of Contemporary Art, 1982. Featuring Gilbert & George, *Four Feelings*, 1980. 16 photographs, 242 × 201 (95¼ × 79⅛) overall. Image courtesy New Museum, Brooklyn. © Gilbert & George

175b Courtesy New Museum, Brooklyn

177 Charley Brown, *Bi Untitled*, 1980. Mixed media, dimensions unknown (installation view). Courtesy the artist and New Museum, Brooklyn

179 James Nares, *Heartbeats*, 1988. Oil on paper, 45.7 × 61 × 2.9 (18 × 24 × 1⅜). Photograph Diego Flores. Image courtesy the artist and Paul Kasmin Gallery, New York

181 Nan Goldin, *Cookie at Vittorio's Casket, NYC, September 16, 1989*, 1989. Cibachrome print. Courtesy the artist. © Nan Goldin

183a Philip-Lorca diCorcia, *Vittorio*, 1989. Ektacolor print. Courtesy the artist and David Zwirner, New York/London. © Philip-Lorca diCorcia

183b Kiki Smith, *All Our Sisters*, 1989. Silkscreen on muslin, 147.3 × 284.5 (58 × 112). Walker Art Center, Minneapolis. Photograph courtesy the artist and Pace Gallery. © Kiki Smith, courtesy Pace Gallery

185 Catherine Opie, *Self-Portrait/Cutting*, 1993. Chromogenic print, 101.6 × 74.8 (40 × 29⁷⁄₁₆). Solomon R. Guggenheim Museum, New York. Purchased with funds contributed by the Collections Council, with additional funds from Mr. and Mrs. Aaron M. Tighe and the Robert Mapplethorpe Foundation, 2012. Courtesy Regen Projects, Los Angeles, and Lehmann Maupin, New York and Hong Kong. © Catherine Opie

187 General Idea, *Baby Makes 3*, 1984/1989. Chromogenic print (Ektacolor), 76.2 × 63.5 (30 × 25). Edition of 3, signed and numbered. Self-published. Image courtesy Esther Schipper

188 Donald Moffett, *You, You, You*, 1990. Cibatransparency in lightbox, 96.5 × 213.4 × 15.2 (38 × 84 × 6). Courtesy the artist. © Donald Moffett

189 Marcel Duchamp, *L.H.O.O.Q.*, 1919. Pencil on reproduction, 19.4 × 12.4 (7⅝ × 4⅞). Private Collection. © Association Marcel Duchamp/ADAGP, Paris and DACS, London 2018

191 Jack Pierson, *Black Jackie*, 1991. Acrylic paint, plywood, silver and black rain curtain, cigarette and ash, dimensions variable. CGAC Photograph Archive, Santiago de Compostela. Photograph Paco Rocha. Courtesy Cheim & Read, New York

194 Tariq Alvi, *The Importance of Hanging*, 2008. Inkjet print, collage, cine gel and tape, 42 × 59.4 (16½ × 23⅜). CGAC Photograph Archive, Santiago de Compostela. Photograph Paco Rocha

195a Nicole Eisenman, *Betty Gets It*, 1992. Ink on paper, 27 × 27 (10⅝ × 10⅝). Hort Family Collection, New York. Courtesy the artist and Anton Kern Gallery, New York. Photograph Object studies. © Nicole Eisenman

195b CGAC Photograph Archive, Santiago de Compostela. Photograph Mark Ritchie

197 Karolina Breguła, *Let Them See Us*, 2003. Cycle of 30 photographs, producer Kampania Przeciw Homofobii. © Karolina Breguła

199 The section "Time of Struggle" in the exhibition "Ars Homo Erotica," National Museum in Warsaw, 2010. Artwork in foreground:

INDEX

AUTHOR BIOGRAPHIES

MAURA REILLY is a curator and arts writer, and executive director of the National Academy of Design in New York. As the founding curator of the Sackler Center for Feminist Art at the Brooklyn Museum, she launched the first exhibition and public programming space in the USA devoted entirely to feminist art, where she organized multiple exhibitions, including the permanent installation of Judy Chicago's *The Dinner Party* and the blockbuster *Global Feminisms* (with Linda Nochlin). Reilly has authored and edited many publications on contemporary art, including, most recently, *Women Artists: The Linda Nochlin Reader* (2015). She is the recipient of a Lifetime Achievement Award from the Women's Caucus for Art and in 2015 was voted one of the fifty most influential people in the art world by both *Blouin Art Info* and *Art+Auction*. She received her M.A. and Ph.D. from the Institute of Fine Arts at New York University.

LUCY R. LIPPARD is an internationally known art critic, activist and curator. She is the author of twenty-four books on contemporary art and cultural criticism, most recently: *Undermining: A Wild Ride through Land Use, Politics and Art in the Changing West* (2014).